CD2枚付

東京大学受験指導専門塾

改訂版

鉄緑会
東大英語
リスニング

鉄緑会英語科 編

JN048580

KADOKAWA

CONTENTS

ii

本書の主な特徴

東大形式のリスニング問題12年分・36問を収録

　本書は，東京大学入試における英語の聞き取り試験（リスニング）攻略のための問題集です。毎年多くの東大合格者を出している鉄緑会が，そのノウハウを結集してオリジナル問題を作成しました。東大で出題されているものと同じ形式の問題を12年分，計36問を収録しています。東大入試を控えた受験生にとっては，本番と同じ感覚で必要十分な量の練習を積める，格好の教材と言えるでしょう。各問題には難易度の表示がありますので，自分の今の実力を測ることが可能です。また，東大のリスニングは，偏りのないオールラウンド型の英語力を求めるものです。東大を目指す学生だけでなく，全ての英語学習者にとって，聴解力，総合的な英語力の向上に大いに役立つでしょう。

知的好奇心をくすぐる良質の英語を厳選

　東大のリスニング問題の特徴を端的に表すなら，とにもかくにも「面白い」という一言に尽きます。大学の入試というと無味乾燥なものを連想しがちですが，東大が出題するのは，知的好奇心をくすぐるような刺激的な問題ばかりです。本書のスクリプト（放送文）作成にあたっては，ただその形式を真似るのではなく，東大が追求しようとしている理想に敬意を払い，それに少しでも近づけるように心がけました。問題を解き終えたあとも繰り返して聴くに値するような，質の高い英語だけを集めてあります。

多彩な話題・形式での出題，話者数は最大7人

　東大のリスニングでこれまで扱われたテーマは，科学技術，社会学，歴史，心理学等，実に多岐にわたります。その形式も多彩で，ラジオインタビュー，大学での講義，日常会話，議会での討論等，ありとあらゆる状況での英語を想定して作られています。また，話者数が多いのも特徴です。1つの問題に3人以上の話者が登場することも多く，過去には5人が登場したこともありました。このような多種多様な内容・形式に慣れてもらうために，本書ではバラエティー豊かなテーマ・状況を用意しました。1問の中での話者数も1人から最大7人までという設定になっています。

思考力を必要とする設問，ポイントをおさえた解説

　東大のリスニングは，その設問にも他には見られない特徴があります。東大では，一部の語句を聞き取っただけで正解に至れるような問題はほとんど出題されません。「聞き取れる」イコール「正解できる」ではないのです。総括的な内容把握力，情報の分析能力，発言の真意を見抜く力等，英語による知的なコミュニケーションに必要なありとあらゆる能力が試されます。本書では，このような東大特有の出題を徹底的に分析し，「骨のある」設問をたくさん用意しました。そして，何に注目して聞けばいいのか，どのように考えれば正解に至れるのかを分かりやすく解説してあります。

アマチュアを含む14名のナレーターを起用，多彩なアクセント

　一般に市販されている英語の音声CDでは，プロのナレーターを使っているため，クリアで聞き取りやすい発音なのが特徴です。一方で，大学の入試問題では，教職員がナレーションを担当していることが多く，市販されている教材との間にはギャップがあります。「市販の英語CDで聞き取りの練習をしたのに，入試本番ではあまり聞き取れなかった」という感想をときどき耳にします。そこで，本書のCD収録には，プロだけでなく，アマチュアを含む計14人のナレーターを起用しました。また，アクセントも北米を中心に，イングランド，スコットランド等を混ぜ，偏りが生じないようにしてあります。さらに，各問題にはスピーカーの出身地を明記しました。

《改訂版での主な変更点》

最新の「5択」に対応！

　東大入試の英語は，2010年代に入り難化したと言われています。その要因の1つが，客観問題での選択肢の増加です。長らく4択を基本としていたのが，この頃を境に5択が標準となりました。リスニング問題も同様で，2018年度から全て5択となっています。

　4択から5択へ―――この変化が受験生に与える負担には見かけ以上のものがあります。単に正解に至る確率が4分の1から5分の1に減るというだけでは

ありません。聞き取り試験の実施時間は変わらず，途中の30秒と1分のポーズの間に吟味すべき選択肢の量が増えるわけですから，これまで以上に速読力が求められます。また選択肢の「下読み」にかかる時間も長くなるため，他の大問にかけられる時間が減り，その結果，英語の試験全体の難易度が上がります。

　以上のような事情をふまえ，東大を目指す受験生は，普段の練習から5択に慣れておく必要があるでしょう。改訂版の本書では，より本番に近い形での演習を積んでもらうために，全ての設問を5択として作り直しました。

東大英語聞き取り試験（リスニング）の概要

　東大入試の英語聞き取り試験（リスニング）は1988年度に導入され，それ以降毎年行われています。2001年度に(A)(B)(C)の3題構成となり，概ね以下のような出題形式が確立されました。

- ●放送時間は約30分。放送は試験開始の45分後から。英文の放送は2回ずつ。1回目と2回目の間に30秒，大問と大問の間に1分間のポーズがある。
- ●(A)(B)(C)の3題構成。このうち2題が内容的に連続していることもある（(A)が「講義」，(B)が「講義の後の討論」等）。
- ●1問の中での話者数は1～5人。
- ●メインは5択のマークシートによる記号選択式。一部にディクテーションが出題されたこともある。
- ●問題文及び選択肢は問題冊子に印刷されてある（問題文が印刷されずに放送されたこともある〈2011年度〉）。

　配点は公表されていませんが，(A)(B)(C)それぞれ10点，計30点の配点となっていると考えられます。英語全体の120点満点のうちの4分の1という比重です。

　スピーカーのアクセントについての公式な発表はありませんが，受験生に聞き取り調査をしたところでは，「標準的なアメリカ英語が中心」「一部イギリス英語も混じっている」というのが実情のようです。2017年度にはナイジェリア出身の作家による回想が出題されました。

　語彙レベルは高くなりすぎないように調整されています。受験者の大半が知らないような難しい単語は使われないか，文脈からある程度の意味を推測できるように配慮されています。

　設問では，放送文についての深い内容理解が試されます。放送文の中の語句が選択肢の中では別の表現に言い換えられてあることが多く，語句レベルの単純な聞き取りだけでは対処できないように配慮されています。

以下は，東大英語リスニングについての「豆知識」です。

- ●選択肢の記号は「アイウエ」が基本だったが，2015年度にマークシートが導入されてから「a) b) c) d)」となった。
- ●選択肢は「4択」を基本としていたが，2018年度に「5択」となった。
- ●記号選択肢の並び順は「選択肢の長さ順」が基本。一番短いものから順に機械的に並べているだけなので，「正解が全てa)」ということも十分にあり得る。
- ●(A)(B)(C)はそれぞれ独立して解けるようになっているのが原則だが，2015年度の(B)では，(A)の放送内容を覚えていないと解けない問題が出題された。
- ●2010年度には，「いずれも一致しない」という選択肢があった。

東大英語リスニング本番での注意点

設問・選択肢の「下読み」が必須！　目標は５〜６分

　聞き取り試験で高得点を上げるには，放送が始まる前に問題文や選択肢の「下読み」をすることが絶対に必要です。できれば10分くらいかけてじっくりと読んでおきたいところですが，そうすると他の問題で時間が不足してしまうでしょう。目標は５〜６分です。放送開始の５〜６分前（試験開始39〜40分後）になったら，それまでやっていた問題を中断し，「下読み」に入りましょう。

放送開始前の「下読み」は(A)を重点的に

　放送が始まるまでに(A)(B)(C)の全てに目を通しておくのが理想ですが，時間的には厳しいのが現実でしょう。(A)と(B)，(B)と(C)の間には１分間のポーズがありますので，その間にもある程度の「下読み」は可能です。放送前には(A)を重点的に，(B)(C)については「できる限り見ておく」という姿勢で臨みましょう。また，この辺りの時間配分については，かなりの個人差があります。本書での練習を通じて，自分に最適な配分を身に付けていきましょう。

「何について語られるか」「何を聞かれるか」に注目

　「下読み」でおさえておくべき大事なポイントは2つ，①「何について語られるか」と，②「何を聞かれるか」です。①については，問題文や選択肢を見ていると，「あ，これは海底資源の活用についての議論だな」というような見当がつくはずです。テーマが分かったら，「海底資源の活用」等と，日本語で大きくメモしておきましょう。英語よりも日本語のメモの方が，目にした瞬間にすぐに頭に飛び込んできます。このような「事前知識」があるとないとでは，聞き取りのしやすさがまるで違います。

「言及されていないものを選べ」タイプに要注意

　②の「何を聞かれるか」に関して，特に注意したいのは，「本文中で言及されていないものはどれか」というタイプの設問です。この種の問題では，全ての選択肢にきちんと目を通す必要があるため，他よりも時間がかかります。このタイプの設問には大きく印を付けておき，選択肢にも目を通して，必要ならば日本語でメモを取っておきましょう。

固有名詞・専門用語をチェックしておく

　放送の内容を追えなくなってしまう原因の1つが，「知らない単語」です。1つの単語が原因で話の流れを見失ってしまうという経験は誰にでもあることでしょう。特に注意すべきなのは人名，地名，会社名等の固有名詞，また扱われているテーマに特有の専門用語です。問題文や選択肢の中でこれらの語を見つけたら，いち早く線を引いておきましょう。こうすることで，その語が読まれたときにも慌てないで対処することができます。

1回目の放送中は「メモの取りすぎ」「選択肢の読みすぎ」に注意

　さて，いよいよ放送開始です。1回目の放送中は，聞き取りに集中しましょう。放送されている内容を具体的に頭の中でイメージすることが大切です。そうすることで内容が記憶に焼き付き，放送後の30秒ポーズや2回目の放送の間に正解を選ぶのが容易になります。1回目の放送で不必要にメモを取ったり選択肢を見たりすると，集中が途切れてしまい，逆効果です。メモを取るのは，数値や年号等の記憶に残りにくい情報のみにとどめてください。また，「下読み」の段階で残しておいた日本語のメモは，特に1回目の放送中にその威力を発揮します。

2回目の放送では，取りこぼした問題を中心に

　2回目の放送では，全体の流れは既に分かっているはずですから，1回目の放送で分からなかった部分を重点的に聞き取ることができます。また，1回目で絞り込めなかった選択肢の吟味も，この2回目の間に行いましょう。

聴解力向上のために

「東大のリスニング問題で高得点を上げるには，とにかく英語をたくさん聞きまくれば良い」と考えている人がいますが，これは大きな誤解です。**東大のリスニング問題は英語の総合力を試すもの**です。単語や表現の知識，読解力，文法知識，そして英語を使った思考力等，様々な能力が必要とされます。「リスニングのテスト」というよりも，むしろ「音声を利用した総合英語力テスト」だと考えましょう。リスニング試験での得点は，英語の総合力を表したものなのです。

「長文読解は得意なのに，リスニングとなるとダメ」という人がいますが，そういう人は，音声学習とそれ以外の英語学習を分けて考えていることが原因となっている可能性が高いです。**全ての英語学習において音声を重視すること**を肝に銘じましょう。単語を覚える際であろうと，長文を読む際であろうと，また文法の問題を解くときでも，常に音を意識し，声に出して発音し，音源があるものはそれをフルに活用しましょう。また，英文を読み聞きするときには，なるべく**日本語を介さずに，英語のままダイレクトに内容をイメージできるように**訓練しましょう。

聞き取りがうまくいかない場合，いくつかの原因が考えられますが，その中でも最も多いのが，「表現を知らない」というものです。**人間の耳は，自分が知らない単語・表現を聞き取ることはできません。**放送文の内容がちんぷんかんぷんなのは，「聞き取れなかった」ではなく，単に「知らなかった」ということが大半なのです。普段の学習時から，できるだけ多くの単語や表現を覚えるように心がけましょう。

正しい発音を身に付けることも大切です。自分で発音ができるようになると，聞き取りの精度も上がってきます。「カッコイイ」発音でなくてもいいのです。大事なのは，それぞれの音の違いが明確に出るように意識することです。「rackと lack」「cold と called」「she と sea」等，日本語では表せないような音の差に特に注意しましょう。発音の練習で大切なのは，英語の音声を「よく聞き」，そして「真似る」ことです。本書の放送文が全く聞き取れないという人は，単語集の例文CD等，短めのものを利用してください。音声を一時停止し

て，それを真似てリピートする練習が最適です。最初のうちは，いわゆる「シャドーイング（音声を聞きながら，同時に発音をしていく練習法）」はお奨めしません。「聞く」という行為が疎かになりがちですし，また，内容を理解しないまま音だけを追う癖がついてしまいます。

本書の使い方

問題演習

●入試本番と同じような緊張感を持って臨んでください！

●**ABC**セットで解きましょう（約30分弱かかります）。

●手元にタイマーやストップウォッチを用意しましょう。

●できれば，イヤホン，ヘッドホンよりもスピーカーで音を出すようにしましょう。

●開始前に，設問と選択肢を下読みする時間を設けてください。慣れないうちは10分程度かけて構いません。最終的には5分にまで縮めることを目標にしましょう。

●放送はそれぞれ2回ずつ。1回目の放送と2回目の放送の間は30秒のポーズ，**A**と**B**，**B**と**C**の間は1分間のポーズを取ってください。

●CDの音声は，実際の入試よりやや速めのスピードで収録されています。入試会場での緊張を考えると，このくらいのスピードで慣れておくべきです。手持ちの機器にスピード調節の機能があるなら，最初のうちは0.8倍速で再生しても構いません。

答え合わせ・実力診断

●問題を解き終えたらまず採点をしましょう。2点×15で計算してください。

●各問題に難易度が表示されています。「総合」の★の数を目安にしてください。目標とする得点率は以下の通りです。

★☆☆：80%
★★☆：70%
★★★：60%

●**ABC**の★の数を合計すると，目標点の目安は以下の通りとなります。

★の合計	目標点
3〜4	24点
5〜6	22点
7〜8	20点
9	18点

復習のしかた

●問題の「やりっ放し」は厳禁です。必ず復習をしましょう。

●まず，放送文のスクリプトを見ながら，2度ほど音声を聞いてください。適宜音声を止めながらで構いません。日本語訳も参照しながら，聞き取れていなかった箇所，理解できなかった箇所をチェックし，その原因を突き止めましょう（「音が聞き取れていなかった」「単語・表現を知らなかった」「スピードについていけなかった」等）。

●🔈では，聞き取りのポイントが示されています。東大のリスニングでは，細部の情報をピックアップするだけでなく，ある程度のまとまりでの要旨を摑むことが必要です。「この辺はだいたいこんなことを言っているな」という大局的な理解を心がけましょう。

●リストアップされている単語や表現をチェックしてください。

●今度はスクリプトを見ずに，全体を通して2度ほど聞きましょう。頭の中で日本語に変換せず，英語のままダイレクトに内容をイメージすること。最初から最後まで無理なく内容を追えるようになったら，いったん聞き取りは終了です。

●次は設問の見直しです。解説を読み，1つひとつ確認していってください。特に間違えた問題に関しては，その原因を突き止めることが大切です。「聞き取れなかったから」なのか，あるいは「設問へのアプローチを間違えたから」なのか，理由を明確に認識してから次へと繋げるようにしましょう。

その後の様々な活用法

　以上で一通りの学習は終了しますが，本書に収録された素材はその後も様々な活用が可能です。

① 通学時の電車の中等で「耳慣らし」

　同じ英語を何度も繰り返し聞くことで，聴解力だけでなく，英作文等も含めた総合的な英語力がアップします。1日15分を目標に，毎日聞き続けるようにしましょう。ただし，BGM的な聞き方をしても全く意味はありません。電車の中でも構いませんので，できる限り集中して聞くようにしましょう。

② ディクテーションの練習

　英語の「音」が聞き取れていない，という人にはディクテーションの練習をお奨めします。本書に収録された放送文の中から，ランダムに10行ほどの1節を選びましょう。適宜音声を停止しながら書き取り，最後に正しく書けているかをチェックします。こうすることで，自分がどのような音を聞き取れていないかが分かり，細かい音にまで注意が行き届くようになります。

③ 発音練習

　上記のディクテーション練習と合わせて行うと効果的です。音声をよく聞き，一時停止してから，真似て発音してみる，ということを繰り返してください。

改訂版 鉄緑会
東大英語リスニング

設問篇

2

Set 1-A CD🅐A-1 解説はP40 📖

これから放送されるのは，あるラジオ番組の一部である。これを聞き，(1)〜(5)の問いに対して，それぞれ正しい答えを一つ選び，その記号を記せ。

(1) What has Steve been reporting on recently?
a) The possibility of life on Mars.
b) A new method for identifying microorganisms.
c) A recent trip to Mars by a Russian space craft.
d) The arrival of small green aliens in Washington.
e) The challenges of bringing back soil samples from Mars.

(2) What is the first potential problem associated with studying the specimens, according to Steve?
a) Martian microbes might contaminate Earth's soil.
b) Martian microbes might die before they reach Earth.
c) Scientists might not have the right tools to analyze them.
d) People from New York City might be afraid of the specimens.
e) Microbes from Mars might become indistinguishable from those from Earth.

(3) What is the second potential problem?
a) The microbes might not really be from Mars.
b) The microbes might damage organisms on Earth.
c) The microbes might be displaced by organisms on Earth.
d) The microbes might be harmed by Earth's native bacteria.
e) The microbes might die before scientists have time to study them.

(4) What is the plan that scientists have come up with for handling the specimens?
a) Put them in a triple-layer box.
b) Put them in three separate boxes.
c) Do not take them off the space ship.
d) Put them in a box with very low air pressure.
e) Put them in three boxes, each with a different pressure.

(5) Which of the following is true about the containment room?
a) The pressure in the middle box is the lowest.
b) The pressure in the innermost box is the lowest.
c) The outermost box has a valve to relieve excess pressure.
d) The innermost box has higher air pressure so that the soil samples will not leak out.
e) The room will prevent the Martian microbes from escaping, but it won't protect them from contamination.

Set 1-B　CD◎A-2　　　　　　　解説はP47 📖

これから放送されるのは，ある製品の発表会の模様である。これを聞き，(1)～(5)の問いに対して，それぞれ正しい答えを一つ選び，その記号を記せ。

(1) Which of the following is true about Computer Connections?
　a) The business was started by Sandra Maynard.
　b) Chris Brown is the company's executive director.
　c) The company employs an African girl as a programmer.
　d) The company's mission is to teach children computer skills.
　e) The company's new product has been featured in many newspapers and magazines.

(2) What is the Learning Lab?
　a) Educational software that facilitates students' independent learning.
　b) A set of computer-based tools that teachers can install in classrooms.
　c) An educational system designed to promote interaction among children.
　d) A system that will allow children to learn even if they don't have teachers.
　e) An educational device that connects poor children in Africa with teachers around the world.

(3) Which of the following is NOT a feature of the Learning Lab?
　a) Educational programs for children of all ages.
　b) A bench for children to sit on while they learn.
　c) Durable materials that withstand rain and dust.
　d) A renewable energy source to provide electricity.
　e) Video screens that allow children to interact with teachers in other countries.

(4) Sandra says, "Don't take my word for it." What does she imply by that?
　a) The user's voice is most important.
　b) Some of the information she gave is wrong.
　c) Reporters shouldn't quote her directly in their articles.
　d) There is something she doesn't understand about the system.
　e) Reporters should visit the community themselves to confirm her comments.

(5) Which of the following statements best describes Hope's experience with the Learning Lab?
　a) She has been studying with it for almost a year.
　b) She first used the kiosk on a class trip led by her teacher.
　c) She has used it to practice English, watch videos, and shop online.
　d) At first she was confused by it, but she quickly learned to use the technology.
　e) Her aunt showed her how to use the computers, but now she can use them on her own.

4

これから放送されるのは、Bに続く質疑応答の模様である。これを聞き、(1)～(4)の問いに対して、それぞれ正しい答えを一つ選び、その記号を記せ。(5)については英語で解答を記せ。

(1) Which of the following is NOT a reason Sandra developed the Learning Lab?
　a) She wanted to help children fulfill their potential.
　b) She saw that there was a shortage of teachers in Kenya.
　c) She realized that an affordable educational system was needed.
　d) There were so many children that she could not teach them all by herself.
　e) She felt that computers could provide higher-quality instruction than human teachers.

(2) Which of the following statements about the experiment in New Delhi is true?
　a) It took the children a long time to figure out how to use the computers.
　b) The goal of the experiment was to prove that digitized education is not effective.
　c) It took the children less than a month to create a simulation model on the computers.
　d) The children were able to learn advanced concepts independently by using the computers.
　e) When adults provided guidance, the children were able to use the computers to study science.

(3) What can be inferred from Hope's answers?
　a) Using the Learning Lab alone is difficult.
　b) She learned to use the computer all by herself.
　c) The Learning Lab can only be used for short periods of time.
　d) Most of the games in the Learning Lab require three or four players.
　e) Using the Learning Lab doesn't require special instruction from adults.

(4) According to Sandra, what is the main challenge her company faces?
　a) Overcoming the limits to machine-centered education.
　b) Securing adequate funding from the donor community.
　c) Convincing teachers to use the new technology in classrooms.
　d) Obtaining permission from the government to use the product.
　e) Expanding the technology to countries where English is not spoken.

(5) Chris says the following sentences at the end of the conference. Fill in the blank with the exact words you hear.
　Please feel free to follow up with me by phone or email if you have any further questions. And _____!

Set 2-A　CD◉A-4　　　　　　　　　　　　解説はP61 📖

これから放送される講義を聞き，(1)〜(5)の問いに対して，それぞれ正しい答えを一つ選び，その記号を記せ。

(1) Which of the following does the lecturer NOT mention as a purpose of bookshelves?
a) To hold books.
b) To show off your wealth.
c) To preserve books for longer periods.
d) To make a room look more attractive.
e) To make it easier to find a book you need.

(2) Which of the following is a classification system used in American libraries?
a) Douglas Digit Classification.
b) Supreme Court Classification.
c) Universal Decimal Classification.
d) Presidential Library Classification.
e) Library of Congress Classification.

(3) According to the lecturer, which of the following is NOT a reason libraries are using digital instead of paper archives?
a) Digital archives are more affordable.
b) Digital archives are more efficient in terms of space.
c) Digital archives can be organized more systematically.
d) Readers in various locations can access digital archives.
e) Readers can access information very quickly with digital archives.

(4) Why were blank books sometimes placed on bookshelves in the past?
a) So they could be used as journals.
b) Because they were easier to handle.
c) Because full bookshelves indicated wealth.
d) Because they were cheaper than real books.
e) Because some people could not read, but wanted to appear smart.

(5) Which statement would the lecturer most likely agree with?
a) Bookshelves serve no purpose in modern society.
b) Bookshelves are an ideal way to store information.
c) Bookshelves should only be used by wealthy people.
d) Bookshelves belong in society as long as books exist.
e) Bookshelves should be used for more practical purposes.

6

Set 2-B　CD🅐A-5　　　　　解説はP68📖

これから放送されるのは，あるラジオ番組での討論の一部である。これを聞き，(1)～(5)の問いに対して，それぞれ正しい答えを一つ選び，その記号を記せ。

(1) What is the main issue the guests on the radio program are debating?
  a) Whether social media sites are beneficial for society.
  b) Whether women use social media in a different way than men.
  c) Whether social media sites are effective for exchanging opinions.
  d) Whether college students should be allowed to use social media sites like Twitter.
  e) Whether the college student who sent the negative tweet should be allowed to return to school.

(2) Which of the following is NOT mentioned regarding Patty's newspaper article?
  a) Many people's lives have been ruined by cyber bullying.
  b) People tend to behave badly when they are part of online crowds.
  c) People are more likely to make sexist comments online than in real life.
  d) Contemporary online bullying is similar to real-life harassment of minorities in the past.
  e) People on social media sites often make hurtful comments without having enough information.

(3) How does Patty feel about the college student from Texas?
  a) What he did should not be tolerated in any way.
  b) He should have apologized publicly to the teacher.
  c) He did the wrong thing, and he deserved the outcome.
  d) He did the wrong thing, but the outcome was too severe.
  e) He is an example of how online bullying can benefit society.

(4) Which of the following best describes Edward's opinion?
  a) Online crowds help to discourage inappropriate behavior.
  b) Online crowds help to spread a biased view on a global scale.
  c) Social media sites contribute to a culture of sexism against women.
  d) Online crowds sometimes improve society, but they more often cause harm.
  e) Online crowds are valuable because they include people from many different cultures.

(5) What does Patty think about Edward's argument?
  a) She agrees that online crowds are helping to create a less sexist society.
  b) She agrees that online crowds can contribute to the good of society as a whole.
  c) She doesn't agree that comments made on social media sites have real-world impacts.
  d) She agrees that the online shaming of one student will teach an important lesson to other college boys.
  e) She doesn't agree that the progress of society as a whole is more important than the human rights of each individual.

Set 2-C CD⊘A-6   解説はP76

これから放送されるのは，会社の同僚であるDevonとJamieの会話である。これを聞き，(1)
〜(5)の問いに対して，それぞれ正しい答えを一つ選び，その記号を記せ。

(1) Which of the following sentences best indicates Jamie's feelings about Sara?
　a) She should open up more at parties.
　b) She was brave to turn up to the party.
　c) She was wrong to participate in the dance routine.
　d) She does not have the ability to complete her MBA.
　e) She should probably switch from accounting to marketing.

(2) Which of the following is NOT true about Sara?
　a) She is studying for an MBA.
　b) She works in the accounting section.
　c) She has won flower-arranging awards.
　d) She is reading a book about shy people.
　e) She prefers to talk in a one-to-one situation.

(3) According to Jamie, how do shy people differ from introverts?
　a) Shy people are often promoted more quickly.
　b) Shy people often judge others in a negative way.
　c) Shy people will speak up more about personal issues.
　d) Shy people feel a greater need to interact with others.
　e) Shy people have absolutely no desire to interact with other people.

(4) What is one issue regarding the workplace that is NOT mentioned?
　a) Introverts are effective in one-on-one situations.
　b) Many offices today are designed to suit extroverts.
　c) Extroverts sometimes push their own ideas too hard.
　d) Introverts are likely to change companies more frequently.
　e) Extroverts tend to be given more opportunities for career advancement.

(5) According to Jamie, which type of people are more likely to make better
leaders, and why?
　a) Extroverts, because they will force their ideas on others.
　b) Extroverts, because they stand out in an open environment.
　c) Introverts, because they will help their staff to fulfill their potential.
　d) Introverts, because they will spend more time organizing their ideas.
　e) Extroverts, because they have more confidence in their own abilities.

8

これから放送される講義を聞き，(1)〜(5)の各文が放送の内容と一致するように，それぞれ正しいものを一つ選び，その記号を記せ。

(1) Before the invention of fake fur,
  a) only rich people could afford fur garments.
  b) animal fur was far more expensive than it is now.
  c) the most popular types of fur were mink and rabbit.
  d) jewelry was the main symbol of wealth and privilege.
  e) animal fur was worn by women who had succeeded in business.

(2) Companies invented fake fur due to
  a) the Great Depression.
  b) the shortage of real animal fur.
  c) pressure from animal rights groups.
  d) a decline in the number of big cats in Africa.
  e) demand from people in the lower and middle classes.

(3) Fake fur was not popular at first, because
  a) it was hard to handle.
  b) it was as expensive as real fur.
  c) it didn't resemble the real thing.
  d) it didn't indicate high social status.
  e) people didn't think wearing real fur was wrong.

(4) The causes of fake fur's rising popularity did NOT include
  a) negative ads about real fur.
  b) the animal rights movement.
  c) general awareness of animal cruelty issues.
  d) cost reduction resulting from mass production.
  e) improvements in the quality of fake fur products.

(5) Today, real fur
  a) is not available in most countries.
  b) is becoming less and less popular.
  c) still symbolizes wealth and privilege.
  d) is becoming more popular than ever.
  e) still has a certain degree of popularity.

Set 3-B　CD⊘A-8　　　解説はP90📖

これから放送されるのは，インドのある都市でのガイド付きツアーにおける会話である。これを聞き，(1)〜(5)の問いに対して，それぞれ正しい答えを一つ選び，その記号を記せ。

(1) Uday refers to Delhi as "a very hectic city." What does the word "hectic" mean?
　a) busy
　b) exotic
　c) large
　d) exciting
　e) polluted

(2) Which of the following statements about air pollution is true, according to Uday?
　a) It is caused mainly by cigarette smoke.
　b) It is a more serious problem in Beijing than in Delhi.
　c) It kills fewer people worldwide each year than cigarette smoke.
　d) It can cause severe health problems that eventually lead to death.
　e) It is no longer a problem in Delhi thanks to the development of smog-eating paint.

(3) According to Uday, how does the smog-eating paint work?
　a) It absorbs chemical pollutants.
　b) It contains tiny micro-organisms that eat air pollution.
　c) It reacts with sunlight and water in a three-step process.
　d) It causes a chemical reaction that energizes harmful substances in the air.
　e) It absorbs pollutants from the air, which workers later wash off using water.

(4) Which of the following is mentioned by Uday as one of the advantages of the technology?
　a) Easy to use.
　b) Great durability.
　c) Relatively low cost.
　d) Non-toxic ingredients.
　e) Attractive appearance.

(5) Which of the following is mentioned by Uday as an application of photocatalysts?
　a) A coating for furniture.
　b) A paint used for vehicles.
　c) Dyeing of clothing materials.
　d) A laundry detergent that coats clothing.
　e) A medical treatment for heart conditions and cancer.

Set 3-C　CD💿A-9　　　　解説はP97📖

これから放送されるのは，友人同士の二人（KatieとDean）による会話である。これを聞き，
(1)〜(5)の問いに対して，それぞれ正しい答えを一つ選び，その記号を記せ。

(1) Which type of gifts do Dean and his brother prefer receiving?
a) Both prefer receiving luxuries.
b) Both prefer receiving practical gifts.
c) Dean prefers receiving luxuries but his brother prefers practical gifts.
d) Dean prefers receiving practical gifts but his brother prefers luxuries.
e) None of the above.

(2) Which of the following does Dean NOT mention as a point to consider when buying a present?
a) What the recipient is like.
b) How the gift will be used.
c) Who will benefit from the gift.
d) How much money he spends on it.
e) The relationship between giver and recipient.

(3) According to Dean, why is cookware inappropriate as a present for a wife?
a) It's not romantic.
b) It's too expensive.
c) It can be used for the benefit of the husband.
d) The giver might not know which brand to buy.
e) The wife might have bought cookware for herself already.

(4) According to Dean, what is the reason that some men give stereotypical gifts?
a) Men are not creative.
b) Their partners have requested them.
c) They have no idea what women want.
d) A combination of pressure to be perfect and fear of offending the recipient.
e) Spending money on jewelry is a sign of how important their relationship is.

(5) Based on Dean's Valentine's Day plans, which statement is most likely true about him and his partner?
a) They are both cheerful people.
b) They do not know each other very well.
c) They both prefer surprises to predictable gifts.
d) They like to give something special to each other.
e) They have been dating for more than a few weeks.

Set 4-A　CD🅰A-10　　　　　　解説はP104📖

これから放送されるのは，ある大学での講義の模様である。これを聞き，(1)～(5)の問いに
対して，それぞれ正しい答えを一つ選び，その記号を記せ。

(1) Choose the correct answer that fills in the blanks: According to "the lipstick
effect" theory, during an economic recession, sales of (X) increase, while
sales of (Y) decrease.
a) (X) necessities / (Y) luxuries
b) (X) luxuries / (Y) necessities
c) (X) cosmetics / (Y) sweets and alcohol
d) (X) affordable luxuries / (Y) expensive luxuries
e) (X) expensive luxuries / (Y) affordable luxuries

(2) What is the word "treat" used to mean in this lecture?
a) A special item you buy for someone else.
b) Something that is done to cure an illness.
c) Something special that gives you pleasure.
d) An item such as ice cream used to reward a child.
e) An expensive item that you would not buy for yourself.

(3) According to the professor, how do people on a budget decide to buy chocolate
or ice cream?
a) They can't control their desire to buy luxuries.
b) They are overwhelmed with an impulse to buy.
c) They compare different brands and choose the cheapest one.
d) They want something that will immediately make them happy.
e) They perceive the purchase as saving money, not as spending it.

(4) What is the phenomenon known as "choice overload"?
a) Shoppers have less interest when their options are limited.
b) The more options a store gives shoppers, the more items it can sell.
c) Consumers are less likely to purchase when offered too many products.
d) When forced to choose between similar products, consumers become fatigued.
e) Consumers end up buying unnecessary items when faced with too many choices.

(5) Based on this lecture, which of the following would be good advice for a shop?
a) Emphasize quality rather than cost.
b) Give consumers as many choices as possible.
c) Make sure prices are lower than at other stores.
d) Place large, expensive items in the most visible spots.
e) Offer sales so consumers feel like they are saving money.

Set 4-B　CD◎A-11　　　　　　　　　　解説はP111📖

これから放送されるのは，Aの翌週に行われた授業の模様である。これを聞き，(1)〜(5)の
問いに対して，それぞれ正しい答えを一つ選び，その記号を記せ。

(1) What factor was most important for Francisca when shopping for lunch?
  a) Satisfaction—she was very hungry.
  b) Price—she wanted something cheap.
  c) Treat—she wanted to reward herself.
  d) Health—she wanted something organic.
  e) Ease—she didn't want to spend time choosing an item.

(2) According to Francisca, what makes customers vulnerable to sales tactics?
  a) Being hungry.
  b) Shopping for items online.
  c) Feeling like they want to reward themselves.
  d) Not having a specific plan or product in mind when shopping.
  e) Not knowing about the methods stores use to encourage purchases.

(3) Why are online shoppers less likely to browse?
  a) Because they can't see the items in person.
  b) Because they are usually on a strict budget.
  c) Because online shops don't have many items.
  d) Because they are often in a rush and can't get distracted.
  e) Because they typically use a search engine to look for items.

(4) Which of the following accurately describes Peter and Francisca's online
    shopping habits?
  a) Peter is not tempted by impulse buys, but Francisca is.
  b) Peter sometimes buys unnecessary items, but Francisca does not.
  c) Francisca is aware of online marketing strategies, but Peter is not.
  d) Peter and Francisca both only buy items they planned to purchase in advance.
  e) Peter and Francisca are both often influenced by advertisements and buy things
      they don't need.

(5) According to the lecture, which strategy do online retailers use to encourage
    purchases?
  a) They send advertisements to consumers via email.
  b) They offer their products at physical stores as well as online.
  c) They match advertisements to the buying patterns of online shoppers.
  d) They post advertisements for many appealing items on their websites.
  e) They keep track of shoppers' purchases and select products that are likely to be
      popular.

Set 4-C　CD🄰A-12　解説はP118📖

これから放送されるのは，あるラジオ番組の一部である。これを聞き，(1)〜(5)の問いに対して，それぞれ正しい答えを一つ選び，その記号を記せ。

(1) Which of the following is NOT a feature of the Divepro?
  a) A window to see outside.
  b) Devices to film the marine environment.
  c) Joints that rotate for effective movement.
  d) Attachments for handling items underwater.
  e) A fin-like apparatus on the back to improve underwater mobility.

(2) Why does Beth think diving down 800 feet in scuba gear would be a bad idea?
  a) It would take too long to descend that far.
  b) It would be too hard to move with dexterity.
  c) It would be too difficult to breathe at that depth.
  d) It would be too cold for the human body to function properly.
  e) It would take too long to recover after returning to the surface.

(3) How is the Divepro different from other ADS suits?
  a) The suit is made of metal rather than plastic.
  b) The suit is more affordable for ordinary fishermen.
  c) The suit enables the diver to recover afterwards in no time.
  d) The suit's joints move more effectively under high-pressure conditions.
  e) The interior of the suit maintains a pressure equivalent to that on land.

(4) Who would be least likely to use a Divepro suit?
  a) A fisherman diving for sea urchins.
  b) A biologist researching fish reproduction.
  c) An archaeologist exploring a sunken ship.
  d) An engineer installing underwater phone lines.
  e) A commercial diver engaging in undersea construction.

(5) According to Beth, why is the Divepro an important technology?
  a) Because many divers and companies are excited about it.
  b) Because it allows divers to work more safely in deep water.
  c) Because it offers both hi-tech features and attractive design.
  d) Because it allows divers to work more efficiently in deep water.
  e) Because it allows divers to descend more deeply than other suits.

14

Set 5-A　CD◉A-13　　　　　　　　　　　　解説はP124📖

これから放送されるのは，あるラジオ番組の一部である。これを聞き，(1)〜(5)の問いに対して，それぞれ正しい答えを一つ選び，その記号を記せ。

(1) According to John, which of the following would NOT be a typical image of nature for an American?
a）A wild river.
b）A dense forest.
c）A grove of redwood trees.
d）A valley full of wildflowers.
e）A grassland where cows graze.

(2) According to Mary's report, in what way is the Japanese view of nature different from the American one?
a）Humans are part of nature just like any other living creatures.
b）To achieve balance with nature, people use resources very carefully.
c）Protecting nature doesn't necessarily mean keeping it free from human influence.
d）To preserve nature, it is necessary to exclude people from important ecosystems.
e）People live in harmony with each other and try to preserve the natural environment.

(3) How do people maintain the grasslands in Aso?
a）By cutting down bushes and trees.
b）By limiting construction in open fields.
c）By planting diverse wildflowers and herbs.
d）By burning, grazing cattle and harvesting grass.
e）All of the above.

(4) According to Mariko, why would biodiversity levels fall if forests spread in Aso?
a）Because the variety of habitats in the area would decrease.
b）Because forests are too dark for most plant species to grow.
c）Because farmers would no longer be able to raise cattle and grow rice.
d）Because fewer types of animals are found in forests than in grasslands.
e）Because certain animals in the forests would destroy the native species.

(5) What did Mary do last spring?
a）Hosted a local volunteer event.
b）Helped Mariko recruit volunteers.
c）Watched volunteers burn grasslands.
d）Went hiking in Aso-Kuju National Park.
e）Tagged the ears of cows for monitoring.

Set 5-B　CD🅐A-14　　　　　　　　　　解説はP130📖

これから放送されるのは，ある大学での講義の一部である。これを聞き，(1)〜(5)の問いに対して，それぞれ正しい答えを一つ選び，その記号を記せ。

(1) What does Janine Benyus mean when she talks about learning from "biological elders"?

a) That elderly people in the community can teach us important lessons about sustainable living.

b) That parents, grandparents, and other older relatives have much to teach the younger generation.

c) That it is important to respect earlier generations of biologists who also turned to nature for inspiration.

d) That the study of biology has a long history and it gives us a lot of insights into how organisms are structured.

e) That plants and animals have been evolving optimal forms and processes for millions of years, and therefore contain valuable hints about good design.

(2) Based on the professor's explanation, which of the following is an example of biomimicry?

a) A realistic drawing of a sea lion.

b) A type of paint made from all-natural ingredients.

c) A robot that can perform the same functions as a human.

d) A necklace made by combining various shapes of seashells.

e) A train whose aerodynamic design is based on the shape of a bird's body.

(3) According to the professor's explanation, why do snails remain clean?

a) Because the tiny bumps on their shells repel dirt.

b) Because the cells in their shells break down contaminants.

c) Because their shells are so smooth dirt cannot stick to them.

d) Because they periodically wash themselves in pools of water.

e) Because the texture of their shells allows dirt to wash off easily.

(4) How is the coating developed by the Japanese company similar to a snail's shell?

a) It contains silica, an element found in soil.

b) When applied to a surface, it creates many tiny valleys that collect water and contaminants.

c) It creates millions of tiny bumps, which collect water and help to keep moisture on the surface.

d) It appears rough to the naked eye, but when viewed under a microscope it is actually very smooth.

e) When applied to a surface, it creates many tiny bumps that reflect light and therefore give the appearance of cleanliness.

(5) How is biomimicry different today from that in the past, according to the professor?

a) It is being applied for more practical purposes.

b) Products are modeled on a wider range of species.

c) It is being used to enhance the sustainability of products.

d) Scientists are collaborating with designers to create new products.

e) Designers are drawing inspiration from smaller and smaller forms.

Set 5-C   CD⑤A-15   解説はP137📖

これから放送されるのは，MarissaとNadineという二人の女性の会話の一部である。これを
聞き，(1)～(5)の問いに対して，それぞれ正しい答えを一つ選び，その記号を記せ。

(1) Why is Marissa upset with her husband Mark?
 a) Because he had dinner with another woman.
 b) Because he wouldn't talk to her cousin at a party.
 c) Because he met with another woman without telling her.
 d) Because he invited another woman to their house for dinner.
 e) Because he looked at her personal emails and text messages.

(2) How are simple jealousy and complex jealousy different?
 a) Complex jealousy is caused by multiple events.
 b) Complex jealousy is caused by insecurity and fear.
 c) Simple jealousy is caused by anger and resentment.
 d) Simple jealousy can positively impact a relationship.
 e) Simple jealousy leads to resentment, anger, and controlling behavior.

(3) Why does Nadine mention the relationship between mother and child?
 a) To point out the root of jealous feelings.
 b) To prove that no one can be free from jealousy.
 c) To illustrate how simple jealousy can benefit people.
 d) To explain how complex jealousy affects a relationship.
 e) To clarify the difference between the two types of jealousy.

**(4) Which of the following is NOT a strategy for reducing complex jealousy,
    according to Nadine?**
 a) Trying to be more compassionate.
 b) Improve your own self-confidence.
 c) Confront your partner about your concerns.
 d) Stop imagining certain scenes over and over again.
 e) Think about situations from your partner's perspective.

(5) How does Nadine's counselor's advice help Marissa?
 a) It helps her to understand her husband's motivation.
 b) It helps her stop thinking obsessively about the situation.
 c) It helps her build up her self-esteem so she is less worried.
 d) It reminds her of some important facts about her husband.
 e) It makes her appreciate her husband's extroverted character.

Set 6-A　CD🅐A-16　　　　解説はP143📖

これから放送される講義を聞き，(1)～(5)の問いに対して，それぞれ正しい答えを一つ選び，その記号を記せ。

(1) How is poetry by Wordsworth different from poetry by modern writers like Larkin?
a) It doesn't rhyme.
b) It is not as emotional.
c) It is less enjoyable to read.
d) It is about emotion, rather than thought.
e) It focuses on beauty rather than deprivation.

(2) Which two words describe both traditional poetry and modern poetry, according to the professor?
a) emotional / rhyming
b) emotional / rhythmical
c) rhyming / pleasurable
d) rhythmical / rhyming
e) pleasurable / rhythmical

(3) How does the professor feel about the poem by William Carlos Williams?
a) It would be more effective if it rhymed.
b) There are several possible interpretations of the poem.
c) It conveys a lot of meaning in a small number of words.
d) It is more moving than poetry by Larkin or Wordsworth.
e) It is difficult to understand because it is broken into eight lines.

(4) Which of the following is true about the poem by William Carlos Williams, according to the professor?
a) It consists of eight words.
b) It was included in a novel.
c) Each line contains two words.
d) It was written in the current century.
e) It is arranged differently than an ordinary sentence.

(5) According to the professor, which of the following is NOT a key definition of poetry?
a) It is moving.
b) It is exciting.
c) It has a beat or tempo.
d) Its arrangement gives meaning.
e) Its words are carefully selected.

Set 6-B　CD◎A-17　　　　　解説はP150📖

これから放送されるのは，Aに続く教授と二人の学生（MartinとCynthia）との会話である。
これを聞き，(1)〜(5)の問いに対して，それぞれ正しい答えを一つ選び，その記号を記せ。

(1) How is the poetry of T. S. Eliot different from that of William Blake?
 a) Eliot deals with a wide variety of subjects, while Blake focuses on a single issue.
 b) Eliot uses strong rhyming words to make his poem appealing, while Blake does not.
 c) Blake's poem communicates history, while Eliot's poem serves a less practical purpose.
 d) Reading Eliot requires extensive cultural and literary knowledge, while Blake's poem is accessible to anyone.
 e) Blake writes about animals, a universally beloved subject, while Eliot writes only about factories and other dreary topics.

(2) Which of the following does NOT describe Martin's feelings about poetry?
 a) Poetry is meant to be heard, not just read silently.
 b) Poetry should be appreciated for the beauty of its style.
 c) Poetry should be written in a style that ordinary people can understand.
 d) Poetry should be written so that people can enjoy the beauty of the words.
 e) Poetry should include images that the listener is able to see in her mind's eye.

(3) According to the professor, how was poetry originally used?
 a) As a medium to spread rumors.
 b) As a way of conveying information.
 c) As a means to dramatize historical events.
 d) As a way of expressing powerful emotions.
 e) As a way to encourage communication between different generations.

(4) Why does Cynthia prefer difficult poetry?
 a) Because it allows her own interpretation of the meaning.
 b) Because it portrays a more accurate image of historical events.
 c) Because it makes her feel like the poet respects her intelligence.
 d) Because it gives her the joy of unraveling the mysteries of the world.
 e) Because it helps her improve her vocabulary and cultural knowledge.

(5) Which of the following best describes Martin's point?
 a) Poetry is meaningless if it is not understood.
 b) Overly complex poetry alienates most readers.
 c) Poets should talk to readers about the kind of poems they like.
 d) People should receive better education so they can enjoy poetry.
 e) Poems about death and dying are too dark for the ordinary reader.

Set 6-C   CD⊘A-18

解説はP157

これから放送されるのは，ある製品の発表会の模様である。これを聞き，(1)～(5)の問いに
対して，それぞれ正しい答えを一つ選び，その記号を記せ。

(1) Which of the following is true?
 a) Some people in the audience came here from overseas.
 b) The new product is already being used in the workplace.
 c) Next Gen Technologies developed the new product alone.
 d) Sandra Thomas is an employee of Next Gen Technologies.
 e) The partnership between the two companies has not been previously announced.

(2) Smith says the new product is "a genuine exception to that rule." What does the
   phrase mean in this context?
 a) Few new products are truly unique, but this one is.
 b) The new product does not follow government regulations.
 c) Many new technologies are revolutionary, including this one.
 d) Technology is evolving quickly, but this product was developed slowly.
 e) It takes time to develop a new product, but this one was made in a short time.

(3) How are the internal smartphone and the conventional smartphone similar?
 a) The screen can be viewed by multiple people.
 b) Both require headphones for private listening.
 c) Both provide access to Internet and telephone networks.
 d) Both can be controlled either by voice commands or touch.
 e) Both can be used simply by purchasing a device and turning it on.

(4) What does Thomas mean when she mentions "two-way control"?
 a) A device that can be operated in two different ways.
 b) A device that can be controlled by two different people.
 c) A situation where the user is given a series of yes-no options.
 d) A situation where a single user can control two devices at once.
 e) A situation where the device controls the user and the user controls the device.

(5) Which of the following is NOT true about the internal smartphone?
 a) It can connect to the Internet.
 b) It is embedded inside the user's body.
 c) It draws energy from the user's body.
 d) It requires an external screen to work.
 e) It responds to thoughts in the user's brain.

Set 7-A　CD⦿B-1　　解説はP163📖

これから放送されるのは，大学における教授と学生（Julia と John）の討論の模様である。これを聞き，(1)〜(5)の問いに対して，それぞれ正しい答えを一つ選び，その記号を記せ。

(1) What was the subject of last week's lecture?
a) The relationship between rules and creativity.
b) The importance of individual creativity in business.
c) The relationship between creativity and competition.
d) The importance of free competition in the marketplace.
e) Policies at companies like Apple and Nike that limit worker freedom.

(2) According to the professor, which of the following statements about Picasso's 11 bulls is NOT true?
a) Picasso created them in 1945.
b) Each print shows a single bull.
c) Nothing else is depicted aside from the bull.
d) With each print, the bull's image became more and more realistic.
e) The 11th bull was drawn as a highly abstract image, with simple lines.

(3) According to Julia's example, how do rules affect creativity?
a) They destroy it because they limit freedom.
b) They ultimately lead to boredom, which hinders creativity.
c) They stimulate creativity by encouraging the artist to break the rules.
d) They hinder creativity, which in turn prompts the artist to experiment.
e) They enhance creativity by encouraging experimentation within the boundaries of the rules.

(4) Which of the following is true about MovieNow?
a) It has an unusual policy for taking time off.
b) The company only has one rule for its workers.
c) The subscribers can rent as many movies as they want.
d) It provides online services to make the home environment more comfortable.
e) It followed the same business model as other companies in the video industry.

(5) According to the professor, why didn't the policy at MovieNow hamper the company's growth?
a) Because the overall economy at that time was very strong.
b) Because employees were still responsible for meeting targets.
c) Because most of the employees didn't choose to take a long vacation.
d) Because the company had many other policies that ensured innovation.
e) Because employee pay was reduced if they took too many vacation days.

Set 7-B　CD ⊘ B-2　　　　　　　　　解説はP170📖

これから放送されるのは，Aの後に行われた三人の学生（Julia, John, Pete）による会話である。これを聞き，(1)～(5)の問いに対して，それぞれ正しい答えを一つ選び，その記号を記せ。

(1) How does John feel about MovieNow's policy?
  a) He is not sure whether it's good or not.
  b) He thinks their teacher should adopt a similar policy.
  c) He believes it suits him because he is lazy by nature.
  d) He likes it because he prefers having a long vacation.
  e) He thinks it may be good for some people, but not for him.

(2) What type of educational system does Julia prefer?
  a) One in which she can continue studying while having fun.
  b) One in which no textbooks or formal classes are provided.
  c) One in which she studies at home but follows a set curriculum.
  d) One in which she is required to complete weekly assignments and tests to monitor her progress.
  e) One in which she is free to study at her own pace during the semester, and take only one major test at the end.

(3) Which of the following accurately describes the unschooling movement?
  a) Children are deprived of the opportunity to learn.
  b) Children study in mini-classrooms in their family homes.
  c) It is based on a belief that children have a natural desire to learn.
  d) Children can decide for themselves whether or not they want to go to school.
  e) Children study a curriculum that is designed to counteract what they have learned in mainstream schools.

(4) Which of the following statements describes Pete's experience with unschooling?
  a) He resents his parents for not giving him the same experiences as other children.
  b) He studied a wider range of subjects than he would have in a conventional school.
  c) He wasted his time learning a lot of things he didn't need to know to get ahead in life.
  d) He enjoyed exploring the forest as a young boy, but he didn't gain the knowledge necessary for success.
  e) He enjoyed the freedom it offered, and was still able to achieve goals such as passing college entrance exams.

(5) What do Julia and John think of unschooling?
  a) They fully approve of it.
  b) They have some doubts.
  c) They are strongly opposed to it.
  d) They wish their parents had tried it.
  e) They think it would be a bad fit for them because it lacks structure.

Set 7-C   CD◉B-3   解説はP177📖

これから放送されるJamesとSarahの会話を聞き，(1)(2)(4)(5)の問いに対しては，それぞれ正しい答えを一つ選び，(3)については英文が放送文の内容と一致するように，正しいものを一つ選び，その記号を記せ。

(1) Which of the following does Sarah NOT mention as an unusual feature of the new overpass?
a) It is very wide.
b) Nobody uses it.
c) There are often traffic jams on it.
d) The area around it is uninhabited.
e) There are many trees and bushes on it.

(2) According to James, why was the overpass built?
a) Wildlife needed a much larger habitat.
b) The number of panthers in the forest had decreased by 65%.
c) Wild animals needed a safe way to move around the forest preserve.
d) Too many people were getting injured when they hit deer with their cars.
e) Pedestrians needed a safe way to get from one part of the forest preserve to another.

(3) The newspaper article James read claimed that
a) some wildlife species risk extinction due to car accidents.
b) many drivers have been attacked by dangerous wild animals.
c) in Texas hunting has greatly reduced the population of ocelots.
d) most of the animals killed by cars are common species like deer.
e) humans are as likely to be injured as animals in roadkill accidents.

(4) Why did rangers monitor the park before building the overpass?
a) To determine which species were most at risk.
b) To map the places where wildlife crossed roads.
c) To track the number of animals getting hit by cars.
d) To make sure the overpass wouldn't interfere with recreation.
e) To decide on the location where car accidents are most likely to occur.

(5) Why was an underpass built on a different section of the road?
a) Because deer are afraid of high places.
b) Because the overpass was not effective.
c) Because the number of car accidents didn't decrease.
d) Because too many animals were trying to use the overpass.
e) Because predators needed a separate place to cross the road.

24

Set 8-A   CD⊘B-4   解説はP183📖

これから放送される講義を聞き，(1)～(5)の問いに対して，それぞれ正しい答えを一つ選び，その記号を記せ。

(1) According to the lecturer, the concepts of "natural" and "unnatural" are:
 a) Surprisingly similar.
 b) Contradictory to each other.
 c) Both necessary to define one another.
 d) Found in cultures throughout the world.
 e) Ideas that did not exist in older civilizations.

(2) Which of the following would the lecturer be LEAST likely to categorize as "natural"?
 a) A river with a dam on it.
 b) A snow-covered mountain.
 c) A cave dug by prehistoric people.
 d) A drought caused by climate change.
 e) A microorganism brought back from outer space.

(3) People who don't eat pork are mentioned as an example of:
 a) Socialized behaviors that are unnatural.
 b) Natural dispositions that humans are born with.
 c) The way in which religion can distort natural behavior.
 d) The changing relationship between humans and the natural world.
 e) The ambiguous line between concepts of "natural" and "unnatural."

(4) According to the lecturer, discussing the definition of nature is:
 a) A purely theoretical exercise.
 b) An important moral obligation.
 c) Frustrating because no clear answers exist.
 d) Relevant only for politicians and public officials.
 e) Of little practical use because it's a purely philosophical matter.

(5) Which of the following is most likely to represent the lecturer's opinion about new types of plants created through genetic engineering?
 a) The plants are clearly unnatural, and therefore should be outlawed.
 b) The plants are unquestionably natural because they are similar to wild species.
 c) The plants represent human mastery of nature, and therefore should be encouraged.
 d) People should stop creating those plants because we are not sure about the implications.
 e) It is a complex ethical issue, in part because the plants are difficult to classify as either natural or unnatural.

Set 8-B　CD◎B-5　　　　　　　　　解説はP189📖

これから放送されるのは，あるコンペティションの模様である。これを聞き，(1)〜(5)の問い
に対して，それぞれ正しい答えを一つ選び，その記号を記せ。

(1) Which of the following is true about the competition?
  a) 15 engineers are taking part in the competition.
  b) John Hart is no longer a member of the jury panel.
  c) There were originally 15 entrants, but four were rejected.
  d) The audience is not allowed to comment on the bridge designs.
  e) The four remaining teams will have to explain more about their designs.

(2) Which of the following is NOT one of the criteria for judging the competition?
  a) The bridge should become a symbol of the local area.
  b) Boats using the river must be able to pass beneath it.
  c) Cars and other vehicles must be able to use the bridge.
  d) People with disabilities must be able to get on the bridge.
  e) The bridge must not have a significant impact on the lives of local people.

(3) From the following illustrations, identify which is the suspension bridge and which
    is the cable-stayed bridge. Then, choose the correct match from the choices below.

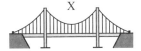 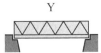 

  a) suspension bridge: X　cable-stayed bridge: Y
  b) suspension bridge: X　cable-stayed bridge: Z
  c) suspension bridge: Y　cable-stayed bridge: X
  d) suspension bridge: Z　cable-stayed bridge: X
  e) suspension bridge: Z　cable-stayed bridge: Y

(4) What criticism does Paul Mason make?
  a) The tiles would not generate a useful amount of electricity.
  b) It would be impossible to cover the whole walkway in tiles.
  c) Covering the whole walkway in tiles would be too expensive.
  d) The number of light bulbs Bluestone proposes to use is too low.
  e) The electric charge created by the crystals could be dangerous.

(5) What is one thing that we learn from this conversation?
  a) Paul Mason believes that the Bluestone bridge is the best option.
  b) John Hart outlined the main rules and requirements for the new bridge.
  c) In terms of cost, a cable-stayed bridge is superior to a suspension bridge.
  d) The width of the River Redmond means the bridge will have to be unusually long.
  e) Amanda Hamilton does not know the difference between cable-stayed and
     suspension bridges.

Set 8-C　CD⊘B-6　　　　　　　　解説はP195📖

これから放送されるのは，Bに続く質疑応答の模様である。これを聞き，(1)～(5)の問いに対して，それぞれ正しい答えを一つ選び，その記号を記せ。

(1) What does Amanda say about the lights on the bridge?
  a) They will be powered partly by wind energy.
  b) They will be powered mainly by solar energy.
  c) They will not be connected to the electricity grid.
  d) They will not use electricity from the piezoelectric tiles.
  e) They will be installed by a company called People Power.

(2) What does Tim Andrews say about the new tiles?
  a) People will not be allowed to walk on them.
  b) Engineers have failed to produce them cheaply enough.
  c) His team has already sold many of them to other businesses.
  d) They use software that can track the number of bridge users.
  e) The applications will shut down automatically when the energy from the tiles fails.

(3) What opinion does John give about the microgeneration aspect of the Bluestone design?
  a) The cost of installing low-energy applications is too high.
  b) Advertisers are unlikely to need the data the software will gather.
  c) The environmental advantages are not as great as Bluestone claims.
  d) People Power might be willing to supply the equipment more cheaply.
  e) The cost of the project will be higher than what People Power estimates.

(4) How does Amanda respond to John's final question?
  a) She dismisses the question as "unrealistic."
  b) She provides John with the assurance that he asked for.
  c) She changes the subject to avoid answering the question.
  d) She denies that the wind will cause vibration in the cables.
  e) She admits that the bridge might have to be closed sometimes.

(5) Which of the following statements is true?
  a) John is not convinced by Tim's comments about the tiles.
  b) John doubts that Amanda's team will win the competition.
  c) John is eager to focus on the structure of the bridge design.
  d) Tim and Amanda are no longer working on the bridge project.
  e) Tim and Amanda's explanation is the best the panel has heard.

Set 9-A　　CD◉B-7　　　　　　　　　　解説はP202📖

これから放送されるのは，あるラジオ番組での公開インタビューの模様である。これを聞き，
(1)〜(5)の問いに対して，それぞれ正しい答えを一つ選び，その記号を記せ。

(1) Why did Mr. Powell decide to write his book about drones?
　a) He wanted the military to stop using drone technology altogether.
　b) He thought that drone technology could be redesigned for military use.
　c) He felt that drone technology was being used for too many military applications.
　d) He wanted the drone technology to be used in many ways, not just for military
　　　 purposes.
　e) He wanted to draw people's attention to the non-military applications of drone
　　　 technology.

(2) Which of the following is NOT mentioned as something drones can do better
　　than humans?
　a) Drones can withstand extreme heat or cold.
　b) Drones can reach areas that humans cannot.
　c) Drones can transport objects quickly and directly.
　d) Drones can receive and interpret electronic signals.
　e) Drones can retrieve information from an aerial perspective.

(3) Which of the following uses of drones does Mr. Powell mention?
　a) Planting seeds
　b) Surveying land
　c) Watering crops
　d) Spreading fertilizer
　e) Investigating crimes

(4) In terms of human influence, what are the two classifications of unmanned
　　aircraft?
　a) intelligent and automatic
　b) semi-automatic and full-automatic
　c) programmable and self-controlling
　d) remote-controlled and autonomous
　e) directly-controlled and artificially-controlled

(5) Which of the following statements would Mr. Powell most likely agree with?
　a) Drones should be used only for military purposes.
　b) Drones are useful for peaceful applications but not military applications.
　c) Drones will replace humans in almost every military and peaceful application.
　d) Drones should only be used for peaceful applications and never for military
　　　 purposes.
　e) Drones can be used as effective weaponry but also have important peaceful
　　　 applications.

28

Set 9-B　CD◎B-8　　　解説はP209📖

これから放送される講義を聞き，(1)(2)(5)については各文が放送の内容と一致するように，それぞれ正しいものを一つ選び，(3)(4)については各問いに対して，それぞれ正しい答えを一つ選び，その記号を記せ。

(1) The professor mentions light
 a) as a contrast to human identity.
 b) as an example of something that cannot be measured.
 c) as an example of what science cannot explain completely.
 d) as an abstract concept which is almost impossible to define.
 e) as a physical phenomenon that has long been a controversial issue among scientists.

(2) According to the professor, the definition of personal identity as a collection of physical matter is problematic because
 a) twins look identical but have separate identities.
 b) people with artificial limbs retain their personal identity.
 c) the human spirit is also an important component of identity.
 d) the components of the human body are replaced continuously.
 e) the human body and mind are so closely interrelated that one cannot be separated from the other.

(3) Which similarity between the Ship of Theseus and the human body does the professor highlight?
 a) They both deteriorate as they age.
 b) They are both composed from many different parts.
 c) They both undergo changes in appearance with the passage of time.
 d) They are both subjects that people have debated since ancient times.
 e) They both contain different physical matter at different points in time.

(4) Which of the following is NOT mentioned as a result of aging?
 a) Changes in DNA.
 b) Increased bone fragility.
 c) Changes in physical attributes.
 d) Growth or shrinkage of the brain.
 e) Changes in the stomach and lungs.

(5) According to the alternative theory of identity described by the professor,
 a) human identity is similar to the hardware of a computer.
 b) human identity is less complex than advanced computer systems.
 c) computers are making progress towards solving the mystery of identity.
 d) human identity is like a set of instructions that determine physical behavior.
 e) human identity is controlled by a kind of software program that is inherent in each person.

Set 9-C　　CD⑦B-9　　解説はP216📖

これから放送されるのは，Bの後で行われた学生三人（Andrew, Brittany, Catherine）の会話である。これを聞き，(1)〜(5)の問いに対して，それぞれ正しい答えを一つ選び，その記号を記せ。

(1) Why does Andrew question the professor's argument that identity is not a physical concept?
 a) Because cells are not actually replaced over time.
 b) Because the argument goes against his religious beliefs.
 c) Because some body parts stay the same throughout life.
 d) Because each individual has unique physical characteristics.
 e) Because physical characteristics are easier to recognize than any other feature.

(2) What does Brittany mean when she says Andrew's 14-year-old body is gone?
 a) His body has matured since his teenage years.
 b) He is a different person now than he was then.
 c) His identity has changed since he became an adult.
 d) He has different cells in his body now than he did then.
 e) His body has become much larger and stronger than it was when he was 14.

(3) Which of the following describes Catherine's belief about the soul?
 a) It determines our physical appearance.
 b) It will be understood by scientists one day.
 c) It is the best explanation for human identity.
 d) It disappears together with our physical body when we die.
 e) It is a spiritual entity that is controlled by each person's identity.

(4) How do the three students react to the professor's explanation of identity?
 a) All three students support his argument.
 b) All three students are skeptical of his argument.
 c) Catherine and Andrew are more critical of it than Brittany.
 d) Catherine agrees with it, but Andrew and Brittany disagree.
 e) Brittany and Catherine don't understand it, but Andrew does.

(5) Why does Catherine mention preachers, priests, and imams at the end of the conversation?
 a) Because she doesn't have much faith in religious leaders.
 b) Because she believes scientists can't solve the mystery of identity.
 c) Because religious leaders are increasingly aware of scientific debates.
 d) Because religious leaders understand patterns of human behavior well.
 e) Because she thinks scientists and religious leaders should work together.

Set 10-A　CD⦿B-10　　　　　解説はP223📖

これから放送されるのは，ある講演の模様である。これを聞き，(1)〜(5)の問いに対して，それぞれ正しい答えを一つ選び，その記号を記せ。

(1) What is the topic of the lecture?
  a) Stories from travel on four continents.
  b) How to travel in places without adequate electricity.
  c) The best places to eat seafood and hear live jazz in New Orleans.
  d) The drawbacks of depending too much on high-tech devices while traveling.
  e) The importance of careful planning in order to have the best experience in a foreign place.

(2) Which of the following accurately describes Mary's first night in New Orleans?
  a) She went to a jazz performance with new friends.
  b) She dined at a restaurant the hotel receptionist recommended.
  c) She used a restaurant review app to find a place to eat dinner.
  d) She got lost on her way to the restaurant, so she went back to the hotel.
  e) She made friends through a travel app and went to a jazz show with them.

(3) Which of the following does Mary NOT mention as a typical way most English people travel today?
  a) Posting reviews of restaurants on online apps.
  b) Using a restaurant review app to find a place to eat.
  c) Staying virtually connected with clients or coworkers.
  d) Using online maps to find their way around new places.
  e) Relying on the Internet to choose what to eat at a restaurant.

(4) What does the term "armed with" mean in the phrase "fully armed with modern gadgets"?
  a) covered in
  b) prepared with
  c) surrounded by
  d) decorated with
  e) loaded down by

(5) According to Mary, why is it better to travel the old-fashioned way?
  a) Traveling without high-tech digital devices is safer, cheaper, and easier.
  b) By referring to books rather than websites, travelers obtain more reliable information.
  c) By not relying on smartphone navigation apps, travelers develop their innate navigational skills.
  d) Without constant access to online information, travelers are more likely to have unexpected experiences.
  e) By going around without high-tech devices, travelers can enjoy their trip at their own pace without being overwhelmed by schedules.

Set 10-B CD◎B-11　　　　　　　　　解説はP230

これから放送されるのは，あるラジオ番組の一部である。これを聞き，(1)〜(5)の問いに対して，それぞれ正しい答えを一つ選び，その記号を記せ。

(1) What does the host assume about the people who created the fake artworks in Spain?
 a) They were trying to make a protest.
 b) They were not motivated by money.
 c) They made huge profits from their work.
 d) They were poorly skilled as forgery painters.
 e) They have not yet been caught by the police.

(2) What was Tom Keating attempting to do?
 a) Make sure that his fake paintings were easy to identify.
 b) Buy poor artists' paintings to help them become famous.
 c) Restore fake paintings and sell them to private collectors.
 d) Change the way the art world dealt with collectors and artists.
 e) Publicize the situation where artists and dealers are working together to make money.

(3) What is one thing we learn about the Fine Art Expert Institute?
 a) Its own artists are able to make fakes that look genuine.
 b) It thinks that radiocarbon dating can damage a painting.
 c) It believes that less than half of the artworks it sees are fakes.
 d) It uses a variety of technologies to see whether paintings are genuine.
 e) Ten to twenty percent of the paintings it examines turn out to be forgeries.

(4) What does Cathy imply about the attitude of many art collectors when she says that "ignorance is bliss"?
 a) They rarely suspect that artworks that they own might be fake.
 b) They choose not to find out whether their artworks are authentic.
 c) They do not trust the accuracy of techniques like radiocarbon dating.
 d) They are unaware of the services offered by the institute in Switzerland.
 e) Whether the artworks they own are genuine or not doesn't matter to them.

(5) What do we learn about the portrait belonging to a museum in Italy?
 a) Experts still disagree about who painted it.
 b) Modern techniques showed it to be genuine.
 c) It was once thought to be a work by Raphael.
 d) It has been put on the market for 30 million euros.
 e) It depicts the face of the great Italian artist Raphael.

Set 10-C CD⊘B-12 解説はP237📖

これから放送される会話を聞き，(1)(4)(5)の問いに対しては，それぞれ正しい答えを一つ選び，(2)(3)については英文が放送文の内容と一致するように，正しいものを一つ選び，その記号を記せ。

(1) Which of the following reasons is NOT given for why the fabricated story was spread?
  a) Reporters failed to check their facts before releasing the story.
  b) Internet tricksters fabricated a story to attract attention to themselves.
  c) Most websites make a profit based on how many hits their articles get.
  d) Readers wanted to share a scandalous news story with all of their friends.
  e) The government cannot restrict news sites from publishing false information.

(2) According to this dialogue, websites propagate false information because
  a) false information makes more money than true stories.
  b) false information is more entertaining for their readers.
  c) fact-checking slows them down and lowers their revenues.
  d) fact-checking is too difficult for their reporters and editors.
  e) they simply can't distinguish between false information and correct information.

(3) According to the speakers, the press can only be held responsible for a hoax if the reporter
  a) knew the information was false and published it for whatever reason.
  b) assumed the information was true and published it without checking the facts.
  c) suspected the information was false and published it to see what would happen.
  d) knew the information was false and published it anyway in order to harm the victim.
  e) suspected the information was false and published it to attract attention and ad revenue.

(4) Why do the speakers believe that the government should not interfere with the press?
  a) Government policy can never prevent the press from doing the wrong thing.
  b) Government policy is determined by a small group of people who dislike the press.
  c) Government policy might cause the press to lose advertising revenue and shut down.
  d) Government policy is hard to change and could potentially restrict important information.
  e) Government policy is subject to change, and therefore the press has difficulty in providing consistent coverage.

(5) Which of the following statements would the speakers most likely agree with?
  a) The information found on news sites is usually false.
  b) Freedom of the press should not apply to news sites.
  c) Fact-checking is too difficult and slow for news sites to attempt.
  d) News sites are only reliable if they carefully verify their information.
  e) In order to protect yourself from fake news, it is important to always check multiple newspapers and choose the most reliable articles.

Set 11-A　CD◎B-13　　解説はP244📖

これから放送されるのは，あるラジオ番組の一部である。これを聞き，(1)〜(5)の問いに対して，それぞれ正しい答えを一つ選び，その記号を記せ。

(1) According to Betsy, which of the following statements about pain is true?

a) The brain is the only organ involved in sensing pain.
b) Its function is to protect us from threats such as fire.
c) The level of pain we feel is always equal to the level of danger facing us.
d) Past experiences do not play a role in determining how much pain we feel.
e) How much pain we feel depends on how much the experience means to you.

(2) What was the cause of the pain Betsy felt a year after the surgery?

a) Her brain's incorrect perception.
b) A psychological trauma from the surgery.
c) A tumor that remained after the operation.
d) Damage to her nerve endings from the surgery.
e) A malfunction in the nerve endings that detect danger.

(3) According to Betsy's account, which of the following is true about nociceptors?

a) Nociceptors can detect a threat that does not exist.
b) Nociceptors remind us of our past experiences with the threat we face.
c) Nociceptors receive information from the brain about the dangers around us.
d) Nociceptors are the part of the brain which is responsible for producing pain.
e) None of the above.

(4) Which of the following does Betsy mention as a reason for writing a book about pain research?

a) She wanted to help people understand their pain.
b) She wanted to understand the pain other people feel.
c) She wanted to help reduce the pain other people feel.
d) She wanted to correct people's misunderstanding about pain.
e) She wanted to write about how other people experience pain.

(5) How does Joe feel about pain, according to the interview?

a) He wishes he had felt less pain from a rib injury last year.
b) He would rather not think about pain because it is too complex.
c) He is thankful for pain because it prevented a rib injury last year.
d) He is confused by pain because it is not always caused by a real injury.
e) He didn't feel so much pain from a rib injury because he didn't have many nociceptors.

34

これから放送されるのは，ある美術館でのガイド付きツアーの模様である。これを聞き，(1)
〜(5)の問いに対して，それぞれ正しい答えを一つ選び，その記号を記せ。

(1) Why does the cashier apologize to the woman?
a) Because she can't join the tour.
b) Because the tickets were sold out.
c) Because he gave her incorrect change.
d) Because she has to pay extra for her tickets.
e) Because she's missed the beginning of the tour.

(2) According to the tour guide, why were *the Thirty-Six Views of Mount Fuji* so
popular when they were first released?
a) Because they were printed using a wide variety of colors.
b) Because they were created by an up-and-coming young artist.
c) Because they used a new blue pigment imported from Europe.
d) Because they depicted a mountain with great spiritual and cultural significance.
e) Because they made effective use of geometric forms such as the conical Mount
Fuji.

(3) According to the tour guide, which of the following is NOT a way in which
Prussian blue differed from traditional blue pigments used in Japan?
a) It was more widely available.
b) It was imported from Europe.
c) It produced more vivid colors.
d) It was derived from chemicals rather than plants.
e) It could be combined with other colors like pink and green.

(4) According to the tour guide, how did the availability of Prussian blue change
Hokusai's work?
a) It made his prints more affordable for a mass audience.
b) It altered the type of landscape element he emphasized.
c) It led him to explore sadder themes associated with blue.
d) It encouraged him to draw in a more realistic, European style.
e) It enabled him to express natural scenes in a more dramatic way.

(5) What was ironic about the European reaction to Hokusai's work, according to
the guide?
a) They thought the prints were more exotic than they actually were.
b) They didn't realize Hokusai had been trained in European techniques.
c) They mistakenly believed that Hokusai was influenced by European art.
d) They didn't know that European artists were also using Japanese indigo.
e) They were excited about the colors rather than the symbolism of the images.

Set 11-C　CD⊘B-15　　　　解説はP258📖

これから放送される講義を聞き，(1)〜(5)の問いに対して，それぞれ正しい答えを一つ選び，その記号を記せ。

(1) **Based on the lecture, which statement would many scientists likely agree with?**
 a) Before long, robots will appear identical to humans.
 b) Robots that resemble humans too closely are dangerous.
 c) In the future, humans will probably be created in factories.
 d) In the not-too-distant future, humans will be replaced by robots.
 e) The key difference between humans and robots is the ability to love.

(2) **What is the "uncanny valley"?**
 a) Negative responses we make to non-human organisms.
 b) The recent unexplained dip in the popularity of robots.
 c) The tendency to reject or fear robots that are too human-like.
 d) A geographical location where many robots are manufactured.
 e) The point at which people stop fearing robots and start liking them.

(3) **Which of the following is NOT mentioned as a reason the uncanny valley effect exists?**
 a) The fact that people may associate robots with death.
 b) The human tendency to experiment with our own appearance.
 c) A natural behavioral tendency that humans share with other animals.
 d) The inability of engineers to make robots that are identical to humans.
 e) The failure of robots to behave as people expect man-made objects to behave.

(4) **What is the argument against the existence of the uncanny valley?**
 a) People often dislike objects that are unfamiliar to them.
 b) People are also afraid of other types of advanced technology.
 c) People get accustomed to an unfamiliar object as soon as they see it.
 d) Most people are actually excited by the possibility of human-like robots.
 e) The entertainment industry has made robots familiar, so they are no longer scary.

(5) **How has the entertainment industry changed, according to the lecture?**
 a) Animators today worry more about declining profits.
 b) Animators in the past drew more realistic characters.
 c) Animators today worry less about drawing overly realistic characters.
 d) Animators in the past worried more about drawing unrealistic characters.
 e) Animators in the past worried less about making audiences uncomfortable.

Set 12-A CD B-16

解説はP265

これから放送される講義を聞き，(1)～(5)の問いに対して，それぞれ正しい答えを一つ選び，その記号を記せ。

(1) **Which of the following was NOT true of the earliest postal systems?**
a) The post was set up mostly for use in governance.
b) Intellectuals often used the post to discuss scholarly questions.
c) Due to the low literacy rate, letter writing was not widespread.
d) The post was sometimes unreliable, in part due to the difficulties of travel.
e) The cost of sending messengers naturally limited letters to the most powerful.

(2) **According to the lecture, what is one reason for the spread of letter writing?**
a) Metal nibs were invented.
b) More people learned to read and write.
c) Transportation systems were developed.
d) Common people gained wealth, allowing them to pay postage.
e) People had larger families that they needed to communicate with.

(3) **How did people in pre-Victorian times save money when writing letters?**
a) They sent only very short messages.
b) They reused checked cloth instead of paper.
c) They used one piece of paper again and again.
d) They wrote in two directions on a single sheet of paper.
e) The letter writer paid the postage, rather than the recipient.

(4) **In what way did Victorian letter writing mimic Victorian society?**
a) Writers had to follow social norms in their letters.
b) People had a great deal of freedom when writing letters.
c) There was no distinction between male and female roles.
d) Women had to obey more rules than men when writing letters.
e) People used typewriters to make their letters look more attractive.

(5) **Based on the lecture, what is probably the best reason that many people today do not use cursive?**
a) Our families are smaller, requiring fewer letters.
b) Computers have made hand-written letters unnecessary.
c) Ornamental handwriting is considered unattractive today.
d) Postage is cheap, so we do not need to write crossed letters anymore.
e) People write far more letters than in the past, so they need to write faster.

Set 12-B　CD◉B-17　　　　　　　　　　解説はP272📖

これから放送されるのは，ある大学での教授による講義である。これを聞き，(1)～(5)の問いに対して，それぞれ正しい答えを一つ選び，その記号を記せ。

(1) **What is one thing the professor says about wolves in his introduction?**
 a) They became extinct in 1926.
 b) They were driven to the brink of extinction in the 1870s.
 c) It is a myth that wolves are too shy to approach human beings.
 d) People's false impressions contributed to the decline in their numbers.
 e) The US government tried to protect the wolf in the early 20th century.

(2) **Which of the following did NOT happen while there were no wolves in the park?**
 a) A large increase in the number of elk.
 b) The removal of soil due to a lack of trees.
 c) The effects called "negative trophic cascade."
 d) The growth of more trees near the riverbanks.
 e) Damage to the areas where fish and birds lived.

(3) **Which view did the 2004 study by Ripple and Beschta support?**
 a) Wolves were getting better at concealing themselves from elk.
 b) Elk behavior changed as a result of the reintroduction of wolves.
 c) After the reintroduction of wolves, the number of trees decreased.
 d) Douglas W. Smith's explanation for the rise in elk numbers was correct.
 e) The growth of young willow trees made it easier for wolves to hunt elk.

(4) **What did the 2005 study tell us?**
 a) Grizzly bears killed more elk than wolves did.
 b) Fewer Americans now watch nature documentaries.
 c) The growth of aspen trees was faster than expected.
 d) Wolves were responsible for a majority of bear deaths.
 e) There was no change in the feeding patterns of elk in response to wolves.

(5) **What is one problem that Arthur Middleton fears may occur?**
 a) People will be less likely to believe scientists in future.
 b) People's attention will be distracted from protecting wolves.
 c) Scientists will advise governments to introduce wolves in other areas.
 d) The case for reintroducing predators to the wild will be strengthened.
 e) Scientists won't be able to get financial support from the government.

38

Set 12-C　CD⊘B-18　　　　　解説はP279📖

これから放送されるのは，Bの後で行われた学生三人（Rachael, Rahim, Graham）の会話である。これを聞き，(1)〜(5)の問いに対して，それぞれ正しい答えを一つ選び，その記号を記せ。

(1) What does Rahim suggest about sharks?
  a) They are actually quite friendly to humans.
  b) They are less territorial than scientists had previously believed.
  c) They get negative coverage even though they rarely pose a threat.
  d) They have become more interesting to scientists since the *Jaws* movie.
  e) They are a good example of an animal that remains a significant danger to humans.

(2) What point does Rachael attempt to make about human nature?
  a) It is important to understand that human nature is not always the same in all places and all situations.
  b) Humans tend to care more for their natural environment than the other two students believe they do.
  c) Humans will always try to dominate other species, even though it may not be in their long-term interests.
  d) Most humans tend to be pessimistic about the future even though there are many conservation movements around.
  e) Humans are superior beings and therefore have the right to control other animals and the environment they are in.

(3) Why does Rahim bring up the subject of conservation?
  a) To claim that some progress is being made.
  b) To show that he remembered last year's lecture.
  c) To point out that Europeans have caused the most problems.
  d) To emphasize how humans totally dominate the environment.
  e) To support Rachael's point about the environment being in trouble.

(4) What is one thing Graham tells us about the cane toad?
  a) The toad was introduced to Australia to protect the cane beetle.
  b) The toad has had less effect on its intended target than was initially predicted.
  c) It would have been better to introduce the toad earlier to protect cane sugar crops.
  d) The cane beetle has now become an endangered species because of the toad's introduction.
  e) The toad is a good example of an animal that was accidentally brought into a foreign ecosystem.

(5) Which of the following sentences is true?
  a) These people all agree that conservation is pointless.
  b) Professor Sanchez's lectures are no longer interesting.
  c) Graham sees some hope as long as humans use science.
  d) Rahim and Rachael have differing opinions about the movie *Jaws*.
  e) Most invasive species have been deliberately brought into foreign environments.

改訂版 鉄緑会
東大英語リスニング

解答・解説篇

Set 1 | 解答

1 A　(1) e　(2) e　(3) b　(4) a　(5) a
1 B　(1) a　(2) d　(3) e　(4) a　(5) d
1 C　(1) e　(2) d　(3) e　(4) b　(5) try not to get too wet as you head out

Set 1-A | 放送文

Space Exploration

❶ Dianne:　Good evening, and welcome to *Science Roundup with Dianne Zollie*, where we bring you the week's top science stories from around the globe. Or in this case, around the universe. Our first guest tonight is reporter Steve Singleton, who's going to tell us how scientists are preparing for an alien invasion. Right Steve?

❷ Steve: Well yes, an alien invasion of sorts. But before any of your listeners out there start panicking, I should clarify. There's no need to worry about little green men descending on Washington en masse. The alien invasion I've been reporting on is a microscopic one. As listeners may recall, Russia announced plans this week for a mission to Mars in 2018 with the goal of bringing back some specimens to study.

❸ Dianne: Soil samples, to be specific.

❹ Steve: Right. Nobody's ever done that before, and as of now we don't even know if there's life of any sort on Mars. But there's a small chance that the soil the Russians bring back will contain microorganisms of some sort, such as bacteria.

❺ Dianne: Martian microbes, so to speak.

❻ Steve: Exactly. Which poses a couple of problems. First, how do we identify these microorganisms? What if the soil becomes contaminated with our own native microbes once it's here on Earth? That could create quite a confusing situation.

❼ Dianne: You wouldn't want scientists saying they'd discovered a Martian life form only to learn later it was actually from New York City!

❽ Steve: No, that would be bad. So they've got to keep that space soil completely isolated and clean.

invasion 名 侵入，侵略
… of sorts 句 …のようなもの
little green men 句 宇宙人（映画やイラストに描かれる，小さな緑色の宇宙人の呼称）
en masse 句 大挙して
microscopic 形 微細な
specimen 名 標本
🔲 Steve の発言の主旨：
　alien invasion といっても，いわゆる「エイリアン」の侵略ではなく，宇宙の微生物を地球に持ち込むこと
soil 名 土，土壌
as of now 句 今のところは，これまで
life 名 生命，生命体
microorganism 名 微生物
microbe 名 微生物
pose a problem 句 問題となる
What if …? 句 もし…だとしたらどうなのか？
contaminated with … 句 …に汚染されている
🔲 土壌サンプルに微生物が含まれていた場合の問題①：
　地球の微生物と区別するのが困難
only to *do* 句 結局…することになる
isolate 他 …を分離する，隔離する

❾ Dianne: Okay, and what about the second problem?

❿ Steve: The second problem is, what if these hypothetical alien microbes are harmful to life on Earth? It would be disastrous if they escaped into the environment and began making us sick or multiplying out of control and displacing Earth's native microorganisms.

⓫ Dianne: Oh, that's a scenario straight out of a horror film. Do scientists have a plan to keep that from happening?

⓬ Steve: They do indeed. This week I had the chance to interview NASA's curator of astromaterials at the Johnson Space Center in Houston, and he told me about a special containment room that his staff has been preparing for the soil.

⓭ Dianne: And how does this containment room work?

⓮ Steve: Well, it's essentially a box in a box in a box. The system makes use of two basic principles. One, microbes move by riding the air. They can't run or walk on their own. Two, air always moves from areas of higher pressure to lower pressure. So here's the plan. The innermost box will have the soil sample in it, and the air pressure in that box will be higher than in the middle box. That means a leak in the innermost box would cause air to flow out, not in, guaranteeing that the soil stays free of contaminants. The outermost box would also have higher air pressure than the middle box, so that air could only flow inwards, never outwards. That would prevent any of the Martian microorganisms from ever escaping the system.

⓯ Dianne: Ingenious. Nothing can escape from the inside of the box, and at the same time no contaminants can get in. Well, that makes me feel a little less nervous about those alien invaders. We'll look forward to more updates as the Mars mission approaches, Steve!

⓰ Steve: Will do.

---

hypothetical 形 仮想の
multiply 自 増殖する
displace 他 …に取って代わる

🔑 土壌サンプルに微生物が含まれていた場合の問題②：微生物が地球環境にとって有害である可能性

curator 名 専門職員, キュレーター
containment 名 封鎖

principle 名 原理, 原則

innermost 形 最も奥の（↔ outermost）

🔑 containment room の構造・仕組み：
・3重の箱
・土壌サンプルは最も内側の箱
・空気圧は外側の箱から順に, 高―低―高
・土壌サンプル内の微生物は外から汚染されることもなく, また外に流出することもない

ingenious 形 創意工夫に富んだ

update 名 最新情報

Set 1-A | 放送文の日本語訳

宇宙探査

❶ダイアン：こんばんは，「ダイアン・ゾリーと科学を総括」へようこそ。ここでは，世界から寄せられた今週一番の科学の話題を紹介します。いや，この場合世界からというよりも宇宙からというべきでしょうか。今晩の最初のゲストは，レポーターのスティーブ・シングルトンさんです。科学者がエイリアンの侵略に対して，どのような準備をしているのか話してくれます。そうですね，スティーブ？

❷スティーブ：はい。まあエイリアンの侵略と言っていいでしょう。でも，リスナーの皆さんがパニックを起こす前に，明確に説明しておきます。緑色をした小さな宇宙人が大挙してワシントンに降り立つといったことを心配する必要はありません。私がレポートしてきたエイリアンの侵略とは，顕微鏡で見ないと分からないほど小さなエイリアンの侵略です。リスナーの皆さんもご存じかもしれませんが，ロシアが研究用の標本を持ち帰る目的で，2018年に火星へのミッションを計画していると今週，発表しました。

❸ダイアン：具体的に言うと，土壌サンプルですね。

❹スティーブ：そうです。これまで，誰もそれを成し遂げたことがないし，現時点では，火星に何らかの生命体が存在するかどうかは分かっていません。しかし，ロシア人たちが持ち帰る土壌にバクテリア等の何らかの微生物が含まれている可能性は，わずかながらあります。

❺ダイアン：要するに，火星の微生物ですね。

❻スティーブ：その通りです。それに伴い，いくつか問題が発生します。第1に，それらの微生物をどのように同定するか？　地球に持ち帰った時点で，地球の土着微生物に汚染されたらどうなるか？　結果的に，ややこしい状況が生まれる可能性があります。

❼ダイアン：科学者が火星の生命体を発見したと言いながら，後でそれが実際にはニューヨークのものだと分かったというのでは困りますね！

❽スティーブ：はい，そんなことになったら問題です。それゆえ，科学者は，宇宙の土壌を完全に隔離し，汚染されないように保つ必要があります。

❾ダイアン：分かりました。では，第2の問題とは？

❿スティーブ：第2の問題は，これらの仮想の地球外微生物が地球上の生物に危害を及ぼすものだったらどうなるか，という点です。それらの微生物が環境中に流出し，我々を病気にしたり，制御不能なほど増殖して地球の土着微生物に取って代わったりし始めたら被害は甚大です。

⓫ダイアン：なんと，まるでホラー映画のシナリオですね。科学者は，そんなことが起きるのを防ぐための対策を考えているのですか？

⓬スティーブ：実際，考えています。今週，ヒューストンのジョンソン宇宙センターでNASAの地球外物質キュレーターにインタビューする機会がありましたが，そうした土壌用としてスタッフが用意している特殊な封鎖室について話してくれました。

⓭ダイアン：その封鎖室は，どのような仕組みになっているのですか？

⓮スティーブ：そうですね，基本的には3重の箱です。このシステムは，2つの基本原則に基づいています。第1は，微生物が空気に乗って移動するという点。微生物は，自分で走行，歩行はできません。第2は，空気が常に圧力が高いところから低いところに移動するという点です。よって，対策とはこうです。最も内側の箱の中に土壌サンプルを収容し，その箱内の空気圧を中間の箱内の空気圧よりも高くします。つまり，最も内側の箱内で漏出が発生しても，空気は流出するだけで流入することがないので，土壌サンプルが汚染されずにすみます。最も外側の箱も中間の箱よりも内部の空気圧を高くし，空気が必ず内側に向けて流れ，外側に向けて流れないようにします。これにより，火星の微生物がこのシステムから漏出するのを防ぐことができます。

⓯ダイアン：うまくできていますね。箱の内側からの漏出があり得ないと同時に汚染物質が流入することもあり得ないわけですね。これで，エイリアンの侵略については，不安感が少し解消されます。スティーブ，火星ミッション間近になったら，もっと最新情報を知らせてください。

⓰スティーブ：分かりました。

《 指針 》

「火星の土壌サンプルを地球に持ち帰る際に生じる問題点と，その対策」をテーマとしたインタビューである。前半部（❶～❺）ではalien invasionという表現が何を指しているのかに注意すること。中盤（❻～⓫）では，火星の微生物を持ち帰った際に生じる2つの問題点とは何かに注目する。後半部（⓬～⓰）ではcontainment roomの構造と仕組みを正確に理解することが求められる。

難易度

放送文	★★☆
設　問	★★☆
総　合	★★☆

☺☹))) **スピーカー情報**

Dianne: 西海岸，カリフォルニア
Steve: 中西部，ミズーリ

44

Set 1-A │ 設問解説

(1) What has Steve been reporting on recently?
スティーブが最近レポートしてきたのは，何についてか。
a) The possibility of life on Mars.
火星に生命が存在する可能性。
b) A new method for identifying microorganisms.
微生物を同定するための新しい方法。
c) A recent trip to Mars by a Russian space craft.
最近行われたロシア宇宙船による火星への旅。
d) The arrival of small green aliens in Washington.
ワシントンでの小さな緑色の宇宙人の出現。
e) The challenges of bringing back soil samples from Mars.
火星から土壌サンプルを持ち帰るという難しい課題。

❷のalien invasionという表現に惑わされないように。Steveが話題にしているのは，いわゆる「エイリアンの地球侵略」ではない。火星の土壌サンプルを地球に持ち帰る際に，それとともに地球外の微生物が地球に入る可能性のことをalien invasionと表現しているにすぎない。正解は e 。challengeは「課題，問題」という意味。ロシアの火星探索計画はまだ計画段階なので c は誤り。

(2) What is the first potential problem associated with studying the specimens, according to Steve?
スティーブによると，標本の研究に関連して発生し得る第1の問題とは何か。
a) Martian microbes might contaminate Earth's soil.
火星の微生物が地球の土壌を汚染する可能性がある。
b) Martian microbes might die before they reach Earth.
火星の微生物が地球に到着する前に死んでしまう可能性がある。
c) Scientists might not have the right tools to analyze them.
科学者が標本を分析するための適切なツールを持っていない可能性がある。
d) People from New York City might be afraid of the specimens.
ニューヨーク市民が標本に恐怖心を抱く可能性がある。
e) Microbes from Mars might become indistinguishable from those from Earth.
火星由来の微生物と地球由来の微生物との区別がつかなくなる可能性がある。

❻では「火星から持ち帰った微生物と地球上の微生物を区別することの難しさ」について語られている。❼でDianneが述べている「火星の微生物だと思ったらニューヨークのものだった」というのは，この問題を分かりやすく喩えたものである。正解は e 。indistinguishable from ...は「…と区別できない」という意味。a は，❿以降で語られる「2つ目の問題」に含まれる。

(3) What is the second potential problem?
発生し得る第2の問題とは何か。
 a) The microbes might not really be from Mars.
  そうした微生物が本当は火星由来のものではない可能性がある。
 b) The microbes might damage organisms on Earth.
  そうした微生物が地球上の生物に危害を及ぼす可能性がある。
 c) The microbes might be displaced by organisms on Earth.
  そうした微生物が地球上の生物によって駆逐されてしまうかもしれない。
 d) The microbes might be harmed by Earth's native bacteria.
  そうした微生物が地球の土着バクテリアにより危害を被る可能性がある。
 e) The microbes might die before scientists have time to study them.
  科学者が研究する暇もなく，そうした微生物が死滅する可能性がある。

❿では「火星の微生物が地球環境に混入して増殖し，地球の環境に有害な影響を与える危険性」について語られている。これを表すbが正解。aは(2)の「1つ目の問題」に含まれる。

(4) What is the plan that scientists have come up with for handling the specimens?
標本を取り扱うために，科学者が考え出した対策とは何か。
 a) Put them in a triple-layer box.
  3重の箱の中に標本を収容する。
 b) Put them in three separate boxes.
  3つの別々の箱の中に標本を収容する。
 c) Do not take them off the space ship.
  宇宙船から標本を運び出さない。
 d) Put them in a box with very low air pressure.
  空気圧が非常に低い箱の中に標本を収容する。
 e) Put them in three boxes, each with a different pressure.
  それぞれ圧力の異なる3つの箱に標本を収容する。

⓮のit's essentially a box in a box in a boxをヒントにaを正解として選ぶ。layerは「層」という意味である。この箱は3重構造になっており，その最も内側の箱に土壌サンプルを格納するのであって，bやeのように3つの箱に入れるのではない。また，土壌を入れる箱の空気圧は高いのでdは誤り。

(5) Which of the following is true about the containment room?
封鎖室について正しいのは，次のうちどれか。
 a) The pressure in the middle box is the lowest.
  中間の箱内の圧力が最も低い。
 b) The pressure in the innermost box is the lowest.
  最も内側の箱の圧力が最も低い。

c) The outermost box has a valve to relieve excess pressure.
最も外側の箱には余分な圧力を逃がすためのバルブがある。

d) The innermost box has higher air pressure so that the soil samples will not leak out.
土壌サンプルが漏出しないように，最も内側の箱内の方が空気圧が高くなっている。

e) The room will prevent the Martian microbes from escaping, but it won't protect them from contamination.
この部屋は，火星の微生物が漏出するのを防ぐが，微生物を汚染から守ることはできない。

❹で述べられているcontainment roomの仕組みを正確に把握すること。全体が3重構造になっており，土壌サンプルは最も内側の箱に入れられる。中間の箱の空気圧は内側の箱より低くなっているため，内側の箱に外部からの空気が入ることはない。また，最も外側の箱の空気圧も高くなっており，内から外へと空気が漏れるのを防ぐようになっている。空気圧が低いのは「中間の箱」であり，a が正解となる。c のvalveについての言及はない。d のThe innermost box has higher air pressureは正しいが，so that the soil samples will not leak outが誤り。空気圧が高いのは「外からの流入を防ぐため」である。e のThe room will prevent the Martian microbes from escapingは正しいが，it won't protect them from contaminationが誤り。外への流出も，また外からの汚染も防ぐ構造になっている。

Set 1-B | 放送文

Digitization of Education 1

❶ Chris: Good morning folks! Thanks for braving the lousy weather today to join me here in Nairobi for a sneak preview of the future of education. My name is Chris Brown, and as most of you know, I'm the communications director for Computer Connections, the company behind a groundbreaking new child-led learning system that we are revealing to the press for the very first time. Here with me this morning is Sandra Maynard, the founder and president of Computer Connections, who will give you some background on the system and tell you why it is so vitally important for children around the world. We also have one more very special speaker with us this morning, Hope Wambui, a young girl who is among the first on-the-ground users of this new system. So I think we are going to send you back to your newsrooms today with some really exciting stories for your readers. Sandra, why don't you get us started?

❷ Sandra: Good morning. Around the world, 134 million children have never been to school. In Africa alone, 32 million go without textbooks, teachers, or classrooms. They are condemned to a life of poverty simply because they were born in a place without schools, and without the money to go elsewhere for an education. This is absolutely unacceptable. Our children deserve more.

❸ That's why I am so excited to be here this morning to show you an incredibly powerful solution to this global problem. What you see in front of you is called a Learning Lab. It is a triangular outdoor kiosk with a computer station on each side. Each of these simple structures includes a built-in video camera, a bench to seat three people, a Wi-Fi connection, and a wide range of educational software for children ages 5 to 15. Up here on the top of the kiosk are solar panels that power the computers so they can be used

brave 他 …に立ち向かう
lousy 形 嫌な
sneak preview 句 内覧会

事実関係の把握：製品を開発したのは Computer Connections。Sandra がその創設者。Chris は広報担当

マスコミ向けの発表会であることが分かる

condemned to … 句 …を余儀なくされている

Sandra の発言の主旨：世界中で多くの子どもが満足な教育を受けられず貧困を強いられている

triangular 形 三角形の
kiosk 名 キオスク（公共の施設にあるマルチメディア端末）

48

in communities that lack electricity. The entire unit is made of durable recycled plastic, and the computers are also coated in plastic to make them waterproof and dustproof. As you can see, even with rain pouring down onto the kiosk like it is right now, they work just fine!

❹　　Last month we installed the very first Learning Lab in an open-air market in Kawangware, a slum here in Nairobi that does not have enough schools or teachers to serve all its children. This kiosk is allowing the community to access a whole new world of education. But don't take my word for it! Let's hear from Hope, a resident of Kawangware who has been using the Learning Lab for the past month.

❺Hope: Hello. My name is Hope Wambui and I am ten years old. I have never been to school. Last month, a Learning Lab just like this one was built down the street from my house. At first I had no idea what it was. I asked my aunt and she said it was a free computer kiosk for children, so I decided to try it out. It was very easy to use. Now my friends and I spend about half an hour playing the learning games on it every day. So far I have learned the alphabet, watched a video about space travel, and used the video camera to talk with a student in Sweden. There is so much more I want to learn! I hope that all children in Kenya have the chance to use a Learning Lab very soon.

❻Chris: Sandra and Hope, thank you so much. Please stay where you are and we will begin accepting questions from the press.

durable 形 耐久性のある

waterproof 形 防水性の
dustproof 形 防塵性の

▶Learning Labの特徴：三角形で，それぞれの面にコンピュータが設置されている。ビデオカメラ，3人がけのベンチ，Wi-Fi接続，5〜15歳向けの教育ソフトを備える。太陽電池で動き，屋外用に防水・防塵処理がされている
install 他 …を設置する
slum 名 スラム街
take someone's word for it 句〈人〉の言うことを信じる
resident 名 住人

▶Hopeの発言の主旨：Learning Labを友人たちと使って色々なことを学べた

Set 1-B | 放送文の日本語訳

教育のデジタル化 1

❶クリス：皆さま，おはようございます。今日は悪天候の中，教育の未来を紹介する内覧会のため，ここナイロビにお集まりいただき，ありがとうございます。私は，クリス・ブラウンと申します。大半の方がご存じのように，コンピュータ・コネクションズ社の広報責任者を務めております。弊社は，画期的な新しい子ども主導の学習システムを考案した企業ですが，そのシステムを今から報道陣の皆さまに初公開いたします。今朝，ここに同席しておりますのは，コンピュータ・コネクションズ社の創業者であり社長であるサンドラ・メイナードです。サンドラからこのシステムの背景と，全世界の子どもたちにとって，このシステムが極めて重要である理由をお話しいたします。もう1人，ここでお話しいただく特別ゲストをお招きしています。この新しいシステムを実際に使用した最初の利用者の1人，ホープ・ワムブイさんです。今日記者の皆さまには，読者が本当に興味をそそられる話題をニュース編集室に持ち帰っていただこうと思います。サンドラ，始めてもらえますか。

❷サンドラ：おはようございます。全世界には，学校に通ったことのない子どもが1億3400万人います。アフリカだけでも，3200万人が教科書，教師，教室を欠いた環境にいます。学校のない地域で生まれ，しかも教育を受けるために他の地域に行くお金もないという理由だけで，貧困生活を余儀なくされています。こんなことは，絶対に許されません。子どもたちは，もっと恵まれてもいいはずです。

❸　ですから，今朝ここに出席し，この世界的問題を解決するための信じられないほど効果的な解決策を皆さまに紹介するのを非常に楽しみにしております。前方に見えるのは，学習ラボというものです。三角形の屋外キオスクで，それぞれの側にコンピュータステーションを設置しています。これらのシンプルな構造物は，おのおのビデオカメラを内蔵し，3人掛けのベンチ，Wi-Fi接続環境，5歳から15歳までの子ども向けの幅広い教育ソフトウェアを完備しています。キオスクの屋根には，コンピュータの電源となるソーラーパネルが取り付けられているので，電気のない地域でもコンピュータを使用できます。このユニット全体が頑丈な再生プラスチックでできており，コンピュータも防水・防塵のため，プラスチックで覆われています。ご覧の通り，今のようにキオスクに雨が降り注いでも，コンピュータは，ちゃんと機能します！

❹　先月，ここナイロビのスラム街であるカワングワレの青空市場に学習ラボ第1号を設置しました。カワングワレには，地域の全ての子どもたちに対応できるだけの学校や教師が揃っていません。このキオスクのおかげで，この地域は，全く新しい教育の世界を手に入れることができます。でも，私の言葉をそのまま鵜呑みにしないでください！　カワングワレに住み，この1ヶ月間，学習ラボを利用してきたホープさんの話を聞きましょう。

❺ホープ：こんにちは。私の名前は，ホープ・ワムブイ，10歳です。学校には通ったことがありません。先月，これと同じような学習ラボが私の家の通りを行った先に設置されました。最初は，これがなんだか分かりませんでした。おばに尋ねると，

50

子ども向けの無料コンピュータキオスクだと言うので，試してみることにしました。とても使いやすかったです。今は，友人と毎日キオスクで30分ほど学習ゲームをして過ごしています。これまでに，アルファベットを学び，宇宙旅行についてのビデオを見たし，ビデオカメラを使ってスウェーデンの生徒とも会話しました。もっとたくさん学びたいことがあります！　ケニアの子どもたち全員が早く学習ラボを利用できるようになることを願っています。

❻クリス：サンドラ，ホープさん，ありがとうございました。そのまま，そこにいてください。今から，報道陣からの質問を受け付けます。

《 指針 》

Learning Labという，子ども向けの学習システムの製品発表である。アフリカ等の貧しい地域で屋外に設置し，学校に通えない子どもたちが独学できるように作られている。前半部（❷）では製品を開発した経緯を把握し，中盤（❸❹）ではこの製品の特徴を理解する。そして最後のHopeの発言では「実際に使ってみてどうだったのか」という感想の要点を摑むようにしたい。

難易度

放送文	★★☆
設　問	★★☆
総　合	★★☆

☺☺))) **スピーカー情報**

Chris: 西海岸，カリフォルニア
Sandra: 西海岸，カリフォルニア
Hope: 西海岸，カリフォルニア

Set 1-B ｜設問解説

(1) Which of the following is true about Computer Connections?
コンピュータ・コネクションズ社について正しいのは，次のうちどれか。

a) The business was started by Sandra Maynard.
サンドラ・メイナードが創業者である。

b) Chris Brown is the company's executive director.
クリス・ブラウンは，同社の専務取締役である。

c) The company employs an African girl as a programmer.
同社はアフリカ人の少女をプログラマーとして雇っている。

d) The company's mission is to teach children computer skills.
同社の使命は，子どもたちにコンピュータ操作技術を教えることである。

e) The company's new product has been featured in many newspapers and magazines.
同社の新製品は，多くの新聞や雑誌で取り上げられてきた。

❶でSandraはthe founder and president of Com0puter Connectionsとして紹介されている。founderは「創設者」という意味であり，a が正解。Chrisはcommunications directorであるからbは誤り。アフリカ人の少女Hope は従業員ではなくLearning Labのユーザーなのでc は誤り。またe はwe are revealing to the press for the very first timeという発言に反する。

(2) What is the Learning Lab?
学習ラボとは何か。
a) Educational software that facilitates students' independent learning.
生徒の自主学習を助ける教育ソフトウェア。
b) A set of computer-based tools that teachers can install in classrooms.
教師が教室に設置できるコンピュータを用いたツール一式。
c) An educational system designed to promote interaction among children.
子どもたちの交流を促進することを目的とした教育システム。
d) A system that will allow children to learn even if they don't have teachers.
教師がいなくても子どもたちが学べるようにするシステム。
e) An educational device that connects poor children in Africa with teachers around the world.
アフリカの貧しい子どもたちと世界中の教師たちとを繋ぐ教育機器。

❷❸からLearning Labの基本コンセプトを読み取る。まず❷では学校に通えない子どもたちが大勢いるという問題が指摘され，さらに❸ではそれに対する解決策としてこの製品を開発したことが示唆されている。以上からd を正解とする。Learning Labは「ソフトウェア」ではないのでa は誤り。子どもたちの「交流」ではなく「学習」を目的としているのでc は誤り。また，無線通信機能が備わっていても，それが「世界中の教師と繋げるため」という説明はなされていないのでe も誤り。

(3) Which of the following is NOT a feature of the Learning Lab?
学習ラボの特徴でないものは，次のうちどれか。
a) Educational programs for children of all ages.
あらゆる年齢層の子ども向け教育プログラム。
b) A bench for children to sit on while they learn.
子どもたちが学習する際に腰掛けるベンチ。
c) Durable materials that withstand rain and dust.
雨やホコリに強い頑丈な素材。
d) A renewable energy source to provide electricity.
再生可能エネルギー源により電源を供給。

e) Video screens that allow children to interact with teachers in other countries.
子どもたちが他の国々の教師たちと対話できるビデオスクリーン。

❸についての問題である。 a はa wide range of educational software for children ages 5 to 15に，bはa bench to seat three peopleに， c はthe computers are also coated in plastic to make them waterproof and dustproofに合致。dのrenewable energy source は solar panels that power the computersを言い換えたものと考えられる。 e についての言及はどこにもない。よって e が正解。

(4) Sandra says, "Don't take my word for it." What does she imply by that?
サンドラが「私の言葉をそのまま鵜呑みにしないでください」と言っているが，それは，何を意味するか。
a) The user's voice is most important.
利用者の声が最も重要である。
b) Some of the information she gave is wrong.
彼女が提供した情報の一部が間違っている。
c) Reporters shouldn't quote her directly in their articles.
記者は，彼女が言ったことを記事に直接引用すべきではない。
d) There is something she doesn't understand about the system.
そのシステムについて彼女に分からないことがある。
e) Reporters should visit the community themselves to confirm her comments.
記者は，自らその地域に出向き，彼女のコメントについて確証を得るべきだ。

❹でSandraがHopeを紹介する際にdon't take my word for itと言っているが，これは「私の言うことを信用しないでください」という意味。もちろん，文字通りの意味ではなく，「私が言うことなんかよりも，実際にLearning Labを使った利用者の生の声を聞いてください」という趣旨での発言である。 a が正解。

(5) Which of the following statements best describes Hope's experience with the Learning Lab?
学習ラボでのホープの体験を最も的確に表している記述は，次のうちどれか。
a) She has been studying with it for almost a year.
1年近くそれを使って勉強をしている。
b) She first used the kiosk on a class trip led by her teacher.
教師が引率したクラス旅行で，初めてキオスクを利用した。
c) She has used it to practice English, watch videos, and shop online.
これまで英語の練習，ビデオ鑑賞，オンラインショッピングに利用したことがある。
d) At first she was confused by it, but she quickly learned to use the technology.
最初は戸惑っていたが，すぐに使い方を習得した。

e) Her aunt showed her how to use the computers, but now she can use them on her own.
おばからコンピュータの使い方を習ったが，今では1人で使いこなすことができる。

❺のHopeの感想を要約すると「先月，家のそばにLearning Labが設置された。最初はそれがなんだか分からなかったが，試してみるととても使いやすく，今では毎日友人たちと色々なことを学んでいる」となる。これに最も近いdが正解。HopeがLearning Labを使って1ヶ月ほどしか経っていないのでaは誤り。Learning LabはHopeの家のそばに設置されたとあるのでbは誤り。cはshop onlineが誤り。eはHer aunt showed her how to use the computersが誤り。

Set 1-C | 放送文

Digitization of Education 2

❶ Chris: Reporters, please say your name and the publication you write for before you ask your question. Yes, in the back.

❷ Celeste: I'm Celeste Arthur from the *Nairobi Daily Press*. This is a question for Sandra. What inspired you to develop this technology?

❸ Sandra: Five years ago, I was working as a volunteer English teacher in a village north of here. The children I was working with were so incredibly eager to learn, so bright, and so dedicated despite the difficult circumstances of their lives. But there was only one of me and hundreds of them. I knew the Kenyan government did not have the funds to hire more teachers, and I thought, wouldn't it be amazing if there were a cheap, digitized educational technology that could provide children with the education they need? Over the following few years I gathered a team of first-rate Kenyan engineers, designers and educators, and together we developed the Learning Lab you see in front of you.

❹ Chris: Yes, second row from the front.

❺ Jim: Jim Stone here from *WPPR News Radio*. Isn't it important for teachers to be involved in teaching? Can a machine really deliver the same quality education as a human being?

❻ Sandra: I do still believe that teachers are important. But many studies have shown that computerized, child-led education is also very effective. In one well-known experiment, scientists installed computers in a New Delhi slum. Within days, children had taught themselves how to use the computers, and within a few more weeks they had begun learning about complex concepts like DNA replication! They did all of that on their own, without any adults to guide them.

❼ Chris: Okay, how about a question for Hope? Yes, the gentleman in the green shirt.

❽ Edward: Hope, how long did it take you to learn how

---

inspire someone to *do* 句 〈人〉に…したい気にさせる

be eager to *do* 句 しきりに…したがっている
dedicated 形 ひたむきな，熱心な
fund 名 資金，財源
digitized 形 デジタル化された
🔁 Sandraの発言の主旨：ケニアの村で，子どもたちが学習意欲に満ちているのに教師がいない状況を目の当たりにして，安価なデジタル教育機器の開発を思いついた

be involved in ... 句 …にかかわる

complex 形 複雑な
replication 名 複製
🔁 Sandraの発言の主旨：コンピュータを用いた子ども主導の学習が効果的だというデータがある

to use the computer?

❾ Hope: About half an hour!

❿ Edward: Great. And did anyone help you?

⓫ Hope: Well, three or four of my friends figured it out together. And now we are showing other children in our neighborhood how to use it.

⓬ Chris: We have time for one final question. How about the lady in the yellow dress?

⓭ Sakura: I'm Sakura Mitani, from *the Japan Daily News*. This is for Sandra. Who pays for the kiosks? And do you have plans to expand them beyond Nairobi?

⓮ Sandra: It costs us just $25 to provide a child with practically infinite educational opportunities, yet fund-raising has been a huge challenge for us. Donors are not excited about child-led, digitized education, perhaps because it goes against the conventional wisdom that kids need teachers and classrooms in order to learn. Currently our costs are covered by donations from individuals in a number of countries, and by a grant from the Kenyan government. We are hoping to raise more funds in the coming year and expand our project to Nicaragua, Mali, and Nepal.

⓯ Chris: Well it looks like we are out of time. Please feel free to follow up with me by phone or email if you have any further questions. And try not to get too wet as you head out!

figure out 句 …を考え出す

▶ Hopeの発言の主旨: Learning Labを短時間で, 大人の手を借りずに使えるようになった

infinite 形 無限の
fund-raising 名 資金集め
challenge 名 難題, 課題
donor 名 寄付者

conventional 形 慣習的な

donation 名 寄付

grant 名 助成金

▶ Sandraの発言の主旨:資金集めが難しい。それはコンピュータによる教育に否定的な見方が多いからだ

Set 1-C | 放送文の日本語訳

教育のデジタル化 2

❶クリス：記者の皆さま，質問される前にお名前と媒体名を名乗ってください。では，後方の方，どうぞ。

❷セレステ：「ナイロビ・デイリー・プレス」のセレステ・アーサーです。サンドラさんに質問します。この技術を開発されたきっかけは何ですか？

❸サンドラ：5年前，私は，ここから北に行ったところにある村でボランティアの英語の教師として働いていました。私が教えていた子どもたちは，信じられないくらい学習意欲が高く，とても頭が良くて，困窮した境遇にありながら，とても熱心でした。しかし，生徒数百人に対し，教師は私1人でした。ケニア政府に，もっと多くの教師を雇う財源がないことは分かっていました。そこで，子どもたちに必要な教育を提供できる安価なデジタル教育技術があれば素晴らしいのにと思いました。その後2，3年かけて，ケニアの一流エンジニア，デザイナー，教育者からなるチームを結成し，前方に見える学習ラボを力を合わせて開発しました。

❹クリス：では，前から2列目の方，どうぞ。

❺ジム：「WPPRニュース・ラジオ」のジム・ストーンです。教育には教師がかかわることが重要ではないですか？　機械が人間と同じように質の高い教育を本当に提供できるのでしょうか？

❻サンドラ：教師が重要だと私も思っています。しかし，多くの研究で証明されているように，コンピュータを使用した子ども主導の教育も非常に効果的です。有名なある実験では，科学者がニューデリーのスラム街にコンピュータを設置しました。すると，数日のうちに，子どもたちは，コンピュータの使い方を独習し，さらに2，3週間のうちに，DNA複製といった複雑な概念について学び始めました！彼らは，大人の指導なしに，独力でその全てを成し遂げたのです。

❼クリス：では，ホープさんへの質問はありませんか。はい，グリーンのシャツを着た男性の方，どうぞ。

❽エドワード：ホープさん，コンピュータの使い方を習得するのに，どれくらい時間がかかりましたか？

❾ホープ：30分ぐらいです！

❿エドワード：それはすごい。誰かに習ったのですか？

⓫ホープ：うーん，3，4名の友人と一緒に使い方を見つけ出しました。そして，今は，近所の他の子どもたちに使い方を教えています。

⓬クリス：では，最後にあと1つ質問をお受けします。黄色の服を着た女性の方，どうぞ。

⓭サクラ：「ジャパン・デイリー・ニュース」のサクラ・ミタニです。サンドラさんにお尋ねします。キオスクの財源は，どこから得ているのですか？　また，キオスク設置をナイロビ以外にも広げる計画があるのですか？

⓮サンドラ：1人の子どもに，ほぼ無限の教育の機会を提供するのに要する費用は，ほんの25ドルですが，資金集めにはとても苦労しました。寄付者の方々は，子ども主導のデジタル教育にはあまり乗り気ではありませ／。おそらく，子どもが学ぶ

には教師と教室が必要だとする社会通念に反しているからでしょう。現在は，様々な国の個人からの寄付金とケニア政府からの助成金で賄っています。来年は，さらに多くの財源を確保し，ニカラグア，マリ，ネパールにも，我々のプロジェクトを広げたいと思っています。

⓯クリス：どうやら，時間切れのようです。他にご質問があれば，ご遠慮なく，電話またはeメールで私にご連絡ください。また，お帰りの際は，あまり濡れないようにご注意ください！

《 指針 》

Bの続きである。話者の数は多いが，1人ずつ順に質問していく形式なので，聞き取りはそれほど難しくないだろう。それぞれの質問と，その答えの要点を簡潔にまとめていくことが求められる。

難易度

放送文	★★☆
設 問	★☆☆
総 合	★★☆

☺😐))) スピーカー情報

Chris: 西海岸，カリフォルニア
Celeste: イングランド
Sandra: 西海岸，カリフォルニア
Jim: 中西部，イリノイ
Edward: 西海岸，オレゴン
Hope: 西海岸，カリフォルニア
Sakura: 西海岸，カリフォルニア

Set 1-C | 設問解説

(1) Which of the following is NOT a reason Sandra developed the Learning Lab?
サンドラが学習ラボを開発した理由に該当しないのは，次のうちどれか。

a) She wanted to help children fulfill their potential.
子どもたちが自分の可能性を発揮するのを手助けしたかった。

b) She saw that there was a shortage of teachers in Kenya.
ケニアでは教師が不足していることを知った。

c) She realized that an affordable educational system was needed.
手頃な料金で利用できる教育システムが必要だと実感した。

d) There were so many children that she could not teach them all by herself.
彼女だけでは教え切れないくらいたくさんの子どもたちがいた。

e) She felt that computers could provide higher-quality instruction than human teachers.
人間の教師よりもコンピュータの方が質の高い指導ができると感じた。

Sandraがケニアの村で英語教師をしていた時にLearning Labの開発を思いついた経緯は❸で述べられている。要点は次の3つ。1.「子どもたちは学習意欲に満ちていた」，2.「教師がいない」，3.「安価なコンピュータ機器による教育が有効だと考えた」。このうち1.はa，2.はbとd，3.はcに該当する。「人間の教師よりもコンピュータの方が質の高い指導ができる」とは言っていないのでeが正解となる。

(2) Which of the following statements about the experiment in New Delhi is true?
ニューデリーで行われた実験についての記述で正しいのは，次のうちどれか。

a) It took the children a long time to figure out how to use the computers.
子どもたちがコンピュータの使い方を会得するのに，かなりの時間がかかった。

b) The goal of the experiment was to prove that digitized education is not effective.
実験の目的は，デジタル教育が効果的でないことを証明することにあった。

c) It took the children less than a month to create a simulation model on the computers.
子どもたちは，1ヶ月もかからずにコンピュータ上でシミュレーションモデルを作成した。

d) The children were able to learn advanced concepts independently by using the computers.
子どもたちは，コンピュータを使い自主的に先進概念を学ぶことができた。

e) When adults provided guidance, the children were able to use the computers to study science.
大人が指導すると，子どもたちは，科学を勉強するのにコンピュータを使いこなすことができた。

ニューデリーでの実験について述べられているのは❻である。children had taught themselves how to use the computersとあるように，子どもが大人の手を借りずに自分たちだけでコンピュータを使いこなし，複雑な概念までも学ぶよ

うになったのである。これに合致するdが正解。aは「数日のうちに独習した」という発言に反する。子どもたちは「DNA複製」について学んだが，「シミュレーションモデルを作成した」わけではないのでcは誤り。子どもたちは大人の手ほどきを受けずに自分たちで学習したのでeは誤り。

(3) What can be inferred from Hope's answers?
　　ホープの回答から何を推察できるか。
a) Using the Learning Lab alone is difficult.
　　1人で学習ラボを使用するのは難しい。
b) She learned to use the computer all by herself.
　　彼女は1人きりでコンピュータを使えるようになった。
c) The Learning Lab can only be used for short periods of time.
　　学習ラボは，短時間しか使用できない。
d) Most of the games in the Learning Lab require three or four players.
　　学習ラボで使えるゲームのほとんどが3，4名のプレーヤーを必要とする。
e) Using the Learning Lab doesn't require special instruction from adults.
　　学習ラボを使用するのに，大人による特別な指導は必要ない。

設問がWhat can be inferred ...となっているので，放送文の中で直接言われていないことが答えとなる可能性もある。⓾のAnd did anyone help you?という質問に対し，HopeはWell, three or four of my friends figured it out together. And now we are showing other children in our neighborhood how to use it.と答えている。直接は言っていないが，Learning Labは子どもたちだけで使えるようになる機械だということが読み取れるだろう。eが正解。Hopeは「3，4名の友人と」学んだのでbの「1人きりで」は誤り。a，c，dはいずれも放送文の内容と大きく異なる。

(4) According to Sandra, what is the main challenge her company faces?
　　サンドラによれば，彼女の会社が直面している主な課題とは何か？
a) Overcoming the limits to machine-centered education.
　　機械中心の教育の限界を克服すること。
b) Securing adequate funding from the donor community.
　　寄付者たちから十分な資金を確保すること。
c) Convincing teachers to use the new technology in classrooms.
　　教師に教室でこの新しい技術を使用するよう説得すること。
d) Obtaining permission from the government to use the product.
　　政府から製品の使用許可を得ること。
e) Expanding the technology to countries where English is not spoken.
　　英語を話さない国にまで，この技術を広めること。

⓮のfund-raising has been a huge challenge for us からbが正解だと分かる。aのlimits to machine-centered educationについては，それが資金集めの障壁

となっていることは述べられているが，「その限界を克服する」ということは言われていない。

(5) Chris says the following sentences at the end of the conference. Fill in the blank with the exact words you hear.

記者会見の最後に，クリスが以下のように言及しているが，聞き取った正確な言葉を空白に書き込め。

Please feel free to follow up with me by phone or email if you have any further questions. And ＿＿＿＿＿＿＿＿＿＿＿＿＿＿＿＿＿＿＿＿＿＿＿＿＿ !

他にご質問があれば，ご遠慮なく，電話またはeメールで私にご連絡ください。また，＿＿＿＿＿＿＿＿＿＿＿＿＿＿＿＿＿＿＿＿＿＿ !

ディクテーションの問題で一番大切なのは，放送中に該当箇所を聞き飛ばさないようにすること。うっかりすると「2回とも聞き飛ばしてしまった」なんていうこともありうる。設問を下読みする際にPlease feel free to follow up というフレーズをチェックしておき，これが読まれたら即座に反応できるように準備しておこう。この問題の聞き取り箇所で難しいのはtの子音が続く部分である。not to get too wetでは，2つのtが1つに繋がって「ナットゥゲットゥウェッ」のように発音されていることに注意したい。

Set 2 | 解答

2A (1) c (2) e (3) c (4) c (5) d
2B (1) a (2) c (3) d (4) a (5) e
2C (1) b (2) d (3) d (4) d (5) c

Set 2-A | 放送文

Bookshelves

❶ The reason for the invention of bookshelves is obvious: they are shelves designed to hold books. However, in addition to their practical use, bookshelves are also pieces of furniture that affect the appearance of a room. Put another way, bookshelves are practical as well as ornamental objects, and have always served both of these purposes.

❷ As a practical object, a bookshelf stores books so that the spines, containing the titles, are clearly visible. This makes it easy for a reader to find, remove, and replace the book she wants without having to rearrange any of the other books on the shelf. The visibility of important information on the spine of the book is particularly important in libraries, where books are stored in greater numbers.

❸ In a library, where the quantity and variety of books is quite large, both books and shelves are arranged conveniently and consistently. In American libraries, the Dewey Decimal Classification or Library of Congress Classification system is used to label the spine of each book so that it can be easily found and replaced in its proper location. Bookshelves lend themselves well to this purpose, as they can be arranged in rows with narrow aisles between them.

❹ Yet no matter how well-organized a library may be, its shelves will always take up a great deal of space. Institutional libraries often have separate buildings designed to house thousands of extra books in their collection. Although these paper books provide some benefits to readers, they are

affect 他 …に影響を与える
put another way 句 言い換えると
ornamental 形 装飾的な
⏩本棚の役割：実用（本を収納する）と装飾（部屋を飾る）
spine 名 本の背
visibility 名 見やすさ，可視性

in great numbers 句 多数，多く
⏩本棚の実用的な役割：本の背にある情報を見やすくする
consistently 副 一貫性をもって
Dewey Decimal Classification 句 デューイ十進分類法
Library of Congress Classification 句 米国議会図書館分類法
lend oneself to … 句 …に役立つ
aisle 名 通路
take up 句 …を占める
institutional 形 公共機関の
house 他 …を収蔵する

not a very efficient way of storing information. The cost of maintaining a library is quite high when compared to the cost of the digital storage systems that modern technology makes possible.

❺ The digital "bookshelf," as we might call it, gives a researcher immediate access to all kinds of relevant information in many different formats. Computers grant researchers access to books, magazines, journals, and even videos from the comfort of their own office. As a result, modern libraries have begun to shift away from physical archives toward virtual ones. In other words, the arrival of digital storage has put the bookshelf-as-practical-object in danger of becoming obsolete. This leaves bookshelves with only their ornamental purpose.

❻ Bookshelves have a long history as furniture pieces. In homes with surplus space, bookshelves were once a way to showcase affluence and refinement. Certain books were manufactured specifically to look good on a shelf, and some companies even produced blank or hollow books designed to take up space on larger bookshelves. In this way, bookshelves became a way for rich homeowners to display their wealth to visitors.

❼ This age-old tradition is now beginning to die out. People are simplifying their lives by living in smaller places with fewer physical possessions. Books take up more space than almost any other form of entertainment, so when space is limited, books and shelves are often the first items to be discarded.

❽ Where affluent homes used to feature expansive libraries, they now showcase expensive technology and entertainment devices. Reading paper books is a leisure activity for the old-fashioned instead of the well-to-do, and a large collection of books now indicates only that the homeowner has enough extra space to store them.

❾ In short, bookshelves are no longer the best way to find information or decorate one's home. Time will tell if bookshelves continue to serve these purposes at all, but as long as physical books

storage 名 貯蔵，収蔵
🔑本棚による収蔵の問題点：デジタル収蔵に比べてスペースが必要であり，コストがかかる
relevant 形 関連している
grant A B 句 AにBを与える

shift away from A toward B 句 Aから離れてBへと変わる
archive 名 収蔵庫，アーカイブ
obsolete 形 時代遅れの
🔑デジタルな書籍収納による結果：本棚の実用性は消え，装飾的目的のみに
surplus 形 余分な
showcase 他 …を見せる，誇示する
affluence 名 豊かさ，富
refinement 名 洗練
manufacture 他 …を製作する
hollow 形 空の，空洞の

die out 句 廃れる

possession 名 所有物

discard 他 …を捨てる，処分する
affluent 形 豊かな，裕福な
expansive 形 膨大な，広範な
🔑本棚の装飾的目的：今日ではテクノロジー機器に取って代わられた

continue to be read, bookshelves will have their place.

have one's place 句 存在意義を持つ

Set 2-A | 放送文の日本語訳

本棚

❶ 本棚の発明の理由は明らかです。本棚は本を入れるために作られた棚です。けれども, その実用的用途に加え, 部屋の見た目を左右する家具でもあります。言い換えれば, 本棚は実用的であると同時に装飾的なものであり, 常にその2つの目的に応えてきました。

❷ 実用的なものとして, 本棚は, 表題を記した背がはっきり見えるように本を収納します。これによって読者は, 棚にある他の本を並べ直す必要もなく, 求める本を容易に見つけ, 抜き取り, そして元に戻すことができます。本の背にある重要な情報の見やすさは, たくさんの本を収蔵する図書館においては特に重要です。

❸ 蔵書の冊数と種類の極めて多い図書館では, 書物と本棚が利便性と一貫性をもって並べられています。米国の図書館では, 本を見つけ, 適切な場所に戻すことが容易にできるよう, デューイ十進分類法あるいは米国議会図書館分類法を用いて, 1冊ずつ背にラベルを貼っています。本棚は狭い通路を挟んで何列も並べられるので, そうした目的に適っています。

❹ しかし, 図書館がどれほど組織化されていようと, 本棚は常に巨大な空間を占有してしまいます。公共図書館にはしばしば, 収容しきれない多数の蔵書を収蔵するための, 独立した建物があります。これらの紙の書物は読者にとって有益な面もありますが, 情報の保管方法としてあまり効率的とは言えません。蔵書を維持するためのコストは, 現代の科学技術によって可能となったデジタルな収蔵システムのコストに比べて, 極めて高いのです。

❺ デジタルな「本棚」とでも呼ぶべきものによって, 調べものをする人は, 多種多様なフォーマットのありとあらゆる関連情報に即時にアクセスできます。コンピュータによって, オフィスにいながらにして, 書籍, 雑誌, 定期刊行物, さらにはビデオにアクセスすることまでできるのです。結果的に, 今日の図書館は物理的な収蔵庫であることをやめ, バーチャルな収蔵庫になりつつあります。つまり, デジタルな収蔵方法の登場によって, 「実用品としての本棚」は時代遅れになろうとしています。かくして本棚には装飾的目的のみが残ることになります。

❻ 本棚は家具としての長い歴史をもっています。余剰空間のある住宅において, かつて本棚は富と洗練の見せ場の1つでした。ある種の本は棚の上での見栄えがいいように特別に作られました。大きな本棚の空きを埋めるための, 中身が白紙だったり空洞だったりする本を作る会社すらありました。このように, 本棚は金持ちが客に自らの富を誇示する方法となったのです。

❼ 今日, こうした古い伝統も廃れつつあります。人々は居住空間を狭め, 物質的所有物を減らすことで, 生活を単純化しつつあります。本はあらゆる娯楽形態のうち最も場所をとるものと言って良いでしょう。したがって, スペースが限られている場合, しばしば本と本棚が真っ先に処分されることとなります。

❽　かつては裕福な家庭といえば膨大な蔵書を誇ったものですが，今日では高額の
テクノロジーや娯楽機器を誇るようになっています。紙の書物を読むことは，金
持ちの道楽ではなく，古臭い人間の道楽です。そして膨大な蔵書は，今やその家
には本を溜め込めるだけの余分なスペースがあることを示しているにすぎません。

❾　要するに，本棚はもはや，情報を得るのにも自宅を飾るのにも最善の方法では
ないのです。本棚がそもそもそうした目的を果たすものであり続けるかどうかは，
時間がたてば分かることです。しかし，物理的な書物が読まれ続ける限り，本棚
は存在意義を保つことでしょう。

《《 指針 》》

「本棚」をテーマとした講義である。「実用」と「装飾」という2つの目的
が，時代とともにどのように失われていったかが説明される。本文の語彙
レベルはやや高いが，論理展開が分かりやすく，文意を摑むのはそれほど
難しくないだろう。設問の(1)や(3)のように，「放送文で言及されていな
いものはどれか」というタイプの問題は，必然的に難易度が高い。選択肢
の下読みを入念に行っておく必要がある。

難易度

放送文	★★☆
設　問	★★★
総　合	★★☆

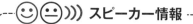 スピーカー情報

Lecturer: 西海岸，オレゴン

Set 2-A ｜設問解説

(1) Which of the following does the lecturer NOT mention as a purpose of
bookshelves?
本棚の目的として講師が言及していないのは，次のうちどれか。

a) To hold books.
本を保持するため。

b) To show off your wealth.
裕福さを誇示するため。

c) To preserve books for longer periods.
書物を長期間保存するため。

d) To make a room look more attractive.
部屋をいっそう魅力的にするため。

e) To make it easier to find a book you need.
必要な本を見つけやすくするため。

❶では本棚の目的として「実用」と「装飾」の2つが挙げられている。前者は，❶の第1文にあるように，「本を入れる」というものと，❷で説明されているように「読みたい本をすぐに見つけられるようにする」というものであり，これが選択肢のaとeに該当する。また「装飾」については，❶で「部屋の見た目を左右する」ということが指摘されており，これがdに該当する。さらに，「装飾」の延長として，❻では，「本棚がかつては a way to showcase affluence and refinement（富と洗練の見せ場）だった」ということが述べられている。これがbに該当する。cへの言及はどこにもない。

(2) Which of the following is a classification system used in American libraries?
米国の図書館で用いられている分類システムは次のうちどれか。

a) Douglas Digit Classification.
ダグラス二進分類法。
b) Supreme Court Classification.
最高裁判所分類法。
c) Universal Decimal Classification.
国際十進分類法。
d) Presidential Library Classification.
大統領図書館分類法。
e) Library of Congress Classification.
米国議会図書館分類法。

❸では，図書館における本の分類法として，米国では Dewey Decimal Classification または Library of Congress Classification が用いられていると述べられている。後者が選択肢のeに合致する。

(3) According to the lecturer, which of the following is NOT a reason libraries are using digital instead of paper archives?
講師によれば，図書館が紙の収蔵庫ではなくデジタル・アーカイブを用いている理由ではないのは次のうちどれか。

a) Digital archives are more affordable.
デジタル・アーカイブの方が費用が安い。
b) Digital archives are more efficient in terms of space.
デジタル・アーカイブの方がスペースの点で効率が良い。
c) Digital archives can be organized more systematically.
デジタル・アーカイブの方がより体系的に整理できる。
d) Readers in various locations can access digital archives.
デジタル・アーカイブは様々な場所の読者がアクセスできる。

e) Readers can access information very quickly with digital archives.
デジタル・アーカイブは読者が情報にたいへん迅速にアクセスできる。

図書館の役割が「デジタル・アーカイブ」に取って代わられつつあることは❹❺で説明されている。その理由の１つはスペースとコストである。紙の本の貯蔵は場所をとるので金がかかるということが❹の後半で述べられている。これが選択肢のａとｂに該当する。さらに❺のThe digital "bookshelf," ... gives a researcher immediate access to all kinds of relevant informationがｅに該当し，Computers grant researchers access to books ... from the comfort of their own officeがｄに該当する。選択肢ｃの「体系的な整理」については，むしろ紙の本について❸で説明されているが，デジタル・アーカイブに関しては特に述べられていない。よってｃが正解となる。

(4) Why were blank books sometimes placed on bookshelves in the past?
かつて何も書かれていない本が本棚に置かれていることがあったのはなぜか。
a) So they could be used as journals.
日記帳として使用することができるように。
b) Because they were easier to handle.
より扱いやすかったから。
c) Because full bookshelves indicated wealth.
隙間のない本棚は豊かさのしるしだったから。
d) Because they were cheaper than real books.
それらは本物の本より安価だったから。
e) Because some people could not read, but wanted to appear smart.
字が読めなくても利口に見られたい者たちがいたから。

かつては「中身が白紙の本（blank books）」が作られていたということは❻で語られている。その目的とはもちろん「読むため」ではなく「見せるため」であり，❻の最後にIn this way, bookshelves became a way for rich homeowners to display their wealth to visitors.とあるように，「金持ちであることを客に誇示するため」であった。これに合致するｃが正解。本棚に立派な本がぎっしりと並んでいることが，ある種のステータスシンボルだったのである。ｄは間違いとは言えないだろうが，そのような本を置いたメインの理由としてはｃに劣る。

(5) Which statement would the lecturer most likely agree with?
講師が最も賛成しそうな主張は次のうちどれか。
a) Bookshelves serve no purpose in modern society.
現代社会において，本棚はいかなる目的にも適わない。
b) Bookshelves are an ideal way to store information.
本棚は情報を保管するための理想的な方法である。
c) Bookshelves should only be used by wealthy people.
本棚は裕福な人たちのみが用いるべきだ。

d）Bookshelves belong in society as long as books exist.
　　本棚は本が存在する限り社会に存在する。

e）Bookshelves should be used for more practical purposes.
　　本棚はもっと実用的な目的に使われるべきだ。

❾では結論が述べられているが，as long as physical books continue to be read, bookshelves will have their placeが選択肢のdに合致する。have one's place「自分の居場所を持つ」つまりは「存在価値を持つ」という意味であり，これがbelong in societyに言い換えられている。belongは「しかるべきところにある」という意味である。本棚がその本来の役割を失ってきているということは指摘されているが，aにあるようなserve no purpose（いかなる目的にも適わない）とまでは言っていない。

Set 2-B | 放送文

Online Crowds

❶ Mary: Good evening and welcome to *Talk-Back Radio*, your weekly debate program. I'm your host Mary McGrady. Tonight we'll be talking about the Internet, social media, and online crowds. These days, you don't need to be a famous writer or politician to share your thoughts with the world. Just about anyone with access to a computer can speak out using tools like Twitter, YouTube, and blogs. But is that a good thing for humanity? I am joined here in the studio by two guests with very different answers to that question. One is Patty Bradley, a journalist who has written about online shaming. Welcome, Patty.

❷ Patty: Thank you Mary, happy to be here.

❸ Mary: My second guest tonight is Edward Salter, a professor of sociology who studies the real-life impacts of social media. Edward, thanks for joining us.

❹ Edward: My pleasure.

❺ Mary: Patty, you recently wrote a newspaper column arguing that virtual crowds such as those that form on Twitter tend to bring out the worst in people. You say we are seeing a new version of an old problem, the so-called "mob mentality" that led to witch hunts and lynching in the past.

❻ Patty: That's right. In the course of my reporting on this topic, I have met so many people whose lives have been ruined by online bullying. Once the online shaming begins, more and more people join in with negative comments, even though they may know very little about the situation or person they are criticizing.

❼ Mary: Give us an example.

❽ Patty: Well, I interviewed a college student from Texas who had a personal blog, and on his blog he had written about the physical appearance of one of his female professors. Basically, he wrote that she was ugly. The blog was shared over and over again on Facebook pages and Twitter feeds,

humanity 图 人類

📗 討論のテーマ：「インターネットでの意見共有は人類にとって良いのか？」

online shaming 句 インターネット上での中傷行為

virtual 形 仮想の

mob 图 群衆
witch hunt 句 魔女狩り
lynching 图 私刑，集団暴行

bullying 图 いじめ

📗 Patty の主張：インターネット上のいじめは人生を破滅させる

basically 副 要するに

and within 24 hours, more than 1,000 people had responded with comments saying he was sexist, a monster, an idiot. Comments came in from Europe, South Africa, Mexico. Some people even wrote death threats. He was expelled from college, lost his financial aid and became extremely depressed.

❾ Mary: Well, he did make an inappropriate comment in a public forum. He was judging his professor for her looks rather than her intelligence.

❿ Patty: True, but did he really deserve the extreme response? We all say or write stupid things sometimes.

⓫ Mary: Edward, what do you think about that example?

⓬ Edward: I agree with Patty that the outcome for the individual student was certainly unfortunate. But I think that cases like this actually improve society as a whole.

⓭ Mary: How so?

⓮ Edward: In the past, the student would probably have made the same kind of sexist comments quite freely in conversations with friends, with no negative consequences whatsoever. Those comments would have contributed to a larger culture of sexism against women. But now, thanks to the Internet, the world is watching. A student in Texas made a sexist comment on his blog, and women in Mexico and London struck back. That had real-world consequences. Because of his case, other college boys will think twice before writing insulting blogs or tweets. That is a good thing for women everywhere. And it's all thanks to the wisdom of the online crowd.

⓯ Mary: Hmm. So you're saying the sacrifice of one student is worth the benefit that online shaming can bring to society as a whole.

⓰ Edward: Well, I wouldn't quite phrase it like that, but yes.

⓱ Patty: I'd like to add a comment here. I think it's extremely dangerous for us to accept the sacrifice of individuals for the so-called "greater good" of society. What about this student's right to an education and a productive life in society? We

---

idiot 名 馬鹿

threat 名 脅し
expel 他 …を追放する
financial 形 経済的な
depressed 形 意気消沈した，鬱の
inappropriate 形 不適切な

📑 Patty の主張：学生に対するインターネット上の反応（いわゆる「炎上」）は度を超している

outcome 名 結果
📑 Edward の主張：ネットの炎上は社会全体を良くする
as a whole 句 全体として

no … whatsoever 句 全く…ない
contribute to … 句 …に荷担する，…を助長する
sexism 名 性差別
consequence 名 影響，結果
insult 他 …を侮辱する
wisdom 名 見識，知恵

📑 Edward の主張：ネットの炎上は人々の愚行を抑止する
sacrifice 名 犠牲

so-called 形 いわゆる
📑 Patty の主張：社会全体のために個人を犠牲にすべきという考え方は危険だ

don't know if other college boys will learn a lesson from his example, but we do know that his life has been destroyed. In my mind that is unacceptable.

⓲ Mary: Okay, let's open up the phone lines and bring some of our listeners into this conversation. If you have a thought you'd like to share, give us a call. But no bullying please!

Set 2-B ｜放送文の日本語訳

インターネット上の群衆

❶メアリー：こんばんは，週刊討論番組「トーク・バック・ラジオ」へようこそ。司会のメアリー・マグレディです。今夜はインターネット，ソーシャルメディア，そしてインターネット上の群衆についてお話ししましょう。近頃では，自分の考えを世界と共有するのに著名な作家や政治家である必要はありません。コンピュータにアクセスできる人であればほとんど誰でも，ツイッターやユーチューブ，ブログといったツールを使って発言することができます。しかしながら，それは人類にとって良いことなのでしょうか？　その疑問に対して大きく異なる答えをお持ちの2人のゲストにスタジオにお越しいただいています。お1人目はパティー・ブラッドリーさん，インターネット上での中傷行為に関する著作をお書きになっているジャーナリストです。ようこそ，パティーさん。

❷パティー：ありがとうメアリーさん，お招きいただいて嬉しいです。

❸メアリー：今夜の2人目のゲストはエドワード・ソルターさん，ソーシャルメディアの現実世界への影響について研究されている社会学者です。エドワードさん，番組に加わってくれてありがとうございます。

❹エドワード：こちらこそ。

❺メアリー：パティーさん，あなたは最近，ツイッター上に形成されるような仮想的な群衆が人々の最も悪い面を引き出す傾向にあると論じた新聞コラムをお書きになりましたね。私たちが目にしているのは，過去に魔女狩りや集団暴行を招いた，いわゆる「群衆心理」という古くからの問題の新しい形だ，とおっしゃっています。

❻パティー：その通りです。このトピックについて取材する過程で，ウェブ上でのいじめによって生活を破壊されてしまった実にたくさんの人々に出会いました。いったんネットでの中傷が始まると，ますます多くの人たちが否定的な意見の書き込みに加わります。批判している状況や人物についてほとんど何も知らないかもしれないのに，です。

❼メアリー：例を挙げてもらえますか。

❽パティー：そうですね，私は個人ブログを持っていたテキサス出身の大学生にインタビューしました。彼は自分のブログに女性教授の1人について身体的な見た目のことを書きました。要するに，彼女が醜いと書いたのです。そのブログはフェイスブックのページやツイッターのリツイートで繰り返しシェアされて，24時間以内に1000人以上の人々が彼は性差別主義者で，怪物で，大馬鹿者だというコメン

トを残しました。コメントはヨーロッパや南アフリカ，メキシコからも書き込まれました。殺すという脅迫を書き込んだ人さえいたのです。彼は大学を退学になり，奨学金を失ってひどい鬱状態になりました。

❾メアリー：彼は実際，公共の場で不適切なコメントをしたんですよね。教授を知性よりも見た目で判断して。

❿パティー：その通りですが，でも彼は本当にそのような極端な反応を受けてしかるべきだったのでしょうか？　私たちは時に，誰でも馬鹿なことを言ったり書いたりします。

⓫メアリー：エドワードさん，この事例についてどう考えますか？

⓬エドワード：その学生個人に起きたことはたしかに不幸だったという点でパティーさんに同意します。しかし私は，このようなケースが実は社会全体を良くするのだと思うのです。

⓭メアリー：説明してもらえますか？

⓮エドワード：昔だったら，その学生はおそらく同じような性差別的な発言をかなり自由に友人との会話の中でして，よくない結果を招くことは全くなかったでしょう。そうした発言は女性に対するより広範な性差別的風潮を助長したかもしれません。しかし現在は，インターネットのおかげで，世界が監視しています。テキサスの学生が自分のブログ上で性差別的な発言をし，メキシコやロンドンの女性たちが反論した。それは現実世界での影響をもたらしたのです。彼の事例によって，他の男子学生たちは侮辱的なブログやツイートを書く前に考え直すことでしょう。それはあらゆる場所にいる女性にとって良いことです。そしてそれは全て，ネット上の群衆の知恵のおかげなんです。

⓯メアリー：うーん。では1人の学生の犠牲は，ネットの中傷行為が社会全体にもたらす利益に値するとおっしゃるのですね。

⓰エドワード：ええ，そういう言葉で表現するつもりはありませんが，そういうことです。

⓱パティー：ひと言付け加えたいのですが。我々が社会におけるいわゆる「より大きな善」のために個人の犠牲を容認するのは，この上なく危険なことだと私は思います。この学生の教育を受ける権利や社会において実りある生活を送る権利はどうなるのでしょう？　彼の事例から他の男子大学生が教訓を得るかどうかは分かりませんが，彼の人生が破壊されてしまったことは確かです。私の考えではこれは容認できません。

⓲メアリー：さあ，電話受付を開始して，リスナーの何人かにこの会話に加わってもらいましょう。共有したい考えがあればお電話ください。でも，いじめはなしでお願いします！

《 指針 》

討論のテーマは「インターネット上の群衆（online crowds）」について。日本ではしばしば「ネットの炎上」といった言葉で語られる。この番組では，1つのテーマに対して対立する意見を持つ2名を招き，司会者（mediatorとも呼ばれる）がそれを調停するというスタイルをとっている。PattyとEdwardがそれぞれどのように意見を対立させているのかに注目しながら聞き取りたい。まずは話者の名前（Mary, Patty, Edward）をメモして，各々の論点を適宜まとめていこう。

難易度

放送文 ★★☆

設 問 ★★☆

総 合 ★★☆

☺☺))) スピーカー情報

Mary: 西海岸，カリフォルニア
Patty: イングランド
Edward: 中西部，ミズーリ

Set 2-B | 設問解説

(1) What is the main issue the guests on the radio program are debating?
ラジオ番組のゲストたちが討論している主な問題は何か。

a) Whether social media sites are beneficial for society.
ソーシャルメディアのサイトは社会にとって有益かどうか。

b) Whether women use social media in a different way than men.
女性は男性とは違ったやり方でソーシャルメディアを使っているかどうか。

c) Whether social media sites are effective for exchanging opinions.
ソーシャルメディアのサイトは意見を交換するのに効果的かどうか。

d) Whether college students should be allowed to use social media sites like Twitter.
大学生はツイッターのようなソーシャルメディアのサイトの使用を許されるべきかどうか。

e) Whether the college student who sent the negative tweet should be allowed to return to school.
否定的なツイートをした大学生は学校に戻るのを許されるべきかどうか。

討論全体のテーマは❶で述べられているように「インターネット上での意見交換が社会にとって有益か否か」である。これと同じ内容のaが正解。設問には「the main issueは何か」とあるので，dやeのように限定的な内容を述べた選択肢を選んではならない。

(2) Which of the following is NOT mentioned regarding Patty's newspaper article?
パティーの新聞記事に関して述べられていないのは次のどれか。

a) Many people's lives have been ruined by cyber bullying.
多くの人の生活がネット上のいじめによって破壊されてきた。

b) People tend to behave badly when they are part of online crowds.
人々はネット上の群衆の一部になった時悪いふるまいをする傾向がある。

c) People are more likely to make sexist comments online than in real life.
人々は現実世界よりもネット上で，より性差別的な発言をする可能性が高い。

d) Contemporary online bullying is similar to real-life harassment of minorities in the past.
現代のネット上でのいじめは過去の現実世界におけるマイノリティーへの嫌がらせに似ている。

e) People on social media sites often make hurtful comments without having enough information.
ソーシャルメディアのサイト上の人々はしばしば十分な情報を持たずに人を傷つけるような発言をする。

Pattyが書いた新聞記事の内容については❺❻で紹介されている。❺のvirtual crowds ... tend to bring out the worst in peopleが b に合致する。witch hunts（魔女狩り）やlynching（集団暴行）が d に合致。また，❻のso many people whose lives have been ruined by online bullyingが a に，even though they may know very little about the situation or person they are criticizingが e に合致する。 c のような事実はどこにも語られていない。

(3) How does Patty feel about the college student from Texas?
テキサス出身の大学生についてパティーはどう感じているか。

a) What he did should not be tolerated in any way.
彼の行ったことはいかなる形でも許されるべきではない。

b) He should have apologized publicly to the teacher.
彼は先生に対して公に謝罪すべきだった。

c) He did the wrong thing, and he deserved the outcome.
彼は間違ったことをしたので，その結果は当然のものだった。

d) He did the wrong thing, but the outcome was too severe.
彼は間違ったことをしたが，その結果は厳しすぎた。

e) He is an example of how online bullying can benefit society.
彼はネット上でのいじめが社会にとって有益であることを示す一例だ。

テキサスの大学生の事例に対するPattyの意見は❿のdid he really deserve the extreme response?に表れている。大学生の行為が不適切であったことは認めつつも，それに対するネットの反応は「行き過ぎだ」としている。d が正解。

74

(4) Which of the following best describes Edward's opinion?
　　エドワードの意見を最もよく言い表しているのは次のうちどれか。

 a) Online crowds help to discourage inappropriate behavior.
　　　ネット上の群衆は不適切なふるまいをやめさせるのに役立つ。
 b) Online crowds help to spread a biased view on a global scale.
　　　ネット上の群衆は，偏見を世界規模で広めるのを助長する。
 c) Social media sites contribute to a culture of sexism against women.
　　　ソーシャルメディアのサイトは女性に対する性差別の風潮を助長する。
 d) Online crowds sometimes improve society, but they more often cause harm.
　　　ネット上の群衆は時に社会を良くするが，害を引き起こすことの方が多い。
 e) Online crowds are valuable because they include people from many different cultures.
　　　ネット上の群衆はたくさんの異なる文化圏の人々を含むので有益だ。

Edwardの基本的な考えは，⓬で語られているように「ネットの炎上は社会を良くする」というものだが，その具体的な理由については⓮で述べられている。Because of his case, other college boys will think twice before writing insulting blogs or tweets.とあるように，「ネットの炎上」には，他の人が不適切な書き込みをするのを思いとどまらせる働きがあるという意見である。a が正解。discourageは「…をやめさせる，思いとどまらせる」という意味である。

(5) What does Patty think about Edward's argument?
　　エドワードの議論についてパティーはどう考えているか。

 a) She agrees that online crowds are helping to create a less sexist society.
　　　ネット上の群衆がより性差別的でない社会を作るのに役立っているということに同意している。
 b) She agrees that online crowds can contribute to the good of society as a whole.
　　　ネット上の群衆が社会全体の善に寄与し得るということに同意している。
 c) She doesn't agree that comments made on social media sites have real-world impacts.
　　　ソーシャルメディアのサイト上でなされた発言が現実の世界に影響を与えるということに同意していない。
 d) She agrees that the online shaming of one student will teach an important lesson to other college boys.
　　　1 人の学生に対するネット上での中傷行為が他の大学生に大切な教訓を与えるだろうということに同意している。
 e) She doesn't agree that the progress of society as a whole is more important than the human rights of each individual.
　　　個々人の人権よりも社会全体の進歩の方が重要であるということに同意していない。

⓯〜⓱では「社会全体のために個人の人生を犠牲にしても良いのか？」が論点となっている。テキサスの大学生はネットで激しい批判を受けて人生を破壊されたが，

「それが社会全体のためには良かった」というEdwardに対して，Pattyは「社会全体のために個人の人生を犠牲にしても良いという考えは危険だ」と反論している。eが正解。agree that …は「…ということに賛成する」という意味でありagree with the opinion that …と同意である。

Set 2-C | 放送文

Introverts

❶ Devon: Hey, Jamie. Did you enjoy the office party last night?

❷ Jamie: Morning, Devon. It was good. Thanks for organizing it.

❸ Devon: You're welcome! I had a great time. I got to know a lot of guys from other departments, too. You left early, right?

❹ Jamie: A little, yeah.

❺ Devon: Well, you missed the special event. I did a Michael Jackson dance routine with Jenny and Tom from marketing!

❻ Jamie: In the spotlight as usual!

❼ Devon: Yeah! ... Hey, even Sara from accounting came. I don't think she really talked to anyone all night, though. Jenny, Tom, and I tried to engage her in conversation. We even tried to chat about her hobby, flower-arranging, but we didn't have much luck.

❽ Jamie: Give her a break. She's just shy, Devon. I've been reading a book about it. She'd probably open up more with you in a quieter one-on-one environment. I sometimes have coffee with her. She's intelligent and very talented. I bet you didn't know that she's won awards for her flower arranging.

❾ Devon: I had no idea.

❿ Jamie: Or that she's studying for MBA in her spare time. You know, it probably took a fair bit of courage for her to go there last night.

⓫ Devon: I guess so. But, you know, it was still hard to get her talking. You seem a bit shy in big groups, too, but at least you make an effort.

⓬ Jamie: I may come across as shy but I would argue that I'm an introvert.

⓭ Devon: So, what's the difference?

⓮ Jamie: Well, most shy people are actually desperate to interact with others, although that might not be obvious to extroverts like you. The problem is that they just find it incredibly difficult to initiate conversation, often through fear of being rejected

---

🔲 事実関係の把握：Devon が主催した会社のパーティーにJamieも参加した。Jamieは途中で帰った

dance routine 句 ダンスの決まった型，ダンスステップ

accounting 名 会計，経理

engage 他 …を関わらせる，引き入れる
🔲 事実関係の把握：経理のSaraもパーティーに来たが，会話にはあまり参加しなかった

one-on-one 形 1対1の

a fair bit of … 句 かなりの…
🔲 事実関係の把握：Saraはフラワーアレンジメントで賞をとったほどの腕前。MBAの勉強をしている

come across as … 句 …に見える
introvert 名 内向的な人 (↔ extrovert)
be desperate to do 句 …しようと必死になっている
interact with … 句 …と交流する
extrovert 名 外向的な人 (↔ introvert)
initiate 他 …を始める

or ridiculed, what the book called the fear of "negative social judgment." We introverts, on the other hand, actually enjoy our own company and often make a conscious effort to be alone to gather our thoughts.

❶⓯ Devon: I do that, too.

❶⓰ Jamie: Well, we all have some extrovert and introvert traits, but you love being the center of attention most of the time.

❶⓱ Devon: You have a point. But listening to you now, no one would really think you're an introvert.

❶⓲ Jamie: Well, that's another thing. The book said that introverts are not antisocial but "differently social." So while we may appear to be withdrawn in larger groups, we can thrive in personal conversations or small groups.

❶⓳ Devon: So it must be quite hard in a big office like ours?

❷⓿ Jamie: Well, the workplace has a big effect on people's lives. Today's workplaces, with their focus on open-plan offices, are designed for maximum group interaction, which suits extroverts like you. This often means that introverts are less likely to be promoted because they don't stand out. The irony is that recent evidence indicates introverts can actually make better leaders for companies.

㉑ Devon: How so?

㉒ Jamie: Well, introvert managers will not only try and spend more one-on-one time with their staff in order to understand them, they'll also let those employees have more freedom to run with their own ideas. Extroverts, on the other hand, often try to dominate and force their own ideas on their staff, rather than allow their staff to take the initiative.

㉓ Devon: I guess I do that sometimes ... Maybe I should change the way I behave ...

㉔ Jamie: Don't change too much, Devon. There's room enough for all of us, and I like you just the way you are!

---

ridicule 他 …を馬鹿にする

one's own company 句 1人でいること

▶shyとintrovertの違い：
・shyな人は他人と交流したがっているが、怖くてそれができない
・introvertは1人でいるのを好み、意図的に1人になろうとする

trait 名 特徴

You have a point. 句 ごもっとも。

antisocial 形 非社交的な

withdrawn 形 引きこもった、内にこもった

thrive 自 繁栄する、うまくやる

maximum 形 最大限の

stand out 句 目立つ

irony 名 皮肉

make 他 …になる

▶Jamieの発言の主旨：introvertは extrovert よりも出世する可能性が低いが、introvertの方が指導者には向いている

dominate 他 …を支配する

force A on B 句 AをBに押しつける

take the initiative 句 主導権をとる

▶Jamieの発言の主旨：introvertの上司は部下の自主性を認める。extrovertの上司は部下に自分の考えを押しつける

room 名 余地、可能性

Set 2-C | 放送文の日本語訳

内向的な人々

❶デヴォン：やあ，ジェイミー。昨晩の会社のパーティー，楽しかった？

❷ジェイミー：おはよう，デヴォン。良かったわよ。企画してくれてありがとう。

❸デヴォン：どういたしまして！　僕も楽しんだよ。別の部署の人たちともたくさん知り合ったしね。君は早くに帰ったよね？

❹ジェイミー：ええ，少し。

❺デヴォン：それじゃあスペシャル・イベントを見逃したね。僕はマーケティング部のジェニーとトムと一緒に，マイケル・ジャクソンのダンスステップをやったんだよ！

❻ジェイミー：いつも通り注目を浴びたのね！

❼デヴォン：そうだよ！　……実はね，経理部のサラまで来たんだよ。彼女は一晩中誰ともあまり話さなかったと思うけどね。ジェニーとトムと僕で，彼女を会話に引き入れようとしたんだ。彼女の趣味の，フラワーアレンジメントについて話してみようとまでしたのだけれど，あまりうまくいかなくて。

❽ジェイミー：分かってあげてよ。デヴォン，彼女は内気なだけなのよ。このところ私はそういうことについての本を読んでいるのよ。おそらく彼女はもっと静かで1対1の環境でなら，あなたにもっと心を開くのじゃないかな。私は時々彼女とコーヒーを飲むことがあるの。彼女は知的だしとても才能のある人よ。あなたは彼女がフラワーアレンジメントで賞を獲っていることなんて絶対に知らなかったでしょう。

❾デヴォン：全然。

❿ジェイミー：空き時間にMBAのための勉強をしていることとかも。たぶん彼女にとっては昨夜のパーティーに行くのもかなり勇気がいったはずよ。

⓫デヴォン：そうだろうね。でもやっぱり，それでも彼女に話してもらうのは難しかったよ。君も大人数の中ではちょっと内気に見えるけれど，少なくとも努力はしているよね。

⓬ジェイミー：内気だと思われるかもしれないけれど，私はむしろ内向的なのだと言いたいわ。

⓭デヴォン：だとすると，違いは何なの？

⓮ジェイミー：そうね，内気な人たちのほとんどは，実は他人と交流しようと必死になっているの。あなたのように外向的な人たちにははっきり分からないかもしれないでしょうけれどね。問題は，彼らにとって会話を始めるというのは信じられないくらい困難なことなのよ。多くの場合，拒絶されたり笑いものにされたりすることへの恐怖のせいでね。私が読んでいる本によると，「否定的社会評価」の恐怖って言うそうよ。一方で，私たち内向性の人間は，実際には1人でいることを楽しんでいて，自分の考えをまとめるために，1人になろうと意識的な努力をしていることが多いの。

⓯デヴォン：僕もそうしているよ。

⓰ジェイミー：ええ，私たちはみんなある程度は外向性と内向性の両方を持っているの。

でも，あなたはだいたいいつも注目の中心にいることが好きよね。

⓱デヴォン：確かに。でも，今の君の話しぶりを聞いていれば，誰も君が内向的だなんて思わないだろうね。

⓲ジェイミー：うーん，それがもう1つの問題なのよ。その本が言うところによれば，内向的な人は非社交的なのではなくて「異なるやり方で社交的」なのだそうよ。だから私たちは，大きなグループの中では内にこもっているように見えるかもしれないけれど，個人同士や小さなグループではうまくやれるのよ。

⓳デヴォン：じゃあ，僕たちの会社みたいな大きなオフィスにいるのは，すごくたいへんだろうね？

⓴ジェイミー：ええ，職場って生活への影響が大きいわよね。今の時代の職場は，開放感のあるオフィスを重視していて，グループでの交流が最大限できるようにデザインされているけれど，こういうのはあなたのように外向的な人に合っているわ。そういうわけで，内向的な人たちは目立たないがゆえに昇進しにくい，ということが多いのよ。皮肉なことに，最近明らかになったところでは，実際には内向的な人の方が会社でより良いリーダーになれるらしいのだけれど。

㉑デヴォン：どうしてそうなるの？

㉒ジェイミー：ええと，内向的なマネージャーはスタッフを理解するために1対1の時間をより多く持とうとするだけじゃなく，従業員が自分自身の考えで動けるように，より大きな自由を与えるの。その一方で，外向的な人は，スタッフに主導権を取らせようとするよりむしろ，支配して，自分の考えを押し付けようとすることが多いということなのよ。

㉓デヴォン：僕も時々そうしてしまっているかもしれない……，ふるまい方を変えるべきかもしれないね……。

㉔ジェイミー：変えすぎなくていいのよ，デヴォン。私たちみんなに十分な可能性があるのだし，私はありのままのあなたが好きよ！

《 指針 》

内向的な人（introvert）と外向的な人（extrovert）の違いがテーマである。introvert／extrovertという単語の意味が分からないと内容把握に苦労するであろう。設問の下読みの段階で，設問や選択肢に出てくる単語の意味を推測しておくことが肝心である。また，この会話は「オフィスパーティーについて」「Saraの性格」「shy peopleとintrovertsの違いについて」「introvertsとextrovertsのどちらがリーダーに向いているか」と，話題が移っていくのが特徴的である。「今は何について話されているのか」ということを常に意識するようにしよう。

難易度

放送文 ★☆☆

設 問 ★☆☆

総 合 ★☆☆

😊😐)))) スピーカー情報

Devon: スコットランド
Jamie: 西海岸，カリフォルニア

Set 2-C │設問解説

(1) Which of the following sentences best indicates Jamie's feelings about Sara?
ジェイミーのサラに対する考えを最もよく示しているのは次のうちどれか。

a) She should open up more at parties.
彼女はパーティーでもっと心を開くべきだ。

b) She was brave to turn up to the party.
パーティーに姿を現すとは彼女は勇気があった。

c) She was wrong to participate in the dance routine.
彼女がダンスステップに参加したのは間違いだった。

d) She does not have the ability to complete her MBA.
彼女にはMBAを取得する能力はない。

e) She should probably switch from accounting to marketing.
彼女はおそらく経理部からマーケティング部に異動するべきだ。

❽❿のJamieの発言を参考にする。❿のit probably took a fair bit of courage for her to go there last nightが直接のヒントとなり，正解はbだと判断できる。他はいずれも会話の内容と大きく異なる。

(2) Which of the following is NOT true about Sara?
サラについて正しくない記述は次のうちどれか。

a) She is studying for an MBA.
彼女はMBAのための勉強をしている。

b) She works in the accounting section.
彼女は経理部で働いている。

c) She has won flower-arranging awards.
彼女はフラワーアレンジメントの賞を獲った。

d) She is reading a book about shy people.
彼女は内気な人々についての本を読んでいる。

e) She prefers to talk in a one-to-one situation.
彼女は1対1の状況で話すことをより好む。

aは❿，bは❼，cとeは❽でそれぞれ触れられている。「内気な人々についての本を読んでいる」のはSaraではなくJamieであるからdが正解となる。

(3) According to Jamie, how do shy people differ from introverts?
　ジェイミーによれば，内気な人々は内向的な人々とどう違うか。
a) Shy people are often promoted more quickly.
　内気な人々はしばしばより早く昇進する。
b) Shy people often judge others in a negative way.
　内気な人々はしばしば他者を否定的に評価している。
c) Shy people will speak up more about personal issues.
　内気な人々は個人的な事柄についてはより多く話すだろう。
d) Shy people feel a greater need to interact with others.
　内気な人々は他者と交流する必要をより強く感じている。
e) Shy people have absolutely no desire to interact with other people.
　内気な人々は他者と交流しようという欲求が全くない。

shy peopleとintrovertsの違いについて語られているのは⓮。most shy people are actually desperate to interact with othersからdを正解とする。aの「昇進が早い」のはextrovertsである。bのnegativeという語は⓮のthe fear of "negative social judgment"で使われているが，これは「(shy peopleが) 社会から否定的に判断されるのを恐れること」という意味である。

(4) What is one issue regarding the workplace that is NOT mentioned?
　職場に関する問題として言及されていないのはどれか。
a) Introverts are effective in one-on-one situations.
　内向的な人々は1対1の状況で力を発揮する。
b) Many offices today are designed to suit extroverts.
　今日の多くのオフィスは外交的な人に合うように作られている。
c) Extroverts sometimes push their own ideas too hard.
　外向的な人々は時々自分の考えを押しつけすぎる。
d) Introverts are likely to change companies more frequently.
　内向的な人々はより頻繁に職場を変えやすい。
e) Extroverts tend to be given more opportunities for career advancement.
　外向的な人々は出世のための機会をより多く与えられる傾向がある。

aについては⓲や㉒の前半で，bは⓴の前半で，cは㉒の後半で述べられている。eは⓴の後半で述べられている。放送文のpromotedがgiven more opportunities for career advancementと言い換えられていることに注意。dについての言及はどこにもない。

(5) According to Jamie, which type of people are more likely to make better leaders, and why?
ジェイミーによれば，どちらのタイプの人々がより良いリーダーになりやすいか，またそれはなぜか？

a) Extroverts, because they will force their ideas on others.
外向的な人々，彼らは他人に自分の考えを押しつけたがるから。

b) Extroverts, because they stand out in an open environment.
外交的な人々，彼らは開放的な環境で目立つから。

c) Introverts, because they will help their staff to fulfill their potential.
内向的な人々，彼らはスタッフが能力を発揮するのを助けたがるから。

d) Introverts, because they will spend more time organizing their ideas.
内向的な人々，彼らはアイデアをまとめるのにより多くの時間を割きたがるから。

e) Extroverts, because they have more confidence in their own abilities.
外向的な人々，彼らは自分自身の能力により自信を持っているから。

❷⓪と❷❷のJamieの発言を手がかりとする。この箇所をまとめると「より良い指導者になるのはintrovertsの方であり，その理由は，スタッフと1対1の会話をし，個人の考えを尊重するから。一方でextrovertsは自分の考えをスタッフに強要することが多い」という内容になる。これに合致するのは c である。help their staff to fulfill their potentialという表現は放送文中には用いられていないが，❷❷の前半部の内容からJamieの発言の要点を摑み，それを最も的確に表した選択肢を選ぶことが求められる。

Set 3 | 解答

3A	(1) a	(2) e	(3) c	(4) d	(5) e
3B	(1) a	(2) d	(3) c	(4) c	(5) d
3C	(1) b	(2) d	(3) c	(4) d	(5) e

Set 3-A | 放送文

A Hairy Situation: The Rise of Fake Fur

❶ Today, when we watch a glamorous Hollywood star walk down the red carpet wearing a floor-length fur coat, it's hard to know if the fur we're looking at is fake or real. Both are equally common at fashion shows and fancy parties alike. But it wasn't always so. A hundred years ago or more, a woman's furs indicated her social status as much as her jewelry did. In order to understand this market shift, we must look back through recent history at the tale of animal skins and the people who wore them.

❷ Before fake fur was invented, only the wealthy could afford to wear fur garments. And it was almost always women who wore them. Because women didn't usually have their own bank accounts back then, they relied on family money to do their shopping. So seeing a woman wearing a mink or rabbit coat meant she had either grown up in a wealthy family, or married a rich husband. Over time, however, ordinary men and women who couldn't afford the glamorous coats and hats of the super rich began to demand an affordable alternative. The clothing industry responded, and in 1929, fake fur was born.

❸ Originally, the product was less than perfect. The fabric was made from looped threads that mimicked the appearance of various animal furs, with varied success. But even when designers in the young industry managed to imitate the look of fur, they had a harder time with its unique texture: anyone who touched fake fur knew instantly that it wasn't real. However, as time passed and techniques improved, differentiating

glamorous 形 魅惑的な，あでやかな
fur 名 毛皮

fancy 形 豪華な
indicate 他 …を示す
shift 名 変化，推移
tale 名 話，物語

📕段落の要旨：現在はフェイクファーも本物の毛皮と同様の扱いだが，以前は本物の毛皮こそが，ステータスシンボルだった
afford to do 句 …する経済的余裕がある
garment 名 衣服
account 名 口座

affordable 形 手頃な価格の
alternative 名 代替品
📕段落の要旨：毛皮はお金持ちの女性のステータスシンボルだったが，庶民からの要望で，フェイクファーが発明された
fabric 名 布地，生地
looped 形 輪になった
thread 名 糸
mimic 他 …を真似する
texture 名 質感
differentiate 自 区別する

📕段落の要旨：フェイクファーは，本物と質感が違うので不人気だったが，品質が向上し，本物と見分けがつかなくなった

84

between true and fake fur became harder.

❹ Animal rights groups and environmental activists contributed to the popularity of fake fur almost from its invention. At first, activists embraced fake fur because it reduced demand for the exotic furs of endangered animals, such as the big cats of Africa. But as long as the fur didn't come from an endangered animal, few people felt there was anything morally wrong about making a coat from it. That changed with time. As fake fur evolved from a cheap alternative to a perfectly good replacement, people began to ask whether it was ever acceptable to kill an animal for its skin.

❺ Soon, environmental groups began to attack the industry as a whole, regardless of whether the fur being sold came from endangered tigers or common rabbits. The fake fur industry took advantage of the situation by going on the offensive and launching attack ads against their competition. At the same time, the real fur industry also had to deal with declining popularity, mainly due to the difficulty of distinguishing fake from real fur and the growing public awareness of animal cruelty issues.

❻ These days, wearing a mink coat no longer signifies a life of luxury and privilege. The elite have found other ways of showcasing their wealth, from diamond rings to shiny Porsches. Nevertheless, the wealthy still tend to favor real fur over fake. Global sales are on the upswing, most likely because living standards are rising around the world. It's clear that despite the invention of fake fur almost one hundred years ago, the real thing is here to stay. What the industry will look like in another hundred years, however, is anyone's guess.

activist 图 活動家
embrace 他 …を受け入れる
exotic 形 珍しい
endangered 形 絶滅の危機にさらされた
evolve 自 進化する
replacement 图 代替品
■段落の要旨：動物保護団体や環境保護活動家の運動によりフェイクファーの人気が促進された

as a whole 句 全体の
regardless of … 句 …とは関係なく
take advantage of … 句 …を利用する
go on the offensive 句 攻勢に出る
launch 他 …を開始する
ad 图 広告(= advertisement)
competition 图 競争相手
distinguish 他 …を区別する
cruelty 图 残酷さ
■段落の要旨：環境保護団体の運動に乗じ，フェイクファー業界が反毛皮の広報活動を行った。フェイクファーの品質向上もあり，毛皮の人気は落ちた

signify 他 …を意味する
privilege 图 特権
showcase 他 …を見せる
nevertheless 副 それにもかかわらず
favor 他 …を好む
on the upswing 句 上向きで
anyone's guess 句 誰にも分からないこと

■段落の要旨：今や本物の毛皮に，金持ちのステータスシンボルとしての役割はないが，それでも，フェイクファーよりは人気があり，根強く残っている

Set 3-A | 放送文の日本語訳

難しい状況：フェイクファーの発達

❶　今の時代，あでやかなハリウッド・スターが床まで届く毛皮のコートを着てレッドカーペットを歩いていくのを観るときに，私たちが眺めているその毛皮が，偽物か本物かを見分けることは容易ではありません。ファッションショーでも豪華なパーティーでも，どちらも同じくらいよく見られます。しかし，いつでもそうだったわけではありません。100年かそれ以上前には，女性の毛皮は，宝石と同じように社会的地位を示すものだったのです。この市場の推移を理解するためには，近年の歴史から，動物の皮とそれを着た人々の物語を振り返らなければなりません。

❷　フェイクファーが発明される前は，裕福な者たちだけに毛皮の衣類を身にまとう余裕がありました。そして，それらを着るのはほとんどいつでも女性でした。女性はその当時，たいてい自分の銀行口座を持っていなかったため，買い物をするのに家族の金を頼っていました。そのため，ミンクかウサギのコートを着ている女性を見ることは，彼女が裕福な家庭に育ったか，金持ちの夫と結婚したかのどちらかを意味していました。しかし，時が経つにつれて，大金持ちの着る華やかなコートや帽子を買うことのできなかったごく普通の男女たちが，手の届く代替品を求めはじめました。それに服飾産業が反応して，1929年，フェイクファーが生まれたのです。

❸　はじめ，その製品は完璧とはいえないものでした。生地は，多様な動物の毛皮の見た目を模した輪っか状の糸から作られ，程度の差はあれよくできていました。しかし，この若い産業におけるデザイナーたちが毛皮の見た目をなんとかうまく模すことができたとしても，その独特の質感に彼らは悪戦苦闘していました。フェイクファーに触れた者であれば誰でも，すぐにそれが本物でないことが分かったのです。しかし，時が経って技術が改良されるにつれて，本物の毛皮とフェイクの毛皮を識別することはより難しくなっていきました。

❹　ほぼそれが発明された時点から，動物保護団体と環境活動家たちは，フェイクファーの人気に貢献していました。はじめは，アフリカの大型ネコ科動物のような，絶滅寸前の動物の珍しい毛皮への需要を減らしてくれるという理由で，活動家たちがフェイクファーを受け入れました。しかし，毛皮が絶滅の危機に瀕した動物から採られたものでない限りは，そこからコートを作ることに道徳上何か問題があると感じる人はほとんどいませんでした。時と共に，それが変わったのです。フェイクファーが安物の代替品から十分に優れた代用品へと進化するにつれ，人々は皮を採るために動物を殺すことがそもそも容認できることなのかを問い掛け始めたのです。

❺　程なくして環境団体は，売られている毛皮が絶滅寸前のトラから採られたか，どこにでもいるウサギから採られたかにかかわらず業界全体を攻撃し始めました。フェイクファー業界は，彼らの競争相手に対して攻勢に出て，攻撃的な広告を打ち出すことで，その状況をうまく利用しました。同時に，本物の毛皮業界の方でも，主にフェイクと本物の毛皮を見分けることが困難であることと，動物虐待問題に関する社会の認識が高まったことによって，低下していく人気に対処することを

強いられました。

❻　昨今では，ミンクのコートを着ることは，もはや贅沢で特権的な生活を意味します。エリートたちは，ダイヤモンドの指輪からピカピカのポルシェに至るまで，自分たちの富を見せつけるための他の手段を発見してきているのです。にもかかわらず，裕福な人々はいまだにフェイクよりも本物の毛皮を好みがちです。世界的な売り上げは上昇傾向にあり，そのもっともありえそうな理由は，世界中で生活水準が上昇しているということです。およそ100年前にフェイクファーが発明されたにもかかわらず，本物の毛皮が普及していることは明らかです。とはいえ，あと100年後に業界がどのようになっているかは，誰にも分からないのです。

《 指針 》

フェイクファー（模造毛皮）をテーマとした講義である。語彙レベルが高く，凝った表現が多用されているため，聞き取りのレベルはかなり高い。語られる話題は「フェイクファーが発明される以前の状況」「フェイクファーが発明された経緯」「当初の不人気」「本物の毛皮への反対運動とフェイクファーの人気上昇」「現在の状況」というように展開していく。それぞれのパートの要旨をしっかりと把握していく必要がある。

難易度

放送文	★★★
設　問	★★☆
総　合	★★☆

☺☹))) スピーカー情報

Lecturer: 西海岸，カリフォルニア

Set 3-A | 設問解説

(1) Before the invention of fake fur,
フェイクファーが発明される前には,

a) only rich people could afford fur garments.
金持ちだけが毛皮の衣類を買うことができた。

b) animal fur was far more expensive than it is now.
動物の毛皮は今よりもはるかに高価だった。

c) the most popular types of fur were mink and rabbit.
もっとも人気のある毛皮の種類はミンクとウサギだった。

d) jewelry was the main symbol of wealth and privilege.
宝石類が富と特権の主な象徴だった。

e) animal fur was worn by women who had succeeded in business.
動物の毛皮はビジネスで成功を収めた女性によって着られていた。

❷冒頭のBefore fake fur was invented, only the wealthy could afford to wear fur garments.がaを正解とする根拠となる。放送文のthe wealthyがrich peopleに書き換えられている以外は,ほぼそのままの記述なので分かりやすいだろう。かつてと現在での毛皮の価格を比較している箇所はないのでbは誤り。❶ではjewelryが社会的地位を示すものだったということが述べられているが,富や特権のmain symbolであったとまでは言っていないのでdはaに劣る。eについてはwho had succeeded in businessが❷の内容に反する。当時は女性が直接お金を稼ぐことは少なかったということが述べられている。

(2) Companies invented fake fur due to
企業がフェイクファーを発明したのは,

a) the Great Depression.
大恐慌のためである。

b) the shortage of real animal fur.
本物の動物の毛皮が不足したためである。

c) pressure from animal rights groups.
動物保護団体の圧力があったからである。

d) a decline in the number of big cats in Africa.
アフリカの大型ネコ科動物が減少したためである。

e) demand from people in the lower and middle classes.
下層階級,中流階級の人々が求めたからである。

フェイクファーが発明されるきっかけについては,❷のordinary men and women who couldn't afford the glamorous coats and hats of the super rich began to demand an affordable alternativeで述べられている。このordinary men and womenがeのpeople in the lower and middle classesに相当する。cの「動物保護団体の圧力」はフェイクファーの人気を促進したが,「発

88

明のきっかけ」ではないので誤り。

(3) Fake fur was not popular at first, because
　　　はじめ，フェイクファーは人気がなかった。なぜなら，
　a) it was hard to handle.
　　　取り扱いが難しかったからだ。
　b) it was as expensive as real fur.
　　　本物の毛皮と同じくらい高価だったからだ。
　c) it didn't resemble the real thing.
　　　本物の毛皮と似ていなかったからだ。
　d) it didn't indicate high social status.
　　　高い社会的地位を表さなかったからだ。
　e) people didn't think wearing real fur was wrong.
　　　人々は本物の毛皮を着ることが悪いとは考えなかったからだ。

フェイクファーが当初不人気だった理由については❸で説明されている。anyone who touched fake fur knew instantly that it wasn't realとあるように，要するに本物の毛皮と質感がまるで違ったのである。cが正解。the real thingはもちろんreal furを指している。

(4) The causes of fake fur's rising popularity did NOT include
　　　フェイクファーの人気が上がった理由に含まれないのは，
　a) negative ads about real fur.
　　　本物の毛皮に対するネガティブな広告。
　b) the animal rights movement.
　　　動物保護運動。
　c) general awareness of animal cruelty issues.
　　　動物虐待問題に対する一般的な意識。
　d) cost reduction resulting from mass production.
　　　大量生産によって生じたコストの低下。
　e) improvements in the quality of fake fur products.
　　　フェイクファー製品の質の改良。

フェイクファーの人気が上昇した理由については❸の最後から❹❺にかけて説明されている。「品質の向上（本物との見分けがつきにくくなった）」「動物保護団体の圧力」「それに乗じたフェイクファー業界のネガティブキャンペーン」の3つであり，これがそれぞれe，b，aに相当する。cについては❺の最後で言及されている。dについての言及はない。

(5) Today, real fur
　　今日，本物の毛皮は，

　a) is not available in most countries.
　　　多くの国では手に入らない。
　b) is becoming less and less popular.
　　　ますます人気が落ちている。
　c) still symbolizes wealth and privilege.
　　　いまだに富と特権を象徴している。
　d) is becoming more popular than ever.
　　　かつてなく人気が高まっている。
　e) still has a certain degree of popularity.
　　　いまだにある程度の人気がある。

　❻の内容把握を問う問題。この段落の内容をまとめると，「今日，本物の毛皮は，かつてのようなお金持ちのステータスシンボルとしての役割はないが，それでもフェイクファーよりは人気があり，世界的には売り上げが増加している」というものになる。要するに「ある程度の人気はある」ということであり，ｅが正解となる。売り上げは増加しているのでｂは誤り。また，富を誇示する手段としては，ダイヤモンドやポルシェなどの他の手段へと移行したとあるのでｃは誤り。

Set 3-B | 放送文

Innovative Architecture

❶ Lucy: Excuse me sir, I'm looking for the guided tour that's supposed to start here at 12:00. I think it's called Exploring Delhi's Green Side.

❷ Uday: You've come to the right place, and you found us just in the nick of time! We're about to get started. I'm Uday Singh, your guide for the afternoon. Let me check you off my list here and then we'll be on our way... What did you say your name was?

in the nick of time 句 ギリギリ間に合って

❸ Lucy: Lucy Green, from England.

❹ Uday: Welcome Lucy! Everybody, please walk behind me in a single file line–Delhi may be an increasingly environmentally friendly place but it's also a very hectic city and I don't want to lose anyone! Our first stop is going to be right across the street, at the new headquarters of one of India's largest electronics companies. Does anyone notice anything unusual about the building?

in a single file line 句 1列になって
environmentally friendly 句 環境に優しい
hectic 形 たいへん忙しい, せわしない
headquarters 名 本部, 本社

❺ Man: Um... the monkey sitting on the roof?

❻ Uday: Ha ha, no, that's not so unusual here in Delhi! Actually it was a bit of a trick question. The building looks entirely normal, but it's coated with a special smog-eating paint that neutralizes air pollution. So just by sitting there, the building counteracts the emissions from 1,000 cars every day. Pretty incredible huh?

coated with ... 句 …でコーティングされている, 覆われている
neutralize 他 …を中和する
counteract 他 …と反対に作用する, …を中和する

❼ Lucy: I've heard a lot about air pollution in places like Beijing, but is it also a big problem in India?

❽ Uday: Unfortunately, Delhi has the worst air pollution in the world. It kills about 10,000 of us Delhiites a year, mostly by causing strokes, heart conditions, and cancer. And as you know, the problem isn't limited to this city. In 2012, seven million people worldwide died from breathing dirty air, which is more than were killed by cigarette smoke!

Delhiite 名 デリーに住む人
stroke 名 発作, 脳卒中
condition 名 病気, 疾患
🔖 事実関係の把握：デリーは大気汚染が世界で最もひどく, 多くの人が病気で死んでいる。また, 世界中で煙草の煙で死ぬ人より, 大気汚染で死ぬ人の方が多い

❾ Man: Wow. So how does the smog-eating paint work?

❿ Uday: Well, it contains titanium dioxide, which is what scientists call a photocatalyst. As some

titanium dioxide 句 二酸化チタン
photocatalyst 名 光触媒

of you may remember from your high school chemistry labs, a catalyst is something that makes chemical reactions happen faster. In this case, when sunlight hits the titanium dioxide paint, a chemical reaction begins that ultimately removes pollutants from the air.

⓫ Lucy: I'm getting a little confused here...

⓬ Uday: Okay, think of it like this. The sunlight kick-starts a chain reaction that turns nasty pollutants into less harmful substances. The process includes several steps. First, light interacts with the titanium dioxide molecules. Next, the energized titanium dioxide molecules react with water molecules in the air, splitting them into two parts. Finally, the split-apart water molecules react with air pollution, making it less harmful to people walking in the streets below. That process happens over and over, millions of times each day.

⓭ Man: Pretty cool. But wouldn't something like that be too expensive for most business owners to afford?

⓮ Uday: Believe it or not, the paint on this building only added about 4% to overall construction costs. And the idea is catching on! There's a similar building in Milan, and in the Netherlands scientists have coated roads with the same type of substance. In England, a clothing designer is working with a chemist to develop titanium dioxide laundry detergent. When you wash your clothes with it, they become coated with photocatalysts. In essence, you become a walking smog eater!

⓯ Lucy: It sounds like I'll need to shop for some new detergent when I get home!

---

catalyst 图 触媒

ultimately 副 最終的には

kick-start 他 …を始める
chain reaction 句 連鎖反応
nasty 形 不快な
substance 图 物質

molecule 图 分子，粒子

☞難しい化学用語が用いられているが，全てを正確に理解する必要はない。「塗料に含まれる化学物質が水を分解し，その水分が汚染物質を無害化する」という程度のおおまかな内容理解で十分である

believe it or not 句 信じられないような話だが
catch on 句 人気を博する，流行る

laundry detergent 句 洗濯洗剤
in essence 句 本質的には，要するに

革新的な建築

❶ルーシー：すみません，12時に開始予定のガイドツアーを探しているのですが。「デリーのグリーンサイド探索」という名前だったと思います。

❷ウダイ：ここで大丈夫ですよ。それに時間ぴったりです！　ちょうどツアーを始めるところでした。私はウダイ・シン，午後のガイドを担当する者です。ここでお名前にチェックを入れて，それから出発しましょう……お名前はなんとおっしゃいましたっけ？

❸ルーシー：イングランドから来ました，ルーシー・グリーンです。

❹ウダイ：ようこそルーシー！　皆さん，1列になって私の後ろを歩いてください——デリーはだんだん環境に優しい場所になってきてはいるのですが，非常にせわしない都市でもあるので，どなたにも迷子になって欲しくないのです。最初に向かうのは，この通りのちょうど反対側にある，インドで最も巨大な電子機器会社の1つの本社です。どなたかこの建物に関して，何か独特な点にお気づきでしょうか？

❺男性：うーん……屋上に猿が座っていること？

❻ウダイ：ははは，違います，ここデリーでは，それはそんなに珍しいことじゃないですからね！　実のところ，ちょっとしたひっかけ問題でした。この建物は完全に普通に見えるのですが，大気汚染を中和する特別なスモッグ吸収塗装で覆われているんです。つまり，この建物はただそこに鎮座しているだけで，1日に自動車1000台分の排出物を中和してくれるのです。全く驚くべきことじゃありませんか？

❼ルーシー：北京みたいな場所での大気汚染については随分耳にしてきましたが，インドでも大きな問題なのですか？

❽ウダイ：残念なことに，デリーは世界で一番大気が汚染されているのです。年間およそ1万人に及ぶ我々デリー市民の命が，大気汚染によって奪われています，多くの場合，脳卒中や心臓病，がん等で。そしてご存じの通り，この問題はこの都市だけには限られません。2012年には，世界で700万人の人々が汚れた大気を吸ったことによって亡くなりました。これは煙草の煙による死者数よりも多いのです！

❾男性：うわあ。それで，スモッグ吸収塗装はどうやって機能するのですか？

❿ウダイ：ええとですね，塗装には，科学者たちが光触媒と呼ぶ，二酸化チタンが含まれています。高校の化学実験でやったことを覚えている人もいるかもしれませんが，触媒とは化学反応が起こるのを早めるものです。この場合は，太陽光が二酸化チタン塗装に当たると，最終的に空気中の汚染物質を取り除くような反応が始まるのです。

⓫ルーシー：ちょっと混乱してきました……。

⓬ウダイ：分かりました，こういう風に考えてみましょう。太陽光が，ひどい汚染物質を害の少ない物質へと変える連鎖反応を促進するのです。この過程には，いくつかの段階が含まれます。第1に，光が二酸化チタンの分子に作用します。次に，エネルギーを得た二酸化チタン分子が空気中の水分子に作用して，水分子を2つの部分に分けます。最後に，分かれた水分子が大気汚染に作用して，汚染物質を，下を歩いている人々にとって害の少ない物質に変えるのです。この過程を何度も

何度も，1日に何百万回も繰り返します。

⓭男性：ほんとうにすごいな。ですが，事業主の多くにとって，そのようなものはお金がかかりすぎるのでは？

⓮ウダイ：まさかと思うかもしれませんが，この建物の塗装による，建設費全体への影響は約4パーセントの上乗せにすぎなかったのです。さらに，この考えは流行しつつあります！ ミラノにも同様の建物がありますし，オランダでは科学者たちが同様の物質で道路を舗装しました。イングランドでは，服飾デザイナーが化学者と協働して，二酸化チタン洗濯洗剤を開発しようとしています。それを使って洗うと，衣類が光触媒に覆われます。要するに，歩くスモッグ吸収者になるわけです。

⓯ルーシー：国に帰ったら，新しい洗剤を買いに行く必要がありそうですね。

《 指針 》

ガイド付きツアーの1場面であるが，話題の中心となるのは大気汚染を中和する建築用塗料についてである。塗料の化学反応についての説明は難しいが，設問では全てを理解することまでは求められていない。おおまかな内容理解だけでも正解することは十分に可能である。専門用語に圧倒されずに，落ち着いて概要を摑むよう心がけたい。

難易度

放送文	★★☆
設　問	★☆☆
総　合	★★☆

☺😐))) スピーカー情報

Lucy: イングランド
Uday: インド（アメリカ，西海岸）
Man: 中西部，ミズーリ

Set 3-B 設問解説

(1) Uday refers to Delhi as "a very hectic city." What does the word "hectic" mean?
ウダイはデリーを "a very hectic city" だと言っている。"hectic" とはどういう意味か。

a) busy
忙しい
b) exotic
異国風の
c) large
大きな
d) exciting
刺激的な
e) polluted
汚染された

hecticという単語を知っていれば何も問題ない。知らない場合は、まず、放送文の該当箇所を聞き飛ばしてしまわないよう、設問の下読みの段階で十分に注意しておくこと。この単語は❹のit's also a very hectic city and I don't want to lose anyoneで用いられているが、ガイドのUdayが心配しているのは「ツアーの客を見失ってしまうこと」だと分かる。とすると、その原因としてデリーが「人や車の通りがとても激しい町」である、すなわちa very busy cityであるということが考えられるだろう。単語の知識がなくても、文脈からの類推で解ける問題である。

(2) Which of the following statements about air pollution is true, according to Uday?
ウダイによると、大気汚染に関する次の説明のうち正しいものはどれか。

a) It is caused mainly by cigarette smoke.
主に煙草の煙によって引き起こされる。
b) It is a more serious problem in Beijing than in Delhi.
デリーよりも北京の方が問題が深刻である。
c) It kills fewer people worldwide each year than cigarette smoke.
毎年世界で大気汚染によって亡くなる人は煙草の煙によって亡くなる人よりも少ない。
d) It can cause severe health problems that eventually lead to death.
最終的に死を招くような深刻な健康被害を引き起こし得る。
e) It is no longer a problem in Delhi thanks to the development of smog-eating paint.
スモッグ吸収塗装のおかげで、デリーではもはや問題が生じていない。

❽で与えられた情報を正確に把握したい。大気汚染によって心臓病やがん等の病気を発症し、毎年多くの人が死んでいるという事実が述べられており、これがdと合致する。デリーの大気汚染は「世界で最悪」と言っているのでbは誤り。また、世界中で煙草の煙よりも大気汚染による死者の方が多いと言っているのでcも誤り。また、smog-eating paintによる効果があったとしても、「大気汚染がもはや問題とはならない」というのは言い過ぎなので、eも誤り。

(3) According to Uday, how does the smog-eating paint work?
ウダイによると，スモッグ吸収塗装はどのように機能するか。

a) It absorbs chemical pollutants.
化学汚染物質を吸収する。

b) It contains tiny micro-organisms that eat air pollution.
大気汚染を食べる小さな微生物を含んでいる。

c) It reacts with sunlight and water in a three-step process.
3段階の過程を経て，太陽光と水に作用する。

d) It causes a chemical reaction that energizes harmful substances in the air.
大気中の有害物質にエネルギーを与える化学反応を引き起こす。

e) It absorbs pollutants from the air, which workers later wash off using water.
大気中から汚染物質を吸収して，その後に作業員が水を使って洗い落とす。

　❿や⓬でのUdayの説明には専門的な用語が多く含まれているため，内容を正確に理解するのは難しいが，設問に答えるには「化学物質が3つのステップを踏んで光や水と反応し，空気中の汚染を無害化する」という程度の理解があれば十分である。専門用語が出てきても慌てずに対処する姿勢が大切だ。⓬ではFirst ... Next ... Finally ...という3つのプロセスが説明されているが，それがcのthree-step processに相当する。dはthat energizes harmful substancesが誤り。energizeされるのはtitanium dioxideである。

(4) Which of the following is mentioned by Uday as one of the advantages of the technology?
この技術の利点の1つとしてウダイが言及しているのは次のうちどれか。

a) Easy to use.
使いやすいこと。

b) Great durability.
優れた耐用性。

c) Relatively low cost.
比較的コストが低いこと。

d) Non-toxic ingredients.
含有物が無害であること。

e) Attractive appearance.
魅力的な外観。

　⓮の冒頭で，この塗装の使用によるコスト増はわずか約4％であると説明されているのでcが正解。その他についてはどこにも触れられていない。

(5) Which of the following is mentioned by Uday as an application of photocatalysts?
光触媒を使用したものとしてウダイが言及しているのは次のうちどれか。

a) A coating for furniture.
家具のコーティング。

b) A paint used for vehicles.
　　 乗り物に使用する塗料。

c) Dyeing of clothing materials.
　　 衣料素材の染色。

d) A laundry detergent that coats clothing.
　　 衣類を覆う洗剤。

e) A medical treatment for heart conditions and cancer.
　　 心臓病やがんの治療。

❹ではこの塗装の様々な使用例について述べられている。紹介されているのは「建物（ミラノ）」「道路（オランダ）」「洗剤（イングランド）」の3つ。このうちの「洗剤」がdに該当する。

Set 3-C | 放送文

Giving Presents

❶ Dean: Hey, Katie! What brings you to the men's side of the department store?

❷ Katie: Oh, hi Dean! I'm just trying to find something for James for Valentine's Day. I have no idea what to get him! I can't decide if a sweater is too practical.

❸ Dean: I think there are two types of gift-givers: those who try to figure out what people want but would never buy for themselves, and those who give items that people need, but dislike buying for themselves.

❹ Katie: Which side do you fall on?

❺ Dean: Well, personally, I tend to like receiving gifts that I hate buying for myself. Who really wants to spend their money on socks or shampoo? But I only give necessities to people who think similarly. Like, my brother recently started his own company, so he's on a strict budget. I purchased a grocery store gift certificate for him so he could get something more than ramen to eat!

❻ Katie: The cost of groceries does add up — that's not a bad idea!

❼ Dean: Right, but not everyone would appreciate that. Can you imagine giving that as a present to your boss, or even someone you just started dating? It would be unacceptable! I think, to choose the best present, you need to consider both the person's character and your relationship with that person. Maybe, you also need to consider what the implications of the gift are.

❽ Katie: Like the old TV scenario where the husband buys the wife a vacuum cleaner and then wonders why she's angry?

❾ Dean: Exactly. If you give a present with the expectation that it will be used to benefit you in some way — like a vacuum cleaner or cookware — then don't be surprised if the recipient isn't overjoyed.

❿ Katie: Are there any exceptions to that?

⓫ Dean: Of course! High-end kitchenware is rather

---

practical 形 実用的な

🔖 プレゼントをあげる人のタイプ：1. 欲しいけれど自分では買わないもの（贅沢品）をあげる，2. 必要だけれど自分では買いたくないもの（必需品）をあげる

fall on ... 句 …に当てはまる

🔖 Deanと弟のタイプ：両者とも「必需品をあげるタイプ」

on a strict budget 句 予算が厳しい
gift certificate 句 商品券

add up 句 大きくなる

implication 名（予想される）影響，結果
🔖 プレゼントを選ぶ時に考慮すべきこと：1. 相手の性格，2. 相手との関係，3. そのプレゼントがどのような結果をもたらすか
vacuum cleaner 句 掃除機
recipient 名 受取人
overjoyed 形 大喜びして
🔖 Deanの発言の主旨：相手が使うことにより自分にとっても利益になるようなプレゼントは好ましくない
kitchenware 名 キッチン用品

expensive, you know? You don't necessarily have to spend a lot to make someone happy, but I know gourmet fans would probably be incredibly happy over an espresso machine — or even just some glasses and coffee beans.

⓬ Katie: I've been hoping for a stand mixer myself, although that coffee machine would be great — if my husband made me coffee every morning with it! But he will probably just buy me some chocolates. Sometimes, it's almost worse than nothing at all. I like chocolate, but it's such a generic gift that it almost feels like he doesn't know what I really want.

⓭ Dean: I think one reason men rely so heavily on the jewelry-and-chocolate standard on Valentine's Day is they don't know what else to get, and the media everywhere makes it seem like women are longing for shiny things and sweets. Or, sometimes we feel paralyzed because people like to pick their own clothing, gift certificates seem impersonal, household appliances are off-limits, and dinner out seems too typical. Added to that is the feeling that you are symbolically representing both the state of your relationship and how well you know your partner in that one gift.

⓮ Katie: When you put it like that, it's no wonder I get chocolates. At least he buys truffles. So, what are you getting your girlfriend?

⓯ Dean: Oh, well, she's easy! Dinner out and some books, and everyone is happy. But then, we've moved beyond the trying-to-impress stage!

gourmet 图 食通，グルメ

📕「好ましくないプレゼント（キッチン用品や掃除機等）」の例外：高性能キッチン用品

generic 形 汎用的な
paralyzed 形 麻痺している，何もできない
impersonal 形 人間味のない，温かみのない
household appliance 句 家電製品
off-limits 形 立ち入り禁止の，踏み込んではいけない

📕男性がありきたりな贈り物をする理由：1. メディアからのプレッシャー，2. 他の何を贈っても問題があるように思える，3. 2人の関係や相手への理解を象徴するようなものを選ばねばならないという意識

put 他 …を言う，表現する
truffle 图 トリュフ（チョコレート菓子）

📕 the trying-to-impress stageの意味：付き合い始めの，相手の気を引こうと努力している段階

Set 3-C | 放送文の日本語訳

プレゼントをする

❶ディーン：やあ，ケイティー！ デパートのメンズ・コーナーで，何しているの？

❷ケイティー：あら，こんにちは，ディーン！ ジェームズのバレンタインのプレゼントを探しているのよ。何にしたらいいか，全然分からなくて。セーターじゃ実用的すぎるかしら。

❸ディーン：プレゼントをする人には2タイプいると思うんだ。欲しいけれど自分では買わないものは何かなと考える人と，必要だけど自分では買いたくないものを贈る人。

❹ケイティー：あなたはどっちのタイプ？

❺ディーン：そうだな，僕は，自分では買いたくないものをプレゼントされたいな。いったい誰が自分のお金を靴下やシャンプーなんかに費やそうと思うだろう。だけど，僕自身は必需品をあげるのは同じような考えの人だけにしてるよ。たとえば，弟は最近会社を興して家計を切り詰めている。だから僕は，食料品店の商品券を買ってあげた。ラーメンよりましなものを買って食べられるようにね。

❻ケイティー：食費ってばかにならないものね。なかなかいい考えだと思うわ。

❼ディーン：そうなんだ。だけど，みんながそれでいいってわけでもない。そんなものを上司に，あるいは付き合い始めたばかりの恋人にプレゼントするなんて，想像できるかい？ そんなものをもらうのは嫌だろう。最適なプレゼントを選ぶためには，相手の性格と，自分と相手とがどういう間柄であるのかの両方を考える必要があると思う。もしかしたら，そのプレゼントがもたらす結果も考えなきゃならない。

❽ケイティー：昔からよくあるテレビ番組のシナリオで，掃除機を買ってあげた妻が不機嫌になるのだけれど，夫にはその理由が分からないというのみたいに？

❾ディーン：そうだよ。掃除機や調理器具を買うってのはまさにこれなのだけれど，相手が使ってくれると自分にも好都合だ等と考えてプレゼントしようとするのなら，相手があまり喜ばなくても当然だね。

❿ケイティー：それには例外はないの？

⓫ディーン：あるよ！ 高性能のキッチン用品って結構高いよね。人を喜ばせるのに必ずしも大金を費やさなければならないってことはないのだけれど，グルメの人なら，エスプレッソ・マシンをあげたら信じられないくらい喜んでくれると思う。ひょっとしたらグラスやコーヒー豆だけでも。

⓬ケイティー：私自身はずっと，スタンド型のミキサーが欲しいのだけれど，そのコーヒーメーカーもいいわね。夫が毎朝それでコーヒーを淹れてくれるのならね！でもきっと，彼はチョコレートを買ってくれるだけのはず。そういうのって，時々，何にもくれないより悪いような気がする。たしかに私はチョコレートが好きよ。でもそういうありきたりなプレゼントをもらうと，私が本当は何が欲しいのか彼は分かってないなって思えてならないの。

⓭ディーン：僕が思うに，男が「バレンタインには宝石やチョコレート」っていう定番にひたすら頼る理由の1つは，他に何を買うべきか分からないってところにあるの

じゃないかな。メディアでも盛んに，女性はキラキラしたものやお菓子が欲しいものだ，みたいに宣伝しているしね。途方に暮れる理由はまだある。みんな自分の服は自分で選びたいだろうし，商品券じゃ温かみがないような気がするし，家電製品は立ち入りすぎかなとか，外食じゃ当たり前すぎるかな，とか。それに，そのプレゼント1つで，相手との間柄も，相手に対する理解度も象徴することになると考えてしまうとね。

⓮ケイティー：今の話からすると，私がチョコレートをもらうのも不思議はないわけね。少なくとも彼はトリュフを買ってくれるし。あなたは彼女に何を買ってあげるの？

⓯ディーン：ああ，そうだな，彼女の場合は簡単なんだ。外で食事して，本を贈って，万事オーケー。ってことは，僕らはもう，互いにアピールしたい段階を過ぎたってことかな。

《《 指針 》》

「良いプレゼントとは何か」についての会話である。「贅沢品がいいか，必需品がいいか」という話題から始まり，「好ましくないプレゼントは何か」，そして「男性がありきたりなプレゼントをする理由」へと移っていく。日常的な会話だが，放送文のレベルはかなり高い。様々な具体例が出てくるが，それぞれが何を表すための例として用いられているのかを見抜く必要がある。

難易度

放送文 ★★☆
設　問 ★★☆
総　合 ★★☆

☺☹))) スピーカー情報

Dean: スコットランド
Katie: イングランド

Set 3-C | 設問解説

(1) Which type of gifts do Dean and his brother prefer receiving?
ディーンと彼の弟がもらいたいのはどちらのタイプのプレゼントか。

a) Both prefer receiving luxuries.
2人とも贅沢品をもらいたい。

b) Both prefer receiving practical gifts.
2人とも実用品をもらいたい。

c) Dean prefers receiving luxuries but his brother prefers practical gifts.
ディーンは贅沢品をもらいたいが、彼の弟は実用品をもらいたい。

d) Dean prefers receiving practical gifts but his brother prefers luxuries.
ディーンは実用品をもらいたいが、彼の弟は贅沢品をもらいたい。

e) None of the above.
上記のどれにも該当しない。

❸でDeanはプレゼントをあげる人のタイプには2つあると言っている。those who try to figure out what people want ...は、いわゆる「贅沢品 (luxuries)」をあげようとする人、those who give items that people need ...は、「必需品・実用品 (necessities／practical gifts)」をあげようとする人だということを理解しよう。そして❺でのI tend to like receiving gifts that I hate buying for myself...という発言からDeanは「必需品・実用品をもらうのが好きだ」ということが分かり、さらに「彼の弟も同じタイプなので商品券をあげた」という内容が続くので、どちらも「必需品派」だということが分かる。正解はb。

(2) Which of the following does Dean NOT mention as a point to consider when buying a present?
次のうち、プレゼントを買う時に考慮すべき点としてディーンが言及していないのはどれか。

a) What the recipient is like.
受け取る相手がどのような人か。

b) How the gift will be used.
そのプレゼントがどのように使われるか。

c) Who will benefit from the gift.
そのプレゼントは誰にとって利益となるのか。

d) How much money he spends on it.
いくら費やすか。

e) The relationship between giver and recipient.
贈る人と受け取る人の間柄。

❼でDeanはyou need to consider both the person's character and your relationship with that person. Maybe, you also need to consider what the implications of the gift areと発言している。この中のthe person's characterがaに、your relationship with that personがeに、what the implications of the gift areがbとcに該当する。implicationとは「予想される結果・影響」という意味で，ここではそのプレゼントがどのように使われるのか（贈り主に利益をもたらすような使い方をされないか，等）という意味合いで使われている。dの「費用」についての言及はない。

(3) According to Dean, why is cookware inappropriate as a present for a wife?
ディーンによれば，調理器具が妻へのプレゼントとして適切でないのはなぜか。
a）It's not romantic.
それはロマンチックではない。
b）It's too expensive.
それは高価すぎる。
c）It can be used for the benefit of the husband.
夫にとって好都合なように用いられる可能性がある。
d）The giver might not know which brand to buy.
贈る人がどのブランドの品を買うべきか分からないかもしれない。
e）The wife might have bought cookware for herself already.
妻は調理器具を自分で既に買ってしまっているかもしれない。

❾ の If you give a present with the expectation that it will be used to benefit you in some way ...から，cを正解とする。掃除機や調理器具等は，使う側（妻）の労働を前提としており，贈る側（夫）の利益（きれいな部屋で過ごせる，美味しい料理が食べられる，等）に繋がるようなものであるから，贈り物としては好ましくないというのである。

(4) According to Dean, what is the reason that some men give stereotypical gifts?
ディーンによれば，一部の男性がありきたりのプレゼントをする理由は何か。
a）Men are not creative.
男性は独創的ではない。
b）Their partners have requested them.
パートナーにリクエストされた。
c）They have no idea what women want.
女性が何を求めているのか全く分からない。
d）A combination of pressure to be perfect and fear of offending the recipient.
完璧でなければならないというプレッシャーと，相手の気分を害することへの恐れの両方による。
e）Spending money on jewelry is a sign of how important their relationship is.
宝石にお金を使うのは自分たちの関係が重要であることの証である。

❸では，男性が女性に贈る「ありきたりの（stereotypical）プレゼント」の代表として「宝石とチョコレート」が挙げられている。そして，男性がそのようなものを贈る理由としては，大きく分けて３つのポイントが指摘されている。1. メディアからの影響，2. 他の何をあげても問題がありそうに思える，3. 2人の関係と相手

への理解を象徴するようなものを選ばねばという意識, の3つである。選択肢dの pressure to be perfect が 3. に, fear of offending the recipient が 2. に該当する。選択肢の e は 3. に近いが,「宝石」に限定している点と,「お金を使うこと」に焦点を当てている点に問題がある。

(5) Based on Dean's Valentine's Day plans, which statement is most likely true about him and his partner?
ディーンのバレンタインデーの予定に基づけば, 彼と彼のパートナーに関して当てはまりそうなのはどれか。

a) They are both cheerful people.
彼らはどちらも快活な人たちである。

b) They do not know each other very well.
彼らは互いをあまりよく知らない。

c) They both prefer surprises to predictable gifts.
彼らはどちらも予想可能なプレゼントよりサプライズが好きである。

d) They like to give something special to each other.
彼らはお互いに特別なものを贈り合うのを好む。

e) They have been dating for more than a few weeks.
彼らは付き合い始めてから数週間以上経っている。

❶❺の Dinner out and some books, and everyone is happy. But then, we've moved beyond the trying-to-impress stage! を手がかりとして, e を正解として選ぶ。この the trying-to-impress stage とは, 付き合い始めの段階, すなわち相手の気を引こうとお互いに努力しているような時期のことを指している。Deanたちの場合は, 既にそのような段階を過ぎ, ある種の円熟期に入っているということである。設問に most likely のような語句が入っている場合には, 放送文の内容をもとにある程度の推測を働かせて解く問題であることが多い。

Set 4 | 解答

4A	(1) d	(2) c	(3) e	(4) c	(5) e
4B	(1) e	(2) d	(3) e	(4) b	(5) c
4C	(1) e	(2) e	(3) d	(4) a	(5) d

Set 4-A | 放送文

Psychology of Shopping 1

❶ Professor Botekin: Good morning, everyone. Today we're continuing our discussion on commercial strategies. Yesterday we talked about why the customer shops, but today we'll be focusing on the sales tactics used to get people to buy, and how those trends have been evolving. Let's review our conclusions from yesterday. Can anyone tell me how the current economic climate has affected consumer spending?

❷ Francisca: In a recession, there is less "big-ticket" spending, and more consumption of smaller goods.

❸ Professor: Good! Yes, this phenomenon has been called "the lipstick effect" because historically, during economic recessions, women purchase a brighter cosmetic as a mood boost, likely instead of more expensive items. Similarly, consumption of sweets and alcohol increases. Although it'd be easy to assume that these luxuries would be first to be cut out when money is tight, it turns out that these purchases are used as relatively inexpensive "treats" for the purchaser.

❹ Peter: Wouldn't it make more sense for those on a budget to cut treats out?

❺ Professor: That's probably true, although thankfully for the economy's sake, people continue to make purchases even on a budget. Most people use a comparative mindset when shopping. Rather than thinking, "this chocolate is two dollars I do not need to spend," it's "I wanted a new shirt, but I can't afford it. Chocolate makes me happy, too, and it's cheaper." It almost feels like a discount, and therefore it's easier to rationalize. Likewise, if you can't afford to get your child that new toy, maybe

commercial 形 商業的な
strategy 名 戦略

tactic 名 戦術，戦略

climate 名 風潮，情勢

recession 名 不況，景気後退
big-ticket 形 高額の

cosmetic 名 化粧品
boost 名 押し上げること

treat 名 ご褒美
☛lipstick effect とは：景気が悪いと，気分を明るくするために，比較的安価な贅沢品の購入が増える

on a budget 句 予算が限られている，家計を切り詰めている
mindset 名 考え方
☛安価な贅沢品を買う心理：より高価なものと比較して，それを買うよりも節約になると考えて自分の購入を正当化する
rationalize 他 …を正当化する，合理化する

an ice cream will be good enough.

❻　Of course, a lot of times this is nearly subconscious—we often feel that we "deserve" a little pick-me-up after a bad day or working hard, and if necessary, we might seek out a cheap way to reward ourselves.

subconscious 形 意識下の，無意識の

seek out 句 …を探し出す

❼　So, let's ask ourselves—how might stores and companies try to use these psychological tendencies to influence our purchasing decisions? Early studies showed several prominent tendencies. For instance, you might think that the more options a shopper had, the better. More choices would equal more sales, right? But it turned out that would-be consumers were more likely to walk away with a purchase when their options were limited. In short, choosing between too many items overwhelmed them. This tendency, called "choice overload," was first revealed in a study of jam sales. The researchers found that when offered a choice of 24 jams versus 6, consumers were ten times less likely to purchase one.

prominent 形 顕著な

would-be 形 …になるつもりの

overwhelm 他 …を圧倒する，困惑させる

▶ choice overloadとは：購入するものの選択肢が多いと，購入意欲が下がる

❽　There may be several reasons behind this. Sometimes, people just want a quick and easy choice. Other times, when the shopper does not know which he likes better—sweet jam? sour jam?—it might be more difficult, or take too much time, for him to compare.

❾　Likewise, for impulse purchases—or, unplanned purchases—convenience may be a key factor. There is a reason supermarkets put magazines and candy bars in highly visible areas near the register. Consumers do not have to expend a lot of thought on these purchases; rather, they perceive them as rewards or treats. Other impulse buys are motivated by appeals such as a lowered price or a new model. There is a reason online discount stores do great business: it's hard to turn down something that appears, on the surface, to be quite cheap. Like our chocolate buyer, this impulse buyer does not consider the actual cost, but rather the discount achieved.

impulse 名 衝動

perceive A as C 句 AがCだと思う

appeal 名 魅力

▶ 衝動買いを行う理由：1. 手軽さ，2. 値引きや新モデルなどの「お得感」

❿　Thus, it's important for us, as consumers, to think about what we are buying, and why.

Just like you shouldn't go to the grocery store
hungry, it's probably wise to ask yourself if you're
shopping to make yourself feel better, or because
you actually need that item.

Set 4-A | 放送文の日本語訳

購買の心理学 1

❶ ボテキン教授：みなさん，おはようございます。今日も商業戦略についての議論の続きです。昨日は，顧客はなぜ買い物をするのかについてお話ししましたが，今日は，人々にものを買わせるために用いられている販売戦略と，それらのトレンドがどのように発展してきたかに焦点を当てます。昨日の結論をおさらいしてみましょう。現在の経済情勢は購買者の支出にどのように影響しているでしょうか。誰か，分かる人。

❷ フランシスカ：景気後退期には，「ビッグチケット」と言われる高額出費への支出が減少し，小物商品の消費が増大します。

❸ 教授：そうですね！　ええと，この現象は「リップスティック効果」と呼ばれています。歴史的にみて，景気後退期には，女性は気分を明るくするため，鮮やかな色の化粧品を購入します。おそらくは，もっと高価な品物の代わりに，です。お菓子やお酒の消費も，同様に増大します。お金に余裕がない時はそうした贅沢品こそ真っ先に切り捨てられるだろうと考えてしまいがちですが，実際にはそれらの品は，購買者自身への比較的安価な「ご褒美」として用いられているのです。

❹ ピーター：家計を切り詰めている人たちは「ご褒美」を切り捨てる方が理に適っているのではないでしょうか。

❺ 教授：おそらくその通りです。しかし，経済にとって幸いなことに，人々は支出を抑えていても買い物をし続けるのです。ほとんどの人々は買い物をする時，相対的な考え方をします。「このチョコレートの2ドルにお金を使う必要はない」ではなくて，「新しいシャツが欲しかったが，買う余裕がない。チョコレートでも私は幸せになれるし，その方が安い」と考えます。それは値引きに近い感覚で，それゆえ正当化するのが容易です。同じように，子供に新しいおもちゃを買ってやる余裕がなければ，アイスクリームで間に合わせるのです。

❻ 　もちろん，たいていの場合これはほとんど無意識に行われています。つまり私たちは，ついてない日や仕事がたいへんだったあとには，ちょっとした元気付けが「あって然るべきだ」と感じ，必要であれば，自分に安上がりの褒美を与える方法を探すようなのです。

❼ 　では，考えてみましょう。店や会社は私たちの購買決定に影響を与えるために，そうした心理的傾向をどのように利用しようとするでしょうか。初期の研究はいくつかの顕著な傾向を明らかにしました。たとえば，買い手にとっての選択肢は多ければ多いほどよいように思えるかもしれません。選択肢が多ければ売り上げも伸びる——とね？　しかし，購買者になるつもりの人は選択肢が限られている場合の方が商品を買って帰る傾向にあることが分かりました。つまり，多すぎる

商品の中から選択するのはうんざりだということです。「選択肢過多」と呼ばれるこうした傾向は，ジャムの販売についてのある研究において初めて確認されました。研究者たちは，ジャムの選択肢を6種類から24種類に増やした場合，購入する人が10分の1になることを発見しました。

❽　これにはいくつかの理由が考えられます。人々は手早く手軽な選択をしたいだけかもしれません。あるいは，買い手が甘めのジャムか，酸味のあるジャムかなどの自分の好みを知らない場合，比較するのが難しいか，比較に時間がかかるかもしれません。

❾　さらに，衝動買い，つまり予定外の買い物の場合，手軽さが重要な要因になるかもしれません。スーパーマーケットが雑誌やキャンディーバーをレジ近くの目立つ場所に置くのには理由があるのです。購買者はこれらの購入に頭を悩ます必要がありません。むしろ彼らはそれらを，報酬あるいは褒美と見なします。衝動買いには，値引きやニューモデルといった魅力が動機となるものもあります。ネットのディスカウント・ストアが流行るのには理由があります。一見すると極めて安価そうな商品を却下するのは困難です。前に述べた，チョコレートを買う人のように，こうした衝動買いをする人は，実際の費用のことを考えているのではなく，なされた値引きのことを考えています。

❿　このように，私たちは購買者として，自分が何を，どうして買おうとしているのかを考えることが重要です。空腹の時には食料品店に行かない方がいいのと同様に，気分をよくするために買い物をしているのか，本当にその品物が必要だから買い物をしているのかを自問してみることが賢明でしょう。

《 指針 》

購買者の心理をテーマとした講義である。いわゆる「リップスティック効果（lipstick effect）」に始まり，「選択肢過多（choice overload）」など，消費者が商品購入を決意するに至るまでの様々な心理プロセスが説明される。語彙レベルは標準的だが，心理学を扱った英文に慣れていない人は，苦戦を強いられるだろう。普段から英文での読書の幅を広げるように心がけたい。

難易度

放送文 ★★★
設　問 ★★☆
総　合 ★★☆

☺☹))) スピーカー情報

Professor Botekin: イングランド
Francisca: 西海岸，カリフォルニア
Peter: 西海岸，オレゴン

Set 4-A ｜設問解説

(1) Choose the correct answer that fills in the blanks: According to "the lipstick effect" theory, during an economic recession, sales of (X) increase, while sales of (Y) decrease.
次の文の空欄を埋めるのにふさわしい語の組み合わせを選べ。
「リップスティック効果理論」によれば，景気後退期には，(X)の売り上げが増加し，(Y)の売り上げが減少する。

a) (X) necessities / (Y) luxuries
(X)必需品／(Y)贅沢品
b) (X) luxuries / (Y) necessities
(X) 贅沢品／(Y)必需品
c) (X) cosmetics / (Y) sweets and alcohol
(X)化粧品／(Y)お菓子やお酒
d) (X) affordable luxuries / (Y) expensive luxuries
(X)手ごろな値段の贅沢品／(Y)高価な贅沢品
e) (X) expensive luxuries / (Y) affordable luxuries
(X)高価な贅沢品／(Y)手ごろな値段の贅沢品

❸で説明される「リップスティック効果」に関する問題である。景気後退期にはリップスティックの売り上げが伸びることからこの名が付けられているが，ここでの「リップスティック」とは，「生活必需品」ではなく，「気分を明るくするようなちょっとした贅沢品」の代表例である。これが選択肢 d の affordable luxuries に該当する。また，❷で In a recession, there is less "big-ticket" spending と言っていることから，高額な商品の売り上げは下がることが分かる。よって d が正解。不況時には，「化粧品」の売り上げは伸びるが，同様にして「お菓子やお酒」の売り上げも伸びるので，c は誤り。

(2) What is the word "treat" used to mean in this lecture?
この講義において，"treat" という語はどのような意味で用いられているか。

a) A special item you buy for someone else.
誰か他の人のために買う特別なもの。
b) Something that is done to cure an illness.
病気を治すためにすること。
c) Something special that gives you pleasure.
喜びを与えてくれる特別なもの。
d) An item such as ice cream used to reward a child.
子供へのご褒美として用いるアイスクリームのようなもの。
e) An expensive item that you would not buy for yourself.
人が自分では買おうと思わない高価なもの。

名詞のtreatは「ごちそう，楽しみ，ご褒美」などの意味を持つ。放送文では❸❹❾で用いられているが，いずれも「自分へのご褒美」という意味で使われている。よって，選択肢のa，b，dは除外できる。また，eも「他人に買ってあげる」という意味が暗に含まれているので，除外する。結局cが正解となる。

(3) According to the professor, how do people on a budget decide to buy chocolate or ice cream?
教授によれば，支出を抑えている時に人々はどのようにしてチョコレートやアイスクリームを買う決断をするのか。

a) They can't control their desire to buy luxuries.
彼らは贅沢品を買いたいという欲望を抑えることができない。
b) They are overwhelmed with an impulse to buy.
彼らは購買衝動に負ける。
c) They compare different brands and choose the cheapest one.
彼らは色々なブランドを比較して，最も安価なものを選ぶ。
d) They want something that will immediately make them happy.
彼らは自分たちをすぐに幸せにするものが欲しい。
e) They perceive the purchase as saving money, not as spending it.
彼らはその買い物を，お金を使っているのではなくお金を節約していると考えている。

❺での教授の説明によると，「高価なシャツは買えないからチョコレート」「おもちゃは買えないからアイスクリーム」というように，他の高価な物と比較して，それらの品物を購入しているとされている。そしてその際には，It almost feels like a discountとあるように，「お金を使っている」というよりも「お金を節約している」という意識が働き，自分の出費を正当化しているのである。これを表したeが正解。cはdifferent brandsが誤り。購買者は色々なブランドを比較しているわけではない。

(4) What is the phenomenon known as "choice overload"?
「選択肢過多」と呼ばれる現象はどのようなものか。

a) Shoppers have less interest when their options are limited.
選択肢が限られていると買い手はあまり興味を持たなくなる。
b) The more options a store gives shoppers, the more items it can sell.
店が買い手に選択肢を与えれば与えるほど，店の売り上げは伸びる。
c) Consumers are less likely to purchase when offered too many products.
購買者は，提供される商品が多すぎると購買しなくなる傾向がある。
d) When forced to choose between similar products, consumers become fatigued.
購買者は，似たような商品の中から選択することを強要されると疲れてしまう。
e) Consumers end up buying unnecessary items when faced with too many choices.
購買者は，多すぎる選択肢に直面すると，結局不要なものを買ってしまう。

110

「選択肢過多（choice overload）」については，❼で説明される。「商品の選択肢が多いと，その商品を買わない可能性が高くなる」というものであり，ｃが正しい。ｄは正解に近いが，forced to choose と become fatigued に問題がある。購買者は選択を「強制される」わけではないし，また選択の結果「疲れる」ということも放送文では説明されていない。

(5) Based on this lecture, which of the following would be good advice for a shop?
　　この講義に基づけば，店に対するアドバイスとして適切なものは次のうちどれか。
　a) Emphasize quality rather than cost.
　　　値段より品質を強調すべきだ。
　b) Give consumers as many choices as possible.
　　　購買者にできるだけ多くの選択肢を与えるべきだ。
　c) Make sure prices are lower than at other stores.
　　　他の店より価格を必ず低くするようにするべきだ。
　d) Place large, expensive items in the most visible spots.
　　　一番目立つところに大きく高価な品物を陳列すべきだ。
　e) Offer sales so consumers feel like they are saving money.
　　　購買者がお金を節約していると実感できるように，特売を行うべきだ。

❾では，人が衝動買いをする理由として「手軽さ（convenience）」と「値引きや新モデルなどの魅力」という２つの点を指摘している。ｄは「手軽さ」に該当するが，すぐ手に取れるように目立つところに置くべきなのは，雑誌やキャンディーバーなどの小物であり，「大きく高価な品物」ではない。ｅが「値引き（lowered price）」に該当し，これが正解となる。値引きされた品物を買うと，購買者はお金を使っているというよりは，得をしている感覚の方が強くなるのである。ｃも正解に近いが，「他の店よりも安い」ということが客に伝わるのかどうか，疑問である。ｅのように特売を行って明確に「値引きされている」ということを示す方がより効果があるだろう。

Set 4-B | 放送文

Psychology of Shopping 2

❶ Professor Botekin: Good morning, everyone. Last week we talked about some of the sales tactics used by stores to encourage customer spending. Today, I want to hear your thoughts on the matter. So, let me begin by asking, when was the last time you impulse-bought an item? Yes, Francisca?

tactic 名 戦術，戦略

❷ Francisca: Hm. Just at lunch, actually. I bought a packet of potato chips at the checkout.

❸ Professor: Good example. Peter, did you have a question?

❹ Peter: Yes. Why would you consider that an impulse buy? It sounds like a logical purchase to me.

logical 形 論理的な，（論理上）必然の
purchase 名 購入

❺ Francisca: Well, I normally don't eat chips. But, it was an organic grocery store and café, and I was extra hungry today. They had some by the register and I just didn't want to bother thinking about another food item to buy instead.

bother *doing* 句 わざわざ…する

❻ Professor: What do you think the store did to encourage you to make that decision ?

🔖 店の戦略：1. 商品を手に取りやすい場所に目立つように置いた，2. 価格を安く設定した

❼ Francisca: First of all, they were placed conveniently near the checkout—and chips bags are usually brightly colored, so they're very visible—and second, they were fairly cheap, so I didn't even think twice about picking them up. Of course, we had just had our lecture, so in the back of my mind I knew the methods stores like to employ. But that didn't seem to affect my actual purchase.

think twice 句 よく考える

❽ Peter: Do you think you considered it a treat for yourself, like we talked about?

❾ Francisca: Not really. I wasn't consciously rewarding myself. But I was tired and hungry, so I think convenience counted the most. I would think, though, that food shopping is rather different than shopping for other products.

consciously 副 意識的に

count 自 重要である，影響力を持つ

❿ Professor: How do you mean?

⓫ Francisca: Well, whenever I go shopping, I usually have something specific in mind that I want or need. For food, though, I'm just thinking "lunch,"

112

which might make me more susceptible to being manipulated.

⓬ Peter: But what about window shopping? Do you ever go into a store to browse, and end up with several items you hadn't planned on buying? Because that often happens to me...

⓭ Francisca: Not often. I do a lot of online shopping, and you don't really browse at most Internet retail sites. Instead, you type the name of the item you need into a search box, so there's not as much chance of getting distracted by potential impulse buys.

⓮ Professor: That's true, but online marketplaces are working very hard to find a way around this problem. Have you ever noticed how, when you're checking email, an advertisement for shoes or lipstick will suddenly pop up on the computer screen, seemingly from out of nowhere?

⓯ Peter: That happens to me all the time, although not with lipstick ads. It seems like every time I surf the Internet, all I see is advertisements for my favorite comic books. I guess that's why I end up buying so many of them!

⓰ Professor: That's exactly what I'm talking about. Online retailers keep track of your purchases, and then find ways to tempt you with similar products —and not only when you're visiting their website! Using recent technology, they're able to locate you when you use certain search engines or email programs. Then they pay the owner of the search engine or email program for the right to present you with an advertisement for those comic books.

⓱ Peter: Wow, I feel so dumb for falling for that!

⓲ Francisca: That kind of thing doesn't tempt me. I have a budget, and I'm not about to get distracted by some silly ad for new earrings.

⓳ Professor: Well Francisca, you're a rare consumer. Most Internet shoppers are extremely vulnerable to pop-up advertisements. The proof is in the incredible rise in online shopping revenue over the past decade!

susceptible to ... 句 …の影響を受けやすい
manipulate 他 …を操作する，操る
browse 自（商品・ネットなどを）見てまわる，冷やかす
▶ Franciscaの発言の主旨：買おうとしている品物が具体的に決まっていないと，店側の戦略にはまりやすい
retail 形 小売りの
distract 他 …の気をそらす
potential 形 潜在的な，可能性がある
a way around ... 句 …を回避する方法
seemingly 副 一見したところ
out of nowhere 句 どこからともなく
ad 名 広告
（＝advertisement）

retailer 名 小売業者
keep track of ... 句 …を追跡する
tempt 他 …を誘惑する
locate 他 …の位置を特定する

present A with B 句 AにBを提示する
▶ ネット・ショップの戦略：客の購入履歴，検索エンジンや電子メールの使用履歴をもとに，その客に特定の商品広告を提示する
dumb 形 ばかな
fall for ... 句 …にだまされる
be not about to do 句 …するつもりはない
vulnerable to ... 句 …に対して弱い
revenue 名 収入，歳入

Set 4-B | 放送文の日本語訳

購買の心理学 2

❶ボテキン教授：おはようございます。先週は，購買者の支出を促進するために店が用いている販売戦略のいくつかについてお話ししました。今日は，この問題について，皆さんの考えを聞きたいと思います。まず，この質問から。一番最近衝動買いをしたのはいつですか？　じゃあ，フランシスカ。

❷フランシスカ：うーん，実はランチの時です。レジのところでポテトチップスを買ってしまいました。

❸教授：いい例ですね。ピーター，質問がありましたか？

❹ピーター：はい。どうして君はそれを衝動買いと思うのかな。僕にはそれは必然的な買い物のように聞こえるけれど。

❺フランシスカ：ええと，私は普段，ポテトチップスは食べません。でもそこはカフェのあるオーガニックの店で，私は今日，とてもお腹が空いていたの。ポテトチップスがレジの脇にあって，単に他のものを考えるのが面倒だったのです。

❻教授：君にその決断をさせるために，店はどのようなことをしたと思いますか。

❼フランシスカ：第1に，手に取りやすいようにレジの近くにありました。ポテトチップスの袋はたいてい派手な色をしているので，とても目立っていました。第2に，値段がかなり安かった。だから，よく考えもせずに買ってしまいました。もちろん，ちょうどこの講義を聴いていましたから，頭では店が採用しようとする手法を知っていました。でもそれは，現実の私の購入に影響しなかったみたいです。

❽ピーター：講義で出てきたように，君はそれを自分への「ご褒美」だと思ったの？

❾フランシスカ：特に思わなかった。意識の上では自分へのご褒美のつもりはありませんでした。むしろ，疲れていて空腹だったので，私にとっては便利さが何より大事でした。でも私は，食べ物の買い物はそれ以外の買い物とはちょっと違うと思っています。

❿教授：どういうことかな？

⓫フランシスカ：ええと，買い物に行く時，私は普通，欲しいものや必要なものを具体的に念頭に置いています。でも食べ物に関しては，「ランチ」とだけ考えているせいで，操作されやすくなっているのかもしれません。

⓬ピーター：でもウィンドーショッピングはどうなの？　君は冷やかしで店に入って，結局，買う予定じゃなかった品を買っていたなんて経験はないの？　というのも，僕はそういうことがしょっちゅうだから……。

⓭フランシスカ：あんまりないわ。私はネット・ショッピングをよく利用します。みんな，インターネットの小売サイトはたいていあてもなく見て回ったりはしないですよね。それよりも，必要な品物の名前を検索ボックスに打ち込みます。だから，衝動買いの可能性があるものに気をとられる機会はそれほどありません。

⓮教授：その通りだ。しかし，ネット市場は，この問題を回避する方法を見出そうと必死に努力している。君たちは，eメールをチェックしているとき，一見何もないところからふいに，コンピュータの画面に靴や口紅のポップアップ広告が現れたなんて経験はないかな。

114

⓯ピーター：よくあります。もっとも口紅の広告じゃないけど。ネット・サーフィンするたびに，僕の大好きな漫画の広告ばかり見ているような気がします。漫画をたくさん買う羽目になるのはそのせいかもしれないな！

⓰教授：私が言っているのは，まさにそのことなんだよ。ネット・ショップは君が買ったものを追跡して，似たような製品で君の気を引こうとしている。しかも，君がそれらのウェブサイトを訪問している間に限らない。最近のテクノロジーを用いて，彼らは君がある検索エンジンやeメールプログラムを使用している時にも君の場所を特定することができるんだ。彼らは検索エンジンやeメールプログラムの所有者にお金を払って，君にその漫画の広告を提示する権利を得ているのだよ。

⓱ピーター：わー，そんなのにだまされていたなんて，なんてまぬけなんだ！

⓲フランシスカ：私はそういった類のものにはひっかからないわ。私は予算を立てているから，新しいイヤリングなんかのばかげた広告に気を取られることはありません。

⓳教授：そうか，フランシスカ，君は珍しい購買者だ。ほとんどのネット・ショッピング利用者はポップアップ広告にはとても弱いものだ。この10年間にネット・ショッピングの収入が信じられないくらい増大していることがその証拠だ！

《〈 指針 〉》

Aに続いて「購買者の心理」をテーマとしているが，今度は話者の具体的な経験をもとに，Aの講義で展開された説が検証される。Aの概要を理解していれば，内容を理解するのにはさほど苦労しないだろう。後半はネット・ショッピングへと話題が進む。2人の学生（FranciscaとPeter）の性格の違いに注目しつつ，ネット広告の仕組みを理解しよう。

難易度

放送文　★★☆
設　問　★★☆
総　合　★★☆

☺☺))) スピーカー情報

Professor Botekin: イングランド
Francisca: 西海岸，カリフォルニア
Peter: 西海岸，オレゴン

Set 4-B | 設問解説

(1) What factor was most important for Francisca when shopping for lunch?
ランチのための買い物をする時，どの要因がフランシスカにとって最も重要だったか。

a) Satisfaction—she was very hungry.
満足——彼女はたいへん空腹だった。

b) Price—she wanted something cheap.
価格——彼女は安価なものが欲しかった。

c) Treat—she wanted to reward herself.
ご褒美——彼女は自分で自分にご褒美をあげたかった。

d) Health—she wanted something organic.
健康——彼女はオーガニックのものが欲しかった。

e) Ease—she didn't want to spend time choosing an item.
手軽さ——彼女は品物を選ぶのに時間をかけたくなかった。

Franciscaがポテトチップスを衝動買いした理由について，❼では「手軽さ」と「価格」が原因だったという分析がなされているが，さらに❾ではI think convenience counted the mostとあり，「手軽さ」が最も大きな要因だったとされている。このconvenienceをeaseに置き換えたeが正解。

(2) According to Francisca, what makes customers vulnerable to sales tactics?
フランシスカによれば，どんな場合に購買者は販売戦略に乗せられるか。

a) Being hungry.
お腹が空いている場合。

b) Shopping for items online.
ネットでものを買う場合。

c) Feeling like they want to reward themselves.
自分自身にご褒美をあげたくなる場合。

d) Not having a specific plan or product in mind when shopping.
買い物をする時に，具体的な予定や商品を念頭に置いていない場合。

e) Not knowing about the methods stores use to encourage purchases.
購買を促進するために店が用いている手法を知らない場合。

❾⓫の内容をもとに，dを正解とする。「ランチ」ということだけで，具体的に購入する品物が決まっていなかったために，店の戦略にはまって不要なものを衝動買いしてしまったという分析である。bの「ネット・ショッピング」で衝動買いをしてしまうのは，FranciscaではなくPeterの方である。

(3) Why are online shoppers less likely to browse?
ネット・ショッピングの利用者があまり見て回らないのはなぜか。

a) Because they can't see the items in person.
彼らは品物をじかに見ることができないから。

116

b) Because they are usually on a strict budget.
彼らは普通，支出を抑えているから。

c) Because online shops don't have many items.
ネットショップの品数は少ないから。

d) Because they are often in a rush and can't get distracted.
彼らはしばしば急いでいるので，気をそらすことがありえないから。

e) Because they typically use a search engine to look for items.
彼らは通常，品物を探すときには検索エンジンを利用するから。

❸でのFranciscaの発言から，ｅが正解だと分かる。通常のウィンドーショッピングとは違って，ネットの場合は購買者が目的の商品を検索して買うので，他の商品を衝動買いする可能性が低いというのである。

(4) Which of the following accurately describes Peter and Francisca's online shopping habits?
ピーターとフランシスカのネット・ショッピングの習慣を的確に描写しているのは次のうちどれか。

a) Peter is not tempted by impulse buys, but Francisca is.
ピーターは衝動買いをしたくなることがないが，フランシスカはある。

b) Peter sometimes buys unnecessary items, but Francisca does not.
ピーターは不必要なものを買うことがあるが，フランシスカはない。

c) Francisca is aware of online marketing strategies, but Peter is not.
フランシスカはネットのマーケティング戦略を知っているが，ピーターは気付いていない。

d) Peter and Francisca both only buy items they planned to purchase in advance.
ピーターとフランシスカはどちらも，あらかじめ買う予定だったものだけを買う。

e) Peter and Francisca are both often influenced by advertisements and buy things they don't need.
ピーターとフランシスカはどちらも広告に流されて不要なものを買ってしまうことが多い。

❶ではPeterが「ネット上の広告を見て漫画を大量に買ってしまう」と告白している。また❸ではFranciscaが「ネット上の広告による戦略に乗せられることはない」と言っている。以上からｂを正解とする。❶から，Peterがオンライン広告の戦略について知らなかったことは分かるが，Franciscaが知っていたかどうかは，この会話から判断することはできない。よってｃは正解とは言えない。

(5) According to the lecture, which strategy do online retailers use to encourage purchases?
講義によれば，購買を促進するためにネット・ショップはどの戦略を用いているか。

a) They send advertisements to consumers via email.
顧客に広告をｅメールで送っている。

b) They offer their products at physical stores as well as online.
商品をネットのほかに実店舗でも提供している。

c) They match advertisements to the buying patterns of online shoppers.
広告をネットの顧客の購買パターンに合わせている。

d) They post advertisements for many appealing items on their websites.
自分たちのウェブサイトに，多数の魅力的な商品の広告を掲載している。

e) They keep track of shoppers' purchases and select products that are likely to be popular.
購買者の購買履歴を追跡し，流行りそうなものを選択する。

ネット・ショップの戦略については❻で説明される。客の購入履歴，検索エンジンやeメールの使用履歴をもとに，その客に特定の商品の広告を提示するという仕組みである。つまり，Peterのように漫画が好きな人がネット・サーフィンをすると，スクリーンには漫画の広告ばかりが表示されることになる。cが正解。dのように自社のウェブサイトに広告を掲載するのは当然だが，それ以外のサイトを閲覧している時にも広告が表示されるというのがポイントである。eの「購買者の購買履歴を追跡する」は正しいが，「流行りそうなものを選択する」が誤り。

Set 4-C | 放送文

Nautical Equipment

❶ Kent: Next up we'll go to our tech reporter Beth Hart, who's been attending the annual diving convention in Miami, Florida, and can fill us in on what's hot and what's not in the world of hi-tech diving equipment. Beth, how's the conference this year?

❷ Beth: Hi Kent. Very good and very wet! I've been in and out of the water all weekend trying out the latest diving suits and I can tell you there are some very exciting developments being rolled out here this year.

❸ Kent: What's caught your eye so far?

❹ Beth: Well certainly the item that diving enthusiasts and corporate buyers seem most excited about is the Divepro. It's a full-body diving suit from a company based out of Vancouver that allows divers to move with complete freedom at a depth of 800 feet for up to 40 hours.

❺ Kent: And tell us what this suit looks like.

❻ Beth: Well, you know how astronauts look when they walk on the moon? That's pretty much what a diver wearing this thing looks like. It's a massive shell made of black metal with white bands along the arms and legs that function as rotating joints. There's a flat window over the face and claw-like hands for manipulating items underwater, along with a whole array of hi-tech features like embedded video cameras and fiber-optic connectivity. It weighs 500 pounds and costs a whopping quarter-million dollars.

❼ Kent: Sounds to me like ordinary scuba gear might be a better option!

❽ Beth: Maybe in terms of the price tag, but if you were to dive 800 feet in a scuba suit you would need about eight days to recover because the pressure at that depth is so intense. Remember we're talking about being the equivalent of 80 stories beneath the water's surface, with the weight of all that water on top of you. That can cause all

convention 图 大会
fill … in on〜 句 …に〜の詳細を伝える
equipment 图 装備
conference 图 会議

try out 句 …を試す

roll out 句 …を披露する, 公開する

enthusiast 图 熱中している人, ファン
corporate 形 企業の

up to … 句 (最大) …まで
astronaut 图 宇宙飛行士
massive 形 巨大な
joint 图 接合部, ジョイント
claw 图 鉤爪
manipulate 他 …を操作する
an array of … 句 ずらりと並んだ…
embedded 形 埋め込まれている
fiber-optic 形 光ファイバーの
connectivity 图 (通信の) 接続性
whopping 形 べらぼうな
gear 图 用具一式
⊿ Divepro の特徴：回転式ジョイント, 水中での操作用の手, ビデオカメラ, 光ファイバー通信
in terms of … 句 …という観点から
intense 形 激しい, 猛烈な
equivalent 图 同等のもの
story 图 (建物の) 階

sorts of health problems if you're not extremely careful.

❾ Kent: So how does this suit get around those problems?

❿ Beth: The inside of the suit maintains the same pressure we have here on land, so the diver doesn't need any special procedures in order to recover afterwards. The technology is called an atmospheric diving system, or ADS, and it's actually existed for over a decade. The real innovation of this suit is in the joints. In earlier ADS suits, high water pressure created friction that hindered joint movement. The suits weren't much use because when divers wore them they became extremely clumsy! The company behind the Divepro has managed to reduce friction by half, which experts here tell me is quite a significant accomplishment.

⓫ Kent: Who might need a suit like this? I'm guessing it's not your average pearl diver.

⓬ Beth: No, definitely not. It's mostly intended for use by scientists studying the deep-sea environment, along with companies that do underwater engineering work. For instance, I've heard divers will use Divepro suits to inspect oil pipelines along the coast of Spain later this year.

⓭ Kent: Very interesting. What else has caught your eye at the convention?

⓮ Beth: Well, there was a very unusual unmanned rover ....

---

get around 句 …を回避する

procedure 名 手順，処置

🔖 Divepro の特徴：ダイバーが深海から地上に戻った時に即座に回復できる

innovation 名 革新，新機軸

friction 名 摩擦

hinder 他 …を妨げる

clumsy 形 不器用な，ぎこちない

🔖 Divepro の特徴：滑らかなジョイントにより，動きやすい

significant 形 大きな，重要な

pearl 名 真珠

🔖 Divepro の用途：科学者による深海調査，企業による海底での工事

inspect 他 …を検査する

unmanned 形 無人の

rover 名 探索車

120

Set 4-C | 放送文の日本語訳

海事装備

❶ケント：次は科学技術レポーター，ベス・ハートの登場です。ベスは今，フロリダ州マイアミのダイビング年次大会の会場にいますが，ハイテクのダイビング用品業界では何が流行っているか，流行っていないかの情報を届けてくれるはずです。ベス，今年の大会はどうなっていますか。

❷ベス：はい，ケント。たいへんすばらしいのですが，びしょ濡れになっています！週末はずっと水を出たり入ったりして，最新のダイビングスーツを試しています。今年こちらでは，非常にわくわくするような最新成果が披露されています。

❸ケント：これまでで目に留まったものは何ですか。

❹ベス：なんと言っても，ダイビング・ファンや企業のバイヤーの方々が一番注目しているようなのは「ダイブプロ」です。これはフルボディのダイビングスーツで，バンクーバー郊外にある企業の製品です。ダイブプロを着用すれば，水深800フィートの場所でも最長40時間，完全に自由に活動することが可能です。

❺ケント：そのスーツは見た目はどんなふうですか。

❻ベス：そうですね，月面を歩行する宇宙飛行士の姿はお分かりですよね。これを着るとちょうどそんなふうに見えます。黒い金属でできた大きな殻とでも言いましょうか。腕と脚の部分に白いバンドがついています。これは回転式のジョイントとして機能します。顔の部分は平らな窓になっています。水中でものを操作するための鉤爪状の手もついています。また，埋め込み型のビデオカメラや，光ファイバー接続等，ハイテクを駆使した装備が満載です。重さは500ポンド，価格はなんと，25万ドルです。

❼ケント：私には普通のスキューバダイビング用品の方がよさそうに思えます！

❽ベス：お値段の点ではそうかもしれません。でも，スキューバ用のスーツで800フィート潜るとすれば，回復までに8日間程度必要です。その深さでの水圧はたいへんなものだからです。そこが水面から建物の80階分下方に相当することを忘れないでください。それだけの水の重量が身体にかかるわけですから。極めて慎重に対応しなければ，ありとあらゆる健康障害が起こり得ます。

❾ケント：では，そのスーツはそうした問題をどう回避しているのでしょうか。

❿ベス：スーツ内部は，私たちが今いるこの陸上での気圧と同じに保たれています。ですから，ダイバーは，回復のために事後に特別な処置を一切する必要がありません。このテクノロジーは大気潜水システム（ADS）と呼ばれています。技術そのものは実は10年以上前から存在していました。このスーツの真の新機軸はと言うと，それはジョイント部分にあるのです。従来のADSスーツだと，高い水圧によって摩擦が生じ，それがジョイント部分の動きを妨げていました。それらはあまり役に立ちませんでした。着用した時，動作がとてもぎこちなくなってしまうからです。ダイブプロを開発した企業は，摩擦を半分に減らすことに成功しました。大会に出席した専門家たちの話では，それは極めて重要な成果だということです。

⓫ケント：このスーツを必要とするのはどういう人たちなのでしょうか。普通の真珠採りの方々ではないと思いますが……。

⑫ベス：ええ，全く違います。これは主に，深海環境を調査する科学者や，水中で土木工事をする会社等の使用を見込んでいます。たとえば，今年の後半，スペイン沿岸部の油送管の点検を行うダイバーがダイブプロを着用する予定だということです。

⑬ケント：とても興味深いお話でした。その他に大会で目についたものはありますか。

⑭ベス：そうですね，たいへん珍しい無人の探査車がありました……。

《 指針 》

Diveproという高性能のダイビングスーツの紹介レポート。製品についての情報伝達がメインである。聞き取る際には，このDiveproの形状等を具体的にイメージすること。頭の中に明確なイメージを浮かべることで，より強く記憶に残り，放送中にメモをとらなくても設問に答えることができるようになるはずである。

難易度

放送文　★★☆
設　問　★☆☆
総　合　★★☆

☺☹))) スピーカー情報

Kent: スコットランド
Beth: イングランド

Set 4-C | 設問解説

(1) Which of the following is NOT a feature of the Divepro?
次のうちダイブプロの特徴ではないものはどれか。

a) A window to see outside.
外を見るための窓。

b) Devices to film the marine environment.
海洋環境を撮影するための機器。

c) Joints that rotate for effective movement.
効果的な動作を可能にする，回転するジョイント。

d) Attachments for handling items underwater.
水中でものを操作するための付属装置。

e) A fin-like apparatus on the back to improve underwater mobility.
水中での移動性を向上させる，背中に付けられたひれ状の装具。

❻で与えられる情報を正確に聞き取ること。a flat window over the faceがa，embedded video camerasがbに合致する。claw-like hands for manipulating items underwaterがd，white bands along the arms and legs that function as rotating jointsはcと合致。eについての言及はない。

(2) Why does Beth think diving down 800 feet in scuba gear would be a bad idea?
ベスが，スキューバダイビング用のスーツで水深800フィートまで潜ることが良くないと考えているのはなぜか。

a) It would take too long to descend that far.
その深さまで下降するのにはたいへん時間がかかるだろうから。

b) It would be too hard to move with dexterity.
機敏に動くことがたいへん難しいだろうから。

c) It would be too difficult to breathe at that depth.
その水深で呼吸することが非常に困難だろうから。

d) It would be too cold for the human body to function properly.
あまりに寒くて人体が正常に機能しなくなるであろうから。

e) It would take too long to recover after returning to the surface.
水面に戻ったあと回復するまでにたいへん時間がかかるだろうから。

❽でのif you were to dive 800 feet in a scuba suit you would need about eight days to recoverからeが正解だと分かる。

(3) How is the Divepro different from other ADS suits?
ダイブプロは他のADSスーツとどのように異なっているか。

a) The suit is made of metal rather than plastic.
このスーツはプラスチックではなく金属で作られている。

b) The suit is more affordable for ordinary fishermen.
このスーツは普通の漁師にとっていっそう買いやすい値段である。

c) The suit enables the diver to recover afterwards in no time.
そのスーツを着れば，ダイバーは潜水後すぐに回復できる。

d) The suit's joints move more effectively under high-pressure conditions.
高圧という条件下で，スーツのジョイント部分がいっそう効果的に動く。

e) The interior of the suit maintains a pressure equivalent to that on land.
スーツ内部の圧力が陸上と同じに保たれている。

❿の内容に関する問題。Diveproが採用しているADSというシステムは10年以上前から存在するものだが，Diveproが他のADSスーツと異なって革新的なのは，ジョイントの摩擦を軽減してより動きやすくした点にある。dが正解。cの「潜水後すぐに回復できる」やeの「水中でも陸上と同じ気圧を保つ」はADS全般の機能であり，Diveproだけに備わる特徴ではない。

(4) Who would be least likely to use a Divepro suit?
ダイブプロを最も使用しそうにないのはどのような人か。
a) A fisherman diving for sea urchins.
海に潜ってウニを採る漁師。
b) A biologist researching fish reproduction.
魚類の生殖を研究する生物学者。
c) An archaeologist exploring a sunken ship.
難破船を探査する考古学者。
d) An engineer installing underwater phone lines.
水中に電話回線を設置するエンジニア。
e) A commercial diver engaging in undersea construction.
海底建設工事に携わる商業ダイバー。

Diveproの用途については⓬で説明されている。まずuse by scientists studying the deep-sea environment（科学者が深海の環境を調査するのに用いる）に該当するのがｂ及びｃである。またcompanies that do underwater engineering work（企業が水中で土木工事を行う）に該当するのがｄとｅである。ａに近い「真珠を採るダイバーによる利用」については⓫⓬で否定されている。

(5) According to Beth, why is the Divepro an important technology?
ベスによれば，ダイブプロはなぜ重要なテクノロジーか。
a) Because many divers and companies are excited about it.
多数のダイバーや企業がそれに注目しているから。
b) Because it allows divers to work more safely in deep water.
ダイバーは，それを着用すると深海でより安全に作業することが可能になるから。
c) Because it offers both hi-tech features and attractive design.
それがハイテクの特徴と魅力的なデザインの両方を具えているから。
d) Because it allows divers to work more efficiently in deep water.
ダイバーは，それを着用すると深海でいっそう効果的に作業することが可能になるから。
e) Because it allows divers to descend more deeply than other suits.
ダイバーは，それを着用すると他のスーツより深く潜ることが可能になるから。

放送文全体に関わる問題である。Diveproの様々な特徴が紹介されているが，最も革新的と言えるのは⓾で述べられている点，すなわち「ジョイントの摩擦を半減したこと」であろう。これによって，深海での作業がより円滑に行えるようになったのである。これを表したｄが正解である。ｅの「他のスーツより深く潜れる」という事実は語られていない。ｃのattractive designへの言及はない。ｂの「安全性」はADS全般に言えることであり，Diveproに固有の特徴ではない。

Set 5 | 解答

5A　(1) e　(2) c　(3) d　(4) a　(5) c
5B　(1) e　(2) e　(3) e　(4) b　(5) e
5C　(1) d　(2) d　(3) c　(4) c　(5) a

Set 5-A | 放送文

Biodiversity and Agriculture

❶ John: Good morning, and welcome to this edition of *Nature News*. I'm John Harper. This week we're going to take a break from our usual lineup of science stories to ask a more basic question. What is nature? Here in the United States, we usually think of nature as untouched wilderness. For example, we might imagine the soaring old-growth redwoods of northern California or the dramatic valleys and mountains of Yosemite National Park. Travel the world, however, and you'll find some very different interpretations of nature. As reporter Mary Davis recently learned on a trip to Japan, people in that country often think of nature as a rural landscape where human beings live in harmony with wild plants and animals. As we'll hear in Mary's report, preserving biodiversity in these landscapes depends not on keeping humans out, but rather on making sure enough people stick around to maintain traditional farming practices and lifestyles.

❷ Mary: I'm standing here in Aso-Kuju National Park, on the island of Kyushu in southern Japan, and looking out at an absolutely stunning landscape. I'm surrounded by acres and acres of silvery grassland. In the distance I can see an active volcano — Mt. Nakadake — sending smoke into the air. I feel like I'm in the midst of a completely wild landscape. But Hiroshi Sato, a ranger here at the park, says that's far from the case.

❸ Hiroshi: These grasslands were created by farmers who have grazed their cows, harvested grass, and practiced controlled burning here for at least 1,000 years.

wilderness 名 荒野，原野
soaring 形 高くそびえる
redwood 名 セコイア，アメリカスギ
interpretation 名 解釈
rural 形 田舎の
landscape 名 景色
in harmony with ... 句 …と調和して
biodiversity 名 生物多様性
stick around 句 その場に居続ける

Johnの発言の主旨：アメリカ人は自然というと「手つかずの自然」をイメージするが，世界には自然について様々な解釈がある。日本では，人間と共存することで保たれる自然がある

stunning 形 息をのむような
acre 名 エーカー（面積の単位）
silvery 形 銀色の
in the distance 句 遠くに
volcano 名 火山
in the midst of ... 句 …の真っただ中に
the case 句 真実，事実

that's far from the case の意味：阿蘇くじゅうの風景は人の手の加わらない自然ではない

graze 他 …を放牧する
harvest 他 …を収穫する

❹ Mary: In fact, some 70,000 people still live in Aso-Kuju National Park today. Many of them raise beef cattle or grow rice inside park boundaries. Sato says that's key for preserving the natural ecosystem here.

cattle 名 牛
boundary 名 境界

❺ Hiroshi: Each spring, members of the local community gather to set fire to dry grass from the previous season. The plains turn black, then green as a rich diversity of wildflowers, grasses, and wild herbs begin to grow back. Because the plant life is so varied, the grasslands provide a habitat for an incredibly wide range of insects, birds, and mammals.

set fire 句 火を付ける

habitat 名 生息地

mammal 名 哺乳類

❻ Mary: Several of the butterfly and wildflower species here are endemic, which means they are not found anywhere else in Japan — or the world. If farmers didn't burn Aso's grasslands, their unique habitat would disappear. Bushes would begin to grow, and then trees. Eventually, the open field where I'm standing right now would be covered with dense forest. Scientists call this process ecological succession. That may not sound like a bad thing, but local conservationist Mariko Ito says having too much forest actually reduces biodiversity.

endemic 形 固有種の

bush 名 低木

dense 形 密度の高い，濃い
ecological succession 句 生態遷移
conservationist 名 自然保護活動家

❼ Mariko: We already have a lot of natural forest here in Kyushu. Grasslands, on the other hand, are extremely rare in modern-day Japan, so we need to do everything we can to preserve them. The biggest threat to this ecosystem is that there aren't enough young farmers living here to carry on traditional land management practices.

📌 Maryの発言の主旨：阿蘇くじゅうの草原を野焼きせず放置しておくと，森林が広がり，固有種の生息域が失われる
threat 名 脅威
carry on 句 …を継続する

❽ Mary: Believe it or not, half of Japan's farmers are more than 70 years old. In some of Aso's villages, the average age is even higher. So Ito is working to bring young volunteers into the area to help with the yearly burning. Last spring, I tagged along with her to one of those volunteer events …

tag along 句 ついて行く

126

Set 5-A｜放送文の日本語訳

生物多様性と農業

❶ジョン：おはようございます。今号の「ネイチャー・ニュース」へ，ようこそ。ジョン・ハーパーです。今週は，通常取り上げる科学の話題から離れ，もっと基本的な質問を問いかけることにします。自然とは何か？　ここアメリカでは，自然を手付かずの原野と思いがちです。たとえば，北カリフォルニアにそびえ立つセコイア原生林やヨセミテ国立公園の雄大な渓谷や山々を思い浮かべるかもしれません。しかし，世界を旅すれば，それとは大きく異なる自然の解釈に出会うでしょう。レポーターのメアリー・デイビスは，最近日本に旅行した時，日本人がよく思い浮かべる自然とは人間と野生の動植物が共生する田園風景であることを知りました。メアリーのレポートの中でも指摘があると思いますが，このような田園風景における生物多様性の保全は，人間を締め出すのではなく，むしろ伝統的な農業のやり方やライフスタイルを維持し続ける人間が十分にいる状態を確保することにかかっています。

❷メアリー：私は，南日本に位置する九州のここ阿蘇くじゅう国立公園に立ち，息をのむような景色を眺めています。私の周りには，広大な銀色の草原が広がっています。遠くには，活火山である中岳が煙を噴き上げているのが見えます。一面原野のような風景の真っただ中にいるような気がします。でも，この公園で自然保護官を務めるサトウヒロシさんによれば，それは，事実から程遠いとのことです。

❸ヒロシ：これらの草原は，少なくとも，1000年もの間，ここで牛を放牧し，牧草を刈り取り，野焼きを行ってきた農民が作り上げたものです。

❹メアリー：実際，阿蘇くじゅう国立公園には現在でも7万人ほどの人々が住んでいます。住民の多くは，公園の境界内で肉牛の飼育や稲作を行っています。サトウさんいわく，それが，ここの自然生態系保全の鍵を握っているそうです。

❺ヒロシ：毎年春になると，地域の住民が集まり，前の季節に生えた乾いた草に火を放ちます。野原は，焼けて黒くなりますが，実に多様な野生の花，牧草，野草が再び生え始めると緑地に変わります。多様性に富んだ植生のため，草原は，信じられないほど多種多様な昆虫，鳥，哺乳動物の生育地となります。

❻メアリー：ここに生息する蝶や野の花の種の一部は，固有種です。つまり，日本，あるいは世界の他の地域では見られません。農業従事者が阿蘇の草原を野焼きしなければ，この特異な生息地は消滅するでしょう。低木が生え始め，次に樹木が生え始めます。最終的に，今私が立っているこの野原は，うっそうとした森林に覆われることになるでしょう。科学者は，このプロセスを生態遷移と呼びます。悪いことではないように思えるかもしれませんが，地元の自然保護活動家であるイトウマリコさんによれば，森林が多すぎると，実際には生物多様性が減少するそうです。

❼マリコ：ここ九州には，既に天然林が豊富に存在します。一方，今の日本には，草原が非常に少なくなっていることから，草原を保全するため，できることは全て行う必要があります。この生態系にとっての最大の脅威は，ここに住み，伝統的な土地管理を実践する若い農業従事者の数が不足している点です。

❽メアリー：なんと，日本の農業従事者の半数は，70歳を超えています。阿蘇の村落の中には，平均年齢がそれよりも高いところもあります。そのため，イトウさんは，若いボランティアをこの地域に呼び込んで，毎年行われる野焼きを手伝ってもらう活動を行っています。昨年の春，私は，彼女に同行して，そうしたボランティア活動の1つを見に行きました。

《 指針 》

「人間の手が加わることで保たれる自然」という切り口から，九州の阿蘇くじゅう国立公園で行われている農業を取材したレポートである。阿蘇くじゅうの生物多様性がどのようにして保たれているのかを正確に把握するように心がけよう。

難易度

放送文	★★☆
設　問	★☆☆
総　合	★☆☆

☺☹))) スピーカー情報

John: 中西部，イリノイ
Mary: 西海岸，カリフォルニア
Hiroshi: 西海岸，カリフォルニア
Mariko: 西海岸，カリフォルニア

Set 5-A ｜設問解説

(1) According to John, which of the following would NOT be a typical image of nature for an American?
ジョンによれば，アメリカ人が自然について抱く典型的なイメージに該当しないのは，次のうちどれか。

a) A wild river.
原生河川。

b) A dense forest.
鬱蒼とした森林。

c) A grove of redwood trees.
セコイア樹林。

d) A valley full of wildflowers.
一面野の花で覆われた渓谷。

e) A grassland where cows graze.
牛が放牧された草原。

❶ではWhat is nature?（自然とは何か）という問いを提起し，それについてアメ

128

リカ人が抱く一般的なイメージを紹介している。放送文では北カリフォルニアのセコイア林やヨセミテ国立公園の渓谷や山々等が例として挙げられているが，それらに共通するのはuntouched（人の手が加わっていない）という要素である。選択肢のa，b，c，dはいずれもこれに該当する。一方でeは人間によって管理された風景であり，この後で紹介される阿蘇くじゅうの自然に近いものである。

(2) According to Mary's report, in what way is the Japanese view of nature different from the American one?
メアリーのレポートによれば，日本人の自然観は，アメリカ人の自然観とどのような点が異なるか。

a) Humans are part of nature just like any other living creatures.
人間は，他のあらゆる生き物と同様，自然の一部である。

b) To achieve balance with nature, people use resources very carefully.
自然とのバランスを取るため，人間が非常に注意深く資源を利用する。

c) Protecting nature doesn't necessarily mean keeping it free from human influence.
自然保護は，必ずしも自然が人間の影響を受けないようにすることを意味しない。

d) To preserve nature, it is necessary to exclude people from important ecosystems.
自然保全のためには，重要な生態系から人間を排除する必要がある。

e) People live in harmony with each other and try to preserve the natural environment.
人間が互いに仲良く暮らし，自然環境の保全に努める。

阿蘇くじゅうに代表される日本独特の自然観については，❶の後半で語られている。preserving biodiversity ... depends not on keeping humans out, but rather on making sure enough people stick aroundとあるように，人間を排除することではなく，むしろ人間が積極的に手を加えることで自然を守るという考え方であり，これが選択肢のcに該当する。dはむしろアメリカ人の自然観である。eのin harmony with ...という語句は，放送文中では「人間が自然と調和して暮らす」という文脈で用いられている。

(3) How do people maintain the grasslands in Aso?
阿蘇では，草原を維持するため，どのような方法が用いられているか？

a) By cutting down bushes and trees.
低木や樹木の伐採。

b) By limiting construction in open fields.
野原における建築制限。

c) By planting diverse wildflowers and herbs.
多様な野の花や草の植栽。

d) By burning, grazing cattle and harvesting grass.
野焼き，牛の放牧及び牧草の刈り取り。

e) All of the above.
上記の全て。

阿蘇くじゅうの草原を保全している方法については❸❺で具体的に述べられている。放牧や牧草の刈り取りに加えて，毎年草原を焼くことで，森林が形成されるのを防ぎ，生物多様性を維持しているのである。これに該当するdが正解。植物を植えているという事実は語られていないので，cは誤り。

(4) **According to Mariko, why would biodiversity levels fall if forests spread in Aso?**
 マリコによれば，阿蘇で森林が広がると，なぜ生物多様性レベルが低下するのか。
 a) Because the variety of habitats in the area would decrease.
   この地域の生息地の多様性が減少するため。
 b) Because forests are too dark for most plant species to grow.
   森林は暗すぎて，ほとんどの植物種が成長できないため。
 c) Because farmers would no longer be able to raise cattle and grow rice.
   農業従事者が牛の飼育や稲作を行うことができなくなるため。
 d) Because fewer types of animals are found in forests than in grasslands.
   草原よりも森林の方が生息する動物の種類が少ないため。
 e) Because certain animals in the forests would destroy the native species.
   森林の特定の動物が在来種を駆逐してしまうため。

❻では，阿蘇くじゅうの草原が，この土地に固有の動植物の生息域となっていることが説明されている。野焼きを行わずに草原を放置してしまうと，森林が広がり，これらの生息域が失われるというのである。これに該当するaが正解。

(5) **What did Mary do last spring?**
 昨年の春にメアリーは，何をしたか？
 a) Hosted a local volunteer event.
   地元のボランティア活動を主催した。
 b) Helped Mariko recruit volunteers.
   マリコがボランティアを募るのを手伝った。
 c) Watched volunteers burn grasslands.
   ボランティアが草原を野焼きするのを見た。
 d) Went hiking in Aso-Kuju National Park.
   阿蘇くじゅう国立公園でハイキングに行った。
 e) Tagged the ears of cows for monitoring.
   モニタリングのため牛に耳標を取り付けた。

❽のLast spring, I tagged along with her to one of those volunteer eventsからcが正解だと判断する。tag along with ...は「…について行く」という意味である。このthose volunteer eventsとは，その直前の文から分かるように，若者たちが毎年行われる野焼きを手伝うことを指している。aの「ボランティア活動の主催」やbの「ボランティアの募集」ではないことに注意。

Set 5-B | 放送文

Designing With Nature

❶ Good morning. Today we'll be picking up from last week's lecture about biomimicry. To refresh your memory, biomimicry refers to design inspired by nature. In fact, the meaning of the term is evident in its components. "Bio" is a Greek term that means life, and is used in words like biology, the study of living beings, or biography, the story of a human life. "Mimicry" means imitating someone or something. Put them together and you have a word that means "imitating life." All too often, we human beings treat nature like it's an enormous warehouse full of the stuff we need for daily life, like water, oil, food, and timber. We take these things with little thought for the environmental harm we're causing. By contrast, designers who practice biomimicry see nature as a mentor who can teach us better ways to live in the world. Janine Benyus, one of the world's leading proponents of biomimicry, points out that nature has been evolving for 3.8 billion years. Through that process, everything from the owl to the oak tree has developed the best, most efficient way of existing in its particular environment. "Humans are a very young organism," she has said. "In biomimicry we are learning from our biological elders, from those 3.8 billion years of experience. These organisms are teachers. There is so much they can tell us."

❷ As I mentioned last week, engineers and inventors have been looking to their biological elders for a very long time. We talked about chopsticks, which are said to have been inspired by the way a bird's beak grasps food, and airplanes, which of course were also modeled on birds. So what is new and different about biomimicry as it's practiced today? One important difference is that designers are examining nature at an increasingly microscopic level. They used to gather ideas from big things like birds' wings or

refresh one's memory 句 記憶をよみがえらせる
term 名 用語
component 名 構成要素
□ biomimicryとは：自然に着想を得たデザイン

all too often 句 たいてい，頻繁に
enormous 形 巨大な
warehouse 名 倉庫
timber 名 木材
by contrast 句 それに対し

mentor 名 師，助言者

proponent 名 提案者
evolve 自 進化する
owl 名 フクロウ
oak 名 楢

organism 名 生物

elder 名 年長者
□ biomimicryの理念：人間は，年長者である自然から多くのことを学べる

look to ... 句 …に頼る

beak 名 くちばし
grasp 他 …を摑む

microscopic 形 微細な
□ 今日のbiomimicryの特徴：顕微鏡レベルでの自然の造形から着想を得ている

beaks. Now they look at cellular structure, DNA, and microbes.

❸　I think an example will help clarify what I'm talking about. Let me ask you something. Have you ever seen a dirty snail? I doubt it. That's because snail shells naturally repel dirt. Although they appear smooth to the naked eye, a microscope will reveal thousands of tiny bumps and valleys all over the shell. Tiny pools of water accumulate in these valleys, and oily contaminants like dirt float on the surface of the pools. When it rains, the dirt simply washes away.

❹　Scientists at a Japanese tile company have adapted this idea by creating a coating that can be painted onto the exterior wall tiles of houses or factories in order to protect them from car exhaust fumes and other pollutants. The coating is made from silica, an element naturally found in soil. When it's painted on, the silica forms millions of microscopic bumps similar to those on a snail's shell. Moisture from the air condenses into tiny pools between the bumps, pollutants accumulate in these pools, and everything is washed away when it rains. It's a brilliant concept that keeps buildings looking clean without any work on the owner's part, and therefore extends their useful lifespan significantly. And that's just one example of how nature is inspiring better design. As you'll see in this week's reading assignment, thousands more exist.

cellular 形 細胞の
microbe 名 微生物
clarify 他 …を明らかにする

snail 名 カタツムリ
repel 他 …をはじく，寄せ付けない
the naked eye 句 肉眼
bump 名 隆起，こぶ
accumulate 自 蓄積する
contaminant 名 汚染物質

🔑カタツムリの殻が汚れない理由：表面に微細な凹凸があり，そこにたまった水滴の水面に汚れが浮き，雨で流される
car exhaust fumes 句 車の排気ガス
pollutant 名 汚染物質
silica 名 二酸化珪素
soil 名 土壌
moisture 名 湿気，水分
condense 自 凝縮する

significantly 副 大いに，著しく
🔑カタツムリの殻の応用：建物の外壁のコーティングに使用。含まれるsilica（二酸化珪素）が微細な隆起をなし，カタツムリと同じ原理で外壁をきれいに保つ

Set 5-B | 放送文の日本語訳

自然に倣ってデザインする

❶ 　おはようございます。今日は先週のバイオミミクリーの講義の続きを行います。復習になりますが，バイオミミクリーとは自然から着想を得たデザインを意味します。実のところ，この語の意味はその構成要素から明らかです。「バイオ」はギリシャ語で「生命」という意味です。これはバイオロジーすなわち生物の研究（生物学）や，バイオグラフィーすなわち人の生涯の物語（伝記）等の語に含まれています。「ミミクリー」は誰かや何かを模倣することを意味します。これらを合わせると「生命を模倣する」という意味の語になります。たいてい私たち人類は，自然を，水，石油，食物，木材等，日常生活で必要とする物で満ちた巨大倉庫であるかのように扱っています。私たちはこれらの物を環境に及ぼす害のことをほとんど顧慮せずに利用しています。これに対し，バイオミミクリーを実践するデザイナーは，自然を，世界の中で生きるより良い方法を我々に教えてくれる師と見なしています。世界におけるバイオミミクリーの指導的な提唱者の1人であるジャニン・ベニュスは，38億年間かけて自然が進化してきたことを指摘しています。この過程を通じて，フクロウから楢の木に至るあらゆるものが，それぞれの環境の中で最良かつ最も効果的な生存形態を発達させました。彼女は言っています。「人類は非常に若い生物である。バイオミミクリーにおいて，我々は生物学上の年長者たちから，つまり38億年間の経験から学んでいる。それらの生物は教師である。彼らが我々に教えるものはたいへん多い」。

❷ 　先週お話しした通り，エンジニアや発明家は大昔から生物学上の年長者たちに頼ってきました。私たちは箸の話題を取り上げました。箸は鳥のくちばしが食物をつまむやり方から着想を得たと言われています。また，航空機についても取り上げました。もちろん，これも鳥を手本にしたものでした。では，今日行われているバイオミミクリーの新しく，他と異なる点とはどのようなものでしょうか。重要な差異は，デザイナーたちが自然をますます微視的に観察するようになっていることです。以前は鳥の翼やくちばしといった大きなものからアイデアを借りていました。今日デザイナーは細胞組織，DNA，微生物に目を向けています。

❸ 　例を挙げると分かりやすいでしょう。皆さんに質問です。皆さんは汚れたカタツムリを見たことがありますか？　ないのではないでしょうか。それは，カタツムリの殻が自然に汚れをはじくからです。殻は肉眼には滑らかに見えますが，顕微鏡で見ると，全体に無数の微小な隆起と溝があることが分かります。それらの溝には小さな水溜りができ，泥等の油性の汚れがその水面に浮かびます。雨が降ると，泥は簡単に流れ落ちます。

❹ 　日本のタイル会社の科学者たちはこのアイデアを導入し，家屋や工場の外壁タイルに塗装して，車の排気ガス等の汚染物質から保護することのできるコーティングを開発しました。このコーティングは二酸化珪素から作られます。これは土壌に自然に含まれている成分です。このコーティングを塗装すると，二酸化珪素によってカタツムリの殻に類似した多数の微細な隆起と溝が形成されます。空気中の水分が凝縮して，隆起と隆起の間に微小な水溜りができ，汚染物質が水溜り

に蓄積し，雨が降った時に全てが洗い流されます。それは，所有者の側では何の努力もすることなく建物の外観をきれいに保ち，それゆえ耐用年数を著しく延長するすばらしい発想です。そしてこれは，いかに自然がより良いデザインの着想のきっかけとなっているかを示す，ほんの一例にすぎません。今週の読書課題によって，この他に無数の事例が存在することが分かるでしょう。

《 指針 》

biomimicry についての講義である。まず最初にこの語の意味が説明されるので，しっかりと聞き取ろう。次に，過去の biomimicry と比べて，現代の biomimicry にはどのような特徴があるのかが語られる。さらに，現代の biomimicry の例として，カタツムリの殻が汚れをはじく原理を外壁タイルの塗装に応用した試みが紹介される。この原理の説明はやや難しい。設問は比較的易しめに作られているが，選択肢に長いものが多いので，時間をかけて下読みをしておく必要がある。

難易度

放送文　★★☆
設　問　★★☆
総　合　★★☆

☺☺))) スピーカー情報

professor: 西海岸，カリフォルニア

134

Set 5-B | 設問解説

(1) What does Janine Benyus mean when she talks about learning from "biological elders"?

ジャニン・ベニュスが「生物学上の年長者たち」から学ぶと言う時，それはどのような意味か。

a) That elderly people in the community can teach us important lessons about sustainable living.

共同体の中の年長者たちは，持続可能な生活に関する重要な教訓を私たちに与えることができるということ。

b) That parents, grandparents, and other older relatives have much to teach the younger generation.

両親，祖父母，その他年長の親族には若い世代に教えることがたくさんあるということ。

c) That it is important to respect earlier generations of biologists who also turned to nature for inspiration.

自然に着想の源を求めた，先行する世代の生物学者たちを尊敬することが重要であるということ。

d) That the study of biology has a long history and it gives us a lot of insights into how organisms are structured.

生物学の研究は長い歴史を持っており，生物がどのように構成されているかについて多くの見識を我々に与えてくれるということ。

e) That plants and animals have been evolving optimal forms and processes for millions of years, and therefore contain valuable hints about good design.

植物と動物は何百万年もの間に最適の形態と過程を進化させてきており，それゆえ良いデザインに関する有益なヒントを含んでいるということ。

❶の後半からの出題である。biomimicryの提唱者であるBenyusによれば，「自然界の生物には，人間よりもはるかに長い時間をかけて進化し，環境に適応してきたものが多く，人間がそこから学べることがたくさんある」ということであり，これがbiomimicryの理念となっている。これに合致するeが正解。biological eldersとは，人間ではなく，自然における「年長者」たる生物のことを指している。学ぶ対象は「生物」であり「生物学」ではないので，dは誤り。

(2) Based on the professor's explanation, which of the following is an example of biomimicry?

教授の説明を踏まえた上で，バイオミミクリーの事例は次のうちどれか。

a) A realistic drawing of a sea lion.
アシカの写実的なスケッチ。

b) A type of paint made from all-natural ingredients.
天然成分だけから作られた塗料。

c) A robot that can perform the same functions as a human.
人間と同じ機能を果たすことのできるロボット。

d） A necklace made by combining various shapes of seashells.
様々な形状の貝殻を組み合わせて作られたネックレス。

e） A train whose aerodynamic design is based on the shape of a bird's body.
鳥の体の形に基づいた空気力学的デザインを持つ列車。

biomimicryの概要は❶で説明され，さらに箸や飛行機等の例が❷で紹介されているが，そのポイントは「自然界の生物を模倣したデザイン」ということである。これに該当するeを正解として選ぶ。選択肢のaは「デザイン」に該当しない。bとcは「自然界の生物を模倣した」に該当しない。dは生物そのものを用いたものであり，「模倣」には該当しない。

(3) According to the professor's explanation, why do snails remain clean?
教授の説明によると，なぜカタツムリはいつもきれいなのか。

a） Because the tiny bumps on their shells repel dirt.
殻の表面の小さな隆起が泥をはじくから。

b） Because the cells in their shells break down contaminants.
殻の細胞が汚れを分解するから。

c） Because their shells are so smooth dirt cannot stick to them.
殻が滑らかなので泥がつかないから。

d） Because they periodically wash themselves in pools of water.
定期的に水溜りで体を洗うから。

e） Because the texture of their shells allows dirt to wash off easily.
殻の表面の構造によって泥が容易に洗い落とされるから。

カタツムリの殻が汚れない理由については，❸で説明されている。「殻の表面に目に見えないような凹凸があり，凹部に水溜りができ，その水面に汚れが浮き，雨が降るとその汚れが流される」という仕組みである。選択肢eのtextureは「表面の肌合い，きめ」を表す語であり，ここでは微細な凹凸のことを指していると考えられる。eが正解。放送文でのTiny pools of waterとは，微細な凹部に溜まる水のことを指しており，いわゆる「水溜り」ではないのでdは誤り。また隆起そのものが泥をはじくわけではないので，aも誤り。

(4) How is the coating developed by the Japanese company similar to a snail's shell?
日本の企業によって開発されたコーティングはカタツムリの殻にどのように類似しているか。

a） It contains silica, an element found in soil.
土壌に含まれる成分である二酸化珪素を含んでいる。

b） When applied to a surface, it creates many tiny valleys that collect water and contaminants.
表面に塗るとたくさんの微小な溝を形成し，そこに水と汚れが集まる。

c) It creates millions of tiny bumps, which collect water and help to keep moisture on the surface.
無数の微少な隆起を形成し，それが水分を集め，表面の湿度を保つのに役立つ。

d) It appears rough to the naked eye, but when viewed under a microscope it is actually very smooth.
肉眼では粗く見えるが，顕微鏡で見ると実際にはたいへん滑らかである。

e) When applied to a surface, it creates many tiny bumps that reflect light and therefore give the appearance of cleanliness.
表面に塗るとたくさんの微小な隆起を形成し，それが光を反射するため，きれいである
という印象を与える。

❹では，日本のある企業がカタツムリの表面の構造を外壁のコーティングに応用した例が紹介されている。両者に共通するのは，「表面の微細な凹凸によって，水が溜まり，汚れを浮かして洗い流す」という仕組みである。これを表したｂが正解。ａはコーティングには当てはまるが，カタツムリには当てはまらない。ｃは「表面の湿度を保つ」が誤り。ｄはroughとsmoothが逆である。

(5) How is biomimicry different today from that in the past, according to the professor?
教授によれば，今日のバイオミミクリーは過去のものとどのように違っているか。

a) It is being applied for more practical purposes.
より実用的な目的で応用されている。

b) Products are modeled on a wider range of species.
製品が手本とする生物種の範囲がますます広くなっている。

c) It is being used to enhance the sustainability of products.
製品の持続可能性を高めるために利用されるようになっている。

d) Scientists are collaborating with designers to create new products.
新製品を開発するために科学者がデザイナーと協働するようになっている。

e) Designers are drawing inspiration from smaller and smaller forms.
デザイナーが着想の源とする形態がますます小さくなっている。

今日と過去のbiomimicryの違いについては❷で説明されている。designers are examining nature at an increasingly microscopic levelとあるように，細胞やDNA等，微細な自然の形態を模倣してデザインをするようになってきているのである。正解はｅ。

Set 5-C | 放送文

Jealousy

❶ Marissa: Hi Nadine, thanks for coming over. I am so mad at Mark right now.

❷ Nadine: Why Marissa, what happened this time?

❸ Marissa: We were at a party on Saturday, and Sarah's cousin from Chicago was there. I swear Mark spent at least half an hour talking to her. It was like they were instant best friends! He even invited her over to our house for dinner next week. I haven't been able to stop thinking about it all week. I just keep imagining him calling her or meeting her without telling me.

❹ Nadine: I'm sorry sweetie. I know how you feel. I used to get really jealous of other women who talked to my husband, too. I would secretly look at his phone and email account all the time. It got to be such a problem that I eventually went to see a counselor about it.

❺ Marissa: Really? Was that helpful?

❻ Nadine: Actually it was. She told me that there are two types of jealousy, simple and complex. Simple jealousy is that really common feeling of insecurity and fear that you might lose your partner to someone else. You usually react by being more loving in order to get your partner to pay attention to you again. Complex jealousy causes more negative feelings, like resentment or anger or a sense of betrayal. You react by attacking your partner or trying to control them. So simple jealousy actually strengthens your relationship, but complex jealousy can destroy it.

❼ Marissa: It's hard to imagine any kind of jealousy making a relationship better!

❽ Nadine: Well think about it for a minute. If jealousy motivates you to do nice things for your partner in order to bring them closer to you, that's good, right? It's similar to how a child feels when a little brother or sister is born. They're sad to lose their mother's attention, so they act extra cute to try to get her back again. Not a bad thing, right?

📌 Marissaの発言の主旨：夫のMarkが他の女性と親しく話していたのが許せない。私に内緒で電話をしたり、会ったりしているのを想像してしまう

jealous of ... 句 …に嫉妬している

eventually 副 最終的には、結局は

jealousy 名 嫉妬
complex 形 複雑な
insecurity 名 不安感

resentment 名 怒り
betrayal 名 裏切り

📌 単純な嫉妬と複雑な嫉妬の違い：
単純な嫉妬：不安感／相手の注意を引こうとする／関係を強化する
複雑な嫉妬：ネガティブな感情／相手を攻撃・支配しようとする／関係を壊す

motivate 他 …を動機付ける

📌 Nadineの発言の主旨：単純な嫉妬は相手との関係を親密にしようとするものなので、良いものだ

❾ Marissa: I guess that makes sense. But which type did you have?

❿ Nadine: I was definitely suffering from complex jealousy. I was obsessive and angry, and it was driving my husband away.

obsessive 形 取り付かれている

⓫ Marissa: That sounds like me! Did your counselor have any tips for how to stop acting that way?

tips 名 役に立つヒント，助言

⓬ Nadine: Yeah, she had a couple of really good suggestions. The first one was to tune out obsessive thoughts. They are just not going to help.

tune out 句 …に耳を貸さない，無視する

⓭ Marissa: Easier said than done!

Easier said than done. 句 言うは易く行うは難し。

⓮ Nadine: I know, but it really does help. Another thing was to build up my own self-esteem so I wasn't constantly worried that I wasn't good enough for my husband. But the most important piece of advice she gave me was to try to be more compassionate.

self-esteem 名 自尊心

compassionate 形 思いやりのある

⓯ Marissa: That's hard when I'm suspicious my husband is cheating on me!

suspicious 形 疑っている
cheat on … 句 …を裏切る

⓰ Nadine: Yeah, but you've gotta do it. The trick is to see the world from his perspective. Try to understand what is motivating him and what might be going through his head.

have gotta *do* = have got to *do*
trick 名 コツ，秘訣
perspective 名 視点，ものの見方

⓱ Marissa: Okay, let me try that. Well, my husband is a much more extroverted person than me, so it's possible that he was just being friendly and trying to make Sarah's cousin feel welcome here.

extroverted 形 外向的な

⓲ Nadine: There you go! That's a much better way to think about it.

There you go. 句 その通り。

Set 5-C | 放送文の日本語訳

嫉妬

❶ マリッサ：こんにちは，ナディーヌ，来てくれてありがとう。今ね，マークにすごく頭にきているの。

❷ ナディーヌ：どうしてなの，マリッサ，今度は何があったの？

❸ マリッサ：土曜日にパーティーに行ったのだけど，シカゴから来たサラのいとこがそこにいたのね。絶対に，マークは彼女と少なくとも30分は話し込んでいたわ。2人は，すぐに一番の親友になったような感じだった！　しかも，彼ったら，来週，彼女を我が家の夕食に招待したのよ。1週間ずっとそのことが気になってしかたがなかった。彼が私に内緒で彼女に電話したり会ったりしているのを想像してばかりいて。

❹ナディーヌ：まあ，かわいそうに。気持ちは分かるわ。私もかつて，他の女性が夫に話しかけると，ひどく嫉妬していたものよ。しょっちゅう，黙って彼の電話やeメールアカウントを盗み見ていた。困り果てて，最終的にカウンセリングを受けたほど。

❺マリッサ：そうなの？　それで，効果があったの？

❻ナディーヌ：実際，効果があったわよ。カウンセラーによれば，嫉妬には，単純なものと複雑なものの2種類があるそうよ。単純な嫉妬とは，パートナーを別の誰かに取られるのではないかという，よくある不安感や恐怖感。もう一度パートナーを自分の方に振り向かせるため，通常は一段と愛情深くなる反応を示すそうよ。複雑な嫉妬は，憤り，怒り，裏切られた気持ち等の，もっとネガティブな感情を呼び起こすらしいわ。パートナーを攻撃したり，支配しようとしたりする反応を示すみたいよ。だから，単純な嫉妬は，実際に関係を強化するけれど，複雑な嫉妬は，関係を壊してしまうことがあるそうなの。

❼マリッサ：関係を良くする嫉妬があるなんて想像できない！

❽ナディーヌ：だって，ちょっと考えてみて。嫉妬が動機となり，パートナーとの距離を縮めるためにパートナーに優しくするならば，それは良いことでしょう？弟や妹が生まれた時の子どもの心情に似ているわね。子どもは，母親に振り向いてもらえないと悲しいので，母親を取り戻そうと，いつも以上に可愛い態度を取るわよね。それは，悪いことじゃないでしょう？

❾マリッサ：確かにそうね。ところで，あなたの嫉妬は，どちらのタイプだったの？

❿ナディーヌ：間違いなく，複雑な嫉妬に陥っていた。強迫観念に取り付かれ，逆上して，そのせいで夫を遠ざけていたわ。

⓫マリッサ：私のことを言われているみたい！　カウンセラーは，そんな態度を取らないようにする方法について，何か助言をしてくれたの？

⓬ナディーヌ：ええ，とても良い助言をいくつかもらったわ。1つ目は，強迫観念を消し去ること。強迫観念は，何の助けにもならないから。

⓭マリッサ：でも，言うは易く行うは難し，よね！

⓮ナディーヌ：そうね。でも，それができれば，本当に役に立つわ。もう1つの助言は，自分が夫にふさわしくないと常に心配しないでいいように自尊心を高めること。でも，彼女がくれた最も重要な助言は，もっと思いやりの心を持つように努めなさいということだった。

⓯マリッサ：夫が自分を裏切っているのではないかと疑っている時に，それを実践するのは難しいわよね。

⓰ナディーヌ：ええ。でも，やるしかないのよ。コツは，夫の視点で世界を見ること。彼に動機を与えているのは何か，彼の頭をよぎっているのは何かを理解しようと努めることね。

⓱マリッサ：分かった，やってみるわ。そうね，夫は，私よりもはるかに外向的な人だから，親切にしていただけで，サラのいとこに歓迎されていると感じてもらおうとしていただけかもしれない。

⓲ナディーヌ：その調子！　そんな風に考えた方がはるかにましよ。

《 指針 》

jealousy（嫉妬）についての会話である。トピックが「夫の行動に腹を立てている理由」「単純な嫉妬と複雑な嫉妬」「嫉妬を軽減する方法」と移行していくが，その流れを見失わないようにすること。また，Nadineの助言に対してMarissaがどのように反応し，どのように悩みを解決したかに注目しよう。

難易度

放送文　★☆☆

設　問　★★☆

総　合　★☆☆

😊😐))) **スピーカー情報**

Marissa: 西海岸，カリフォルニア
Nadine: イングランド

Set 5-C ｜設問解説

（1）Why is Marissa upset with her husband Mark?
マリッサは，なぜ夫のマークに腹を立てているのか。

a) Because he had dinner with another woman.
彼が別の女性と夕食を食べたから。

b) Because he wouldn't talk to her cousin at a party.
彼がパーティーで彼女のいとこと話そうとしなかったから。

c) Because he met with another woman without telling her.
彼が彼女に内緒で別の女性に会ったから。

d) Because he invited another woman to their house for dinner.
彼が自宅での夕食に別の女性を招待したから。

e) Because he looked at her personal emails and text messages.
彼が彼女の個人的なeメールや携帯電話のメールを盗み見たから。

❸ではMarissaが夫のMarkに対して腹を立てていることが語られているが，その理由は「パーティーで夫が他の女性と仲良くし，夕食にまで招待したから」である。dが正解。cについては，そういう状況をMarissaが想像しているだけであって，実際にあったことではない。

⑵ How are simple jealousy and complex jealousy different?
　単純な嫉妬と複雑な嫉妬は，どう違うか。

　a）Complex jealousy is caused by multiple events.
　　　複雑な嫉妬の原因は，複数の事象にある。
　b）Complex jealousy is caused by insecurity and fear.
　　　複雑な嫉妬の原因は，不安感や恐怖感にある。
　c）Simple jealousy is caused by anger and resentment.
　　　単純な嫉妬の原因は，怒りや憤りにある。
　d）Simple jealousy can positively impact a relationship.
　　　単純な嫉妬は，関係に良い影響を及ぼし得る。
　e）Simple jealousy leads to resentment, anger, and controlling behavior.
　　　単純な嫉妬は，憤り，怒り，支配的な態度に繋がる。

「単純な嫉妬」と「複雑な嫉妬」の違いは❻で述べられている。前者は「相手を失うのではないかという不安が原因となり，相手の注意を引こうとする行動に出るため，関係を強化することになる」というもの。一方の「複雑な嫉妬」は「ネガティブな感情を呼び起こし，相手を攻撃・支配しようとするため，関係を壊すことになる」というものである。「単純な嫉妬」は2人の関係をより強める可能性があるので，dが正解。bの「不安感や恐怖感によって引き起こされる」のは「単純な嫉妬」の方である。

⑶ Why does Nadine mention the relationship between mother and child?
　ナディーヌが母親と子どもの関係に言及するのは，なぜか。

　a）To point out the root of jealous feelings.
　　　嫉妬心の根源を指し示すため。
　b）To prove that no one can be free from jealousy.
　　　嫉妬と無縁でいられる人はいないことを証明するため。
　c）To illustrate how simple jealousy can benefit people.
　　　単純な嫉妬がどのように人に良い効果をもたらし得るか例証するため。
　d）To explain how complex jealousy affects a relationship.
　　　複雑な嫉妬が関係にどのような影響を及ぼすかを説明するため。
　e）To clarify the difference between the two types of jealousy.
　　　2種類の嫉妬の違いを明確にするため。

❽ではNadineが「母と子の関係」に触れているが，これが「単純な嫉妬」の例として用いられていることを読み取ろう。「弟や妹が生まれた時に，母親の注意を引こうとして可愛く振る舞う」という傾向は，❻での「単純な嫉妬」の説明に合致する。cが正解。また❽の発言は，❼でMarissaが「嫉妬が関係を良くすることはありえない」と言ったことへの反論であり，eの「2種類の嫉妬の違いを明確にする」ことが目的なのではない。

(4) Which of the following is NOT a strategy for reducing complex jealousy, according to Nadine?
ナディーヌによれば，複雑な嫉妬を緩和するための戦略に該当しないのは，次のうちどれか。

a) Trying to be more compassionate.
もっと思いやりの心を持つようにする。

b) Improve your own self-confidence.
自信を高める。

c) Confront your partner about your concerns.
自分の心配事をめぐってパートナーとぶつかる。

d) Stop imagining certain scenes over and over again.
特定の場面を何度も繰り返し想像するのをやめる。

e) Think about situations from your partner's perspective.
パートナーの視点で状況を考える。

「複雑な嫉妬」を撃退する方法としてNadineが紹介しているものは3つある。まず⓬の「強迫観念を消し去ること」。これがdに該当する。obsessive thoughtsとは，ある1つのことについて考え続けることである。⓮の「自尊心を高める」がbに該当する。同じく⓮の「もっと思いやりの心を持つ」がaに該当し，そして⓰の「相手の視点から考える」がeに該当する。cについての言及はない。

(5) How does Nadine's counselor's advice help Marissa?
ナディーヌのカウンセラーの助言は，マリッサにとってどのように役立つか。

a) It helps her to understand her husband's motivation.
彼女が夫の動機を理解するのに役立つ。

b) It helps her stop thinking obsessively about the situation.
彼女が状況について，くよくよ考えるのをやめるのに役立つ。

c) It helps her build up her self-esteem so she is less worried.
彼女が不安の軽減に繋がるよう自尊心を高めるのに役立つ。

d) It reminds her of some important facts about her husband.
彼女に，夫についてのいくつかの重要な事実を思い出させてくれる。

e) It makes her appreciate her husband's extroverted character.
彼女が夫の外向的な性格を高く評価するように仕向ける。

⓱でMarissaは，Nadineの「相手の視点から考える」という助言に従って夫の心理を分析する。そして「夫は外向的な人間だから，その女性が気詰まりな思いをしないように親切にしていただけだ」という結論に至り，安心する。つまり，夫が相手の女性と親しくした「動機」が決してやましいものではないということを理解し，嫉妬心をやわらげることができたのである。これに該当するaが正解。

Set 6 | 解答

6A	(1) e	(2) b	(3) c	(4) e	(5) b
6B	(1) d	(2) b	(3) b	(4) c	(5) b
6C	(1) e	(2) a	(3) c	(4) e	(5) d

Set 6-A | 放送文

Poetry 1

❶　What is poetry? The question is a deceptively difficult one. Everyone thinks they know the answer, but ask for a clear definition of poetry and most people find themselves at a loss. We're going to start out today's lecture by seeing if the dictionary provides any useful guidance. According to Dictionary.com, poetry is "the art of rhythmical composition, written or spoken, for exciting pleasure by beautiful, imaginative, or elevated thoughts."

❷　Taking the second half of that definition first, we have the claim that the purpose of poetry is to create a pleasant experience for the reader. That may be true enough for traditional poets like Shakespeare or Wordsworth, but I doubt that many modern poets would agree that their purpose is to provide pleasure. Philip Larkin, one of the greatest English poets of the twentieth century, once said, "Deprivation is for me what daffodils were for Wordsworth." He meant that while poets like Wordsworth who lived in an earlier era found meaning in describing beauty, he on the other hand found meaning in writing about poverty and suffering and torment. I think, then, that our dictionary needs correcting. Poetry doesn't necessarily evoke pleasure, but it always has emotional content. It might make us smile, but it might just as well make us shudder, cry, or simply pause for a moment of peaceful contemplation. As Wordsworth himself said, poetry is "the spontaneous overflow of powerful feelings." It is born from the emotion of the poet and in turn inspires emotion of some sort in the reader. In

deceptively 副 見かけによらず

definition 名 定義

composition 名 構成物, 作文
imaginative 形 想像力に富んだ
elevated 形 崇高な, 高められた

doubt that … 句 …ではないと思う

deprivation 名 窮乏
daffodil 名 ラッパズイセン
A is for B what C is for D 句 BにとってのAは, DにとってのCと同じだ
torment 名 苦痛
need *do*ing 句 …する必要がある
evoke 他 …をかき立てる
shudder 自 身震いする
contemplation 名 瞑想, 黙想
spontaneous 形 自発的な
in turn 句 そして今度は
inspire 他 … (感情) を呼び起こす

144

contrast to a textbook or an advertisement, a poem is at its core an emotional text.

❸ But what about the first part of that dictionary definition, which tells us that poetry is "the art of rhythmical composition"? Note that it says rhythmical, not rhyming. As children you probably learned that the last word of each line in a poem must rhyme. "The cat / sat on a mat / teasing a rat." Cat, mat, rat – that's a poem, right? Wrong. Quite a lot of contemporary poetry does not rhyme at all. But it does usually have a rhythm to it, a sort of beat or tempo that moves through the sentence and makes you pause at certain places rather than others.

❹ Let's take a look at a very famous poem from the mid-twentieth century by William Carlos Williams and see if it gives us any other hints about what a poem is. Close your eyes and listen while I read it. "So much depends / upon / a red wheel / barrow / glazed with rain / water / beside the white / chickens." That's it. That's the entire poem. It sounds almost like a sentence that you would find in a novel, doesn't it? Yet so much meaning and depth is contained in that single sentence. Although there are no obvious rhymes, there is a bit of rhythm. I'd argue that there are two other things that make this a poem as opposed to an ordinary sentence. One is the care with which Williams chose each word. There are 16 words in that poem and each one is clearly essential. The second point is the way in which he arranged the words on the page. If you open up your textbooks and look at the poem, you'll see that it is broken into 8 separate lines. The line breaks tell us where to pause, and help us guess which words are important.

❺ So there you have it: my definition of poetry. One, it has emotional content. Two, it has rhythm. Three, each word is carefully chosen. And four, lines are arranged on the page in a way that adds to the meaning of the poem.

---

in contrast to … 句 …とは対照的に
advertisement 名 広告
at one's core 句 根本的には
rhyme 自 韻を踏む
contemporary 形 現代の

📓 辞書による詩の定義その1：読者に喜びを与えるもの

📓 定義その1に対する答え：過去の詩には当てはまるが，現代の詩には当てはまらない

📓 詩の新たな定義：詩とは感情のこもった文章である

📓 辞書による詩の定義その2：詩はリズムを持つ

📓 定義その2に対する答え：正しい（詩はリズムを持つ）

barrow 名 手押し車
glazed 形 つやつやと光っている

as opposed to … 句 …とは対照的に

📓 通常の文と比較した詩の特徴：1. 1語1語が注意深く選ばれている，2. 行の分け方によってどの語が重要かが分かる

📓 詩の新たな定義（まとめ）：1. 感情にうったえる内容，2. リズムを持つ，3. 1語1語が注意深く選ばれている，4. 行の配置によって意味が加わる

Set 6-A | 放送文の日本語訳

詩 1

❶ 詩とは何でしょうか？ 見た目以上に難しい問題です。誰もが答えを知っていると思っていても，詩の明確な定義を尋ねるとほとんどの人は途方に暮れてしまいます。辞書が何らかの有効な指標を与えてくれるか確かめることから，今日の講義を始めることにしましょう。ディクショナリー・ドットコムによれば，詩とは，「書かれるか話されるかした，リズムの整った構成物による芸術。美しく，想像力に富んだ，あるいは高められた思考によって，喜びをかきたてるために作られたもの」ということです。

❷ まずその定義の後半をとってみれば，詩の目的とは読者に対して喜ばしい経験を創造することだ，と言うことができます。シェイクスピアやワーズワースといった伝統的な詩人については，それで十分に正しいかもしれませんが，喜びをもたらすことが目的であるということに多くの現代の詩人たちが同意するかどうかは，私は疑わしいと思います。20世紀イギリスの最も偉大な詩人の1人であるフィリップ・ラーキンは，かつてこう言いました。「私にとって窮乏とは，ワーズワースにとってスイセンが意味していたものと同じだ」。彼が言いたかったのは，ワーズワースのようなより古い時代に生きた詩人は美を描き出すことに意味を見出していたが，一方ラーキンは貧しさや苦悩や苦痛について書くことに意味を見出したということです。思うに，そうであるなら，私たちの辞書を訂正する必要があります。詩は必ずしも喜びをかきたてはしませんが，常に感情にかかわる内容を含んでいるのです。私たちを微笑ませるかもしれませんが，それと同様に，私たちを戦慄させたり，泣かせたり，あるいはしばし平穏な黙想をすべくただ立ち止まらせるかもしれません。ワーズワース自身が言ったように，詩とは「力強い感情の自発的な氾濫」なのです。詩は詩人の感情から生まれ，そして今度は読者になんらかの感情を呼び起こします。教科書や広告文とは対照的に，詩は根本的に情緒的な文章なのです。

❸ しかし，詩とは「リズムの整った構成物による芸術」であるという，辞書の定義の前半はどうでしょうか？ 韻を踏んだ，ではなく，リズムの整った，と言っている点に注意してください。子どもの頃，おそらく詩の各行の末尾の語は韻を踏んでいなければならないと習ったのではないでしょうか。「猫は／敷物に座り／鼠をからかう」。キャット，マット，ラット——これが詩というものだ，と。そうではないのです。現代の詩の実に多くが韻を全く踏んでいません。しかしたいていの場合，リズムは持っています。文の中で進行し，ある特定の箇所でひと息つかせる，ある種のビートやテンポです。

❹ ウィリアム・カーロス・ウィリアムズによる，20世紀中葉の非常に有名な詩を取り上げて，詩とは何かについて他になんらかのヒントを与えてくれるかどうか見てみましょう。私が読む間，目を閉じて聞いてください。「たくさんのものがゆだねられた赤い手押し車。つやつやと雨水で光る，そばには白いにわとりたち（So much depends／upon／a red wheel／barrow／glazed with rain／water／beside the white／chickens.)」。以上。これが詩の全部です。ほとんど小説の中で

出会う一文のように聞こえるのではないでしょうか。しかしながら，この1つの文の中に実にたくさんの意味と深みが含まれています。明白な韻はなくても，かすかなリズムがあります。この文を普通の文章ではなく詩にしているものが他にも2つあると言わせてください。1つ目は，ウィリアムズが1語1語を選んだその配慮。詩の中には16の単語がありますが，その1つひとつが明らかに必要不可欠なものです。2点目は，彼がページに単語を配置したやり方です。教科書を開いてこの詩を目にすれば，詩が8つのばらばらの行に分かれていることが分かるでしょう。改行箇所がどこで言葉を区切れば良いかを教えてくれ，どの語が重要かを推測するのを助けてくれます。

❺　　さあそこで，これが私の詩の定義です。1つ，詩は感情にうったえる内容を持っている。2つ，詩にはリズムがある。3つ，1語1語が注意深く選びとられている。そして4つ，各行がその詩に意味を与えるようなやり方でページ上に配置されている。

《 指針 》

「詩の定義」をテーマとした講義である。「辞書による詩の定義」からスタートし，それを実際の詩を例に引きながら検証し，最終的には4つの要素に集約される詩の新たな定義を示している。放送文の難易度は高いが，設問は易しめに作られている。分からない箇所があったとしても，全体の大枠を摑めば正解を選ぶことができるはず。

難易度

放送文	★★★
設　問	★★☆
総　合	★★☆

☺☹))) **スピーカー情報**

Professor：中西部，イリノイ

Set 6-A | 設問解説

(1) How is poetry by Wordsworth different from poetry by modern writers like Larkin?
ワーズワースの詩は，ラーキンのような現代の書き手の詩とどのように異なっているか。

a) It doesn't rhyme.
韻を踏んでいない。

b) It is not as emotional.
それほど感情にかかわるものではない。

c) It is less enjoyable to read.
読んだ時の喜びが少ない。

d) It is about emotion, rather than thought.
思考よりもむしろ感情を題材としている。

e) It focuses on beauty rather than deprivation.
窮乏よりも美に焦点を当てている。

❷では，Wordsworthは昔の詩人の代表として，Larkinは現代の詩人の例として引き合いに出されている。そして「詩は読者に喜びを与えるか否か」という問いに対して，Wordsworthの詩は美しいものを描いて読者に喜びを与えるものであるのに対し，Larkinは貧困や苦痛等について書いている，という違いが指摘されている。これに合致するeが正解である。韻については❸で説明されるが，「韻を踏まない」のはむしろ現代の詩であるから，aは誤り。

(2) Which two words describe both traditional poetry and modern poetry, according to the professor?
教授によれば，どの2語が伝統的な詩と現代的な詩の両方を説明しているか。

a) emotional / rhyming
感情にかかわる／韻を踏んでいる

b) emotional / rhythmical
感情にかかわる／リズムが整っている

c) rhyming / pleasurable
韻を踏んでいる／喜びをもたらす

d) rhythmical / rhyming
リズムが整っている／韻を踏んでいる

e) pleasurable / rhythmical
喜びをもたらす／リズムが整っている

❷❸での説明から，「伝統的な詩は韻を踏むのに対して，現代的な詩は韻を踏まない。伝統的な詩は喜びをもたらすのに対し，現代的な詩は喜びをもたらさない」ということが読み取れれば，a，c，d，eの選択肢は全て除外できる。両方の詩に共通する特徴として「感情にかかわる」ということは❷で，「リズムが整っている」ということは❸で説明されている。bが正解である。

(3) How does the professor feel about the poem by William Carlos Williams?
ウィリアム・カーロス・ウィリアムズの詩について，教授はどう感じているか。

a） It would be more effective if it rhymed.
韻を踏んでいればもっと効果的だろう。

b） There are several possible interpretations of the poem.
その詩にはいくつかの解釈があり得る。

c） It conveys a lot of meaning in a small number of words.
少ない数の単語でたくさんの意味を伝えている。

d） It is more moving than poetry by Larkin or Wordsworth.
ラーキンやワーズワースの詩よりももっと感動的だ。

e） It is difficult to understand because it is broken into eight lines.
8行に分かれているので理解するのが難しい。

❹ではWilliamsの詩が朗読され，それについての考察が語られるが，so much meaning and depth is contained in that single sentenceとあるように，わずか1文の中に多くの深い意味が込められていることが指摘されている。これに合致するcが正解。「韻は踏んでいない」という指摘はあるが，それが感動を損ねているというようなことを含意する発言はないので，aは誤り。

(4) Which of the following is true about the poem by William Carlos Williams, according to the professor?
教授によれば，ウィリアム・カーロス・ウィリアムズの詩について正しいのは次のうちどれか。

a） It consists of eight words.
8語からなる。

b） It was included in a novel.
小説の中に含まれていたものだ。

c） Each line contains two words.
各行に2単語が含まれている。

d） It was written in the current century.
今世紀に書かれた詩である。

e） It is arranged differently than an ordinary sentence.
普通の文とは違うやり方で配置されている。

Williamsの詩について❹で新たに述べられている特徴は2つ。「1語1語が注意深く選ばれている」という点と，「特殊な改行のしかたによって，詩に意味を加えている」という点である。このうちの後者が選択肢のeに該当する。「まるで小説の中で出会うような文だ」ということは言われているが，実際の小説の中の一節ではないので，bは誤り。また「20世紀中葉の詩」として紹介されているので，dも誤り。

(5) According to the professor, which of the following is NOT a key definition of poetry?
教授によれば，詩の重要な定義でないものは次のどれか。

a) It is moving.
感情を揺さぶる。

b) It is exciting.
刺激的だ。

c) It has a beat or tempo.
ビートあるいはテンポがある。

d) Its arrangement gives meaning.
その配置には意味がある。

e) Its words are carefully selected.
語が注意深く選ばれている。

教授による詩の新たな定義は❺にまとめられている。1. 感情にうったえる内容，2. リズムを持つ，3. 1語1語が注意深く選ばれている，4. 行の配置によって意味が加わる，の4つに集約される。1.はa，2.はc，3. はe，4. はdに該当する。bのexcitingという語は，喜びや興奮等のポジティブな感情を引き起こすことを意味するが，❷では詩には悲しみ等のネガティブな感情を引き起こす力もあることが指摘されている。一方でaのmovingは涙を誘うような感動をも表すので， aではなくbを正解とする。

Set 6-B | 放送文

Poetry 2

❶Professor: But now I'd like us to direct our attention to another question. Should poetry be quote-unquote "difficult"? Do obscure references and veiled meanings make a poem better than if it uses simple, straightforward language that even a child can grasp? Some of the 20th century's most respected poets created incredibly dense, difficult-to-understand work. Take the great American-born writer T. S. Eliot. His famous poem *The Waste Land* includes references to over a dozen different writers, not to mention cultural topics ranging from eastern religion to children's songs. Reading the poem is like trying to solve a very complex puzzle. On the other hand, look at William Blake, who lived about a century before Eliot. His poem *The Tyger* begins like this: Tyger tyger burning bright / In the forests of the night. Simple words, strong rhythms, and powerful images have made *The Tyger* one of the most famous poems in the English language. Yet many scholars today look down on this sort of poetry as being unrefined or unintellectual. So what do you think? Do you prefer, the complex texture of Eliot's *Waste Land*, or the straightforward power of Blake's *Tyger*? Yes, Martin?

❷Martin: I definitely prefer Blake. I think poetry is meant to be read out loud and enjoyed by the people who are listening to it. It's about hearing the beauty of the spoken words and seeing the images they create in your mind. If you can't understand the meaning of the poem when you hear it, how can you enjoy it?

❸Professor: Good point. Long ago, one of the functions of poetry was to communicate information to people who couldn't read. For instance, stories about important battles would be turned into poems and passed from one generation to the next. It was easier to remember something that rhymed, so a poem had a greater chance of being passed along than a story whose sentences had no

---

quote-unquote 形 括弧付きの，いわば
obscure 形 不明瞭な，よく知られていない
reference 名 引用
veiled 形 隠された
straightforward 形 分かりやすい
dense 形 難解な
not to mention 句 …は言うまでもなく
range from A to B 句 AからBに及ぶ
unrefined 形 洗練されていない（↔ refined）
unintellectual 形 知的でない（↔ intellectual）
texture 名 手ざわり

📌問題提起：難解な詩と分かりやすい詩のどちらが優れているのか

📌難解な詩の例：Eliot——様々な知識を背景とし，謎解きが必要

📌分かりやすい詩の例：Blake——平易な言葉と強いリズム

about … 前 …を本質としている

📌Martinの主張：詩は分かりやすいものが良い
　根拠：詩は言葉の音とそれが喚起するイメージを楽しむものだから

📌教授の発言の主旨：（Martinの意見への補足として）元来詩は情報伝達の手段であり，リズムを持つことで記憶を容易にしていた

rhythm or pattern to them. Cynthia, do you have a question?

❹ Cynthia: Yes. I don't see why that matters today. Just about everyone in the developed world can read, so why should poems serve as our newspapers and history books? I think they should be more like sparkling jewels that challenge us to think about the meaning of life.

❺ Professor: But would you agree with Martin that the best poems are those that are easy to understand when read out loud?

❻ Cynthia: Not at all! For me, the more difficult the poem, the better. I like to feel as though the poet has faith in my intelligence as a reader, and that she believes I will be able to decipher the hidden meanings she weaves into her poem. I like to research a poem almost as if I'm trying to solve a mystery.

❼ Professor: Martin, do you have anything to say in response to Cynthia?

❽ Martin: I'd say she's condemning the art of poetry to an untimely death! The vast majority of ordinary people are like me. They prefer to buy books of poems that they can enjoy without getting a PhD in English literature. We need more poets who speak to the common man instead of catering to an intellectual elite!

❾ Professor: Well said. I think you both have valid points that deserve further exploration.

🔀 Cynthiaの主張：難解な詩の方が良い
　根拠：識字率の高い現代では，詩には伝達手段としての役割はない。詩は人生の意味を考えさせるものだ

sparkling 形 輝いている
challenge someone to *do* 句〈人〉に…することに挑ませる

have faith in … 句 …を信頼する
decipher 他 …を解読する
weave A into B 句 AをBに織り込む

🔀 Cynthiaの主張：作者が詩にこめた意味を読者が解き明かすものである

condemn A to B 句 AにB（刑）を宣告する，AをBに追いやる
untimely 形 時機を逸した，時期尚早の
PhD 略 博士号
cater to 句 …の要望に応じる

🔀 Martinの主張：詩は，専門知識を持つ一部の人ではなく，一般の人のためにあるべきだ

valid 形 有効な，もっともな

152

Set 6-B｜放送文の日本語訳

詩2

❶教授：しかし今度は，別の問題に注意を向けてみたいと思います。詩は，いわば「難しく」あるべきでしょうか？　子どもでも分かるような単純で分かりやすい言葉を使うよりも，誰にも分からないような引用や隠された意味が詩をより優れたものにするでしょうか？　20世紀に最も尊敬を集めた詩人たちの幾人かは，信じられないくらい難解で理解するのが難しい作品を書きました。アメリカ生まれの偉大な作家，T・S・エリオットを挙げてみましょう。彼の有名な詩篇『荒地』は，東洋の宗教から童謡にまで及ぶ文化的主題は言うまでもなく，十数人の様々な作家に対する言及を含んでいます。その詩を読むのはとても複雑なパズルを解くのに挑むようなものです。一方で，エリオットの約1世紀前に生きた，ウィリアム・ブレイクを見てみましょう。彼の『虎』という詩は次のように始まります。「明るく燃える虎よ，虎よ(Tyger tyger burning bright)／夜の森の中で(In the forests of the night)」。シンプルな言葉に強いリズム，そして力強いイメージが，『虎』を英語で書かれた詩の中で最も有名な作品の1つにしてきました。しかしながら今日では，洗練されていない，あるいは知的でないとして，多くの学者がこういった詩を低く見ています。さて，君たちはどう思いますか。エリオットの『荒地』の複雑な手ざわりと，ブレイクの『虎』の真っ直ぐな強さと，どちらが好きでしょう。どうぞ，マーティン君。

❷マーティン：僕は確実にブレイクが好きですね。詩は大きな声で朗誦して，聞いている人たちに楽しんでもらうものだと思うのです。詩の本質は，話された言葉の美しさを聞いて，それらの言葉が心の中に作り出すイメージを見るということです。聞いた時に詩の意味が分からなかったら，どうやって楽しんだらいいでしょう。

❸教授：いい指摘ですね。ずっと昔には，文字を読めない人たちに情報を伝えることが詩の役目の1つでした。たとえば，重要な戦いについての物語が詩になって，1つの世代から次の世代へと伝わっていたのです。韻を踏んでいるものを覚える方が簡単だから，リズムやパターンを持たない文章で書かれた物語に比べて，詩は遥かに伝播する可能性が高かったのですね。シンシアさん，質問がありますか。

❹シンシア：はい。今の時代になぜそういうことが重要なのか分かりません。先進地域のほとんど全ての人が文字を読めるのですから，なぜ詩が新聞や歴史書のような役割を負うべきなのでしょうか。詩はむしろ，人生の意味について考えることに挑ませるような，輝く宝石のようなものであるべきだと思います。

❺教授：でもマーティン君の，最良の詩は朗誦した時に理解しやすいものという意見には賛成ですか。

❻シンシア：全く違います！　私にとっては，詩は難しいほどいいのです。読者としての私の知性を詩人が信頼しているかのように感じ，詩の中に織り込んだ隠された意味を，私が読み解くことができると詩人が信じているのだと感じるのが好きなのです。ほとんど謎解きに挑むみたいにして，詩を探究するのが好きです。

❼教授：マーティン君，シンシアさんに対して言いたいことはありますか。

❽マーティン：僕に言わせれば，彼女は詩という芸術を早死にに追い込んでいるので

はないでしょうか！　普通の人たちの大半は僕みたいな人間です。彼らは英文学の博士号をとらなくても楽しめる詩集を買う方が好きですよ。知的なエリートに応えるのではなく，ありきたりの人間の心に訴えかけるような詩人が，僕らにはもっと必要なんです。

❾教授：いいですね。2人とも，さらに探求するに値するもっともな論点を持っていると思います。

《《 指針 》》

Aでは「詩とは何か」がテーマだったが，今度は一歩進んで「難解な詩と分かりやすい詩のどちらが良いか」という論点をめぐって討論がなされている。「分かりやすい詩」を支持する Martin と「難解な詩」を支持する Cynthia の意見の対立に注目し，それぞれがどのような根拠を提示しているかを把握しよう。

難易度

放送文　★★☆

設　問　★★☆

総　合　★★☆

☺☹ 》》 **スピーカー情報**

Professor: 中西部，イリノイ
Martin: 西海岸，カリフォルニア
Cynthia: 西海岸，カリフォルニア

Set 6-B | 設問解説

(1) How is the poetry of T. S. Eliot different from that of William Blake?
　　T・S・エリオットの詩は，ウィリアム・ブレイクの詩と，どのように異なっているか。

 a) Eliot deals with a wide variety of subjects, while Blake focuses on a single issue.
　　エリオットは多様な主題を扱うが，ブレイクはたった1つの問題に焦点を当てる。

 b) Eliot uses strong rhyming words to make his poem appealing, while Blake does not.
　　エリオットは詩を魅力的にするために強く韻を踏む語を使っているが，ブレイクはそうではない。

 c) Blake's poem communicates history, while Eliot's poem serves a less practical purpose.
　　ブレイクの詩は歴史を伝えるが，エリオットの詩の実用性はもっと低い。

 d) Reading Eliot requires extensive cultural and literary knowledge, while Blake's poem is accessible to anyone.
　　エリオットを読むには文化や文学に関する広範な知識が要求されるが，一方ブレイクの詩は誰にとっても分かりやすい。

154

e) Blake writes about animals, a universally beloved subject, while Eliot writes only about factories and other dreary topics.
ブレイクは動物という普遍的に愛される主題について書いているが，一方でエリオットは工場やその他の憂鬱なテーマについてばかりを書いている。

❶では「難解な詩」の代表としてEliotのThe Waste Landが，「分かりやすい詩」の代表としてBlakeのThe Tygerが紹介されている。前者は意味を読み解くためには様々な知識を必要とするが，一方の後者は平易な言葉と力強いリズムで誰にでも理解できるように書かれている。dが正解。eについては，確かにBlakeは「虎」という動物を扱っているが，ここで問題とされているのはスタイルの違いであり，扱っているテーマの違いではない。

(2) Which of the following does NOT describe Martin's feelings about poetry?
マーティンの詩に対する考えを説明していないのは次のうちどれか。
a) Poetry is meant to be heard, not just read silently.
詩はただ黙って読むのではなく，耳で聞かれるようにできている。
b) Poetry should be appreciated for the beauty of its style.
詩はその形式の美しさが評価されるべきだ。
c) Poetry should be written in a style that ordinary people can understand.
詩は一般の人が理解できる形式で書かれるべきだ。
d) Poetry should be written so that people can enjoy the beauty of the words.
詩は人々が言葉の美しさを楽しめるように書かれるべきだ。
e) Poetry should include images that the listener is able to see in her mind's eye.
詩は聞き手が心の目で見ることのできるイメージを含んでいるべきだ。

❷でMartinは「分かりやすい詩」を支持しているが，その根拠として「詩とは，音読された言葉の美しさと，そこから頭に浮かぶイメージを楽しむものである」という考え方を述べている。これに合致するa，d，eは正しい。また，If you can't understand the meaning of the poem when you hear it, how can you enjoy it?と問いかけていることからcも正しい。bはthe beauty of its styleが誤り。Martinは「声に出して読まれた言葉の美しさを楽しむべきだ」と言っているのであって，「スタイルの美しさ」を問題にしているのではない。

(3) According to the professor, how was poetry originally used?
教授によれば，元来詩はどのように使われていたか。
a) As a medium to spread rumors.
噂を広めるための媒体として。
b) As a way of conveying information.
情報を伝える手段として。
c) As a means to dramatize historical events.
歴史上の出来事を劇的に表現する手段として。

d) As a way of expressing powerful emotions.
強烈な感情を表現する手段として。
e) As a way to encourage communication between different generations.
異なる世代間のコミュニケーションを助ける手段として。

❸で，教授はMartinの意見の補足として，「元来詩の役割は，文字が読めない人に情報を伝達することだった」と述べている。これに合致するｂが正解である。詩のリズムが情報を記憶するのに役立ったとあるが，ｃのように「劇的に表現する」のが目的だったわけではない。また，ｅがやや紛らわしいが，詩の元来の役割は「情報を次の世代に伝えること」であり，「世代間のコミュニケーションの促進」ではないので誤り。

(4) Why does Cynthia prefer difficult poetry?
なぜシンシアは難しい詩を好むのか。
a) Because it allows her own interpretation of the meaning.
彼女独自の意味の解釈を可能にするから。
b) Because it portrays a more accurate image of historical events.
歴史上の出来事のより正確なイメージを描いているから。
c) Because it makes her feel like the poet respects her intelligence.
詩人が彼女の知性に敬意を払っているように感じられるから。
d) Because it gives her the joy of unraveling the mysteries of the world.
世の中の神秘を解き明かす喜びを与えてくれるから。
e) Because it helps her improve her vocabulary and cultural knowledge.
語彙や文化に関する知識を向上させる助けになるから。

「難解な詩」を支持するCynthiaの意見は❹と❻で述べられている。その主旨は「詩には人生の意味が織り込まれており，詩人は知的な読者がそれを解明してくれることを想定している」というもの。I like to feel as though the poet has faith in my intelligence as a readerという発言がｃと合致する。Cynthiaが重視しているのは「作者が詩に込めた意味を読者が解読すること」であり，ａのような「読者自身の解釈」ではないことに注意したい。ｄはやや紛らわしいが，Cynthiaは「詩に込められた意味を読み解くこと」をsolve a mysteryと表現しているのであり，これは「世の中の神秘を解き明かす」のとは異なるので，誤り。

(5) Which of the following best describes Martin's point?
マーティンの論点を最もうまく言い表しているのは次のどれか。
a) Poetry is meaningless if it is not understood.
詩は理解されなくては意味がない。
b) Overly complex poetry alienates most readers.
過度に複雑な詩はほとんどの読者を遠ざける。
c) Poets should talk to readers about the kind of poems they like.
詩人たちは自分の好きな種類の詩について読者に話すべきだ。

156

d) People should receive better education so they can enjoy poetry.
　人々は詩を楽しめるように，より良い教育を受けるべきだ。

e) Poems about death and dying are too dark for the ordinary reader.
　死や死ぬことについての詩は一般の読者には暗すぎる。

❽でMartinが言いたいのは，「詩は専門家ではなく一般の人のためにあるものだ」ということである。she's condemning the art of poetry to an untimely death という表現がやや難しいが，Cynthiaが支持するような難解な詩は一般の読者には理解できないため，詩という芸術が読者を遠ざけて衰退してしまうということであり，それをuntimely death（早死に）という言葉で表現しているのである。これを表したbが正解。alienateは「遠ざける」という意味である。aもMartinの考えに近いが，彼は「より多くの人に理解できる詩が必要だ」とは言っているが，「理解されない詩は無意味だ」とまでは言っていないので，bに劣る。

Set 6-C | 放送文

Towards a New Technological Frontier

❶ Smith: Good morning. It's my pleasure to welcome you here in Palo Alto, California. I'm also pleased to welcome those who are participating remotely from London and Tokyo. My name is John Smith, the senior vice president for Next Gen Technologies. Joining me here today is Sandra Thomas, creative director at Pelham Communications.

❷ As I think all of you are aware, technology is evolving at a breakneck pace. However, most so-called breakthroughs are simply variations on older products. We're here today to announce a genuine exception to that rule. We'll be telling you about a partnership between Next Gen Tech and Pelham Communications, as well as our first product together. Both have been in the works for quite a while now, and we're excited to finally make them public. With that, I'd like to turn the stage over to Ms. Thomas.

[Applause]

❸ Thomas: Thank you for the introduction, John. It's an honor to be here. I'd like to direct your attention to the screen behind me. As you can see, it's an ordinary screen. The image projected onto it shows a smartphone home screen. There are icons for email, phone, Internet access, music, and various other functions. You'll also notice that there's a slight blue haze covering the right side of my face, which signals that our new device is on.

❹ Okay, so what exactly am I doing? To put it simply, I'm demonstrating the world's first internal smartphone. Everything you see on the screen behind me is a projection of what I'm seeing in front of my right eye. I control the device through thoughts or voice commands. Say, for instance, I want to look up my friend Jane's phone number and call her. I can either imagine Jane's face, think of her name, or say "Jane" out loud. A

---

remotely 副 遠く離れて，ネット経由で
senior vice president 句 シニア・バイスプレジデント，上席副社長

evolve 自 進化する
breakneck 形 危険なほど速い
breakthrough 名 飛躍的進歩
genuine 形 真の

in the works 句 とりかかって，進行中で

turn A over to B 句 AをBに引き渡す

📌 Smithの発言の主旨：2社が共同で開発した製品を初めて公開する

haze 名 もや，かすみ

to put it simply 句 簡単に言うと

📌 製品の概要：世界初の体内スマートフォン

screen then appears in front of my eye—or in my mind's eye, you might say—showing her name and phone number. I think or say "call," and we are connected just as if I were holding a cell phone in my hand. If I want to listen to an album by my favorite band, I simply think of the album's name, say "play," and the music begins to stream in my head—again, just as if I were wearing headphones plugged into a smartphone. The difference, of course, is that it's all happening in my mind. No one else can hear my conversation with Jane, and no one knows what album I'm listening to. So the product offers everything you could ever want in a handheld device, except it's projected inside your brain for you, and only you, to see.

❺ But how does it work? Well, users undergo minor, non-invasive surgery to implant the device under their skin, where it links with and is powered by their nervous system. The device uses radio waves to connect their brain to the cloud network through which all our services are run. Additionally, none of our hardware allows for any sort of two-way control—it's all one-way from the user to the device. It goes without saying that we've consulted with top security and medical professionals around the world while developing this product.

📲製品の機能：声や思考による命令で動く。映像や音声は脳内で再生される

undergo 他 …(手術等)を受ける
minor 形 小さい，重要でない
non-invasive 形 非侵襲性の（生体を傷つけないような）
surgery 名 外科手術
implant 他 …を埋め込む
power 他 …に電力を供給する
📲製品の仕組み：手術によって皮下に埋め込む。神経組織から電力を受ける。電波によって脳と外部ネットワークを接続
allow for … 句 …を許す，可能にさせる
consult with … 句 …に相談する
📲製品の安全性：機械が身体をコントロールすることはない

Set 6-C | 放送文の日本語訳

テクノロジーの最前線へ

❶スミス：おはようございます。皆様，カリフォルニア州パロアルトへようこそ。またロンドンと東京からネットでご参加の皆様も，ようこそ。ジョン・スミスと申します。ネクストジェン・テクノロジーズのシニア・バイスプレジデントです。そして本日ご参加くださっているのは，ペルハム・コミュニケーションズのクリエイティブ・ディレクター，サンドラ・トマスさんです。

❷ 皆様ご承知のことと思いますが，テクノロジーは恐るべき速度で進歩しています。しかし，一般に飛躍的進歩と呼ばれるもののほとんどは，従来品のバリエーションにすぎません。さて，本日のこの席は，そうした法則の真の例外を公表するために設けられました。私どもは皆様に，ネクストジェン・テクノロジーズとペルハム・コミュニケーションズの提携ならびに，両社の共同開発になる初の製

品についてお知らせいたします。いずれもかなり長期にわたって準備して参りましたが，ついに公表できますことを，喜ばしく思います。では，この後はトマスさんにお任せしたいと思います。

[一同拍手]

❸ トマス：ジョン，ご紹介ありがとうございます。本日はお招きいただき光栄です。皆様，私の後ろにありますスクリーンにご注目ください。ご覧の通り，ごく普通のスクリーンです。今映っているのは，スマートフォンの待受画面ですね。eメール，電話，インターネット・アクセス，音楽，その他各種機能のアイコンが並んでいます。また，私の顔の右半分がかすかに青味がかっているのがお分かりですか。これは，私どもの新製品が起動している印です。

❹ さて，私は今何をしているのでしょう。簡単に申しますと，私は今，世界初の体内スマートフォンをご紹介しています。私の後ろのスクリーンに映っているのは，全て私の右目の前に見えているものなのです。私はこの機器を思考と音声による命令によってコントロールしています。たとえば，私が友人のジェーンの電話番号を調べて，電話をかけたいと思ったとしますね。そういう時は，彼女の顔を想像するか，彼女の名前を思い浮かべるか，「ジェーン」と口に出して言うかします。すると，私の目の前に，つまり私の頭の中の目にと言いましょうか……スクリーンが現れて，彼女の名前と電話番号が表示されます。私が「通話」と考えるか言うかすると，まるで携帯電話を手に持っているかのように，電話がかかります。大好きなバンドのあるアルバムを聴きたいと思った時は，そのタイトルを思い浮かべ，「演奏」と言うだけで音楽が頭の中に流れ始めます。まるでスマートフォンにつないだヘッドフォンをしているかのようにです。もちろん，違いは，全てが私の頭の中で起こっているという点にあります。ジェーンとの会話は他の誰にも聞こえませんし，私が何というアルバムを聴いているのかも，誰にも分かりません。つまり，この製品は，私たちが携帯用の機器に求める全てのものを提供してくれます。ただしそれは，脳内に投影され，自分に見える，自分だけに見えるものなのです。

❺ では，それはどのように作動するのでしょうか。ユーザーは簡単な，非侵襲的な手術をして，皮下に機器を埋め込む必要があります。皮下においてユーザーの神経組織と連結し，そこから電力を受け取ります。この機器は，電波を使って，ユーザーの脳と私どもがサービスを提供しているクラウド・ネットワークとを接続します。さらに申し上げれば，私どものハードウェアは全て，いかなる種類の双方向的コントロールも行うことがありません。コントロールは，ユーザーから機器へという一方向のみです。またもちろん，この製品の開発にあたっては，世界中の一流のセキュリティー専門家及び医療専門家から意見を求めました。

《 指針 》

「世界初の体内スマートフォン」の製品発表会の模様である。想像の上を
いくような製品であるが，その具体像をどこまで正確に把握できたかが
勝負となる。「機能」「仕組み」「安全性」という順で説明されていくので，
放送文を聞きながらそれぞれのイメージを頭の中で描いていくようにしよ
う。

難易度

放送文　★★☆

設　問　★★★

総　合　★★☆

☺☹))) **スピーカー情報**

Smith: 西海岸，カリフォルニア
Thomas: 西海岸，カリフォルニア

Set 6-C | 設問解説

(1) Which of the following is true?
次のうち正しいものはどれか。

a) Some people in the audience came here from overseas.
聴衆の中には海外からここに来た人もいる。

b) The new product is already being used in the workplace.
その新製品はすでに職場で使用されている。

c) Next Gen Technologies developed the new product alone.
ネクストジェン・テクノロジーズはその新製品を単独で開発した。

d) Sandra Thomas is an employee of Next Gen Technologies.
サンドラ・トマスはネクストジェン・テクノロジーズの社員である。

e) The partnership between the two companies has not previously announced.
2つの企業の提携は事前に公表されていなかった。

❶❷でのSmithによる導入についての問題。❷にBoth have been in the works
for quite a while now, and we're excited to finally make them public.とあ
るが，このBothとは「2社の提携」と「共同開発した製品」を指している。つまり，
2社の提携を発表するのは今回が初めてであり，eが正解となる。in the worksは
「進行中で」という意味であり，bにあるような「職場で使用されている」という意
味ではない。また，ロンドンと東京からの聴衆はネットを通じて参加しているので，
aは誤り。

(2) Smith says the new product is "a genuine exception to that rule." What does the phrase mean in this context?
スミスは，その新製品は「そうした法則の真の例外」であると言っている。上の文脈において，この言葉はどのような意味か。

a) Few new products are truly unique, but this one is.
真にユニークな新製品というものはほとんどないが，これはそれにあたる。

b) The new product does not follow government regulations.
その新製品は政府の規制に従っていない。

c) Many new technologies are revolutionary, including this one.
これも含め，多くの新しいテクノロジーは革命的である。

d) Technology is evolving quickly, but this product was developed slowly.
テクノロジーは急速に進歩しつつあるが，この製品は時間をかけて開発された。

e) It takes time to develop a new product, but this one was made in a short time.
新製品の開発には時間がかかるが，この製品は短時間で作られた。

a genuine exception to that rule（その法則の真の例外）というフレーズは❷でSmithによって用いられる。that ruleとは，その直前のmost so-called breakthroughs are simply variations on older productsを指している。つまり，「世に言う『飛躍的進歩』の大半は，従来の製品を少し変えたものにすぎないが，これから紹介する製品は真の『飛躍的進歩』と言えるものである」という趣旨の発言である。これに合うaが正解。

(3) How are the internal smartphone and the conventional smartphone similar?
体内スマートフォンと従来のスマートフォンはどのように類似しているか。

a) The screen can be viewed by multiple people.
スクリーンを複数の人で見ることができる。

b) Both require headphones for private listening.
どちらも，自分1人で聞くためにはヘッドフォンが必要である。

c) Both provide access to Internet and telephone networks.
どちらも，インターネットと電話のネットワークへのアクセスを提供している。

d) Both can be controlled either by voice commands or touch.
どちらも，音声による命令とタッチの両方によってコントロールされることが可能である。

e) Both can be used simply by purchasing a device and turning it on.
どちらも，単に機器を購入して電源を入れれば使用することができる。

「体内スマートフォン」の主な機能については❸❹❺で説明されている。❸では，待受画面に通常の「電話」や「インターネット・アクセス」のアイコンがあると言っているので，従来のスマートフォンと同様のネットアクセスや電話の機能があることが分かる。また，電話の機能については❹でも説明されている。cが正解。スクリーンは「頭の中に」現れ，本人にしか見えないからaは誤り。❹では「音声は頭の中で流れる」とあるのでbも誤り。「体内スマートフォン」への命令は思考または声によってするものであり，dの「タッチ」は含まれない。また❺で説明されてい

るように「体内スマートフォン」は手術によって皮下に埋め込んで使用するものなので，eの記述も誤り。

(4) What does Thomas mean when she mentions "two-way control"?
トマスの言う「双方向的コントロール」とはどのような意味か。

a） A device that can be operated in two different ways.
2つの異なる方法で操作することが可能な機器。

b） A device that can be controlled by two different people.
2人の異なる人によってコントロールされることが可能な機器。

c） A situation where the user is given a series of yes-no options.
ユーザーが一連のイエス／ノーの選択肢を与えられている状況。

d） A situation where a single user can control two devices at once.
1人のユーザーが2つの機器を同時にコントロールできる状況。

e） A situation where the device controls the user and the user controls the device.
機器がユーザーをコントロールし，ユーザーが機器をコントロールする状況。

❺でのAdditionally, none of our hardware allows for any sort of two-way control—it's all one-way from the user to the device.という発言からeを正解とする。two-way／one-wayの違いは，機器と人間が相互にコントロールし合うか，あるいは人間が機器を一方的にコントロールするかの違いである。機器が人間をコントロールするとなると，安全面での様々な懸念が生じてくるはずであり，Thomasは「体内スマートフォン」の安全性を強調するために，one-way controlであることに言及しているのであろう。

(5) Which of the following is NOT true about the internal smartphone?
体内スマートフォンに関して，次のうち正しくないのはどれか。

a） It can connect to the Internet.
インターネットに接続できる。

b） It is embedded inside the user's body.
ユーザーの身体の内部に埋め込まれている。

c） It draws energy from the user's body.
ユーザーの身体からエネルギーを引き出している。

d） It requires an external screen to work.
作動するためには外部のスクリーンが必要である。

e） It responds to thoughts in the user's brain.
ユーザーの脳内の思考に反応する。

❹では，「体内スマートフォン」の画像は全て頭の中に浮かぶとあるので，dの記述は正しくない。この発表会では，観客に見せるために，頭の中と同じ画像を外部スクリーンに投影しているのである。❺でit links with and is powered by their nervous systemとあり，神経系から電力をもらっていることが分かるので，cは正しい。また，aは❸で，bは❺で，eは❹で説明されている事柄に合致する。

Set 7 | 解答

7A　(1) b　(2) d　(3) e　(4) a　(5) b
7B　(1) e　(2) d　(3) c　(4) e　(5) a
7C　(1) c　(2) c　(3) a　(4) b　(5) e

Set 7-A | 放送文

Creative Thinking 1

❶ Professor: Okay everybody, have a seat and we'll get started. Today I want to continue our discussion about how businesses use creativity to their advantage. As you'll remember from last week's lecture, most successful companies today realize that in order to keep creating innovative products they must foster out-of-the-box thinking among their employees. We looked at a couple of the most famous examples of innovative companies, like Apple, Nike, Toyota, and Amazon, and talked about how all of these companies have policies in place to encourage creativity on an individual level. But one of the trickiest challenges every company struggles with is what to do about rules. Is it better to have more rules or less? Do rules hinder creativity by limiting the freedom of employees? Or do they provide the necessary framework for creativity to flourish? That is the question we will be discussing today. So, can anyone give me a historical example of when a rule actually helped an artist or inventor to come up with new ideas? Yes, Julia.

❷ Julia: Picasso's 11 bulls?

❸ Professor: Picasso's bulls, excellent example. For those of you who aren't as familiar with his work, Picasso made 11 lithographs in 1945, each with a single bull in the center of the paper. The first print is just a sketchy image. The next three or four are more realistic, but after that Picasso starts to break down the bull and create more and more abstract versions of it. By the time he gets to the final image he's left with just a very simple line drawing that manages to capture the animal's

innovative 形 革新的な
foster 他 …を促進する
out-of-the-box 形 形にとらわれない，型破りの

struggle with … 句 …に取り組む
hinder 他 …を妨げる

framework 名 枠組み
flourish 自 開花する，栄える

🔖議論のテーマ：ルールは創造性を妨げるのか，あるいは促進するのか？

lithograph 名 石版画
sketchy 形 大雑把な
abstract 形 抽象的な
capture 他 …をとらえる

🔖ピカソの「11枚の雄牛」の概要：1匹の雄牛を描いた石版画。11の連作で，雄牛は次第に抽象化され，本質をとらえていく

essence perfectly. So Julia, what was the rule in this case?

❹ Julia: Um, each print must show a black-and-white bull, and nothing else.

❺ Professor: And where did creativity come in?

❻ Julia: It almost seems like the rule pushed Picasso to think more and more deeply about what a bull is. It would have been boring to draw the same image over and over again, so he began to experiment with new ways of drawing it.

❼ Professor: Right. In business, too, employees sometimes need rules in order to help them focus and take the next step towards experimentation. It's counterintuitive, isn't it? But now let's look at a contrasting example. Most of you have heard of the popular video streaming company MovieNow, right? That company has essentially done away with the traditional video store industry and created a new model where anybody can rent any movie they want from the comfort of their own home, via the Internet. Very successful company. But does anyone know what the vacation policy at MovieNow is? John?

❽ John: They don't have one. The workers can take as many vacation days as they want, whenever they want, and their salary stays the same. I read about it in the newspaper. It sounds pretty awesome to me.

❾ Professor: Exactly. So in this area of policy, the company has no rules. Yet this clearly has not created chaos, because MovieNow now has 10 million subscribers. How did they manage that? I'd like to suggest that MovieNow actually does have a rule related to vacations, but it's a very simple one. The rule is this. Get your work done. Doesn't matter when or how, just get it done. That one rule maximizes both the freedom and the responsibility of employees. And that is the key: finding rules that set boundaries, but at the same time give people the freedom to find new ways of achieving goals. That is where creativity at the workplace begins.

---

essence 名 本質

☞「11枚の雄牛」の意義：ルールの存在が，実験的な試みを促した

employee 名 従業員

counterintuitive 形 直感に反する，意外な
contrasting 形 対照的な

do away with … 句 …を処分する，捨てる

via 前 …を通して

awesome 形 素晴らしい

chaos 名 混乱
subscriber 名 加入者，予約購読者

maximize 他 …を最大化する
boundary 名 境界線

☞MovieNowの狙い：単純なルールを設けることで，従業員の自由と責任感を最大化する

Set 7-A | 放送文の日本語訳

創造的思考 1

❶教授：はい皆さん，席に着いてください。始めましょう。今日は，いかにしてビジネスが，利益を生むために創造性を利用しているかについての議論を続けたいと思います。先週の講義を覚えていると思いますが，今日成功している企業のほとんどは，革新的な製品を生み出し続けるためには，従業員たちの形にとらわれない思考を促進しなければならないということに気付いています。私たちは，アップルやナイキ，トヨタ，アマゾンといった，もっとも有名な革新的企業の例をいくつか見ましたし，これら全ての企業がどのようにして，個人レベルでの創造性を後押しする方針を採っているのかについて話しました。しかし，あらゆる企業が取り組んでいる一番厄介な課題の1つが，ルールをどうするべきか，ということなのです。より多くのルールがあった方がいいのか，少ない方がいいのか。ルールは，従業員の自由を制限することで創造性を妨げるのか。あるいは，ルールは，創造性を開花させるために必要な枠組みを与えてくれるのか。それが，今日私たちが議論する問いです。それでは，ルールが実際に，芸術家や発明家が新しいアイデアを生み出すのを助けた歴史的事例を挙げられる人は誰かいますか？　はい，ジュリアさん。

❷ジュリア：ピカソの11枚の雄牛はどうですか。

❸教授：ピカソの雄牛，素晴らしい事例ですね。彼の作品にあまり親しんでいない皆さんのために説明すると，ピカソは1945年に11枚の石版画を作成し，それぞれ紙の真ん中に1頭の雄牛を描きました。最初の版は，ただの大雑把な絵です。その次の3枚か4枚は，より写実的なものですが，その後，ピカソはその雄牛を壊し，どんどん抽象的なバージョンの雄牛を創り始めるのです。最後の絵に至る頃に，彼に残されているのは，かろうじてその動物の本質を完璧にとらえている，極めて単純な線のみによる描画です。さて，ジュリアさん，この事例におけるルールとはなんだったのでしょうか。

❹ジュリア：ええと，それぞれの版で，白黒の雄牛を表現しなければならなくて，それ以外には何も描いてはいけないということです。

❺教授：それで，どこに創造性が生じたのでしょう。

❻ジュリア：そのルールが，ピカソに雄牛とはなんであるかをより一層深く考えるように促したように思えます。同じ絵を何度も繰り返し描くのは退屈だったでしょうから，それで彼は絵を描くための新しい方法を実験し始めたんです。

❼教授：その通り。ビジネスにおいても従業員は時として，実験に向けた次のステップを集中して踏み出す手助けとなるようなルールを必要とします。これは直感に反することなのではないでしょうか。しかし，ここで対照的な事例を見てみましょう。皆さんの多くは，ムービーナウという有名なビデオ配信会社について聞いたことがありますよね。この会社は，伝統的なビデオ販売産業を本質的に捨て去り，インターネットを通じて，誰もが，観たいどんな作品でも，自宅にいながらにして借りられるという新しいモデルを作りました。とても成功している企業です。しかし，ムービーナウの休暇の方針がどのようなものか，誰か知っていますか？　ジ

166

ョン君，どうですか。

❽ジョン：彼らは方針を持っていません。社員たちは望むままに好きな日数だけ，いつでも好きな時に休暇を取ることができて，給料が同じなのです。このことは新聞で読みました。すごく素晴らしいように思えます。

❾教授：まさしくその通り。つまり，この領域の方針においては，この企業はルールを持っていません。それでも，そのことが混乱を生み出していないのは明らかです。ムービーナウは，今や1000万人の加入者を抱えているのですからね。彼らはどうやってそんなことをやり遂げたのでしょうか。ムービーナウには，実のところ休暇に関するルールが1つあって，ただしそれはとても単純なルールだ，ということを示してみたいと思います。そのルールとはこういうものです。仕事をやり遂げよ。いつ，どうやって，といったことは問題ではない。とにかく仕事をやり遂げよ。この1つのルールが，従業員の自由と責任の両方を最大化させるのです。そして，それが鍵となります。すなわち，境界線を設定すると同時に，目標を達成する新しい方法を見つけるための自由を人々に与えるようなルールを見つけ出すこと。ここから，職場における創造性が始まるのです。

《 指針 》

「創造的な思考」というテーマのクラス内討論である。最初に「ルールは創造性を妨げるのか，あるいは促進するのか？」という問いが提起される。それに対し，「ピカソの11枚の雄牛」と「MovieNowという会社のルール」という2つの例が提示される。それぞれが，先の問いに対してどのような結論を示唆しているのかに注目しながら聞き取ろう。

難易度

放送文	★★☆
設 問	★★★
総 合	★★☆

☺☹))) スピーカー情報

Professor: 西海岸，オレゴン
Julia: 西海岸，カリフォルニア
John: イングランド

Set 7-A | 設問解説

(1) What was the subject of last week's lecture?
先週の講義のテーマはなんだったか。

a) The relationship between rules and creativity.
ルールと創造性の関係。

b) The importance of individual creativity in business.
ビジネスにおける個人の創造性の重要性。

c) The relationship between creativity and competition.
創造性と競争の関係。

d) The importance of free competition in the marketplace.
市場における自由競争の重要性。

e) Policies at companies like Apple and Nike that limit worker freedom.
社員の自由を制限するアップルやナイキ等の企業の方針。

先週の講義については，❶の As you'll remember from last week's lecture, … で述べられている。most successful companies … to encourage creativity on an individual level. から，「企業にとっては，従業員の創造性をいかに高めるかが死活問題であり，各企業はどのような取り組みをしているか」というような内容であったと想像できる。b が正解。a は先週のテーマではなく，まさにこれから扱おうとしているテーマである。c は正解に近いが，中心テーマは「創造性を高めるための企業の取り組み」であり，「創造性と競争との関係」ではない。

(2) According to the professor, which of the following statements about Picasso's 11 bulls is NOT true?
教授によると，ピカソの11枚の雄牛に関して，以下の説明のうち正しくないものはどれか。

a) Picasso created them in 1945.
ピカソはそれらの絵を1945年に制作した。

b) Each print shows a single bull.
1つの版には雄牛が1匹だけ描かれている。

c) Nothing else is depicted aside from the bull.
雄牛の他には何も描かれていない。

d) With each print, the bull's image became more and more realistic.
版を重ねるごとに，雄牛の絵はどんどん写実的になった。

e) The 11th bull was drawn as a highly abstract image, with simple lines.
11番目の雄牛は極めて抽象的な絵であり，単純な線によって描かれた。

ピカソが描いた11枚の雄牛の石版画については，❸及び❹で語られている。選択肢の a，b，e については❸で，c については❹で触れられている。この連作は次第に抽象化していったものであるが，d の記述はこれと正反対の内容になっている。

(3) According to Julia's example, how do rules affect creativity?
ジュリアが挙げた例によると，ルールはどのように創造性に影響するか。

a) They destroy it because they limit freedom.
自由を制限することによって，ルールが創造性を破壊する。

b) They ultimately lead to boredom, which hinders creativity.
ルールが究極的には退屈をもたらし，それによって創造性が抑え付けられる。

c) They stimulate creativity by encouraging the artist to break the rules.
芸術家にルールを破るように促すことで，ルールが創造性を刺激する。

d) They hinder creativity, which in turn prompts the artist to experiment.
ルールは創造性を阻害し，それに触発されて芸術家は実験をしようとする。

e) They enhance creativity by encouraging experimentation within the boundaries of the rules.
ルールの境界内での実験を促すことで，ルールが創造性を高める。

設問のJulia's exampleとはピカソによる11枚の石版画のことを指している。この連作では，「白黒の版画で雄牛を1頭のみ描く」というルールが，ピカソをより実験的な描画へと導いた。つまり「ルールが創造性を促進した」ということになる。選択肢の中からcとeの2つに絞れるが，ピカソの例では，ルールを破ろうとしたのではなく，ルールの及ぶ範囲内で実験的な試みを行ったのであるから，eの方が正解となる。

(4) Which of the following is true about MovieNow?
ムービーナウについて，以下のうち正しいものはどれか。

a) It has an unusual policy for taking time off.
休みを取ることに関して，独特の方針を採っている。

b) The company only has one rule for its workers.
この企業は，社員に対するルールを1つしか持っていない。

c) The subscribers can rent as many movies as they want.
加入者は好きなだけたくさんの映画をレンタルすることができる。

d) It provides online services to make the home environment more comfortable.
自宅の環境をより快適にするようなオンラインサービスを提供している。

e) It followed the same business model as other companies in the video industry.
ビデオ産業の他の企業と同じビジネスモデルを後追いした。

MovieNowという会社の試みについては❼❽❾で説明されている。❼ではThat company has .... created a new modelとあり，他者とは違った新しいビジネスモデルを創出したことが分かるのでeは誤り。また，同じくanybody can rent any movie they want from the comfort of their own homeとあるが，この the comfort of their own homeは「自宅でくつろぎながら」といった意味であり，dの内容とは異なる。❽の「好きなだけ休暇を取って良く，給料も変わらない」というのがaのan unusual policy for taking time offに該当する。bは紛らわしいが，MovieNowには従業員の休暇を定めるルールは「ない」のであり，誤りである。

そもそも，MovieNowの「休暇に関する方針」については語られているが，その他のルールがあるか否かについては触れられていないので，ｂを正解と断定することはできない。

(5) According to the professor, why didn't the policy at MovieNow hamper the company's growth?
　教授によると，ムービーナウの方針が，企業の成長を妨げなかったのはなぜか。

a) Because the overall economy at that time was very strong.
　当時の経済全体が極めて好況だったから。

b) Because employees were still responsible for meeting targets.
　それでも従業員は目標を達成するという責任を負っていたから。

c) Because most of the employees didn't choose to take a long vacation.
　大半の従業員は長い休暇を取らなかったから。

d) Because the company had many other policies that ensured innovation.
　この企業が，革新を保証する他の方針を多数採用していたから。

e) Because employee pay was reduced if they took too many vacation days.
　従業員が休暇を取りすぎると，給料が減らされたから。

「好きなだけ休暇を取って良い」というMovieNowの方針が成功した理由については❾の後半で説明されている。この方針が従業員の自由と，そして目標を達成することへの責任感を促進することに繋がったのである。よってｂが正解。❽で「どれだけ休んでも給料は同じ」とあるのでｅは誤り。ａ，ｄについては全く言及がない。

Set 7-B | 放送文

Creative Thinking 2

❶ Julia: John, what did you think of today's lecture?

❷ John: I thought it was interesting. To tell the truth, though, I don't know if I could handle a situation like the one at MovieNow. I've always needed a lot of structure to get anything done. I'd probably end up taking like two months of vacation, not finishing any work, and getting fired!

❸ Julia: I'm the same. That's actually one reason I like this class. The weekly quizzes and journal assignments that the professor gives us really help me stay on track with my studying. Imagine if he gave us complete freedom to study or not throughout the semester, and then gave us one big test at the end. I know I'd put off studying to the last minute. I just don't have that kind of self-discipline.

❹ John: What about you, Pete? You don't seem to be much of a procrastinator.

❺ Pete: You're right, I'm not. I can't take much credit for it though – it's all thanks to my parents!

❻ Julia: How so?

❼ Pete: I might not have told you this before, but my family was part of the unschooling movement when I was growing up.

❽ John: What's that?

❾ Pete: It's an educational philosophy established in the 1960s by a guy named John Holt. It's actually similar in some ways to the MovieNow model. The basic idea is that children are born with a natural curiosity about the world, and they will learn enough without adults telling them what to do. Unschooled kids don't go to school. We decide what to study, or even if we want to study at all.

❿ Julia: Is that similar to the home schooling movement? I've heard of that before.

⓫ Pete: It's similar in that both home-schooled kids and unschooled kids don't go to ordinary schools with teachers and classrooms. But most home-school families create a kind of mini-classroom in

structure 名 構造，枠組み
fire 他 …を解雇する
🔲 John の 発 言 の 主 旨：
MovieNow の自由な方針
は自分には向かない。規則
がないと仕事をしなくなっ
てしまう

journal 名 日誌
on track 句 順調に進んで
いる
semester 名 学期

self-discipline 名 自制心
🔲 Julia の発言の主旨：John
に同意。授業で毎週の課題
を出されなければ，勉強を
先延ばしにしてしまうだろ
う

not much of a … 句 大した
…ではない
procrastinator 名 ぐずぐず
と先延ばしにする人
take credit for … 句 …を自
分の手柄にする

establish 他 …を設立する，
創始する

their home. They give their kids textbooks and homework, and follow a set curriculum. I didn't have any of that.

⑫ John: Wow, that's crazy.

⑬ Pete: Only from your modern perspective! Believe it or not, until 1852, children in the United States weren't required to go to school. A lot of them stayed home and helped their parents run the family farm or business. And even after 1852, kids were only required to be in school for three months a year!

⑭ Julia: Okay, so give me an example of a typical unschooled day for you when you were, say, a 10-year-old boy.

⑮ Pete: Well, I grew up on a farm, so I'd usually get up at dawn and help my mom collect eggs. After breakfast, my brother and I would head out to the woods. We'd go fishing or pick berries or build shelters. It was super fun.

⑯ John: Wait a second. You're here in college with us now. If you didn't have to study math or science or history like the rest of us, how did you end up here?

⑰ Pete: When I got to be a teenager, I naturally got interested in some of those things. For instance, if I wanted to build a tree house, I needed to know geometry to draw up the plans. In fact, I loved building so much that I eventually decided I wanted to be an architect, and I knew I'd need a college degree for that. So I studied on my own for the entrance exams. I didn't need anyone looking over my shoulder telling me what to do.

⑱ Julia: And here you are, a sophomore getting straight As and putting John and me to shame!

⑲ John: I guess the no-rules approach does work after all.

---

set 形 決められた
curriculum 名 カリキュラム

🔗 home schooling と un-schooling の違い：home schooling は学校に近い教育を家庭で行う。unschooling は学校で行われるような学習をさせない

perspective 名 視点, 考え方

say 副 たとえば

dawn 名 夜明け

woods 名 森
shelter 名 隠れ家

geometry 名 幾何学
architect 名 建築家
degree 名 学位
look over someone's shoulder 句 …を肩越しに見る, 監視する

🔗 Pete の発言の主旨：自分のやりたいことに必要な勉強を自発的に行い, 大学まで行った

sophomore 名 2年生
put someone to shame 句 〈人〉に恥をかかせる

172

Set 7-B｜放送文の日本語訳

創造的思考2

❶ジュリア：ジョン君，今日の講義についてどう思った？

❷ジョン：興味深いと思ったよ。でも，正直に言うと，自分がムービーナウのような状況をうまく扱えるかどうかは分からないな。僕はいつも何かをやり遂げるために，多くの枠組みを必要としてきたから。たぶん，僕は結局，休暇を2ヶ月とか取って，仕事を何も終わらせられずに解雇されることになるのじゃないかな！

❸ジュリア：私も同じ。実際，それがこのクラスが好きな理由の1つだし。毎週ある小テストと教授が出してくれる日誌の宿題が，間違いなく私が勉強をきちんと進めていくための手助けになってるわ。もし先生が学期中，勉強するかどうかは完全に自由だということにして，それで学期の最後に大きなテストを1回実施するとしたら，と想像してみてよ。私ならきっとぎりぎりまで勉強を先延ばしにするわ。そういう類の自制心が全くないのよね。

❹ジョン：君はどう，ピート君。あまり何でも先延ばしにするような人には見えないけれど。

❺ピート：その通り，僕はそうではないな。ただ，それを自分の手柄にすることはできないけれど。全て僕の両親のおかげだから！

❻ジュリア：どうしてそうなの？

❼ピート：これまで話していなかったかもしれないけれど，子どもの頃，僕の家族は非学校教育運動に参加していたんだ。

❽ジョン：それって何？

❾ピート：ジョン・ホルトという男性によって，1960年代に創始された教育哲学。実のところ，ある意味ではムービーナウのモデルと似ているんだ。子どもたちは世界に対する自然な好奇心を持って生まれてくるもので，大人たちが何をすべきかを指示しなくても十分に学ぶことができるはずだ，というのが基本的な考えでね。非学校教育の子どもは学校に通わない。自分たちで何を勉強するかを決め，あるいはそもそも勉強したいかどうかさえも決めるんだ。

❿ジュリア：それってホームスクール運動と似ているのかしら。以前に聞いたことがあるのだけど。

⓫ピート：ホームスクールの子どもたちも，非学校教育の子どもたちも，教師と教室が用意された普通の学校に通わないという点では似ているね。でも，ホームスクールの家庭の多くでは，家の中に一種の小さな教室を作る。子どもたちに教科書と宿題を与えて，決められたカリキュラムに従う。僕にはそういったものは一切なかった。

⓬ジョン：わあ，そりゃ普通じゃない。

⓭ピート：君の現代的な視点だけから見ればね！　信じられないかもしれないけれど，1852年まで，アメリカ合衆国の子どもたちにとって学校に通うことは必須ではなかった。子どもたちの多くが，家に留まって，両親が農場やビジネスを管理するのを手伝っていたんだ。それに，1852年以降であっても，子どもたちに求められていたのは，年に3ヶ月間学校に通うことだけだったのだから！

⑭ジュリア：そう，それじゃあ，あなたが，たとえば，10歳の少年だった時の，非学校教育の典型的な1日がどんなものだったか教えて。

⑮ピート：ええと，僕は農場で育ったから，普段は夜明けに起きて，母が卵を集めるのを手伝っていた。朝食の後には，兄と一緒に森に出かけた。釣りに行ったり，ベリーを採集したり，隠れ家を建てたりしていたな。ものすごく楽しかった。

⑯ジョン：ちょっと待って。君は今僕たちと一緒にこうして大学にいるよね。君以外の僕たちみんなのように，数学とか科学とか歴史を勉強しなくても良かったとしたら，どうやってここに行き着いたんだ？

⑰ピート：10代になった頃に，自然とそういったことのいくつかに興味を持つようになったんだ。たとえば，木の家を建てたいと思った時，設計図を描くために幾何学を知ることが必要だった。実際，僕は家を建てることがあまりに大好きだったために，結局建築家になりたいと決めて，そのためには大学の学位が必要だろうということが分かった。それで，僕は入学試験のために自力で勉強したんだ。僕には，肩越しに見張ってて，何をすべきか指示するような誰かは不要だったんだ。

⑱ジュリア：それであなたはここにいるというわけね。成績はAばかりとって，ジョン君と私に恥をかかせる大学2年生として！

⑲ジョン：やっぱりルールなしのやり方は確かにうまくいくわけだね。

《 指針 》

Aの続きである。「規則は必要か」というテーマを引き継いではいるが，話題は大きく転換して「教育において規則は必要か」という方向へと進み，後半からはunschooling（非学校教育）についての会話となる。unschoolingと，それに似たhome schoolingとの違いに注意しながら聞き取りを進めよう。

難易度

放送文	★☆☆
設問	★★☆
総合	★★☆

☺😐))) スピーカー情報

Julia: 西海岸，カリフォルニア
John: イングランド
Pete: 西海岸，オレゴン

Set 7-B | 設問解説

(1) How does John feel about MovieNow's policy?
ムービーナウの方針について，ジョンはどう感じているか。

a) He is not sure whether it's good or not.
その方針が良いか悪いか，彼には分からない。

b) He thinks their teacher should adopt a similar policy.
自分たちの教師も同じような方針を採用するべきだと考えている。

c) He believes it suits him because he is lazy by nature.
自分は生来怠け者なので，その方針は自分に合っていると思っている。

d) He likes it because he prefers having a long vacation.
長い休暇を取ることが好きなので，その方針を気に入っている。

e) He thinks it may be good for some people, but not for him.
その方針に合う人もいるかもしれないが，彼には合わないと考えている。

❷のI thought it was interesting. To tell the truth, though, I don't know if I could handle a situation like the one at MovieNow. という発言から，John は MovieNow の方針を認めているが，自分には向かないと考えていることが分かる。正解は e 。

(2) What type of educational system does Julia prefer?
ジュリアはどのようなタイプの教育制度を好んでいるか。

a) One in which she can continue studying while having fun.
楽しみながら勉強を続けられるような制度。

b) One in which no textbooks or formal classes are provided.
教科書も型通りの授業も全く与えられない制度。

c) One in which she studies at home but follows a set curriculum.
家で勉強しながら，決められたカリキュラムには従う制度。

d) One in which she is required to complete weekly assignments and tests to monitor her progress.
学習の進み具合を監視するための宿題とテストを，毎週こなすことが求められる制度。

e) One in which she is free to study at her own pace during the semester, and take only one major test at the end.
学期中，自分のペースで自由に勉強して，最後に1回だけ大きな試験を受ける制度。

❸の発言から，Julia も John と同じく「規則がないと怠けてしまう」タイプだと認めていることが分かる。授業で，小テストや日誌の課題を毎週出されているからこそ，勉強を進めていくことができているという主旨の発言をしており，これが d に該当する。b や e のような自由な授業は，Julia の好みとは正反対である。

（3）**Which of the following accurately describes the unschooling movement?**
以下のうち，非学校教育運動を正確に説明しているのはどれか。

a）Children are deprived of the opportunity to learn.
子どもたちは学習する機会を奪われる。

b）Children study in mini-classrooms in their family homes.
子どもたちは，自分たちの家の中の小さな教室で学習する。

c）It is based on a belief that children have a natural desire to learn.
子どもたちは学ぶことに対する生まれつきの欲求を持っている，という信条に基づいている。

d）Children can decide for themselves whether or not they want to go to school.
子どもたちは，学校に通いたいかどうかを自分で決めることができる。

e）Children study a curriculum that is designed to counteract what they have learned in mainstream schools.
子どもたちは，主流の学校で学んだことに対抗するように意図されたカリキュラムを学習する。

unschooling movementについての説明は❾と⓫でなされているが，これとhome schooling movementとの違いを正しく理解しよう。どちらも「通常の学校には通わない」という共通点はあるが，home schoolingは「学校と同じような教育を家庭で行う」のに対し，unschoolingでは「宿題，教科書，カリキュラムといったものを一切使わない」というのである。選択肢のbはhome schoolingに該当する。また，unschoolingでは，子どもは学校にも通わないし決まったカリキュラムも持たないのでd，eは誤りである。また，❾で言われているように，子どもに自然かつ自由に学習させることが狙いなので，aも誤り。cは❾のThe basic idea is that children are born with a natural curiosity about the world, and they will learn enough without adults telling them what to do.と合致する。

（4）**Which of the following statements describes Pete's experience with unschooling?**
以下のうち，ピートの非学校教育における経験を表しているのはどれか。

a）He resents his parents for not giving him the same experiences as other children.
他の子どもたちと同じ経験を与えてくれなかったという理由で，両親に腹を立てている。

b）He studied a wider range of subjects than he would have in a conventional school.
従来型の学校で習うはずの科目よりも，幅広い範囲の科目を学んだ。

c）He wasted his time learning a lot of things he didn't need to know to get ahead in life.
出世するのに必要のないたくさんのことを学んで時間を無駄にした。

d）He enjoyed exploring the forest as a young boy, but he didn't gain the knowledge necessary for success.
少年の頃，森の探検を楽しんだが，成功するために必要な知識を得ることはなかった。

176

e) He enjoyed the freedom it offered, and was still able to achieve goals such as
passing college entrance exams.
彼はそこで与えられた自由を謳歌し，それでも大学の入学試験に受かるというような目
標を達成することができた。

Pete自身のunschoolingの経験は**⑮⑰**で述べられている。「強制的に勉強をさせ
られたのではなく，自分が興味を持った方向に進む上で必要な勉強を自発的に行い，
大学まで進んだ」という内容である。これに合致するeが正解。bの「従来の学校
よりも幅広い科目を学んだ」という事実は語られていない。むしろ，好きな科目だ
けを学んだのだから，その幅は狭いはずである。また，dは後半が誤り。自由な遊
びを通じて，幾何学等を学んだということが語られている。

(5) What do Julia and John think of unschooling?
ジュリアとジョンは非学校教育をどう思っているか。
 a) They fully approve of it.
十分に認めている。
 b) They have some doubts.
いくらか疑問に思っている。
 c) They are strongly opposed to it.
強く反対している。
 d) They wish their parents had tried it.
自分たちの両親がその教育を試してくれれば良かったと思っている。
 e) They think it would be a bad fit for them because it lacks structure.
その教育は枠組みを欠いているため，自分たちには合わないであろうと思っている。

unschoolingに対してJuliaとJohnは直接的な意見は述べていないが，**⑱⑲**での反
応から，2人ともPeteの経験を全面的に肯定していることが分かる。aが正解であ
る。dも同じ方向性の内容だが，「自分の親にもunschoolingを試してほしかった」
と思っているということを窺わせる発言はない。また，eの記述は，MovieNowの
方針については当てはまるが，unschoolingについて2人がこのような意見を持っ
ているかは断定できない。

Set 7-C | 放送文

Roads and Wildlife

❶ James: Good morning Sarah. Sorry I'm a little late getting into the office. The traffic was so bad today. It took me almost half an hour to get downtown!

❷ Sarah: It's okay James, I got stuck in that traffic jam too. It must be the roadwork they're doing on Main Street. Which reminds me, have you been down Route 43 lately?

❸ James: No, why?

❹ Sarah: Well, if you drive a couple of miles out of town, out towards the forest preserve, there's a really wide new bridge over the road. It must be 150 feet wide and it has all sorts of trees and bushes planted on it. I've been trying to figure out why they built it because I drive down that road all the time, but I've never seen anybody using it. There aren't any houses nearby so I don't know who it's for!

❺ James: Oh, I read about that in the newspaper! It's a wildlife overpass.

❻ Sarah: A what?

❼ James: Apparently a lot of deer, bobcats, and foxes were getting hit by cars when they tried to cross Route 43. That road goes right through the middle of the forest preserve and I guess the animals would get hit as they were trying to get from one side of the park to the other. Anyway, last March the city council approved funds to build a bridge for them. According to the article there are thousands of wildlife overpasses like this one in the US now.

❽ Sarah: I had no idea roadkill was such a big problem. Now that you mention it, though, I've seen quite a few dead foxes and raccoons on that road.

❾ James: The article had some pretty unbelievable statistics in it. The annual figures for roadkill nationwide are in the millions, and it's not just ordinary animals like deer that get hit. If I'm remembering this correctly, 65% of the

roadwork 名 道路工事	
forest preserve 句 森林保護区	
bush 名 灌木，低木	
📝橋の特徴：幅150フィート。木が植えてある。人が使っている気配はない	
wildlife overpass 句 野生動物陸橋	
bobcat 名 ボブキャット	
📝橋の目的：森林保護区の野生動物が車に轢かれずに道路を渡るためのもの	
city council 句 市議会 fund 名 予算，資金	
quite a few 句 かなりの数の raccoon 名 アライグマ	
statistics 名 統計 in the millions 句 数百万の	

endangered panthers in Florida have been killed by cars, and drivers have reduced the number of endangered ocelots in Texas to less than 100 animals.

⑩ Sarah: Wow. I know hitting an animal can be dangerous for humans too. Just a few months after my daughter got her driver's license last year, she was driving home late at night and hit a deer. The deer was killed and my daughter had serious neck problems from the force of the impact for almost six months.

⑪ James: Yeah, I've heard stories like that too. For these wildlife overpasses to work, you have to put them in places that the target species is actually going to find. The newspaper article I read said that rangers at the park spent over six months monitoring the corridors that foxes, bobcats and deer use to get around the park before they decided on the location of the bridge. Actually, the bridge is primarily for the deer. There's also an underpass about a mile down the road that was built for the foxes and bobcats.

⑫ Sarah: That makes sense. Things wouldn't work out very well if predators and prey had to use the same bridge!

⑬ James: Right. And now that everything is in place, the rangers are tracking the numbers of animals using the structures to see how well they work.

⑭ Sarah: Cool. I'll have to keep my eye out for updates in the paper!

---

endangered 形 絶滅の危機に瀕した
panther 名 パンサー
ocelot 名 オセロット

▸Sarahの発言の主旨：動物を轢くのは人間にとっても危険だ

ranger 名 森林警備隊，レンジャー
monitor 他 …を観察する，監視する
corridor 名 廊下，通り道

underpass 名 地下通路

▸Jamesの発言の主旨：特定の野生動物の通り道に橋を設置するために，事前に調査を行う。捕食者と獲物が別の通路を使うように配慮されている

predator 名 捕食者
prey 名 獲物

Set 7-C | 放送文の日本語訳

道路と野生動物

❶ ジェームズ：おはよう，サラ。出社がちょっと遅くなってしまってごめんね。今日は道路がとても混んでいたんだ。中心街に着くのに，30分近くもかかってしまって。

❷ サラ：大丈夫よ，ジェームズ，私もその渋滞に引っかかったわ。メイン・ストリートで行われている道路工事のせいね。そういえば，最近43号線を走ったことはある？

❸ ジェームズ：いや，なぜ？

❹ サラ：あのね，街を抜けて森林保護区の方に2〜3マイルも走ってみると，道路にすごく幅の広い新しい橋が渡してあるのよ。幅が150フィートはあるはずで，そしてその上にはあらゆる種類の木や灌木が植えられているの。いつもその道を通るのに，その橋を使っている人を見たことがないから，なぜその橋を造ったのかなって思っていたのよ。近くには民家も全くないし，誰のためのものなのか分からないのよ！

❺ ジェームズ：ああ，それについては新聞で読んだよ！　野生動物陸橋だよ。

❻ サラ：何ですって？

❼ ジェームズ：どうやら，たくさんのシカや，ボブキャットや，キツネが43号線を横断しようとして車に轢かれてしまっていたらしい。43号線は森林保護区のちょうど真ん中を走っているから，動物たちが保護区の片側から反対側へ移動しようとして轢かれてしまっていたのじゃないかな。ともかく，去年の3月に市議会が動物用の橋を造る予算を認めたんだ。その記事によれば，今アメリカにはその橋みたいな野生動物陸橋が何千もあるらしいよ。

❽ サラ：動物の道路での事故死がそんなに大きな問題になっているなんて思いもしなかったわ。でもそう言われてみると，その道路で，死んでいるキツネやアライグマを相当な数見たことがあるわ。

❾ ジェームズ：その記事にはにわかには信じられないような統計が載っていたよ。国内の動物事故死の年間件数は数百万に上っていて，しかも轢かれているのはシカのようなよくいる動物だけじゃないんだ。僕の記憶が正しければ，絶滅の危機に瀕しているフロリダのパンサーの65パーセントは車によって死亡していて，絶滅危惧種のテキサスのオセロットの数が100頭以下にまで減ってしまったのも車のせいなんだ。

❿ サラ：まぁ。動物を轢くことは人間にとっても危険よね。去年私の娘が，運転免許を取ってほんの数ヶ月後に，夜遅くに車で帰宅する途中シカを轢いてしまったの。シカは死んでしまって，私の娘は衝突の衝撃で6ヶ月近く首にひどい問題を抱えていたわ。

⓫ ジェームズ：ああ，僕もそういった話を聞くことがあるよ。野生動物陸橋を機能させるためには，対象となる種が実際に見つけてくれるような場所に橋を設置しなければいけないんだ。僕が読んだ新聞記事によると，橋を造る場所を定める前に保護区の森林警備隊員たちが6ヶ月以上かけて，キツネやボブキャットやシカが保護区の中を移動するのに使う通り道を観察したらしい。実は，その橋は主にシカのためのものなんだ。道路を約1マイル行った先にも地下を通る通路があって，こ

ちらはキツネやボブキャットのために造られたんだ。

⓬ サラ：それは理にかなっているわね。捕食者と獲物が同じ橋を使わなくちゃいけな
かったらあまりうまくいかないでしょうから！

⓭ ジェームズ：そうだね。いまやもう全てが整って，森林警備隊員たちは橋や通路が
どのくらい機能しているか調べるために，利用している動物の数を追っているんだ。

⓮ サラ：それはすごい。最新の情報がないか新聞に目を留めておかないといけないわね。

《 指針 》

野生動物陸橋（wildlife overpass）についての会話である。野生動物陸
橋とは，森林保護区の野生動物が道路を渡る際に車に轢かれるのを防ぐた
めに作られた陸橋である。各種の動物の通り道を研究した上で適切な位置
に設置し，さらに捕食者と獲物が同じ橋を使わないようにする等の配慮が
されている。放送文，設問ともに平易であり，高得点が狙える問題である。

難易度

放送文　★☆☆

設　問　★☆☆

総　合　★☆☆

☺☺))) スピーカー情報

James: スコットランド
Sarah: イングランド

Set 7-C │ 設問解説

(1) Which of the following does Sarah NOT mention as an unusual feature of the
new overpass?
新しい高架橋の独特の特徴としてサラが挙げていないのはどれか。

a) It is very wide.
とても幅が広い。

b) Nobody uses it.
誰も利用していない。

c) There are often traffic jams on it.
しょっちゅう渋滞が起きている。

d) The area around it is uninhabited.
その周辺には人が住んでいない。

e) There are many trees and bushes on it.
橋の上にたくさんの木や灌木がある。

a，b，d，eは全て**❹**のSarahの発言の中で触れられている。cの「渋滞」については**❶❷**で話題にされているが，これは全く別の道についての話である。

(2) According to James, why was the overpass built?
　　ジェームズによれば，その高架橋が造られたのはなぜか？
　a）Wildlife needed a much larger habitat.
　　野生動物がもっと広い生息域を必要としていたから。
　b）The number of panthers in the forest had decreased by 65%.
　　森のパンサーの数が65パーセントも減ってしまっていたから。
　c）Wild animals needed a safe way to move around the forest preserve.
　　野生動物が森林保護区を動き回るのに安全な通り道を必要としていたから。
　d）Too many people were getting injured when they hit deer with their cars.
　　あまりに多くの人々がシカを車で轢いた時に怪我をしていたから。
　e）Pedestrians needed a safe way to get from one part of the forest preserve to another.
　　歩行者が森林保護区の一方から別の方へ移動するのに安全な通り道を必要としていたから。

野生動物陸橋が作られた経緯については**❼**でJamesが説明している。野生動物が森林内を移動しようとして道路を横断する際に車に轢かれるのを防ぐのが狙いである。cが正解。bのパンサーについては**❾**で触れられているが，これはフロリダの話であり，ここで問題となっている高架橋とは直接関係ない。

(3) The newspaper article James read claimed that
　　ジェームズが読んだ新聞記事の主張では，
　a）some wildlife species risk extinction due to car accidents.
　　車の事故が原因でいくつかの野生の種が絶滅に瀕している。
　b）many drivers have been attacked by dangerous wild animals.
　　多くのドライバーが危険な野生動物に襲われている。
　c）in Texas hunting has greatly reduced the population of ocelots.
　　テキサスでは狩猟がオセロットの生息数を大幅に減らしてきた。
　d）most of the animals killed by cars are common species like deer.
　　車によって殺される動物のほとんどはシカのような一般的な種である。
　e）humans are as likely to be injured as animals in roadkill accidents.
　　道路での動物死亡事故では，動物たちと同じように人間も怪我をしがちである。

❾ではJamesが新聞記事に載っていた統計について述べているが，車との事故によってパンサーの65%が死に，テキサス州のオセロットに至っては個体数が100頭に満たなくなったとあるので，aの記述が正解となる。cのhuntingはcar accidentsに変えなくてはならない。eの「人間の負傷」については**❿**でSarahが語っているが，これは新聞記事とは無関係である。

(4) Why did rangers monitor the park before building the overpass?
高架橋を建設する前に森林警備隊員たちが保護区を観察したのはなぜか？
a) To determine which species were most at risk.
どの種が最も危機に瀕しているかを決めるため。
b) To map the places where wildlife crossed roads.
野生動物が道路を渡った場所をマッピングするため。
c) To track the number of animals getting hit by cars.
車に轢かれる動物たちの数を調べるため。
d) To make sure the overpass wouldn't interfere with recreation.
高架橋によって娯楽活動が妨げられないようにするため。
e) To decide on the location where car accidents are most likely to occur.
交通事故が最も起こりやすい場所を選ぶため。

森林警備隊員たちの働きについては⓫で説明されている。彼らが森林を観察した理由は，you have to put them in places that the target species is actually going to findとあるように，特定の動物の通り道に橋を設置するためである。bが正解。

(5) Why was an underpass built on a different section of the road?
その道路の別の箇所に地下を通る通路が造られたのはなぜか。
a) Because deer are afraid of high places.
シカが高いところを恐れるため。
b) Because the overpass was not effective.
高架橋が効果を上げていなかったから。
c) Because the number of car accidents didn't decrease.
交通事故の数が減らなかったから。
d) Because too many animals were trying to use the overpass.
あまりに多くの動物たちが高架橋を使おうとしていたから。
e) Because predators needed a separate place to cross the road.
捕食動物が道路を横断するための別の場所を必要としたから。

シカが通るための高架橋とは別に，キツネやボブキャット用の地下通路が約１マイル先に作られた理由は，Things wouldn't work out very well if predators and prey had to use the same bridge!とSarahが指摘したように，捕食者と獲物が同じ通路を通らないようにするためである。eが正解。

Set 8 | 解答

8A　(1) c　(2) c　(3) e　(4) b　(5) e
8B　(1) e　(2) c　(3) b　(4) a　(5) b
8C　(1) b　(2) d　(3) d　(4) e　(5) c

Set 8-A | 放送文

The Shifting Meaning of Nature

❶ "Nature" is a slightly vague concept, all the more so when viewed in the context of humanity. This is because humanity defines the natural by giving birth to its opposite, the unnatural.

❷ Just like there is no light without darkness, a concept is meaningless if it has no limits. Nature is no exception: without the artificial acting as a contrasting presence, everything on Earth would fall under the definition of the natural, effectively making that definition meaningless. Of course, humans are the only beings with the intellectual capacity to even distinguish between natural and artificial objects. But even more importantly, if humans hadn't invented unnatural objects, they would never have needed the contrasting concept of "natural." It is extremely ironic that humans, ourselves naturally occurring organisms, created the concept of nature.

❸ What is interesting, then, is that humans, the very beings that invented the idea of nature, have such varied opinions about it. While most everyone can agree on the big picture, we often disagree on the details of just what is and isn't included in the scope of "nature." Mt. Everest, the Mariana Trench, blizzards, and the aurora in the Arctic zone. Geography and weather are beyond doubt within the boundary of nature, as are the various naturally occurring plant and animal species. Similarly, skyscrapers, highways, and automobiles clearly fall within the scope of the unnatural, the manufactured.

❹ Not all things, however, are so easily split into black and white. Once human influence enters

vague 形 曖昧な
humanity 名 人類
define 他 …を定義する
give birth to … 句 …を生む

the artificial 句 人工のもの
(↔ the natural)
contrasting 形 対照的な
effectively 副 事実上
intellectual capacity 句 知的能力

📎 発言の主旨：「自然」という概念は，「非自然・人工」という対概念があって初めて生まれる

ironic 形 皮肉な
organism 名 生物

scope 名 範囲，領域
blizzard 名 猛吹雪，ブリザード
aurora 名 オーロラ
beyond doubt 句 疑う余地なく
boundary 名 境界，範囲
skyscraper 名 摩天楼，超高層ビル

the realm of nature, boundaries begin to blur. How, for instance, to classify animals that have been bred by humans so extensively that they no longer resemble their counterparts in the wild? Into which category should we place man-made organisms, which closely resemble naturally occurring life forms but are clearly built by humans? On an even more theoretical level, can socialized behaviors such as avoiding pork for religious reasons truly be called natural? Is religion a naturally occurring phenomenon, or an invented one? Questions such as these shatter the traditional definition of "nature."

❺ This uncertainty becomes increasingly important as humanity begins to push the boundaries of what is possible. While on the surface a discussion of definitions appears to be purely philosophical, it is inseparably linked to complicated questions about morality and the role of humans as guardians of the planet. For example, do we have a moral obligation to treat artificial organisms the same as naturally occurring ones? Are landscapes altered by humans, such as farms and cities, less deserving of conservation than purely natural ones like rainforests and savannahs? Our answers to these questions significantly impact both public policy and personal actions. It is therefore essential that regardless of—or perhaps because of—the ambiguities inherent in the discussion, humankind pay particular attention to the boundaries and implications of the natural versus the unnatural.

realm 名 領域
blur 自 ぼやける
breed 他 …を繁殖させる，交配する
extensively 副 広範囲に，大規模に
counterpart 名 同等のもの

theoretical 形 理論的な

🗨 発言の主旨：人間の影響が及ぶと，何が自然で，何が自然でないかの境界は曖昧である
shatter 他 …を打ち砕く，壊滅させる

philosophical 形 哲学的な

morality 名 道徳
guardian 名 守護者

obligation 名 義務
landscape 名 風景

🗨 「自然」対「非自然」の境界を考えることは，地球環境を守る立場にある人間にとって重要である

inherent in … 句 …に固有の
implication 名 (予想される) 影響, 結果

Set 8-A ｜放送文の日本語訳

変化している「自然」の意味

❶ 　「自然」というのはいささか曖昧な概念です。人類という文脈からみると，なおさらです。人類は自然というものを，それとは反対のもの，すなわち非自然を生み出すことによって定義しているからです。

❷ 　闇がなければ光もないことと全く同じように，なんらかの概念というものは，何も制限を持たない状態では意味をなしません。自然も例外ではありません。対照的な存在として振る舞う人工的なものがなければ，地球上のあらゆるものが自然

の定義に当てはまってしまい，実質的にその定義の意味がなくなってしまうでしょう。もちろん，人間は自然の事物と人工的な事物を区別することさえもできる知的能力を備えた唯一の存在です。しかしよりいっそう大事なのは，もし人間が非自然的なものを生み出していなかったら，「自然」という対照的な概念も決して必要とされなかっただろうということです。自分たち自身が自然に存在する生命体である人間が，自然という概念を「創造した」というのは極めて皮肉なことです。

❸　そうなると興味深いのは，自然という考え方を発明した張本人である人間が，自然についてかくも多様な意見を持っているということです。ほとんど全ての人がその全体像には同意できる一方で，具体的に何が「自然」という範囲に含まれて何が含まれないのか，という詳細については，意見が分かれることが多いでしょう。エベレスト山，マリアナ海溝，猛吹雪，北極圏のオーロラ，といった地形や気候は疑う余地もなく自然の範囲内ですし，自然に存在する様々な植物や動物の種も同じです。同様に，摩天楼や高速道路や自動車は，明確に非自然・人工物の範囲に分類されます。

❹　しかしながら，全てのものがいとも簡単に黒と白に分けられるわけではありません。ひとたび人間の影響が自然の領域に及ぶと，境界線はぼやけ始めます。たとえば，人間が激しい異種交配をさせて，もはや野生の元の姿とは似ていない動物たちを分類するとどうなるでしょうか？　自然に存在する生物形態とそっくりであっても，明らかに人の手で作られた人工的な生命体は，どちらの分類に位置付けるべきでしょう？　あるいは，よりいっそう理論的なレベルでは，宗教的な理由から豚肉を避けるような社会的振る舞いは本当に自然だと言えるのでしょうか？　宗教は自然に生じた現象なのか，それとも発明された現象なのか？　こうした疑問は，「自然」の伝統的な定義を破壊してしまうものです。

❺　この不確かさは，人類が可能なことの境界を押し広げ始めるとともに，次第に重要になってきています。表面上は，定義についての議論は純粋に哲学的なものに思えますが，道徳やこの惑星の守護者としての人間の役割に関する複雑な問題と密接に繋がっているのです。たとえば，私たちは人工的な生命体に対して，自然に存在する生命体と同じ道徳的責任を負っているのでしょうか？　農場や都市のように人間の手によって変貌した風景は，熱帯雨林やサバンナ地帯のように純粋な自然の風景に比べて保護に値しないものなのでしょうか？　こうした疑問に対する私たちの答えによって，公共政策も個人の行動も重大な影響を受けます。したがって，この議論に特有の曖昧さにもかかわらず，いや，その曖昧さゆえにというべきかもしれませんが，人類が「自然」対「非自然」の境界とそこからもたらされる影響に特別な関心を注ぐことは，絶対に必要なことなのです。

難易度

放送文　★★★
設　問　★★☆
総　合　★★☆

☺☹))) **スピーカー情報**

Lecturer: 中西部，ミズーリ

Set 8-A｜設問解説

(1) According to the lecturer, the concepts of "natural" and "unnatural" are:
講師によると，「自然」という概念と「非自然」という概念は……

a) Surprisingly similar.
驚くほど似ている。

b) Contradictory to each other.
互いに矛盾している。

c) Both necessary to define one another.
互いを定義するために両方必要である。

d) Found in cultures throughout the world.
世界中の文化の中に見出される。

e) Ideas that did not exist in older civilizations.
古い文明には存在しなかった考え方である。

unnaturalという概念がnaturalという語を前提としているのは当然として，❶に humanity defines the natural by giving birth to its opposite, the unnatural とあるように，naturalという概念もまた，unnaturalを生み出すことによって成立している，というのがこの講義の前半のポイントである。正解は c である。この問題はさらに❷でも突き詰めて考察されている。

(2) Which of the following would the lecturer be LEAST likely to categorize as "natural"?
講師が最も「自然」に分類しそうにないのは次のうちどれか。

a）A river with a dam on it.
ダムが設置された川。

b）A snow-covered mountain.
雪に覆われた山。

c）A cave dug by prehistoric people.
先史時代の人間が掘った洞窟。

d）A drought caused by climate change.
気候の変化がもたらした干ばつ。

e）A microorganism brought back from outer space.
宇宙から持ち帰ってきた微生物。

❸❹では，「自然」と「非自然」の境界線について，いくつかの例を引き合いに検証がなされている。「地形や天候」等は明らかな「自然」として，また「超高層ビル」や「車」等は，人間が作り出した「非自然」として分類される。一方，「人間が交配を重ねて作り出した動物」等は，その分類が疑問視されている。つまり，1.「人の手が全く加わっていないもの（＝自然）」，2.「人間が作り出したもの（＝非自然）」，3.「人間の手によって改変されたもの（＝分類が曖昧）」，の３つに分けられる。bは1.に，ａとdは3.に該当し，ｅは1.もしくは3.に該当する。一方のｃの「洞窟」は人間が作り出したものであり，2.に該当する。よってｃが正解。

(3) People who don't eat pork are mentioned as an example of:
豚肉を食べない人々が言及されたのは……

a）Socialized behaviors that are unnatural.
非自然的な，社会化された振る舞いの例としてである。

b）Natural dispositions that humans are born with.
人間が持って生まれた自然な性質の例としてである。

c）The way in which religion can distort natural behavior.
宗教によって自然な振る舞いが歪められる方法の例としてである。

d）The changing relationship between humans and the natural world.
人間と自然世界の変わりゆく関係の例としてである。

e）The ambiguous line between concepts of "natural" and "unnatural."
「自然」と「非自然」という概念の曖昧な境界線の例としてである。

❹では，「自然」と「非自然」の境界線が曖昧であることを，様々な例を挙げて説明している。「宗教上の理由から豚肉を避ける」という行為もその一例であり，ｅが正解となる。語り手は「自然と呼べるだろうか」という疑問を呈しているだけであって，ａのように「非自然的だ」と結論付けてはいない。

(4) According to the lecturer, discussing the definition of nature is:
　講師によれば，自然の定義を議論することは……

a) A purely theoretical exercise.
　純粋に理論的な営みである。

b) An important moral obligation.
　重要な道徳的責務である。

c) Frustrating because no clear answers exist.
　明確な答えが存在しないために苛立たしい。

d) Relevant only for politicians and public officials.
　政治家と役人だけにしか関係ない。

e) Of little practical use because it's a purely philosophical matter.
　純粋に哲学的な問題なので，実用性はほとんどない。

❺の it is inseparably linked to complicated questions about morality and the role of humans as guardians of the planet から b を正解とする。「自然」対「非自然」の問題が今日とりわけ重要になるのは，地球環境を守るという道徳的な責務が人間に課せられているからだ，と語り手は主張している。

(5) Which of the following is most likely to represent the lecturer's opinion about new types of plants created through genetic engineering?
　遺伝子工学によって作られた新種の植物についての講師の意見を表すであろうと最も思われるのは次のうちどれか。

a) The plants are clearly unnatural, and therefore should be outlawed.
　その植物は明らかに非自然なものであり，それゆえ法律で禁止するべきだ。

b) The plants are unquestionably natural because they are similar to wild species.
　その植物は野生の種と似ているのだから，疑問の余地なく自然に属する。

c) The plants represent human mastery of nature, and therefore should be encouraged.
　その植物は人間の自然への支配の表れであり，それゆえ奨励されるべきだ。

d) People should stop creating those plants because we are not sure about the implications.
　結果がどうなるか分からないので，そのような植物を作るのはやめるべきだ。

e) It is a complex ethical issue, in part because the plants are difficult to classify as either natural or unnatural.
　その植物を自然に分類することも非自然に分類することも困難だという理由からも，複雑な倫理的問題である。

設問の「遺伝子工学によって作られた新種の植物」は，❹で「自然なのか非自然なのか白黒付け難いもの」の一例として用いられている man-made organisms に極めて近いものである。また，❺では，そのような微妙な境界線に注意を払っていくことが，地球環境を守る人間にとっては道徳的な問題としてのしかかってきているという主張がなされている。以上から e を正解として選ぶ。

Set 8-B | 放送文

Bridge Design 1

❶ John: OK, let's make a start. I'm John Hart, the Chairperson of the jury panel for the River Redmond Crossing design competition. As you know, the purpose of this competition is to find an ingenious team of engineers to create a bridge spanning the River Redmond between Thornton and Springfield. So far, the panel has narrowed the field down from 15 initial entrants to four finalists. During today's public meeting, representatives from the four teams will answer questions from the audience and the panel.

❷ The fundamental design challenge is to create a bridge that can accommodate both pedestrians and cyclists and also provide adequate headroom for river traffic. In addition, the project brief sets out various other requirements, and the jury panel will evaluate each proposal based on how well it meets those criteria. For instance, the bridge should be of an innovative and distinctive design that will come to characterize this part of the city. Yet it must have a minimal impact on the lives of local residents and the wider environment. It must also comply with anti-disability discrimination legislation, ensuring that it is accessible to all.

❸ First, I'd like to turn to Amanda Hamilton from Bluestone Design Consultants. Your company is planning to build a cable-stayed bridge. An audience member asked earlier how they differ from suspension bridges.

❹ Amanda: Well, cable-stayed bridges share certain similarities with suspension bridges like the Golden Gate Bridge in San Francisco. Both types of bridge feature roadways that are hung from cables, and both have towers. However, the principles behind their design are rather different. The main cables of a suspension bridge ride freely over the towers and are anchored at each end to the ground on the sides of the river. Smaller cables connect the roadway to the main cables, and the forces acting on the roadway are transferred through the cables to the ground at the anchor points and also to the

jury panel 旬 審査員団,
審査委員会
ingenious 形 独創的な
span 他（橋が）…にかかる
narrow A down to B 旬 A
をBに絞り込む
initial 形 最初の
entrant 名 参加者
representative 名 代表者
📗 コンペティションの目的：
　Redmond 川の橋のデザイ
　ンチームを決める
fundamental 形 基本的な,
根本的な
challenge 名 課題
accommodate 他 …を収容
する, …に対応する
pedestrian 名 歩行者
adequate 形 十分な
headroom 名 頭上の空間
brief 名 概要, 要綱
requirement 名 要求
evaluate 他 …を評価する,
審査する
criteria 名 基準
innovative 形 革新的な
distinctive 形 独特の
minimal 形 最小の
comply with … 旬 …（要
求・規則）に従う
anti-disability
discrimination legislation
旬 障害者差別禁止法
ensure that … 旬 …という
ことを保証する
feature 他 …を特徴とする
principle 名 原理

anchor 他 …を固定する

towers. In cable-stayed bridges, by contrast, the cables are attached directly to the towers. This means that no anchor points are required and that the towers bear the weight of the roadway alone.

❺ John: Thank you. Next, I believe that Paul Mason from the jury panel has a question.

❻ Paul: Yes, your design notes claim that the Bluestone bridge will incorporate features that will make it the most environmentally efficient bridge in the country. One is the piezoelectric tiles in the pedestrian walkway. As I understand it, the tiles contain crystals. When somebody steps on them, an electric charge is created. The electricity is then stored and used to help power the lights on the bridge. Isn't it the case, though, that this is little more than a gimmick? It's estimated that on average 800 pedestrians will use the bridge every day. Even if you covered the entire walkway in piezoelectric tiles, which would be costly, wouldn't you struggle to power more than a few light bulbs?

❼ John: OK, thanks, Paul. Let's hear Amanda's response …

☞ 2つの橋の違い：
suspension bridgeでは，メインケーブルが川の両側で固定され，そのメインケーブルから小さなケーブルで通行路を吊る。重さは塔や固定点に分散される
cable-stayed bridgeでは，塔から直接ケーブルで通行路を吊る。重さは全て塔にかかる

incorporate 他 …を組み込む
efficient 形 効率的な
piezoelectric 形 圧電性の
crystal 名 水晶
electric charge 句 電荷
gimmick 名 巧妙な仕掛け

☞ Paulの発言の意図：piezo-electric tilesを使用しても，大した発電量にはならない。単なる仕掛けにすぎないのではないか

Set 8-B｜放送文の日本語訳

橋のデザイン１

❶ ジョン：よろしいですか，では始めましょう。私はジョン・ハート，レッドモンド川の橋デザイン・コンペティション審査委員会の議長をしております。ご存じの通り，このコンペティションの目的は，ソーントンとスプリングフィールドの間を流れるレッドモンド川に架かる橋を作るための独創的なエンジニアのチームを見つけ出すことです。これまでに，委員会では最初の15の参加チームから4つの最終候補にまで絞ってきました。今日の公開会議では，4チームの代表者たちに，聴衆と委員会からの質問に答えていただきます。

❷ このデザインにおける基本的な課題は，歩行者と自転車通行者の両方に対応し，かつ河川の交通にとって十分な頭上の空間が提供される橋を作るということです。加えて，プロジェクトの概要書は他にも様々な要求を設定しており，審査委員会は，それらの基準をいかに満たしているかに基づいて各チームの案を評価します。たとえば，橋は町のこの場所を特徴付けるようになる革新的で特色のあるデザインであるべきです。しかし，地域の住民やより広い環境に与える影響は最小限でなければなりません。また，障害者差別禁止法に従って，全ての人がアクセス可能であることを保証しなければならないのです。

❸ 最初は，ブルーストーン・デザイン・コンサルタンツのアマンダ・ハミルトンさんにお尋ねしましょう。あなたの会社は斜張橋の建設を計画していますね。聴衆のお1人が先立って，斜張橋は吊り橋とどう違うのかと質問していました。

❹アマンダ：そうですね，斜張橋はサンフランシスコのゴールデンゲートブリッジのような吊り橋といくつかの類似点があります。どちらの種類の橋も，ケーブルに吊り下げられた通行路を特徴とし，両者とも塔があります。しかし，それらのデザインの背後にある原理はかなり異なっているのです。吊り橋のメインケーブルは塔の上に掛かっていて，両端が川の両側の地面で固定されています。より小さなケーブルが通行路とメインケーブルを結び付けており，通行路にかかる力は，そのケーブルを通して地面の固定点や塔にも伝わります。斜張橋では，対照的に，ケーブルは直接塔に付けられているのです。つまり，固定点は必要なく，塔が単体で通行路の重さを支えるということを意味します。

❺ジョン：ありがとうございます。続いて審査委員会のポール・メイソンさん，質問がおありですね。

❻ポール：ええ，あなた方のデザインノートでは，ブルーストーン社の橋は，この橋をこの国で最も環境面での効率が良いものとするような特徴を組み込むと主張されていますね。その1つが，歩行者用通路における圧電性物質タイルです。私が理解する限りでは，このタイルは水晶を含んでいます。誰かがそれを踏むと，電荷が作り出されます。次に電気が蓄えられて，橋の上の照明に電力を供給するために使われるわけです。しかし，これは関心をひくための仕掛け程度のものでしかないというのが事実ではないですか？　毎日，平均800人の歩行者が橋を使うと見積もられています。たとえ歩行者用通路全体を圧電性物質タイルで覆うとしても，それはコストが高くつくでしょうし，2〜3個以上の電球に電力を供給するのにも四苦八苦するのではないですか。

❼ジョン：分かりました，ありがとうございます，ポールさん。アマンダさんの答えを聞いてみましょう……。

《〈 **指針** 〉》

橋のデザインを選ぶコンペティションの模様である。まず最初にコンペの概要と選考基準の説明がなされ，さらに，あるデザイン案についての質疑応答へと続く。質疑応答の中では，2種類の橋の構造についての説明が難しいが，設問で示されているイラストを見ておくことで，かなり理解しやすくなるはずだ。また2つ目の質問では，質問者が何に対してどのような批判をしているのかを把握しよう。

難易度

放送文 ★★★

設　問 ★★☆

総　合 ★★★

--☺☺))) スピーカー情報--------

John: 西海岸，カリフォルニア
Amanda: 西海岸，カリフォルニア
Paul: 中西部，イリノイ

Set 8-B | 設問解説

(1) Which of the following is true about the competition?
コンペティションについて正しい説明は，以下のうちのどれか。

a) 15 engineers are taking part in the competition.
コンペティションには15人のエンジニアが参加している。

b) John Hart is no longer a member of the jury panel.
ジョン・ハートは既に審査委員会のメンバーではない。

c) There were originally 15 entrants, but four were rejected.
最初に15の参加チームがあったが，そのうち4つが落選した。

d) The audience is not allowed to comment on the bridge designs.
聴衆は橋のデザインについて意見を述べることが認められていない。

e) The four remaining teams will have to explain more about their designs.
残った4チームは，自分たちのデザインについてさらに説明しなければならない。

❶ではこのコンペの概要が述べられている。「15の参加チームから，既に4チーム
に絞られており，その4チームがこれから質問に答える」という内容。cは誤りで
あり，eが正しい。参加したのは「15人のエンジニア」ではなく「15組のチーム」
なので，aは誤り。Johnは審査委員会の議長なのでbは誤り。また，「聴衆からの
質問に答える」とあるのでdも誤り。

(2) Which of the following is NOT one of the criteria for judging the competition?
コンペティションで審査を行う基準として正しくないのは，以下のうちどれか。

a) The bridge should become a symbol of the local area.
橋はその地域を象徴するものになるべきである。

b) Boats using the river must be able to pass beneath it.
川を走る船が橋の下を通れなければならない。

c) Cars and other vehicles must be able to use the bridge.
車や他の乗り物が橋を使えなければならない。

d) People with disabilities must be able to get on the bridge.
障害を持った人々が橋を使えなければならない。

e) The bridge must not have a significant impact on the lives of local people.
橋は地元民の生活に大きな影響を与えてはならない。

❷では審査の基準が述べられている。1.「歩行者と自転車通行者の両方に対応できる」，2.「船が航行するのに十分な頭上スペースがある」，3.「地域を特徴付けるような革新的で特色のあるデザイン」，4.「環境への影響は最小にとどめる」，5.「障害者差別禁止法に従う」の5つである。選択肢のaは3，bは2，dは5，eは4に該当する。cについては特に言及されていない。

(3) From the following illustrations, identify which is the suspension bridge and which is the cable-stayed bridge. Then, choose the correct match from the choices below.
次のイラストのうち，吊り橋と斜張橋を表したものはそれぞれどれか。正しい組み合わせの選択肢を選べ。

X 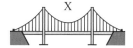　Y 　Z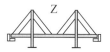

a) suspension bridge: X　　cable-stayed bridge: Y
　　吊り橋：X　　斜張橋：Y

b) suspension bridge: X　　cable-stayed bridge: Z
　　吊り橋：X　　斜張橋：Z

c) suspension bridge: Y　　cable-stayed bridge: X
　　吊り橋：Y　　斜張橋：X

d) suspension bridge: Z　　cable-stayed bridge: X
　　吊り橋：Z　　斜張橋：X

e) suspension bridge: Z　　cable-stayed bridge: Y
　　吊り橋：Z　　斜長橋：Y

suspension bridge（吊り橋）とcable-stayed bridge（斜張橋）の共通点，相違点については❹で説明されている。通行路をどのようにして吊っているかに決定的な違いがある。suspension bridgeでは，Smaller cables connect the roadway to the main cablesとあるように，メインケーブルから出た小さなケーブルで通行路を吊っているのに対し，cable-stayed bridgeではthe cables are attached directly to the towersとあるように，塔から直接ケーブルで通行路を吊っている。前者はX，後者はZのイラストが正しい。

(4) What criticism does Paul Mason make?
ポール・メイソンはどのような批判をしているか。

a) The tiles would not generate a useful amount of electricity.
　　タイルは役立つ程の量の電気を作り出さないだろう。

b) It would be impossible to cover the whole walkway in tiles.
　　タイルで歩道全体を覆うのは不可能だろう。

c) Covering the whole walkway in tiles would be too expensive.
　　歩道を全てタイルで覆うのはお金がかかりすぎるだろう。

194

d) The number of light bulbs Bluestone proposes to use is too low.
ブルーストーン社が使おうと提案している電球の数が少なすぎる。

e) The electric charge created by the crystals could be dangerous.
水晶によって作り出される電荷は危険かもしれない。

Bluestone Design Consultantsの案の「売り」の1つは, piezoelectric tiles（圧
電性物質タイル）を使用した, 通行人の歩行によって発電するシステムである。こ
れに対するPaulの批判とは, ❻でEven if you covered the entire walkway in
piezoelectric tiles, … wouldn't you struggle to power more than a few light
bulbs?とあるように,「2〜3個の電球を点灯させるくらいの電力しか得られない
のではないか」というものである。これが a に該当する。a few light bulbs（2〜
3個の電球）というのは, 電力が少ないことを表すために提示されているものであり,
電球の使用数を批判しているわけではないので d は誤り。また「（歩道を全てタイル
で覆うと）お金がかかる」ということは述べているが, コストそのものを問題とし
ているわけではないので c も誤り。

(5) What is one thing that we learn from this conversation?
この会話から分かることは何か。

a) Paul Mason believes that the Bluestone bridge is the best option.
ポール・メイソンはブルーストーン社の橋が最良の選択肢だと信じている。

b) John Hart outlined the main rules and requirements for the new bridge.
ジョン・ハートは新しい橋に関する主要なルールと条件の要点を述べた。

c) In terms of cost, a cable-stayed bridge is superior to a suspension bridge.
費用の点では, 斜張橋は吊り橋より優れている。

d) The width of the River Redmond means the bridge will have to be unusually
long.
レッドモンド川の幅に沿うには, 橋が通常よりも長くなくてはならない。

e) Amanda Hamilton does not know the difference between cable-stayed and
suspension bridges.
アマンダ・ハミルトンは斜張橋と吊り橋の違いを分かっていない。

放送文全体を対象とした設問である。Paul MasonはBluestoneのデザインに対し
てむしろ懐疑的なので a は誤り。b は❶❷でのJohnの説明と合致する。これが正
しい。橋の長さについての言及はないので d は正解とは言えない。2つの橋の違い
を説明しているのがAmanda自身なので e は誤り。

Set 8-C | 放送文

Bridge Design 2

❶ Amanda: Yes, I would be happy to respond to Mr. Mason's point about the piezoelectric tiles. The tiles will be supplied and installed by a local start-up called People Power. It specializes in what is known as microgeneration, the small-scale production of electricity using alternative sources of energy such as solar and wind power. The company will also provide solar panels for the side of the roadway. The majority of the energy required by the lights and other electrical equipment on the bridge will be sourced from these panels, and the piezoelectric tiles will make a contribution, but just a minor one. Of course, cloudy conditions or reduced pedestrian traffic could result in a shortfall, so energy will be drawn from the regular electricity grid when necessary in order to keep the lights illuminated constantly during the hours of darkness.

❷ However, I think the important point about the tiles is not the amount of electricity they generate, but rather the additional benefits they bring. My colleague Tim Andrews can give you some more details about that.

❸ Tim: Thank you, Amanda. Well, the tiles will be placed along the pedestrian walkways on each side of the bridge. People Power has built software into the tiles that records every footstep in real time. …

❹ John: Excuse me for interrupting, but could you be brief? We are short of time, and I want to get back to the structure of the bridge.

❺ Tim: Certainly. Well, the tiles are connected to a number of low-energy electronic applications on the bridge, including signs, vending machines, and advertising displays. When no one is near one of these applications, it shuts down automatically and only powers up again when someone approaches. This results in considerable savings in electricity consumption. What is more, the software would

start-up 图 新興企業

microgeneration 图 マイクロ発電
alternative sources of energy 句 代替エネルギー源

shortfall 图 不足

📌 Amandaの発言の主旨：
橋の電力供給は太陽光発電や通常の電力供給網からなされる。piezoelectric tiles による電力供給はわずかしかない

considerable 形 かなりの
consumption 图 消費

enable us to compile detailed statistics showing how many people use the bridge at different times of day and even how long people spend at certain points. We could pass this data on to businesses to help them decide when and where to place advertisements.

❻John: Thank you, Mr. Andrews. You and Ms. Hamilton have provided a convincing explanation of the environmental and commercial benefits of the microgeneration aspect of your design. Questions remain over the cost, though. As I understand it, the work that People Power will do accounts for 5 percent of the initial budget. Since the bridge would provide a showcase for their products, it seems possible that you could persuade the company to revise its estimate downwards. Now, I want to return to the structure of the bridge. As we know, the weather conditions along this part of the river are normally good, but there are sometimes strong winds during certain times of year. Can you assure us that the bridge will be safe to use in all weather conditions?

❼Amanda: Compared to suspension bridges, cable-stayed bridges are less vulnerable to high winds. Nevertheless, there might be occasions when the wind causes the cables to vibrate in a way that leads to excessive movement of the roadway. One important safety feature of our design is the large number of sensors attached at various points to the bridge's cables. These detect vibration and transmit information wirelessly to a central computer. Based on this information, officials could prevent access to the bridge promptly should it become necessary to do so.

❽John: I see. Thank you very much for your answers. Let's take a break now before we turn our attention to the next design.

---

compile 他 …を集める
statistics 名 統計
⚓piezoelectric tiles の役割：1. 歩行者の有無を感知し，不要な電気機器の使用を止めることで節電できる。2. 歩行データを集め，広告設置の参考にできる

convincing 形 説得力のある
commercial 形 商業的な

account for … 句 …を占める
initial 形 初期の
showcase 名 展示する場

revise 他 …を修正する
estimate 名 見積もり
⚓John の発言の主旨：People Power 社にとっては自社製品の宣伝の場になるのだから，もっとコストを抑えるよう要求できるはずだ
assure 他 …に保証する

vulnerable to … 句 …に対して弱い

vibrate 自 揺れる，振動する

detect 他 …を検出する，感知する
transmit 他 …を送信する
promptly 副 即座に
⚓Amanda の発言の主旨：強風によって橋が揺れた場合は，ケーブルに取り付けられたセンサーが揺れを検知して情報を中央に送り，交通を止める措置がとられる

Set 8-C ｜ 放送文の日本語訳

橋のデザイン 2

❶アマンダ：はい，圧電性物質タイルについてのメイソン氏の指摘に喜んでお答えします。このタイルは，ピープル・パワーという名前の地元の新興企業によって供給され，取り付けられます。この企業は，マイクロ発電として知られる，太陽光や風力等の代替エネルギー源を使った小規模な発電を専門としています。この企業はまた，通行路の脇に太陽光パネルを供給します。橋の上の照明やその他の電気設備が必要とするエネルギーの大部分はそれらのパネルから供給され，圧電性物質タイルも貢献はしますが，その役割は小さなものです。もちろん，天候が曇りがちだったり歩行者が減少したりすれば電力不足を招くので，必要な時には，夜間に照明を点け続けられるように通常の電力供給網からもエネルギーを使用します。

❷　しかしながら，このタイルについて重要な点は，それらが生み出す電気の量ではなく，そこからもたらされる他の利益にあると思うのです。同僚のティム・アンドリューズが，これについてもっと詳しくお話しします。

❸ティム：アマンダ，どうもありがとう。そうですね，タイルは橋の両側の歩行者用通路に沿って設置されます。ピープル・パワー社は全ての足跡をリアルタイムで記録するソフトウェアをタイルに埋め込みました……。

❹ジョン：遮ってすみませんが，簡潔にお願いできますか。時間が足りませんし，橋の構造の話にも戻りたいので。

❺ティム：もちろんです。さて，タイルは，標識や自動販売機や広告看板を含む橋の上のいくつかの低エネルギー電子アプリケーションに繋がっています。こうしたアプリケーションのいずれの近くにも人がいない時には自動的に電源が切れて，誰かが近付いた時にだけ再び電源が入ります。これは，かなりの電力消費の抑制に繋がります。さらにこのソフトウェアは，1日のうちの異なる時間帯にどれだけの人が橋を利用するか，特定の場所でどれだけの時間を過ごすかまでも示す詳細な統計データを集めることを可能にしてくれるのです。私たちはこのデータを企業に提供して，いつどこに広告を設置すべきかを決める手助けをすることもできるでしょう。

❻ジョン：ありがとうございます，アンドリューズさん。あなたとハミルトンさんは，あなた方のデザインのマイクロ発電という側面における環境面，及び商業的な利益について説得力のある説明を提供してくれました。しかし，コストに関する疑問は残っています。私が理解する限り，ピープル・パワー社が行う業務は初期予算の5パーセントを占めています。この橋が彼らの製品にとっての展示場となるでしょうから，見積もりを下方修正するように説得してもらうことは可能であるように思えます。さて，橋の構造に戻りたいと思います。ご存じの通り，この辺りの川沿いの気象条件は通常穏やかですが，1年のうち特定の時期には時々強風が吹きますね。あらゆる気象条件のもとで，橋を利用することが安全であると保証できますか。

❼アマンダ：吊り橋と比べて，斜張橋は強風に対しての脆弱性が低いのです。それで

もなお，風によっては，通行路を過度に動かすほどケーブルが揺れる場合もある
かもしれません。私たちのデザインにおいては，重要な安全策の1つとして，橋の
ケーブルの様々な箇所に多数のセンサーを付けています。センサーが揺れを感知
して，情報を中央コンピュータに無線で送ります。この情報に基づいて，必要と
なった場合は，職員が橋への交通を即座に止めることができるのです。

❽ジョン：分かりました。答えをありがとうございました。次のデザインに目を向け
る前に，ここで休憩をとりましょう。

《 指針 》

Bの質疑応答の続きである。前半はBで話題に出た piezoelectric tiles
を設置する意義について，後半は強風に対する橋の耐性について語られて
いる。(4)のように，発言の具体的な内容ではなく，発言同士の関係性を
問う問題に注意したい。

難易度

放送文	★★★
設 問	★★★
総 合	★★★

☺☹))) スピーカー情報

Amanda: 西海岸，カリフォルニア
Tim: 中西部，ミズーリ
John: 西海岸，カリフォルニア

Set 8-C 設問解説

(1) What does Amanda say about the lights on the bridge?
橋の照明についてアマンダが述べていることは何か。

a) They will be powered partly by wind energy.
照明は一部風力エネルギーによって作動する。

b) They will be powered mainly by solar energy.
照明は主に太陽光エネルギーによって作動する。

c) They will not be connected to the electricity grid.
照明は電力供給網とは繋がれない。

d) They will not use electricity from the piezoelectric tiles.
照明は圧電性物質タイルからの電気を利用しない。

e) They will be installed by a company called People Power.
照明はピープル・パワーという企業によって設置される。

❶の内容についての問題。「橋での電力供給は主に太陽光によってまかなわれ，通常の電力供給網からも一部供給される。piezoelectric tilesによる発電はごく一部にすぎない」という内容から，bが正解で，a，c，dが誤りだと分かる。eはやや紛らわしいが，People Power社が設置するのは照明ではなく，piezoelectric tilesやsolar panels等の発電機器であるので，誤り。

(2) What does Tim Andrews say about the new tiles?
新しいタイルについてティム・アンドリューズが述べていることは何か。

a) People will not be allowed to walk on them.
人々がタイルの上を歩くことは許可されない。

b) Engineers have failed to produce them cheaply enough.
エンジニアたちはタイルを十分に安く製造することができなかった。

c) His team has already sold many of them to other businesses.
彼のチームは既にタイルの多くを他の企業に販売した。

d) They use software that can track the number of bridge users.
橋の利用者の数を記録できるソフトウェアを使用している。

e) The applications will shut down automatically when the energy from the tiles fails.
タイルからのエネルギーが不足するとアプリケーションは自動的に停止する。

piezoelectric tilesが果たす役割についての説明は❺でなされている。「歩行者の有無を感知し，不要な電気機器の使用を止めることで節電できる」「歩行データを集め，広告設置の参考にできる」という2点がポイント。このうち後者がdに該当する。bの費用に関する指摘は，この後でJohnによってなされる。電気機器がシャットダウンするのは「歩行者がいない場合」であり，「エネルギーが不足した場合」ではないのでeは誤り。また，「集めた歩行データを広告主に渡す」ということは言われているが，cのように「タイルを他の企業に販売した」という事実は語られていない。

(3) What opinion does John give about the microgeneration aspect of the Bluestone design?
ジョンはブルーストーン社のデザインにおけるマイクロ発電の側面に関してどのような意見を表明しているか。

a) The cost of installing low-energy applications is too high.
低エネルギーのアプリケーションを設置するコストが高すぎる。

b) Advertisers are unlikely to need the data the software will gather.
広告主たちが，ソフトウェアが収集するデータを必要とすることはありそうもない。

c) The environmental advantages are not as great as Bluestone claims.
環境面での利点は，ブルーストーン社が主張するほど優れていない。

d) People Power might be willing to supply the equipment more cheaply.
ピープル・パワー社はもっと安い値段で設備を供給しようとするかもしれない。

e) The cost of the project will be higher than what People Power estimates.
プロジェクトのコストはピープル・パワー社が見積もるよりも高くつくだろう。

タイル設置についての問題点の指摘は❻でなされている。「設置を請け負うPeople Power社にとっては，自社の製品を宣伝する絶好の機会となるのだから，コストをもっと抑えるように要求できるのではないか」という内容である。これに合致するdが正解。Johnが問題にしているのは「タイルを設置するコスト」であり「low-energy applicationsを設置するコスト」ではないので，aは誤り。

(4) How does Amanda respond to John's final question?
ジョンの最後の質問にアマンダはどのように応答しているか。

a) She dismisses the question as "unrealistic."
その質問を「非現実的だ」としてはねつけている。

b) She provides John with the assurance that he asked for.
ジョンが求めた保証を与えている。

c) She changes the subject to avoid answering the question.
質問に答えることを避けるために話題を変えている。

d) She denies that the wind will cause vibration in the cables.
風がケーブルの揺れに影響することを否定している。

e) She admits that the bridge might have to be closed sometimes.
時々は橋を閉鎖しなければならないかもしれないことを認めている。

「強風があった場合でも橋は安全に使用できるのか」というJohnの質問に対して，Amandaは❼で「cable-stayed bridgeは風に対して強いが，それでも激しく揺れる場合はある。その時はケーブルに設置したセンサーが揺れの情報をセンターに送り，即座に交通を止める等の措置をとることが可能だ」という返答をしている。「安全に使用できるか」という問いに対して「使用できなくなることもある」と答えているわけだから，bではなくeが正解となる。

(5) Which of the following statements is true?
以下の説明のうち正しいものはどれか。

a) John is not convinced by Tim's comments about the tiles.
ジョンはタイルについてのティムのコメントに納得していない。

b) John doubts that Amanda's team will win the competition.
ジョンはアマンダのチームはコンペで優勝しないと思っている。

c) John is eager to focus on the structure of the bridge design.
ジョンは橋のデザインの構造の問題に焦点を当てたがっている。

d) Tim and Amanda are no longer working on the bridge project.
ティムとアマンダはもはや橋のプロジェクトに関わっていない。

e) Tim and Amanda's explanation is the best the panel has heard.
ティムとアマンダの説明は委員会が聞いたうち最良のものである。

放送文全体に関わる問題である。❹の I want to get back to the structure of the bridge や❻の Now, I want to return to the structure of the bridge. から，John は橋の構造を話題の中心にしようとしていることが分かる。c が正解。John は費用については疑問を抱いているものの，❻で You and Ms. Hamilton have provided a convincing explanation と言っていることから，a は誤り。

Set 9 | 解答

9A	(1) e	(2) d	(3) b	(4) d	(5) e
9B	(1) c	(2) d	(3) e	(4) e	(5) d
9C	(1) d	(2) d	(3) c	(4) c	(5) b

Set 9-A | 放送文

Drones

❶ Host: Good afternoon, and thank you all for joining us for this week's distinguished author interview. We will be continuing our ongoing series of discussions about military technology. Today I am interviewing author David Powell, who recently published a new book entitled *More Than a Weapon: Peaceful Applications of Unmanned Aircraft*. Please welcome Mr. Powell to the stage.

❷ Powell: Thank you very much. It's a pleasure to be here.

❸ Host: Mr. Powell, I'd like to start by asking what motivated you to write this book.

❹ Powell: When most people talk about unmanned aircraft, they usually discuss military applications, such as the hundreds of drone strikes the United States has made in the Middle East within the past decade. A great deal of international focus has been directed on these attacks, and I felt as if the drone technology itself was being held responsible for these attacks in some way. I wanted to remind readers that drone technology is a tool with a wide variety of uses, and a tool is entirely subject to the whims of the people who use it, for better or worse.

❺ Host: And you think that those peaceful applications deserve more attention.

❻ Powell: Absolutely. Most drones are not being used for military applications at all, but we rarely discuss those peaceful uses. I think there are three primary objectives that drones can accomplish better than humans: transporting objects quickly and directly, retrieving information from an aerial perspective, and reaching areas that humans

---

distinguished 形 著名な
ongoing 形 現在進行中の

unmanned 形 無人の

drone 名 無人機，ドローン

hold ... responsible 句 …に責任があるとみなす
be subject to ... 句 …の影響を受けやすい
whim 名 思いつき，気まぐれ
for better or worse 句 良くも悪くも

📕本を書いた狙い：ドローンの軍事利用ばかりに注目が集まっている風潮に対し，他の平和的利用法があるという事実を広めたかった

objective 名 目標，目的
retrieve 他 …を回収する，収集する
aerial 形 空の，空中の

cannot.

❼ Host: Could you provide us with some examples of these applications?

❽ Powell: Of course. Drones have been used to deliver a number of items for various companies, including things like pizza, groceries, and medicine, without regard for traffic or other obstacles. As for retrieving information, drones, like airplanes and satellites, are excellent at conducting surveillance and finding targets from the sky. Although this clearly has military applications, it is also useful for land surveying, climate observation, and searches for missing persons, among other things.

❾ Host: I see. And what about the drones' ability to reach areas that humans cannot?

❿ Powell: Unlike humans, drones, even expensive models, are replaceable. Drones can withstand extreme heat or cold, radioactivity, and extreme winds. If a drone is shot down or blown up, the only losses are financial. Drones expand our ability to explore by opening up the dangerous places where humans cannot go.

⓫ Host: Interesting point. Now, your book talks about two major categories of drones, in terms of human influence and control. What are those categories?

⓬ Powell: Unmanned aircraft can be classified as either autonomous or remote-controlled, based on how much direction they receive from a human pilot. A remote-controlled drone is fairly self-explanatory; it is controlled entirely by a human with some kind of remote control. Autonomous drones are pre-programmed to pilot themselves based on their surroundings.

⓭ Host: But there are some legal issues with autonomous drones, right?

⓮ Powell: Yes. Using an autonomous drone is still illegal in most jurisdictions because they can malfunction and cannot be easily reprogrammed or redirected while in flight. However, they have non-military applications as well, and I think we will begin to explore those applications in the coming years.

⓯ Host: Well, I'll be fascinated to see how things progress. We need to take a short break now, but the

---

🔧 ドローンの3つの利用目的：1. ものを速く直接運搬する，2. 上空から情報を収集する，3. 人間が行けないところに行く

without regard for … 句 …を気にせずに
obstacle 名 障害物
satellite 名 人工衛星
surveillance 名 監視，調査

land surveying 句 土地測量
among other things 句 特に

replaceable 形 取り替え可能な
withstand 他 …に耐える
radioactivity 名 放射能
blow up 句 …を爆破する

autonomous 形 自律的な

self-explanatory 形 自明の

🔧 2種類のドローン：自律的なものと遠隔操作によるもの

jurisdiction 名 法的管轄区域
malfunction 自 誤作動する

204

audience will be able to ask their own questions after we return.

Set 9-A ｜放送文の日本語訳

ドローン

❶司会：こんにちは。今週の注目の著者へのインタビューにご参加いただき，ありがとうございます。軍事技術についての議論をシリーズで行っていますが，引き続きこのテーマです。本日お迎えしたのはデービッド・パウエルさんです。ご著書『武器を超えて──無人飛行機の平和利用』を出されたばかりです。パウエルさんをステージにお迎えしましょう。

❷パウエル：ありがとうございます。お招きいただいて光栄です。

❸司会：パウエルさん，まず始めに，この本を書こうと思われたきっかけをお話しいただけますか。

❹パウエル：人々が無人飛行機について話す時，たいてい軍事利用についての議論になります。たとえば，この10年以内に合衆国が中東で行ったドローンによる何百回という攻撃等です。国際的な関心の大部分がこうした攻撃に向けられており，私は，ドローン技術自体がそうした攻撃の責任の一端を負わされているような気がしました。ドローン技術は様々に使える1個の道具にすぎず，道具は，良くも悪くも，それを使用する人間の思いつき次第でどうにでもなるものなのだということを人々に思い出してもらいたいと思ったわけです。

❺司会：そして，様々な平和的な利用法も，もっと注目されてしかるべきだと思われたのですね。

❻パウエル：その通りです。ドローンのほとんどは軍事利用とは全く無縁ですが，私たちがそのような平和利用について議論することはほとんどありません。私は，ドローンが人間より首尾よく遂行することのできる主な目的が3つあると思います。ものを迅速かつ直接的に運搬する，上空の視点から情報を収集する，人間が行くことのできない場所に行く，この3つです。

❼司会：そうした利用法の例を挙げていただけますか。

❽パウエル：もちろんです。ドローンは様々な企業のために，ピザ，食料雑貨，薬等いくつかの品物を，交通量やその他の障害を気にせず配達するのに利用されています。情報収集について言えば，ドローンは飛行機や人工衛星と同様に，上空から監視したり，目標物を発見したりするのに優れています。これは明らかに軍事的に利用することもできますが，それはまた，特に土地の測量，気候観測，行方不明者の捜索に役立っています。

❾司会：なるほど。では，ドローンの，人間が行くことのできない場所に行く能力についてはいかがですか。

❿パウエル：人間とは違って，いかに高価なモデルであってもドローンは替えが利きます。ドローンは，極度の高温あるいは低温，放射能，極度の風速にも耐えられます。ドローンが撃ち落とされたり，爆破されたりしたとしても，損害は金銭的なものでしかありません。ドローンは，人間が行くことのできない危険な場所へ

の道を開くことで，人類の探査の能力を拡大しています。

⓫司会：興味深い点ですね。さて，ご著書には，人間の影響と制御という観点からのドローンの主要な2分類についての議論があります。それはどのような分類なのでしょうか。

⓬パウエル：無人飛行機は，人間の操縦士からどれだけ命令を受け取るかに応じて，自律的なものか遠隔操作によるものかに分けることができます。遠隔操作のドローン，これはほとんど自明ですね。何らかの遠隔操作を通じて，1人の人間によって完全に制御されているものです。自律的ドローンは，周囲の状況に応じて自らを導くことができるよう予めプログラムされているものです。

⓭司会：しかし，自律的ドローンには法的問題があるのですよね。

⓮パウエル：そうなんです。ほとんどの法的管轄区域において，自律的ドローンの使用は依然として違法です。誤作動を起こす可能性がありますし，飛行中にプログラムや方向を変更することが容易ではないからです。しかしながら，自律的ドローンは非軍事的に利用することも可能なので，今後私たちはそうした利用法を探求していくことになると思います。

⓯司会：そうですね。今後の進展を楽しみにしたいと思います。ではここで一旦休憩をはさんで，そのあと，観客の皆さんからのご質問をお受けします。

《《 指針 》》

テーマとなっている「ドローン(drone)」という言葉は，無人の航空機を指すものとして日本でもある程度は定着している。放送文中では unmanned aircraft とほぼ同義で使われている。インタビューのトピックは，「本を書いた目的」「ドローンの3つの目的」「2種類のドローン」の3つであり，いずれも平易な英語で説明されているので，聞き取りに苦労する箇所は少ないはずである。

難易度

放送文　★☆☆

設　問　★☆☆

総　合　★☆☆

☺☺))) スピーカー情報

Host: 西海岸，カリフォルニア
Powell: イングランド

206

Set 9-A | 設問解説

(1) Why did Mr. Powell decide to write his book about drones?
パウエル氏はどうしてドローンについての本を書くことにしたのか。

 a）He wanted the military to stop using drone technology altogether.
　軍にドローン技術の使用を完全にやめてほしいと考えた。

 b）He thought that drone technology could be redesigned for military use.
　ドローン技術は軍事利用に向けて再設計できると考えた。

 c）He felt that drone technology was being used for too many military applications.
　ドローン技術が軍事目的に利用されすぎていると感じた。

 d）He wanted the drone technology to be used in many ways, not just for military purposes.
　ドローン技術を軍事的な目的だけでなく多方面で利用してもらいたいと考えた。

 e）He wanted to draw people's attention to the non-military applications of drone technology.
　ドローン技術の非軍事利用に対して人々の注目を喚起したいと思った。

本を書いた動機については❹から❻にかけて説明されている。「ドローンの話題になると、ほとんどの人は軍事利用について話す。実際には他の平和的な利用があることを分かってほしかった」というものである。これに合致するeが正解。Powellが正したいと思ったのは、人々の偏った見方であり、実際の使用における偏りではないので、cやdは誤り。

(2) Which of the following is NOT mentioned as something drones can do better than humans?
次のうち、ドローンが人間より上手に行うことができることとして言及されていないものはどれか。

 a）Drones can withstand extreme heat or cold.
　ドローンは極度の高温や低温に耐えることができる。

 b）Drones can reach areas that humans cannot.
　ドローンは人間が行くことのできない場所に行くことができる。

 c）Drones can transport objects quickly and directly.
　ドローンはものを迅速かつ直接的に運搬することができる。

 d）Drones can receive and interpret electronic signals.
　ドローンは電子信号を受信し解読することができる。

 e）Drones can retrieve information from an aerial perspective.
　ドローンは上空の視点から情報を収集することができる。

ドローンが人間に優る3つの点については❻で述べられている。「ものを速く直接運搬できる」「上空から情報を収集できる」「人が行けないところにも行くことができる」の3つであり、それぞれc、e、aとbに該当する。dについての言及はない。

(3) Which of the following uses of drones does Mr. Powell mention?
次のドローンの利用法のうちパウエル氏が言及しているのはどれか。

a) Planting seeds
種まき

b) Surveying land
土地の測量

c) Watering crops
作物への散水

d) Spreading fertilizer
肥料の散布

e) Investigating crimes
犯罪捜査

❽のit is also useful for land surveyingという発言からｂを正解とする。その他の選択肢についての言及はない。

(4) In terms of human influence, what are the two classifications of unmanned aircraft?
人間の影響という観点において，無人飛行機の2分類とはどのようなものか。

a) intelligent and automatic
インテリジェントとオートマチック

b) semi-automatic and full-automatic
半自動と全自動

c) programmable and self-controlling
プログラム可能とセルフコントロール

d) remote-controlled and autonomous
遠隔操作と自律的

e) directly-controlled and artificially-controlled
直接的制御と人工的制御

❿のUnmanned aircraft can be classified as either autonomous or remote-controlledから，ｄが正解だと分かる。

(5) Which of the following statements would Mr. Powell most likely agree with?
次の主張のうち，パウエル氏が最も賛成しそうなのはどれか。

a) Drones should be used only for military purposes.
ドローンは軍事的な目的だけに使われるべきだ。

b) Drones are useful for peaceful applications but not military applications.
ドローンは平和利用には役立つが，軍事利用には役立たない。

c) Drones will replace humans in almost every military and peaceful application.
ドローンは，軍事利用と平和利用のほとんど全てについて，人間に取って代わるだろう。

d) Drones should only be used for peaceful applications and never for military purposes.
ドローンは平和目的にのみ使用されるべきであり，決して軍事目的に使用されてはならない。

e) Drones can be used as effective weaponry but also have important peaceful applications.
ドローンは効果的な兵器として使用され得るが，重要な平和的利用法もある。

❹や❻で明らかにされているように，Powellがこの本によって伝えたかったのは，「ドローンには軍事以外の利用法がある」ということである。軍事，平和的利用のどちらかに賛成あるいは反対するといった立場は表明していない。eが正解である。

Set 9-B | 放送文

Identity 1

❶ Science is capable of addressing many important philosophical questions about the nature of reality, yet it struggles with concepts that defy physical explanation. Scientists prefer measurable quantities, repeatable experiments, and easily-defined concepts over abstract metaphysical problems. For example, the physical behavior of light has been well established through many centuries of scientific experimentation, but the nature of light itself remains almost impossible to describe.

❷ Another problem that escapes scientific explanation is the concept of human identity. At first, the concept seems simple to define because it is so integral to our daily lives. Names, faces, voices, and personalities all come together to produce our unique identities. The ability to recognize these features is so central to human nature that the inability to comprehend human identity is a sign of severe mental disability or psychosis.

❸ Beneath the surface, however, the scientific concept of identity is much harder to define. The human body is a physical construct composed of various atoms and molecules, so the simplest answer would be to define a human being as a collection of physical matter. Although this definition seems intuitive, it falls apart almost immediately.

❹ All of the matter within the human body is replaced every seven years, and some of that matter, such as the food in one's stomach and the air in one's lungs, is replaced even more frequently, from day to day or even minute to minute. Does that matter become part of one's identity for that time, or is it just passing through? In other words, does every breath or meal alter one's identity? Most people, including scientists, would suggest otherwise.

❺ This paradox has been debated by philosophers since antiquity. The ancient Greeks discussed the

address 他 …に取り組む

struggle with … 句 …に苦労する
defy 他 …に反抗する，を拒む
abstract 形 抽象的な
metaphysical 形 形而上的な
🔖発言の主旨：科学では説明できない概念がある
be integral to 句 …にとって不可欠な，と一体化している
human nature 句 人間の性質
comprehend 他 …を理解する
mental disability 句 精神障害
psychosis 名 精神病
🔖仮説1：自己同一性は，物理的物質の集合体によって決まる
construct 名 構造物
composed of … 句 …から成る
atom 名 原子
molecule 名 分子
intuitive 形 直感的な，直感で理解できる
fall apart 句 崩壊する

🔖仮説1の反証：人間の体内にある物質は絶えず入れ替わっている

alter 他 …を変える

paradox 名 矛盾，逆説
antiquity 名 古代

Ship of Theseus, a ship where each individual piece is replaced over time, and debated whether it could still be called the same ship.

❻ For humans, the question is this: If nothing is left of your original body, are you really the same person? The intuitive answer is yes. Therefore, if physical matter does not define one's identity, then what does? Body structure is another clear possibility, because the structure of an adult's body remains largely the same in the short term.

❼ However, aging induces a wide variety of changes from infancy to adulthood to old age. In fact, it is impossible to find a physical or biological characteristic that does not change, even the ones we consider permanent. The skeleton becomes weakened by calcium loss, the weight and structure of the brain gradually change with age, and even DNA mutates and becomes altered by retroviruses. Every physical attribute is temporary and subject to change.

❽ Even the most steadfast rationalist has to concede that identity cannot be explained purely as a physical phenomenon. Therefore, there must be something more abstract at work.

❾ One comparison we can make is to a computer program, an immaterial collection of instructions and procedures that are carried out on a physical medium. In a way, software is a kind of pattern, reproducible by physical hardware without being physical itself.

❿ If the human body is hardware, then identity might be a kind of abstract software that defines and controls it, running constantly despite the tiny, continuous changes in its hardware. Although human identity is clearly more sophisticated than any piece of software humans have yet created, science may someday simulate human identity with a program that could almost be called human despite its man-made hardware.

⓫ In the meantime, the human body is the only "machine" capable of containing human identity, although that "machine" still seems to be more than the sum of its physical parts.

⬛仮説2：自己同一性は，体の構造によって決まる

induce 他 …を誘発する，引き起こす

permanent 形 永久的な
skeleton 名 骨格
mutate 自 変異する
retrovirus 名 レトロウィルス
attribute 名 特質
⬛仮説2の反証：体の構造は年齢とともに変わる
steadfast 形 確固たる，不動の
rationalist 名 合理主義者
concede that … 句 …と認める，譲歩する
at work 句 作用している
⬛新たな説：自己同一性と身体の関係はコンピュータのソフトウェアとハードウェアの関係に類似している

sophisticated 形 洗練された
simulate 他 …を模倣する，シミュレーションする

in the meantime 句 その一方で

sum 名 合計

Set 9-B | 放送文の日本語訳

自己同一性 1

❶ 　科学は，現実の本質についての多くの重要な哲学的問いに取り組むことができます。しかし，物理的な説明を拒むような概念に取り組むのには苦労します。科学者は，抽象的な形而上的問題よりも，計測可能な量，反復可能な実験，定義が容易な概念を好みます。たとえば，光の物理的な作用は何世紀にもわたる科学実験を通して実証されていますが，光そのものの本質はほとんど説明することが不可能です。

❷ 　科学的に説明できないもう1つの問題は，人間の自己同一性という概念です。はじめ，この概念は容易に定義できるように思えます。私たちの毎日の生活にあまりにも一体化しているからです。名前，顔，声，性格の全てが一緒になって，私たちの自己同一性を生み出しています。これらの特徴を認識する能力は人間の性質にとって極めて中心的なものであり，人間の自己同一性を理解できないことは深刻な精神障害か精神病の兆候となるほどです。

❸ 　しかし，深く考えると，自己同一性の科学的概念は，定義することがはるかに難しいものです。人間の肉体は，様々な原子や分子から成り立つ物理的な構築物であり，それゆえ最も単純な答えは，人間の存在を物理的物質の集合として定義することでしょう。この定義は直感的に思えますが，ほぼ即座に破綻してしまいます。

❹ 　人体の中の物質は7年ごとに全て入れ替わり，胃の中の食べ物や肺の中の空気等，一部の物質はより頻繁に，毎日，あるいは毎分のペースでさえも入れ替わっていきます。こうした物質はその間にも自己同一性の一部となるのか，それともただ単に通り過ぎていくだけなのか？　言い換えると，あらゆる息や食物が，人の自己同一性を変化させるのでしょうか？　科学者を含むたいていの人々が，そうではないと言うでしょう。

❺ 　この矛盾は，古代から哲学者たちによって議論されてきました。古代ギリシャ人は，個々の部品が徐々に入れ替えられる船，「テーセウスの船」について議論し，それでも同じ船と呼べるのかどうかを討議しました。

❻ 　人間については，次のような疑問になるでしょう。もともとの肉体から残っているものが何もないとしたら，それでも本当に同じ人間なのだろうか？　直感的な答えは「イエス」です。そうすると，物理的な物質が人の自己同一性を決めないとして，では何がそれを決めるのでしょうか？　体の構造というのが，もう1つの明快な可能性です。なぜなら，成人の体の構造は，短い期間においては大部分が同じままだからです。

❼ 　しかし，年齢を重ねることによって，幼児から大人，そして老齢まで，様々な変化が引き起こされます。実際，変化のない物理的もしくは生物的な特徴を見つけることは不可能なのです。私たちがいつまでも変わらないと思っている特徴でさえも。骨格はカルシウムを失うことで弱くなり，脳の重さや構造も年齢とともに徐々に変化し，DNAさえもレトロウィルスによって変異したり変化したりします。あらゆる物理的な特質は，一時的なものであり変化するものなのです。

❽　どんなに揺るぎない合理主義者であっても，自己同一性は純粋に物理的な現象としては説明できないと認めざるを得ません。それゆえ，もっと抽象的な何かが作用しているに違いないのです。

❾　我々が相似を見出せる対象のひとつが，コンピュータプログラムです。コンピュータプログラムは，物理的なメディア上で実行される非物質的な命令と手続きの集合です。ある意味で，ソフトウェアというのは一種のパターンであり，それ自体が物理的になることなく，物理的なハードウェアによって復元可能なものです。

❿　人間の肉体がハードウェアであるなら，自己同一性は，体を特徴付けてコントロールする一種の抽象的なソフトウェアであり，ハードウェアが継続的に小さく変化しても常に作動し続けています。人間の自己同一性の方が，これまでに人間が生み出したいかなるソフトウェアよりも洗練されているのは明らかですが，科学もいつの日か，ハードウェアは人の手によるものであっても，ほとんど人間と呼べるようなプログラムによって，自己同一性をシミュレーションするかもしれません。

⓫　その一方で，人間の体は人間の自己同一性を内包することができる唯一の「機械」ということになります。その「機械」にしても，物理的な部品の合計以上のものであるように思えるのですが。

《 指針 》

identityは「自己同一性」と訳されるが，カタカナで「アイデンティティ」と言った方が分かりやすいだろうか。「ある人が，その人たる所以」というような意味であり，たとえば「今の私」が，肉体的にも精神的にも異なる「10年前の私」と同じ人物であると言えるのはなぜだろうか，という素朴な疑問に端を発するものである。放送文では，「自己同一性とは何か」について2つの仮説を紹介し，それを1つずつ反証した上で，教授自身による新しい説を紹介している。それぞれの仮説の問題点は何か，そして教授の説はどのようにしてその問題点を克服しているのかに注目して聞き取ろう。

難易度

放送文	★★☆
設　問	★★☆
総　合	★★☆

☺☺))) スピーカー情報

Professor: 西海岸，カリフォルニア

Set 9-B | 設問解説

(1) The professor mentions light
　教授が光に言及したのは……
　a) as a contrast to human identity.
　　人間の自己同一性と対照的なものとしてである。
　b) as an example of something that cannot be measured.
　　計測することができないものの例としてである。
　c) as an example of what science cannot explain completely.
　　科学では完全に説明できないことの例としてである。
　d) as an abstract concept which is almost impossible to define.
　　ほとんど定義することが不可能な抽象的な概念としてである。
　e) as a physical phenomenon that has long been a controversial issue among
　　scientists.
　　科学者たちの間で昔から物議をかもしている物理的現象としてである。

　❶では，「自己同一性」というテーマへの導入として，「科学では説明できない抽象
概念」について述べられ，その一例として「光」が挙げられている。「光の物理的
作用」は科学的に説明できても，より抽象的な「光の本質」は説明するのが不可能
である，という文脈である。ｃが正解。ここでは「定義できるか否か」ではなく
「科学的に説明できるか否か」が問題とされているので，ｄは誤り。また，この問題
が昔から物議をかもしているということも述べられていないので，ｅも誤り。

(2) According to the professor, the definition of personal identity as a collection of
　physical matter is problematic because
　教授によれば，物理的な物質の集合として個人の自己同一性を定義することには問題があ
　る。なぜなら……
　a) twins look identical but have separate identities.
　　双子は同一に見えるが，それぞれの自己同一性を持っているから。
　b) people with artificial limbs retain their personal identity.
　　人工的な手足を持った人々も個人的な自己同一性を保っているから。
　c) the human spirit is also an important component of identity.
　　人間の精神もまた，重要な自己同一性の構成要素だから。
　d) the components of the human body are replaced continuously.
　　人間の体の構成要素は絶えず入れ替わるから。
　e) the human body and mind are so closely interrelated that one cannot be
　　separated from the other.
　　人間の肉体と精神は相互に密接に関係しあっているため，一方を他方と分けることはで
　　きないから。

　❸では，自己同一性の定義として「a collection of physical matter（物理的物質
の集合）である」という仮説が立てられ，これが❹で反証される。その根拠は，All

of the matter within the human body is replaced every seven years とある
ように、「人体の物質はどんどん入れ替わるものであるから」である。これを表した
d が正解。

(3) Which similarity between the Ship of Theseus and the human body does the
professor highlight?
教授が強調した「テーセウスの船」と人間の体の類似点はどれか。

a) They both deteriorate as they age.
どちらも年を経ると劣化する。

b) They are both composed from many different parts.
どちらも多くの異なる部分から成り立っている。

c) They both undergo changes in appearance with the passage of time.
どちらも時間の経過とともに外見が変化する。

d) They are both subjects that people have debated since ancient times.
どちらも古代から議論されてきた主題である。

e) They both contain different physical matter at different points in time.
どちらも異なる時には異なる物理的物質を含んでいる。

「テーセウスの船」と人間の体の類似点については❺❻で説明されている。この船は、
個々の部品が次々に取り替えられるという点で、「中の物質が7年ごとに全て入れ替
わる」という人間の体とパラレルな関係にある。そして、「パーツが入れ替わっても、
同じ船（人）だと言えるのか」という問題が提起されるのである。e が正解。その
他はどれも、記述として間違いではないだろうが、教授が強調したいポイントとは
異なる。

(4) Which of the following is NOT mentioned as a result of aging?
年を取ることの結果として言及されていないのは次のうちどれか。

a) Changes in DNA.
DNAの変化。

b) Increased bone fragility.
骨が壊れやすくなること。

c) Changes in physical attributes.
身体的特性の変化。

d) Growth or shrinkage of the brain.
脳の拡張あるいは縮小。

e) Changes in the stomach and lungs.
胃と肺の変化。

❼では、「人間の自己同一性とは体の構造である」という仮説に対し、「人間の体
は年を取るにつれて変化する」ということを根拠に反証を行っている。その具体
例としては「骨格の劣化」「脳の重さ・構造の変化」「DNAの変異」の3つが挙げ
られており、これがそれぞれb、d、aに該当する。またこれらを総合してEvery

physical attribute is temporary and subject to change. と述べられており，これが c に該当する。e についての言及はない。

(5) According to the alternative theory of identity described by the professor,
教授によって説明された自己同一性についての別の説によれば……

a) human identity is similar to the hardware of a computer.
人間の自己同一性はコンピュータのハードウェアに似ている。

b) human identity is less complex than advanced computer systems.
人間の自己同一性は高度なコンピュータシステムほど複雑でない。

c) computers are making progress towards solving the mystery of identity.
コンピュータは自己同一性の謎を解くための進化を遂げてきている。

d) human identity is like a set of instructions that determine physical behavior.
人間の自己同一性は物理的な行動を決定する指示の集合のようなものである。

e) human identity is controlled by a kind of software program that is inherent in each person.
人間の自己同一性は，各人に生まれつき備わっている一種のソフトウェアプログラムによって制御される。

❾❿では，自己同一性について，教授が独自の説を披露する。その内容とは，人間の身体は一種のハードウェアであり，自己同一性はそれを動かすソフトウェアである，というものである。❾では，コンピュータのプログラム（ソフトウェア）を an immaterial collection of instructions and procedures that are carried out on a physical medium と表現しており，これが d の記述と一致する。a は hardware が誤り。正しくは software である。また，自己同一性そのものをソフトウェアになぞらえているのであって，e の「自己同一性がソフトウェアに制御されている」というのは誤り。

216

Set 9-C | 放送文

Identity 2

❶ Andrew: I'm still trying to figure out what the professor was talking about when he said that identity can't be described as a physical concept. Don't we all have physical bodies, and don't our physical bodies contain our identities? Did you get what he was saying, Brittany?

get 他 …を理解する

❷ Brittany: I'm not exactly sure what he meant, either, Andrew. I think the professor wanted us to think about how, even though our physical bodies change as we age, our identity remains the same.

❸ Andrew: So what kind of changes are we talking about?

❹ Brittany: Imagine you're looking at a snapshot of yourself after you were born. Every part of your body is bigger now than when you were born, right?

❺ Andrew: Actually, I read that our eyeballs stay the same size from birth until death. Eyeballs are the only body part that never grows as we age.

❻ Brittany: Okay, so everything except your eyeballs has grown since you were born. Are you still the same person?

❼ Andrew: I think so. I'm still the same person, just older.

❽ Brittany: Right, you have the same identity. But your entire body has changed. Every seven years, all of the cells in your body are replaced. You're 21 now, right? That means that your 14-year-old body is entirely gone.

cell 名 細胞

🔲 Andrewの立場：自己同一性の中心となるのは物理的特性である

❾ Andrew: That may be true, but I still look pretty much the same as I did back then. My nose may be made of different cells, but it's still an Andrew-shaped nose. No one else in the world has a nose that looks exactly like mine. And the same goes for my brain. The physical matter is different, but the form that matter takes—the neurons and thought pathways that determine my personality —is unique to me. That makes me think physical attributes are central to identity. What do you

the same goes for … 句 同じことが…についても言える
neuron 名 ニューロン
pathway 名 経路

attribute 名 特性

think, Catherine?

❿ Catherine: For me, identity is more of a spiritual question. My family taught me that God gives each one of us a soul that lasts forever, even after we die. The soul is what animates our physical body and makes each of us who we are, no matter how much our outer appearance or even our thought patterns and neurons change.

⓫ Brittany: But don't you think we have to address these questions scientifically? We can't just rely on some religious theory that doesn't make sense on a scientific level.

⓬ Catherine: I don't know. I think there are some things in life that defy scientific explanation. Wasn't that exactly what the professor was saying when he talked about scientists being able to explain the behavior of light but not its underlying nature? That's why we have religion—because there are some things even the best scientists can't explain.

⓭ Brittany: Personally, I thought the professor's comparison between human identity and the software on a computer was pretty convincing.

⓮ Andrew: Really? That went completely over my head.

⓯ Brittany: If I understood him correctly, he was suggesting that our identity is a sort of pattern that determines how we grow, what we think, and what we do—in other words, pretty much everything about us.

⓰ Catherine: But where is that pattern encoded, if not in the physical structure of our bodies and brains?

⓱ Brittany: That is a question for the scientists of the future.

⓲ Catherine: Or perhaps the priests and preachers and imams.

spiritual 形 精神的な

soul 名 魂
animate 他 …に生命を与える，動かす
🔖 Catherineの立場：自己同一性を決めるのは「魂」である
address 他 …に取り組む

defy 他 …に反抗する，を拒む
🔖 Catherineの根拠：科学では説明できないことがある
underlie 自 根底にある

comparison 名 比較

convincing 形 説得力がある
go over someone's head 句〈人〉には理解できない

encode 他 …をコード化する
🔖 教授の説に対する3人の反応：Brittanyは賛成，AndrewとCatherineは懐疑的

imam 名（イスラム社会の）導師

218

Set 9-C | 放送文の日本語訳

自己同一性 2

❶アンドリュー：教授が，自己同一性は物理的な概念としては説明できないと言った時に話していたことについて，ずっと理解しようとし続けているんだ。僕たちみんな，物理的な体を持っていないか？　そして僕たちの物理的な体は自己同一性を含んでいないか？　ブリタニー，彼が言っていることを理解した？

❷ブリタニー：アンドリュー，私も彼が意図したことを正確には分かっていないわ。私が思うに，教授は，たとえ私たちの物理的な肉体が加齢に伴って変化しても，自己同一性は同じまま保たれるということを考えてもらいたかったのじゃないかな。

❸アンドリュー：それで今，僕たちが話している変化というのはどういう種類のものなの？

❹ブリタニー：生まれてすぐのスナップ写真を見ていると想像してみて。体のどの部分も生まれた時より大きくなっているわよね？

❺アンドリュー：実際のところは，眼球は生まれてから死ぬまで同じ大きさのままだと読んだことがある。眼球が，年齢に伴って決して大きくならない唯一の部分なんだって。

❻ブリタニー：いいわ，では眼球以外の全ては生まれて以来大きくなってきている。あなたはそれでも同じ人物？

❼アンドリュー：そう思うよ。僕は今でも同じ人物だよ。ただ年を取っただけで。

❽ブリタニー：その通り，あなたは同じ自己同一性を持っている。でも，あなたの肉体の全ては変化したわ。7年ごとに，体の中の全ての細胞が入れ替わる。あなたは21歳よね？　それはつまり，14歳の頃のあなたの肉体は完全になくなってしまっているということよ。

❾アンドリュー：それは正しいかもしれないけれど，それでも僕は当時の僕とほとんど同じような見た目をしているよ。僕の鼻は違う細胞でできているかもしれないけれど，それでも「アンドリューの形」の鼻だよ。世界中の誰も，僕と全く同じような鼻を持ってはいない。僕の脳にも同じことが言える。物理的な物質は違っても，その物質がまとう形——僕の性格を決定するニューロンや思考回路——は僕に固有のものだ。だから，僕は物理的な特性こそが自己同一性の中核だと思うんだよ。キャサリン，どう思う？

❿キャサリン：私にとっては，自己同一性はより精神的な問いなの。私の家族は，神が私たち1人ひとりに死後でさえも永遠に続く魂を与えてくれるのだって教えてくれたわ。魂というのは，いかに外側の見た目や，思考回路やニューロンさえ変化したとしても，私たちの物理的な肉体に生命を与え，私たち1人ひとりが誰であるかを形造ってくれるものなのよ。

⓫ブリタニー：でも，こういう問題には科学的に取り組まなければいけないとは思わない？　科学的なレベルで意味をなさない宗教論に頼って済ますわけにはいかないわ。

⓬キャサリン：そうかしら。世の中には，科学的な説明を拒むような物事もあると思う。それこそがまさしく，科学者たちは光の作用については説明できてもその根本に

ある本質は説明できないと話した時に，教授が言わんとしていたことではなかったのかしら？　だからこそ，私たちには宗教があるのよ。どんなに優れた科学者でも説明できない物事があるのだから。

⓭ブリタニー：個人的には，教授が行った人間の自己同一性とコンピュータ上のソフトウェアの比較はとても説得力があると思ったわ。

⓮アンドリュー：本当に？　僕には全く理解不能だったよ。

⓯ブリタニー：もし私が彼を正しく理解できていたとしたらだけど，彼が示唆していたのは，私たちの自己同一性というのは，私たちがどう成長するか，何を考えるか，何をするか，言い換えれば自分たちに関するおよそ全てのことを決定する，一種のパターンだ，ということよ。

⓰キャサリン：でもそのパターンは，肉体や脳の物理的構造の中でないとしたら，どこでコード化されているの？

⓱ブリタニー：それは未来の科学者にとっての問題ね。

⓲キャサリン：それか，神父や牧師や導師にとって，かもしれないわね。

《 指針 》

Bの講義についての学生たちの会話である。日常的な会話であり，聞き取りはそれほど難しくないはずだ。教授の講義を受けて，3人がそれぞれ違った立場を表明している。その主張・根拠の違いを理解することが何よりも大切である。特に設問(4)には注意したい。細かな情報よりも，まずは各人の論の大まかな方向性を掴むようにしよう。

難易度

放送文　★★☆
設　問　★★☆
総　合　★★☆

☺☺))) **スピーカー情報**

Andrew: 中西部，ミズーリ
Brittany: 西海岸，カリフォルニア
Catherine: イングランド

Set 9-C | 設問解説

(1) Why does Andrew question the professor's argument that identity is not a physical concept?

自己同一性は物理的な概念ではないという教授の主張にアンドリューが疑問を抱くのはなぜか。

a) Because cells are not actually replaced over time.
細胞は実際には時間と共に入れ替わりはしないから。

b) Because the argument goes against his religious beliefs.
その論点は彼の宗教的信仰に反するから。

c) Because some body parts stay the same throughout life.
人生を通して同じままである体の部分もあるから。

d) Because each individual has unique physical characteristics.
それぞれの人間が固有の物理的特質を持っているから。

e) Because physical characteristics are easier to recognize than any other feature.
身体的特徴は他のどんな特徴よりも認識しやすいから。

Andrewの主張は❶に始まって❾まで続く。その論拠が最も強く出ているのは❾であろう。The physical matter is different, but the form that matter takes ... is unique to me.と言っているように，細胞等の物質は入れ替わったとしても，顔や脳等の特徴はその人固有のものであり続けるから，というのである。dが正解。cは正解に近いが，Andrewが言っているのは「体の部分そのものが変わらない」ということではなく，「体の部分の特徴が変わらない」ということであるから，dを正解として選ぶ。

(2) What does Brittany mean when she says Andrew's 14-year-old body is gone?
アンドリューの14歳の体は失われていると言った時，ブリタニーが意図しているのはどんなことか。

a) His body has matured since his teenage years.
彼の肉体は10代の日々以来，成熟してきている。

b) He is a different person now than he was then.
現在は当時とは異なる人間である。

c) His identity has changed since he became an adult.
大人になってから彼の自己同一性は変化した。

d) He has different cells in his body now than he did then.
現在は当時とは異なる細胞で体ができている。

e) His body has become much larger and stronger than it was when he was 14.
彼の肉体は，14歳のときとくらべてずっと大きく，そして強くなった。

❽のEvery seven years, all of the cells in your body are replaced. You're 21 now, right? That means that your 14-year-old body is entirely gone.というくだりから，すぐにdが正解だと分かる。

(3) Which of the following describes Catherine's belief about the soul?
　　キャサリンの魂に関する考えを説明しているのは次のうちどれか。

　a) It determines our physical appearance.
　　　物理的な外見を決定している。

　b) It will be understood by scientists one day.
　　　いつの日か科学者によって解明されるだろう。

　c) It is the best explanation for human identity.
　　　人間の自己同一性を最も適切に説明するものである。

　d) It disappears together with our physical body when we die.
　　　死ぬ時に物理的な肉体と共に消滅する。

　e) It is a spiritual entity that is controlled by each person's identity.
　　　各人の自己同一性によってコントロールされる精神的な存在である。

「自己同一性とは何か」についてのCatherineの立場は❿で表明されている。「魂が人間の自己同一性を説明するものである」と直接的には言っていないが，The soul is what ... makes each of us who we are の who we areとはまさに「自己同一性」のことであり，ｃが正解だと分かる。自己同一性の正体が魂と言っているが，ｅのように「魂が自己同一性にコントロールされる」とは言っていない。

(4) How do the three students react to the professor's explanation of identity?
　　3人の学生は，自己同一性についての教授の説明にどう反応しているか。

　a) All three students support his argument.
　　　3人の学生全員が彼の議論を支持している。

　b) All three students are skeptical of his argument.
　　　3人の学生全員が彼の議論に懐疑的である。

　c) Catherine and Andrew are more critical of it than Brittany.
　　　キャサリンとアンドリューはブリタニーに比べて批判的である。

　d) Catherine agrees with it, but Andrew and Brittany disagree.
　　　キャサリンは賛成しているが，アンドリューとブリタニーは反対している。

　e) Brittany and Catherine don't understand it, but Andrew does.
　　　ブリタニーとキャサリンは理解していないが，アンドリューは理解している。

自己同一性をコンピュータのソフトウェアにたとえた教授の説に対し，まず⓭でBrittanyが「説得力がある（convincing）」と賛意を表すと，Andrewは⓮で「理解できない」と反論する。さらに⓰ではCatherineも疑問を呈する。Catherineは，「自己同一性は一種のパターンであり，物理的なものではない」という教授の説に対し，「結局，そのパターンも体とか脳とかの物理的な場所でコード化されるのではないか」と反論しているのである。全面的に賛成しているのはBrittanyのみで，他の2名は懐疑的なので，ｃが正解。

222

(5) Why does Catherine mention preachers, priests, and imams at the end of the conversation?
会話の最後にキャサリンが牧師，神父，導師に言及するのはなぜか。

a) Because she doesn't have much faith in religious leaders.
宗教指導者をあまり信用していないから。

b) Because she believes scientists can't solve the mystery of identity.
科学者には自己同一性の謎が解けないと信じているから。

c) Because religious leaders are increasingly aware of scientific debates.
宗教指導者は科学的な議論を次第に意識するようになってきているから。

d) Because religious leaders understand patterns of human behavior well.
宗教指導者は人間の行動パターンをよく理解しているから。

e) Because she thinks scientists and religious leaders should work together.
科学者と宗教指導者はともに仕事すべきだと考えているから。

Catherineの基本的な立場は「自己同一性の正体は魂である」というものであり，⓫でBrittanyに「科学的でない」と批判されたのに対し，⓬で「科学では説明できないこともある」と反論している。つまり，このテーマに関しては，科学的な解釈よりもスピリチュアルな理解を重視していることが分かる。⓱でBrittanyが「この問題（自己同一性を司るパターンがどこでコード化されているかという問題）は科学者に委ねられている」と言ったのに対し，⓲でCatherineが「神父，牧師，導師に委ねられている」と訂正したのも同じ流れであり，「自己同一性の問題については科学では解決できないので，精神的なアプローチが必要だ」ということが言いたいのである。正解はｂ。選択肢のｄは，patternという語を放送文とは別の文脈で用いてしまっている。

Set 10 | 解答

10A (1) d (2) a (3) a (4) b (5) d
10B (1) b (2) d (3) d (4) b (5) b
10C (1) d (2) c (3) d (4) d (5) d

Set 10-A | 放送文

Travel

❶ Host: Good evening, and welcome to the San Francisco City Club's "World Explorer" lecture series. Tonight I have the pleasure of introducing one of my favorite travel writers, Mary Hodgeson. Mary is a London-based author who writes about Asia, Latin America, Europe, and even Antarctica. In today's high-tech world, she is known for her low-tech approach to travel: no smartphone, no constant Twitter updates, no blogging. The title of her talk tonight is *Traveling Unplugged: Why It's Still the Best Way to Go.* Welcome Mary!

[Applause]

❷ Mary: Thank you so much. I'm delighted to be here. I'd like to start by telling you a story. Last month I visited New Orleans for the first time in my life. The night I arrived, I wanted to find a great local fish restaurant for dinner, so I asked the hotel receptionist for a suggestion. This turned into a 20-minute discussion of various options. She ended up making me a hand-drawn map to her favorite gumbo spot. Unfortunately, I got lost on the way there. Well, I say "unfortunately," but actually, I ended up wandering into an absolutely wonderful section of the French Quarter. Street musicians were playing jazz, flowers were blooming on balconies, and people were laughing and talking in the streets. I found a restaurant that looked good and went in. I didn't know what to order, so I asked the couple at the table next to me if they had a suggestion. It turned out they were visiting from France, and they invited me to join them at a jazz show after dinner, which I did. All in all, a fantastic evening!

Antarctica 名 南極大陸

unplug 他 …のプラグを抜く

end up *do*ing 句 しまいには…する
gumbo 名 ガンボ（アメリカ南部のオクラを使った料理）
wander into … 句 …に迷い込む
bloom 自 (花が) 咲く

it turns out (that) … 句 …ということが分かる
all in all 句 全体的に見て

224

❸   Now let's rewind that scene and imagine I was traveling the way that most English people do these days: fully armed with modern gadgets that ensure nothing unexpected ever happens. I arrive at my hotel and need to find a dinner spot, so I type "good fish in New Orleans" into the restaurant review app on my smartphone. Over a hundred choices pop up, and I choose one near me. To find my way there, I use the navigation app on my phone, which shows me the fastest walking route. I get to the restaurant in 15 minutes flat. Next, what to order? Well, time to check the restaurant review app on my phone again to see what other diners have tried and liked. But while I'm checking, I notice I have three new emails from an editor at a magazine I write for. I read them. Turns out she needs an article rewritten as soon as possible. I eat in a hurry and rush back to my hotel room to do the work. I fall into bed exhausted and feeling just as stressed out as I do back home in London.

❹   I think you see my point. There are literally hundreds of digital tools available today that make traveling far easier, cheaper, and safer than it was even 10 years ago. In some cases those tools may improve the quality of our experiences. But I firmly believe that the main effect these devices are having is to drastically reduce the amount of spontaneous human contact and adventure we stumble upon during our travels. That's why I urge you, no matter how hard it seems, to unplug from technology the next time you take a trip. I promise, you'll be glad you did.

Set 10-A | 放送文の日本語訳

旅

❶ホスト：こんばんは，ようこそサンフランシスコ・シティ・クラブの「世界の探検家」レクチャー・シリーズへ。今夜は，私の好きな紀行作家のお1人，メアリー・ホジソンさんをご紹介できることを喜ばしく思います。メアリーさんは，アジアやラテンアメリカ，ヨーロッパ，南極大陸についてまでも執筆を行っている，ロンドンに拠点を置く作家です。今日のハイテクな世界の中で，彼女は旅に対してローテクなアプローチをとっていることで知られています。つまり，スマートフォンもなし，ツイッターの定期的な更新もなし，ブログの投稿もなし，ということです。彼女の今夜の講演タイトルは，「テクノロジーのプラグを抜いて旅すること――なぜそれが今でも最良のやり方なのか」。メアリーさん，ようこそ！

　　　［拍手］

❷メアリー：どうもありがとうございます。お招きいただき嬉しいです。ある体験をお話しすることから始めましょう。先月，私は人生で初めてニューオーリンズを訪ねました。到着した夜，夕食をとるために，素晴らしい地元の魚料理のレストランを見つけたかったので，ホテルの受付係に提案を求めたんです。このことは様々な選択肢をめぐる20分にわたる議論になりました。結局彼女は，彼女のお気に入りの南部料理ガンボがあるお店までの手描きの地図を作ってくれました。不運なことに，そこへ行く途中で私は道に迷ってしまいました。さて，「不運なことに」と言っても，実は私は，フレンチ・クオーターの本当に素敵な一角に迷い込むことになったのです。ストリートミュージシャンたちがジャズを演奏していて，バルコニーには花が咲き誇っていて，人々は路上で笑ったり話したりしていました。私は良さそうなレストランを見つけて，そこに入りました。何を注文すべきか分からなかったので，隣のテーブルにいたカップルに提案があるかどうか尋ねました。彼らはフランスからやって来ていたことが分かり，さらに夕食後のジャズの公演に一緒に来ないかと誘ってくれて，私は行きました。全体的に見て，とても素晴らしい夜でした！

❸　今度は，その場面を巻き戻して，たいていのイギリス人が昨今行っているやり方で私が旅をしていたと想像してみましょう。つまり，予想外のことが一切起こらないことを保証してくれる現代的装置をすっかり装備したやり方ということです。私はホテルに着いて，夕食をとる場所を見つける必要があると，スマートフォンのレストラン評価アプリに，「ニューオーリンズの美味しい魚」と打ち込みます。100以上の選択肢が表示されて，私は近いところを選びます。そこまでの行き方を把握するために，携帯電話の地図アプリを使うと，最も早い徒歩での経路が示されます。私はそのレストランに，15分きっかりで到着します。次は，何を注文すべきかです。さあ，今度は他の食事客が何を試して何を好んだかを調べるために，再び携帯でレストラン評価アプリをチェックします。ところが調べている最中に，私が執筆を行っている雑誌の編集者から新しいeメールが3通来ていることに気がつきます。私はそれを読みます。彼女が至急記事の書き直しを求めていることが判明します。急いで食事を済ませ，その仕事にかかるために大慌てでホ

226

テルの部屋に引き返します。疲れ果てて，自宅のあるロンドンでと全く同じように
ストレスを抱えながら，ベッドに倒れこみます。

❹　私の言いたいことが分かってもらえるのではないでしょうか。今日では，10年
前と比べてさえも，はるかに簡単で，安くて，安全な旅を可能にする，文字通り
何百ものデジタルツールが手に入ります。場合によっては，そうしたツールが私
たちの経験の質を高めてくれるかもしれません。ですが，こうした装置が及ぼし
ている主な影響は，旅の最中に遭遇する自然発生的な人との接触や冒険の数を劇
的に減らしてしまうことであると，私は堅く信じています。そういうわけで，そ
れがどれほど困難に思えるとしても，皆さんが次に旅行をする時には，テクノロ
ジーのプラグを抜くことを強く奨励させてもらいます。約束しましょう，そうし
てよかったと思えることを。

《 指針 》

Traveling Unpluggedというタイトルの講演である。文字通り「プラグ
を抜いて」，すなわちデジタル機器を持たず，インターネットへのアクセ
スを断って旅することを奨励する内容になっている。発言の半分以上が自
分の体験談等の具体例だが，この実例を以て話者が何を言おうとしている
のかを考えること。

難易度

放送文	★☆☆
設　問	★☆☆
総　合	★☆☆

☺☺))) スピーカー情報

Host: 西海岸，カリフォルニア
Mary: イングランド

Set 10-A | 設問解説

(1) What is the topic of the lecture?
講演のテーマは何か。

 a) Stories from travel on four continents.
四大陸の旅についての物語。

 b) How to travel in places without adequate electricity.
十分な電気のない場所をあちこち旅する方法。

 c) The best places to eat seafood and hear live jazz in New Orleans.
ニューオーリンズでシーフードを食べ，生演奏のジャズを聴くのに最適な場所。

 d) The drawbacks of depending too much on high-tech devices while traveling.
旅の間，ハイテクな装置に頼りすぎることの欠点。

 e) The importance of careful planning in order to have the best experience in a
foreign place.
異国の地で最高の体験をするために入念な計画を立てることの大切さ。

放送文全体に関わる問題である。❶では，この講演のタイトルがTraveling Unpluggedであると紹介されているが，これは「デジタル機器を持たずに旅をすること」というような意味合いである。unplugとは文字通り「プラグを抜く」という意味であり，ここではハイテク機器を持たずに，ネット環境を断つことを指している。❸や❹でも述べられているように，デジタルツールを持つことで，旅に驚きがなくなってしまうという「欠点（drawbacks）」があるというのである。これを表したdが正解。

(2) Which of the following accurately describes Mary's first night in New Orleans?
ニューオーリンズでのメアリーの最初の夜について正確に説明しているのは次のうちどれか。

 a) She went to a jazz performance with new friends.
新しくできた友人たちと，ジャズの演奏を聴きに行った。

 b) She dined at a restaurant the hotel receptionist recommended.
ホテルの受付係が薦めたレストランで食事をとった。

 c) She used a restaurant review app to find a place to eat dinner.
夕食をとる場所を探すために，レストラン評価アプリを使った。

 d) She got lost on her way to the restaurant, so she went back to the hotel.
レストランまでの道の途中で迷ったため，ホテルに戻った。

 e) She made friends through a travel app and went to a jazz show with them.
旅行アプリを通じて友人を作り，一緒にジャズのショーに行った。

ニューオーリンズでの夜については❷で語られている。「ホテルの受付係に薦めてもらったレストランに行こうとしたが，途中で道に迷った。そして，素敵な界隈に迷い込み，そこで良さそうなレストランに入った。フランス人のカップルと知り合い，食後にはジャズの演奏に招待された」という内容。最後の部分がaに合致する。結

局ホテルの受付係が薦めたレストランには行かなかったので，bは誤り。

(3) Which of the following does Mary NOT mention as a typical way most English people travel today?
今日たいていのイギリス人が旅行する典型的な方法として，メアリーが言及していないのは次のうちどれか。
a) Posting reviews of restaurants on online apps.
オンラインのアプリに，レストランの評価を投稿すること。
b) Using a restaurant review app to find a place to eat.
レストラン評価アプリを使って食事をする場所を探すこと。
c) Staying virtually connected with clients or coworkers.
仕事の依頼主もしくは同僚と，バーチャルに繋がり続けること。
d) Using online maps to find their way around new places.
新しい土地で道を調べるためにオンラインの地図を使うこと。
e) Relying on the Internet to choose what to eat at a restaurant.
レストランで何を食べるか選ぶためにインターネットに頼ること。

❸では，Maryの過ごした一夜を，現代の一般的なイギリス人ならどのように過ごすだろうかという「想像上の場面」が語られている。「評価アプリを使って近くのレストランを検索する」「地図アプリを使ってそこまで行く」「評価アプリを参考に食べるものを決める」「仕事のメールをチェックする」といった行為が挙げられているが，aの「レストランの評価を投稿する」は述べられていない。

(4) What does the term "armed with" mean in the phrase "fully armed with modern gadgets"?
"fully armed with modern gadgets"（「現代的装置をすっかり装備した」）という表現の中で，"armed with"（「…を装備した」）という語句は何を意味しているか。
a) covered in
…に覆われた
b) prepared with
…を備えた
c) surrounded by
…に囲まれた
d) decorated with
…で装飾した
e) loaded down by
…を満載した

armed with ...は「…で武装している」という意味だが，この文脈ではむろん武器を持っているということではなく，比喩的に「…を備えている」という意味を表している。これに近いbが正解。

(5) According to Mary, why is it better to travel the old-fashioned way?
メアリーによれば，なぜ古風なやり方で旅をした方が良いのか。

a) Traveling without high-tech digital devices is safer, cheaper, and easier.
ハイテクなデジタル装置を使わずに旅することは，より安全で，より安価で，より簡単である。

b) By referring to books rather than websites, travelers obtain more reliable information.
ウェブサイトよりも本を参照することで，旅行者たちはより信頼できる情報を得られる。

c) By not relying on smartphone navigation apps, travelers develop their innate navigational skills.
スマートフォンの地図アプリに頼らないことで，旅行者はもともと自分に備わっている経路探査能力を高めることができる。

d) Without constant access to online information, travelers are more likely to have unexpected experiences.
オンラインの情報を絶えず利用しないことで，旅行者たちが予期しなかった経験を持てる可能性が高まる。

e) By going around without high-tech devices, travelers can enjoy their trip at their own pace without being overwhelmed by schedules.
ハイテク機器を持たずに回ることで，旅行者はスケジュールに追われることなく，自分のペースで旅行を楽しめる。

❹ではMaryが自分の経験から得た結論を述べている。「デジタル機器を持って旅をすると便利だが，旅の間に遭遇する人との出会いや冒険が減ってしまう」というもの。言い換えると，デジタル機器を持たないで旅した方が予想外の経験が増えるということであり，これがdに相当する。

Set 10-B | 放送文

History of Art Forgery

❶ Host: We recently heard in the news about the arrest in Spain of nine people involved in the production and sale of fake works of art. Spanish police seized 271 paintings and drawings that the gang were planning to pass off as works by well-known artists such as Pablo Picasso. Here to discuss the case and other aspects of art forgery is art historian Cathy Gordon. Cathy, can you give us some more details about the Spanish forgeries?

seize 他 …を押収する
pass off A as B 句 AをB だとして押し通す
forgery 名 贋作，偽造

❷ Cathy: Well, according to the police, the works were of high quality. However, the forgers weren't particularly well rewarded for their efforts. They received as little as 50 or 100 euros for each piece from middlemen, who went on to sell them at galleries or on the Internet at hugely inflated prices.

forger 名 偽造者
middleman 名 中間業者，ブローカー
go on to *do* 句 さらに…する
inflated 形 暴騰した，膨れ上がった
☛発言の主旨：偽造者たちの報酬は少なかった

❸ Host: So the forgers themselves weren't out to make a profit.

be out to *do* 句 …しようとしている

❹ Cathy: Well, it's hard to be sure, but forgers do sometimes say they have other motivations. Tom Keating, for example, who was one of the best known forgers of recent times, claimed he was trying to make a protest. Keating, who worked as an art restorer, felt that the art world was corrupt. He accused art critics and dealers of working together to get rich at the expense both of naive collectors and poor artists. Hoping to disrupt and change the system, he put large numbers of his fakes into art auctions throughout the 1950s and 60s.

motivation 名 動機
make a protest 句 抗議する
art restorer 句 美術品の修復家
corrupt 形 腐敗している
accuse A of B 句 Bの理由でAを非難する
naive 形 うぶな，騙されやすい
disrupt 他 …を混乱させる，破壊する
☛発言の主旨：キーティングは腐敗した美術界への抗議として贋作を市場に流した

❺ Host: How did his activities come to light?

come to light 句 明るみに出る

❻ Cathy: He went public in 1970 and admitted that there were over 2,000 of his creations in circulation. To the annoyance of many in the art world, though, he refused to list them.

to the annoyance of … 句 …にとって困ったことには

❼ Host: So some people might still be in possession of one of his forgeries thinking it's the real thing.

in possession of … 句 …を所有して

❽ Cathy: Without doubt, but it is not just Keating's forgeries that collectors have to worry about.

Switzerland's Fine Art Expert Institute recently revealed that 70 to 90 percent of the pieces that it examines turn out not to be by the artist claimed. The institute uses various cutting-edge techniques to determine whether paintings are genuine. For example, forgers sometimes paint over other works because of the need to use a canvas from an appropriate time period, but this can easily be revealed using an infrared scan. Also, radiocarbon dating can show whether the paint is of the correct period.

turn out to be … 句 …であることが分かる
cutting-edge 形 最新の
genuine 形 本物の

infrared scan 句 赤外線スキャン
radiocarbon 名 放射性炭素

❾ Host: I imagine that some collectors might be reluctant to use that kind of service even if they have doubts about the authenticity of their art. After all, if you had paid millions for a Rembrandt or Van Gogh, you probably wouldn't want to be told that you had wasted your money.

be reluctant to *do* 句 …したがらない
authenticity 名 正統性

❿ Cathy: I think you're right. For many collectors, ignorance is bliss. But these techniques can also bring good news. A museum in Italy recently analyzed a portrait of a young woman. Previously, experts had said it was a copy made in the style of the great Italian artist Raphael. As such, it was considered to be of little value. The analysis results, though, proved conclusively that the portrait was the work of the master himself, and the museum believes it to be worth 30 million euros or more.

Ignorance is bliss. 句 知らぬが仏。
analyze 他 …を分析する

as such 句 そういうものとして
analysis 名 分析
conclusively 副 決定的に

⓫ Host: Extraordinary. Well, that's a positive note to end on. Thank you, Cathy.

end on a positive note 句 明るい雰囲気で終わる

Set 10-B | 放送文の日本語訳

美術品偽造の歴史

❶司会者：最近，スペインで偽物の美術品の製造と販売に関与した9人が逮捕されるという出来事をニュースで耳にしました。スペイン警察は，ギャングがパブロ・ピカソのような有名アーティストの作品と偽ることを目論んでいた絵画作品271点を押収しました。この事件や，美術における贋作の他の側面について議論するために，美術史家のキャシー・ゴードンさんがいらっしゃっています。キャシーさん，このスペインの贋作について，もう少し詳しく教えてもらえますか。

❷キャシー：ええ，警察によると，これらの作品は質の高いものでした。しかし，偽造犯たちは努力の割りにはたいした見返りを得ていなかったのです。彼らがブローカーたちから受け取ったのは，それぞれの作品につきわずか50ユーロか100ユーロでしたが，ブローカーたちはそれらをギャラリーで，もしくはインターネット上で，不当に釣り上げた値段で売っていたというわけです。

❸司会者：つまり，偽造犯たち自身は利益を得ようと思ってはいなかったということですね。

❹キャシー：確かめるのは難しいことですが，しかし偽造犯たちが，別の動機があるという場合があることも確かです。たとえば，トム・キーティングという人物は近年の最も有名な偽造犯の1人ですが，自分は抗議を行おうとしたのだと主張しました。キーティングは美術品の修復者として働いていましたが，美術の世界は腐敗していると感じていたのです。彼は，美術批評家やディーラーたちが一緒になって，騙されやすい収集家と貧乏な美術家の両方を犠牲にして金持ちになろうとしていると非難しました。このシステムを破壊し，変革しようとして，キーティングは1950年代から60年代を通して数多くの偽物を美術オークションに送り込んだのです。

❺司会者：どうやって彼の活動が明るみに出たのですか。

❻キャシー：1970年に彼は，2000を超える彼の創作物が流通していることを公表したのです。しかし，美術界の多くの人々にとって困ったことに，彼はそれらをリストアップすることを拒んだのです。

❼司会者：つまり，彼の模造品の1つを本物だと思っていまだに所有している人がいるかもしれないというわけですか。

❽キャシー：間違いなくそうです。でも，収集家たちが心配しなければならないのはキーティングの偽造品だけじゃありません。スイスの美術専門家協会は最近，協会が検査する作品の70パーセントから90パーセントが，作り手だと言われていたアーティストの手によるものではないと判明したことを明らかにしました。この協会は，絵画が本物かどうか決定するために多様な最新の技術を使っています。たとえば，偽造犯は時々，適切な時代のキャンバスを用いる必要性から他の作品の上に重ね描きをしますが，これは赤外線スキャンを用いることで容易に明らかにすることができます。さらに，放射性炭素年代測定法によっても，絵がその通りの時代のものかどうかが分かります。

❾司会者：収集家の中には，たとえ自身の美術品の正統性に疑問を持っていても，そ

うした類のサービスを使いたがらない人もいるのではないかと思います。結局の
ところ，レンブラントやゴッホの絵に何百万も払っていたとしたら，お金をドブ
に捨てていたなんてことを言われたくはないでしょうからね。

❿キャシー：その通りだと思います。多くの収集家にとって，知らずにいることが何よ
りの幸せなのです。しかし，こうした技術が良いニュースをもたらすこともあり
ます。イタリアのある美術館は最近，ある若い女性の肖像画を分析しました。そ
れ以前には，専門家たちはこの絵がイタリアの偉大な芸術家ラファエロのスタイ
ルを模倣して作られた模写だと言っていたのです。そういうものとして，絵はほ
とんど価値がないものだとみなされていました。しかし，その分析結果は最終的に，
その肖像画が巨匠本人の作品であることを証明することとなり，美術館は今では
その絵に3000万ユーロかそれ以上の価値があるとしています。

⓫司会者：素晴らしいですね。締めくくりにふさわしい，明るい話題でした。キャシ
ーさん，どうもありがとうございました。

《 指針 》

スペインでの美術品偽造事件についての話題から始まって，贋作の動機に
ついて，そして美術品の分析や収集家の心理まで，「贋作」を巡る興味深
い話が展開されている。キーワードとなるforgery／forgerの意味が分か
らないと厳しい。この語を知らない人にとっては，どれくらい早い段階で
意味を推測できるかが勝負所である。設問は素直なものが多く，全体とし
ては取り組みやすい問題となっているはずだ。

難易度

放送文	★★☆
設　問	★★☆
総　合	★★☆

☺☻))) スピーカー情報

Host: 西海岸，カリフォルニア
Cathy: 西海岸，カリフォルニア

Set 10-B | 設問解説

(1) What does the host assume about the people who created the fake artworks in Spain?
司会者は，スペインで偽物の美術品を作った人々についてどのように推測しているか。

a) They were trying to make a protest.
彼らは抗議を行おうとしていた。

b) They were not motivated by money.
彼らの動機は金ではなかった。

c) They made huge profits from their work.
彼らはその仕事によって大きな利益を得た。

d) They were poorly skilled as forgery painters.
彼らの偽造品画家としての技術は劣っていた。

e) They have not yet been caught by the police.
彼らはまだ警察に逮捕されていない。

❸の So the forgers themselves weren't out to make a profit. という発言から，司会者は，偽造者が贋作を市場に流出させたのは，金儲けが目的ではなかったのではないかと推測していることが分かる。b が正解。❹では，美術界への抗議活動として贋作を描いた例が紹介されているが，これは Cathy による説明であり，司会者の推測ではないので a は誤り。e は❶の内容と矛盾する。

(2) What was Tom Keating attempting to do?
トム・キーティングはどんなことをしようと試みていたか。

a) Make sure that his fake paintings were easy to identify.
彼が作った偽造絵画を容易に判別できるようにすること。

b) Buy poor artists' paintings to help them become famous.
貧しい画家たちの作品を買って，彼らが有名になる手助けをすること。

c) Restore fake paintings and sell them to private collectors.
偽物の絵画を修復して，個人的な収集家たちに売ること。

d) Change the way the art world dealt with collectors and artists.
美術界の収集家と美術家に対する扱い方を変革すること。

e) Publicize the situation where artists and dealers are working together to make money.
芸術家とディーラーが協力してお金を稼いでいる状況を公表すること。

Tom Keating という人物については❹で説明されている。大量の贋作を市場に流通させた人物であり，その目的は「騙されやすい収集家や貧しい芸術家を搾取している美術界に抗議するため」であった。d が正解。❻では，彼が自分の手による贋作のリストを公開しなかったとあるので，a は誤り。また，ディーラーと協力しているとされているのは「芸術家」ではなく「批評家」なので，e は誤り。

(3) **What is one thing we learn about the Fine Art Expert Institute?**
美術専門家協会について分かることは何か。

a) Its own artists are able to make fakes that look genuine.
専属のアーティストたちは，本物そっくりの偽物を作ることができる。

b) It thinks that radiocarbon dating can damage a painting.
放射性炭素年代測定法は絵画を傷付ける可能性があると考えている。

c) It believes that less than half of the artworks it sees are fakes.
調査する美術品のうち偽物は半分に満たないと信じている。

d) It uses a variety of technologies to see whether paintings are genuine.
絵画が本物かどうか調べるために多様な技術を用いている。

e) Ten to twenty percent of the paintings it examines turn out to be forgeries.
調査する絵画の10〜20％が贋作であると判明している。

Fine Art Expert Institute については❽で説明されている。The institute uses various cutting-edge techniques to determine whether paintings are genuine. という発言がｄと合致する。この協会が検査する作品の「70〜90％が贋作だと判明する」と言っているのでｃやｅは誤りである。

(4) **What does Cathy imply about the attitude of many art collectors when she says that "ignorance is bliss"?**
「知らずにいることが何よりの幸せ」という発言によって，キャシーが多くの美術品収集家の態度について示唆しているのはどんなことか。

a) They rarely suspect that artworks that they own might be fake.
彼らは自分が所有している美術品が偽物かもしれないとはめったに疑わない。

b) They choose not to find out whether their artworks are authentic.
彼らは自分たちの美術品が本物かどうか調べないことを選ぶ。

c) They do not trust the accuracy of techniques like radiocarbon dating.
彼らは放射性炭素年代測定法のような技術の正確さを信用していない。

d) They are unaware of the services offered by the institute in Switzerland.
彼らはスイスの協会が提供しているサービスを知らずにいる。

e) Whether the artworks they own are genuine or not doesn't matter to them.
自分たちが所有する美術品が本物であるかどうかは，彼らにとってどうでもいいことだ。

Ignorance is bliss. はことわざであり，そのまま日本語に訳せば「無知とは至福である」となる。❾で司会者が「自分が所有する美術品が本物かどうか疑っていても，それを判定する検査を受けたがらない人がいるのではないか」と言ったのに対して，❿でCathyがこのフレーズを用いている。そこに含意されるのは「自分が大金を失ったという事実が明るみに出るのを避けるために，あえて検査を受けずにいる」という見方である。ｂが正解。❾で司会者が even if they have doubts about the authenticity of their art と言ったのに対し，Cathy は I think you're right. と肯定しており，自分が所有する作品が贋作だと疑っている人のことを念頭に置いていることが分かる。したがってａは誤り。

(5) What do we learn about the portrait belonging to a museum in Italy?
イタリアの美術館に収められている肖像画について分かることは何か。

a) Experts still disagree about who painted it.
誰がその絵を描いたか，専門家の意見はいまだに一致していない。

b) Modern techniques showed it to be genuine.
新しい技術が，その絵が本物であることを明らかにした。

c) It was once thought to be a work by Raphael.
それはかつてラファエロによる作品だと考えられていた。

d) It has been put on the market for 30 million euros.
市場に3000万ユーロで売りに出されている。

e) It depicts the face of the great Italian artist Raphael.
偉大なイタリア人画家，ラファエロの顔を描いている。

❿では，これまでラファエロの模倣だと思われていた絵画が分析を受け，実は真作であると判明した例が紹介されている。bがその内容を的確に表している。「3000万ユーロ」というのは，美術館の見積もりであり，実際の市場価格ではないのでdは誤り。また，ここで話題となっているのは，ラファエロ「が」描いた絵であって，ラファエロ「を」描いた絵ではないのでeも誤り。

Set 10-C | 放送文

Hoaxes

❶ A: Did you read the story about the nude pictures of that famous actress that were leaked onto the Internet? It's terrible that someone chose to violate her privacy like that.

❷ B: Actually, that story turned out to be false. It seems that a group of Internet tricksters wanted to see if people would be fooled by a rumor based on the leaks of other celebrities' private pictures.

❸ A: I had no idea the story was fabricated. Why do people do things like that?

❹ B: I think some of them like the attention the story gets and enjoy seeing how it can get everybody online in an uproar. The more controversy they can stir up, the more important they feel. Personally, I don't think the problem lies with the creators of the hoax as much as the sites that spread these rumors without proper verification.

❺ A: I know what you mean. At this point, I've stopped believing most of what I read on the Internet, even on the respectable sites.

❻ B: You certainly should be skeptical about anything you read online. Remember that most websites profit from the number of hits their articles receive, so reposting popular stories means that they make money regardless of whether or not the story itself is true.

❼ A: In other words, their goal is always to make money first and verify factual information second.

❽ B: Right. All the major websites want to be the first to feature a story, so they are spending less time verifying details and more time propagating whatever information they have available. If they take the time to check their facts, they might not be the first website to publish the information, and the traffic will go to the other sites. Their revenues will drop and their site will suffer the financial consequences.

❾ A: Why don't the people mentioned in these fabricated stories step in and demand a change? Can't they

---

leak 他 …を漏らす

violate someone's privacy 句 〈人〉のプライバシーを侵害する
trickster 名 詐欺師
fool 他 …をだます
celebrity 名 有名人
fabricate 他 …を捏造する

📄 捏造記事を広げる理由：詐欺師たちが騒動を起こして悦に入ろうとする

uproar 名 騒動
controversy 名 論争，議論
stir up 句 …をかき立てる

hoax 名 でっち上げ，作り話
verification 名 確認

respectable 形 まともな，立派な
skeptical 形 懐疑的な

regardless of … 句 …とは関係なく

verify 他 …を検証する，確かめる
feature 他 …を特集する，記事にする
propagate 他 …を広める

📄 捏造記事が出回る理由：ウェブサイトが，閲覧回数を稼ぐことを優先し，事実確認を行わずに記事を掲載する
revenue 名 収入，歳入

step in 句 介入する，行動に出る

take action to remove false information from these websites?

❿ B: Because of the freedom of the press, it's very difficult for individuals to take action against reporters and news sites. The victim of a false story has to prove that the reporter deliberately spread false information with malicious intent. That's a heavy burden of proof for anyone to establish.

⓫ A: Well, what good is a free press if it behaves so irresponsibly? I can't see why the ability to spread lies about people is protected by the government.

⓬ B: I think the potential for government abuse is even worse than what journalists might do. As consumers, we have the power to affect these websites by refusing to visit them. Government policy is more difficult to change, especially when it requires the government to surrender control to the people.

⓭ A: I guess I should just stop checking news sites, then.

⓮ B: You should definitely stop checking the sites that knowingly publish false information. If you support the sites that do the right thing, they will become more prominent and successful. There's no reason that we can't have trustworthy news sites that check their facts.

⓯ A: I will do some research on my own and look for sites that check all the facts before rushing to print a false story.

⓰ B: I think that's the best way to prevent problems like this from happening again.

take action 句 行動に出る、訴訟を起こす

freedom of the press 句 報道の自由

deliberately 副 故意に
malicious 形 悪意のある
intent 名 意図
burden of proof 名 立証責任

▶捏造記事に対し訴訟を起こすのが難しい理由：悪意をもって故意に誤情報を広めたことを立証しなくてはならない

potential 名 (潜在的な) 可能性
abuse 名 濫用
surrender A to B 句 AをBに譲り渡す

knowingly 副 故意に

prominent 形 有名な
trustworthy 形 信頼のおける

Set 10-C｜放送文の日本語訳

捏造記事

❶A：あの有名女優のヌード画像がネット上に流出したって記事を読んだ？　誰かがあやって彼女のプライバシーを侵害しようとしたのね。ひどいわ。

❷B：実は，あの記事は捏造だってことが分かったんだ。ネット詐欺グループが，別のセレブのプライベートな写真をリークしたものに基づく噂話で人々をだませるかどうかやってみたらしい。

❸A：記事が作り物だなんて思いもしなかった。なぜそんなことするのかしら。

❹B：記事が注目されて，それがネット上でみんなを騒ぎに巻き込むのを見て喜んでいる奴もいるのじゃないかな。議論が大きければ大きいほど，自分たちが大物だと思うのだろう。僕としては，記事を捏造した当人よりも，しかるべき事実確認を行わずに噂を流したサイトの方に，むしろ責任があると思う。

❺A：そうね。もう，ネット上の記事のほとんどが信じられないわ。たとえまともなサイトでもね。

❻B：ネット上のものに対しては，常に疑いをもってかかるべきなんだよ。いいかい，ほとんどのウェブサイトが，掲載記事が獲得した閲覧回数で儲けている。だから，中身が真実であろうとなかろうと人気のある記事を載せることが儲けに繋がるんだ。

❼A：つまり，彼らの目指すところは，何よりもまず儲けであって，事実に基づく情報であることの確認は二の次ってわけね。

❽B：そうなんだ。主要なウェブサイトはどれも，他のどこよりも先に記事を掲載したいと思っている。だから彼らは，細部の確認より，どんなものであれ入手した情報を広めることの方に時間を割くんだ。事実確認に時間をかければ，情報を公表する最初のサイトになれないかもしれない。そうなるとアクセスが他のサイトに流れてしまう可能性がある。収入は減少し，そのサイトは財政的な打撃を受けることになる。

❾A：そういう捏造記事で書かれた当事者たちはなぜ，進み出て現状の変更を求めないのかしら。訴訟を起こして，そういうサイトから嘘の情報を消去させることはできないの？

❿B：報道の自由ってものがあるからね。個人が記者やニュースサイトを相手取って訴訟を起こすのはとても難しい。捏造記事の被害者は，記者が故意に悪意をもって嘘の情報を流したということを証明しなければならない。そんな立証責任の遂行は，誰にとっても困難だ。

⓫A：そんなに無責任なことで，何が自由な報道よね？　なぜ政府が，国民について嘘を広める能力を保護しているのか分からない。

⓬B：政府による濫用の可能性はジャーナリストの場合よりずっと悪いと僕は思う。僕ら消費者は，そうしたウェブサイトに影響を与える力をもっている。そういうサイトを訪れないようにすればいいんだ。政府の政策を変える方が難しい。特に政府が権力を国民に譲り渡すことが必要な場合には。

⓭A：じゃあ，ニュースサイトを読むのをやめればいいわけね。

240

⓮B：故意に嘘の情報を流しているサイトを読むのは断じてやめるべきだ。正しいことをしているサイトを支持すれば，そういうサイトが有名になって成功するだろう。僕らが，事実確認を行う信頼できるニュースサイトを持てない理由はないよ。

⓯A：私も自分で調べてみて，嘘の記事を急いで載せる前に事実確認を完全に行っているサイトを探してみるわ。

⓰B：今回のような問題が再び起こらないようにするには，それが一番だね。

《 指針 》

「インターネット上での捏造記事」についての会話である。前半は「捏造記事が出回る理由」が，後半は「捏造記事への対策」が話題の中心となる。2名の話者が意見を対立させることはないので，論点の違いに気を配る必要はないが，その一方で語彙のレベルは高い。また，(1)や(5)のような全体に関わる質問と，(3)のような細部の理解を問う質問とが混在している。ミクロとマクロの両レベルでの理解が求められる，難易度の高い問題である。

難易度

放送文　★★☆
設　問　★★★
総　合　★★★

☺😐))) **スピーカー情報**

A: 西海岸，カリフォルニア
B: スコットランド

Set 10-C | 設問解説

(1) Which of the following reasons is NOT given for why the fabricated story was spread?
次のうち，捏造記事が広まった理由として挙げられていないものはどれか。

a）Reporters failed to check their facts before releasing the story.
記者が記事を公表する前に事実確認をするのを怠った。

b）Internet tricksters fabricated a story to attract attention to themselves.
ネット詐欺グループが自分たちへの注目を集めるために記事を捏造した。

c）Most websites make a profit based on how many hits their articles get.
ほとんどのウェブサイトは，記事のアクセス数に応じて利益を得ている。

d）Readers wanted to share a scandalous news story with all of their friends.
読者が中傷的なニュース記事を全ての友人と共有することを望んだ。

e）The government cannot restrict news sites from publishing false information.
政府はニュースサイトが嘘の情報を公表することを制限することができない。

捏造記事が広まった理由については，放送文の各所で述べられている。a について
は❽で，b については❹で，c については❻で説明されている。また，e について
は❿で触れられている。d への言及はどこにもない。

(2) According to this dialogue, websites propagate false information because
この対話によれば，ウェブサイトが嘘の情報を流す理由は

a）false information makes more money than true stories.
嘘の情報は真実の物語より儲かるからである。

b）false information is more entertaining for their readers.
読者にとっては嘘の情報の方がおもしろいからである。

c）fact-checking slows them down and lowers their revenues.
事実確認は作業速度を落とし，収入を減少させるからである。

d）fact-checking is too difficult for their reporters and editors.
事実確認をすることが記者や編集者にとって難しすぎるからである。

e）they simply can't distinguish between false information and correct information.
嘘の情報と正しい情報を区別することが絶対にできないからである。

❽の内容把握を問う問題である。「ウェブサイトがアクセス数を稼ぐには，他のサイ
トよりも早く記事を掲載しなくてはならない。事実確認を行うと，掲載が遅れ，利
益の低下に繋がる」という内容である。これを表した c が正解。「お金を儲けるた
め」ということは各所で言われているが，「早く掲載すると儲かる」のであって，a
にあるように「嘘の情報だから儲かる」のではない。

242

(3) According to the speakers, the press can only be held responsible for a hoax if the reporter
対話している人物たちによれば，捏造記事の責任が報道機関にあるとされる唯一の場合は，記者が

a) knew the information was false and published it for whatever reason.
その情報が嘘であることを知りつつ，理由は何であれそれを公表した場合。

b) assumed the information was true and published it without checking the facts.
その情報が正しいと思い，事実確認をせずにそれを公表した場合。

c) suspected the information was false and published it to see what would happen.
その情報が嘘ではないかと思いつつ，何が起こるか見るためにそれを公表した場合。

d) knew the information was false and published it anyway in order to harm the victim.
その情報が嘘であることを知りつつ，犠牲者を傷つけようという意図をもってそれを公表した場合。

e) suspected the information was false and published it to attract attention and ad revenue.
その情報が嘘ではないかと思いつつ，注目を集め，広告収入を得るためにそれを公表した場合。

❿の The victim of a false story has to prove that the reporter deliberately spread false information with malicious intent.を正確に聞き取ろう。deliberately spread false information（故意に嘘の情報を流す）と with malicious intent（悪意をもって）という2つの条件を満たす選択肢を選ぶ。a，c，d，eは「故意に嘘の情報を流す」に該当するが，「悪意をもって」に当てはまるのはdのみである。

(4) Why do the speakers believe that the government should not interfere with the press?
対話している人物たちが，政府が報道機関に干渉すべきでないと考えているのはなぜか。

a) Government policy can never prevent the press from doing the wrong thing.
政府の政策は，決して，報道機関が不正を働くことを阻止することができないから。

b) Government policy is determined by a small group of people who dislike the press.
政府の政策は報道機関に反感をもつ少数の人々によって決定されているから。

c) Government policy might cause the press to lose advertising revenue and shut down.
政府の政策は報道機関に広告収入を失わせ，それを休業に追い込むかもしれないから。

d) Government policy is hard to change and could potentially restrict important information.
政府の政策は変更が難しく，潜在的に，重要な情報を制限する可能性をもつから。

e) Government policy is subject to change, and therefore the press has difficulty in providing consistent coverage.
政府の政策は変更されやすく，それ故に報道機関は一貫した報道をするのが困難であるから。

❶❷のI think the potential for government abuse is even worse ...では，政府が報道に干渉することへの懸念が示されている。このgovernment abuseとは政府が権力を濫用して報道・メディアを規制することを指しており，それがジャーナリストによる捏造記事の掲載よりも危険である理由は，As consumers, we have the power to ...以下で述べられている。それは，「一般の報道なら，我々がウェブサイトを閲覧しないことで打撃を与えることができるが，権力を握っている政府に対してその政策を変えさせるのは容易ではない」というもの。ここでは政府が権力を武器に，都合良く情報を操作する可能性が示唆されている。以上から d を正解とする。

(5) Which of the following statements would the speakers most likely agree with?
次の主張のうち，対話している人物たちが最も賛成しそうなものはどれか。

a) The information found on news sites is usually false.
ニュースサイトに載っている情報は，たいてい嘘である。

b) Freedom of the press should not apply to news sites.
報道の自由はニュースサイトには適用すべきでない。

c) Fact-checking is too difficult and slow for news sites to attempt.
事実確認は困難で時間がかかるため，ニュースサイトにはできない。

d) News sites are only reliable if they carefully verify their information.
ニュースサイトが信頼できるのは，それらが情報の真実性を入念に立証している場合のみである。

e) In order to protect yourself from fake news, it is important to always check multiple newspapers and choose the most reliable articles.
捏造記事から身を守るためには，常に複数の新聞をチェックし，最も信頼できる記事を選ぶことが大切だ。

❸〜❻の内容をもとに判断する。❸でAが「ニュースサイトを見るのをやめるべきだ」と言ったのに対し，❹ではBが「全てのニュースサイトを否定するのではなく，事実確認をしっかりやっているところ・やっていないところを調べて，前者を利用すべきだ」という趣旨の発言をしている。したがって，選択肢のaは言い過ぎであり，dが正解となる。また，❿や⓫では「報道の自由 (the freedom of the press)」に懐疑的になっているが，bのように「ニュースサイトには適用すべきではない」とまでは言っていない。

Set 11 解答

11A	(1) b	(2) a	(3) e	(4) a	(5) a
11B	(1) e	(2) c	(3) e	(4) b	(5) a
11C	(1) a	(2) c	(3) b	(4) a	(5) c

Set 11-A 放送文

Pain

❶ Joe: Good morning and welcome to *Book Talk with Joe Jones* on WKPR Radio. Our guest this morning is Betsy Hillcrest, a renowned scientist who has devoted her life to studying a topic most of us would rather forget exists at all: pain. Betsy, welcome to the show, and congratulations on your new book.

❷ Betsy: Thank you Joe, it's a pleasure to be here.

❸ Joe: Now Betsy, your new book, *The Puzzle of Pain*, introduces readers to cutting-edge research happening at hospitals and science labs around the world, but you write that your own interest in this topic grew out of a very personal experience.

❹ Betsy: That's right. When I was about ten years old, I began to experience severe pain in my right shoulder. My mother took me to the doctor, and x-rays revealed a cancerous tumor causing the pain. I underwent surgery to remove the tumor, and the pain stopped.

❺ Joe: So the story ended happily?

❻ Betsy: Not quite. About a year later, I once again began experiencing pain in my arm. This time, however, there was no tumor, and the doctor told me something very surprising.

❼ Joe: What was that?

❽ Betsy: She said that the pain was caused by my fear that the tumor would return.

❾ Joe: By your fear, not by an actual injury. Explain that.

❿ Betsy: Well, the function of pain is to warn our body about threats, such as extreme heat or cold or harm from a cut or a cancerous tumor.

⓫ Joe: In other words, its job is to protect us.

⓬ Betsy: Right. But the odd thing is that the level of

renowned 形 著名な
devote 他 …を捧げる
⏢文の構造：いわゆる「関係詞連鎖」が用いられている。a topic (which) <most of us would rather forget>exists at all の<>内を抜いてみると分かりやすい
congratulations on … 句 …についておめでとう
cutting-edge 形 最先端の

reveal 他 …を明らかにする
cancerous 形 がん性の
tumor 名 腫瘍
undergo 他 …を受ける
surgery 名 手術

threat 名 脅威

odd 形 奇妙な

the threat does not necessarily match up with the level of pain. In my case, my brain was trying to protect me from the threat of cancer even though it didn't exist anymore!

⑬ Joe: Wait a second, I thought it was our nerves that sense pain, but it sounds like you're saying it's our brain.

⑭ Betsy: It's both. Our bodies are packed with nerve endings called nociceptors that are responsible for detecting danger. If I put my hand on a hot stove, nociceptors send a message to my brain that says "Danger! Danger! Produce pain!" I feel that pain and react by moving my hand away from the hot surface, thereby avoiding the risk. But my brain also gets information about danger from other sources. For instance, I may remember burning my hand on a hot stove as a child, or see the color of the red-hot surface. Research has shown that these bits of information increase my sensation of pain, even though they have nothing to do with my nerve endings. So it's very complicated – and that's why I decided to write this book exploring the research. My hope is that it will help other victims of pain understand what they are experiencing.

⑮ Joe: And I'm very glad you did write it. I suffered through a broken ribcage last year, and I can certainly say I'd rather have a few less nociceptors myself.

⑯ Betsy: Be careful what you wish for, Joe. Remember, nociceptors are our danger detectors, and without them we'd have a very hard time protecting ourselves. People who can't feel pain often suffer frequent bone fractures, scarring and even premature death!

⑰ Joe: Hmmm. Being thankful for pain, that's an interesting concept. Well, we're just about out of time. Thanks very much for joining us today, Betsy.

⑱ Betsy: Thank you, Joe.

Betsy が手術後にも痛みを感じた理由：もはや存在しない脅威を感じて、脳が脅威を感じ、守ろうとした

nerve 名 神経

nerve ending 句 神経終末
nociceptor 名 侵害受容器
detect 他 …を検出する

thereby 副 それによって

sensation 名 感覚

ribcage 名 胸郭，肋骨

Joe の発言の主旨：nociceptors が少なければ，昨年肋骨を折った時に苦しまないで済んだかもしれない

bone fracture 句 骨折
scarring 名 傷
premature 形 時期尚早の

Set 11-A | 放送文の日本語訳

痛み

❶ジョー：おはようございます，WKPRラジオがお送りするジョー・ジョーンズの
ブック・トークにようこそ。今朝のゲストは，著名な科学者で，私たちのほとん
どが存在することすら忘れておきたいトピック，痛みの研究に人生を捧げている，
ベッツィー・ヒルクレストさんです。ベッツィーさん，番組へようこそ，そして
新しい著書のご出版おめでとうございます。

❷ベッツィー：ありがとうジョーさん，お招きいただいて嬉しいです。

❸ジョー：さてベッツィーさん，あなたの新刊『痛みの謎』は，世界中の病院や研究
所で行われている最先端の研究を読者に紹介していますが，あなたはご自身のこ
の話題への関心が極めて個人的な経験から生まれたのだと書いていますね。

❹ベッツィー：その通りです。10歳くらいの時，私は右肩にひどい痛みを感じ始めま
した。母が私を医者へ連れて行ってくれて，レントゲンでがん性腫瘍が痛みを引
き起こしていると分かったのです。腫瘍を切除する手術を受けて，痛みは治まり
ました。

❺ジョー：ではその件は無事落着したのですね。

❻ベッツィー：そうでもないのです。1年くらい経って，私は再び腕に痛みを感じ出
しました。しかし，今回は腫瘍は見つからず，医者は私にびっくりするようなこ
とを言ったのです。

❼ジョー：なんだったのですか。

❽ベッツィー：彼女は，腫瘍が再発するのではという私の怖れによって痛みが引き起
こされていると言いました。

❾ジョー：実際の症状ではなく，あなたの恐怖心によるものだというのですね。説明
してくださいますか。

❿ベッツィー：ええ，痛みの機能とは，私たちの体に脅威を警告することなのです。極
度の熱さや冷たさ，あるいは切り傷やがん性腫瘍からの害といったものを。

⓫ジョー：言い換えると，その働きは私たちを守ることだというわけですね。

⓬ベッツィー：そうです。しかし不思議なのは，脅威のレベルと痛みのレベルは必ず
しも一致しないということです。私のケースでは，腫瘍はもう存在していなかっ
たというのに，脳ががんの脅威から私を守ろうとしていたのです！

⓭ジョー：ちょっと待ってください，痛みを感じるのは神経だと思っていたのですが，
痛みを感じるのは脳なのだとおっしゃられているように聞こえます。

⓮ベッツィー：両方なんです。私たちの体は，危険を察知する働きをする侵害受容器
と呼ばれる神経終末でいっぱいになっています。もしも，私が熱くなったコンロ
に手を置けば，侵害受容器が「危険！　危険！　痛みを生成せよ！」というメッ
セージを脳に送ります。私は痛みを感じて，熱い表面から手を離すという反応を
します。それによって危険を避けるのです。しかし私の脳は別のところからも危
険についての情報を得るのです。たとえば，私は子どもの頃に熱いコンロで手を
やけどしたことを思い出すかもしれないし，赤く熱をもったコンロの表面の色を
見るかもしれません。研究によって，神経終末とは何も関係がなくても，こうし

た情報の断片が痛みの感覚を増大させるのだと分かってきました。つまり，とても複雑なんです——そういうわけで私は，研究についてよく調べてこの本を書くことにしました。私の願いは，この本が，痛みに苦しんでいる他の方々が自分たちの経験していることを理解する助けとなることなのです。

⑮ジョー：あなたが実際に書いてくれて本当に良かったと思います。私は昨年肋骨骨折に苦しめられたのですが，確かに言えるのは，自分の侵害受容器が少なかったらいいなということです。

⑯ベッツィー：自分が何を望んでいるのか，よく注意してください，ジョーさん。覚えておいてくださいね，侵害受容器というのは私たちの危険探知器であり，それらがなかったら自分の身を守るのにすごく苦労しますよ。痛みを感じることのできない人の中には，ひんぱんに骨折や怪我をする人や，早死にする人さえいるのです。

⑰ジョー：ううむ。痛みに感謝するというのは，興味深い考えですね。それでは，そろそろお時間です。今日はご出演どうもありがとうございました，ベッツィーさん。

⑱ベッツィー：ありがとうございました，ジョーさん。

《 指針 》

pain（痛み）をテーマとしたインタビューである。痛みが発生する仕組みについて，脳と神経がそれぞれどのように機能しているのかを理解する必要がある。放送文も容易ではないが，設問には複数の箇所を手がかりとするものもあり，難しい。細部の聞き取りだけでなく，総括的な内容理解が求められる。

難易度

放送文	★★☆
設　問	★★★
総　合	★★☆

☺☹))) **スピーカー情報**

Joe: スコットランド
Betsy: 西海岸，カリフォルニア

Set 11-A ｜設問解説

(1) According to Betsy, which of the following statements about pain is true?
ベッツィーの話によると，痛みについての次の説明のうち正しいものはどれか。

a) The brain is the only organ involved in sensing pain.
脳は痛みの知覚にかかわる唯一の臓器である。

b) Its function is to protect us from threats such as fire.
痛みの機能とは，火等の脅威から私たちを守ることである。

c) The level of pain we feel is always equal to the level of danger facing us.
私たちが感じる痛みのレベルは，直面している危険のレベルと常に等しい。

d) Past experiences do not play a role in determining how much pain we feel.
過去の経験は，私たちがどれほどの痛みを感じるかの決定に関係しない。

e) How much pain we feel depends on how much the experience means to you.
どれくらいの痛みを感じるかは，その経験がどれだけの意味を持つかによる。

放送文全体にまたがる問題である。ｂは❿の内容と合致する。ａは⓭から⓮にかけて「痛みを感じるのは脳と神経終末の両方である」と言われていることに反する。ｃは⓬の内容に反する。ｄは⓮の後半の「記憶が痛みの感覚を増すことがある」という内容に反する。ｅについての言及はない。

(2) What was the cause of the pain Betsy felt a year after the surgery?
手術の1年後にベッツィーが感じた痛みの原因は何だったか。

a) Her brain's incorrect perception.
彼女の脳の間違った知覚。

b) A psychological trauma from the surgery.
手術からくる心理的トラウマ。

c) A tumor that remained after the operation.
手術後に残っていた腫瘍。

d) Damage to her nerve endings from the surgery.
手術による神経終末の損傷。

e) A malfunction in the nerve endings that detect danger.
危険を感知する神経終末における機能不全。

Betsyが手術後にも痛みを感じた理由については❽～⓬で述べられているが，直接のヒントとなるのは⓬のmy brain was trying to protect me from the threat of cancer even though it didn't exist anymoreである。脳が，もはや存在しない脅威に対して，がんの脅威だと認識してしまったことが原因である。これがａのincorrect perceptionに相当する。これは脳の誤動作が原因であり，神経の問題ではないので，ｅは誤りである。

⑶ According to Betsy's account, which of the following is true about nociceptors?
　ベッツィーの説明によると，侵害受容器について正しいのは次のうちのどれか。

　a）Nociceptors can detect a threat that does not exist.
　　　侵害受容器は，存在しない脅威を発見することがある。
　b）Nociceptors remind us of our past experiences with the threat we face.
　　　侵害受容器は，直面している危険に関する過去の経験を思い出させる。
　c）Nociceptors receive information from the brain about the dangers around us.
　　　侵害受容器は，脳から私たちをとりまく危険についての情報を受け取る。
　d）Nociceptors are the part of the brain which is responsible for producing pain.
　　　侵害受容器は，痛みを作る働きをする脳の一部である。
　e）None of the above.
　　　上記のいずれでもない。

nociceptors（侵害受容器）については⓮で説明されている。危険を検出し，その情報を脳に送る神経終末のことである。a はむしろ脳の働きに該当する。b は nociceptors ではなく，⓮の後半で述べられる「脳が参考にする別の情報」に該当する。c は関係が逆。危険についての情報は nociceptors から脳へと送られるのである。また nociceptors は身体中にあるものであり，脳の一部ではないので d も誤り。よって e が正解となる。

⑷ Which of the following does Betsy mention as a reason for writing a book about pain research?
　痛みの研究についての本を書いた理由として，ベッツィーが挙げているのはどれか。

　a）She wanted to help people understand their pain.
　　　人々が自分たちの痛みのことを理解するのを助けたかった。
　b）She wanted to understand the pain other people feel.
　　　他人が感じている痛みを理解したかった。
　c）She wanted to help reduce the pain other people feel.
　　　他人が感じている痛みを和らげるのを助けたかった。
　d）She wanted to correct people's misunderstanding about pain.
　　　人々の痛みについての誤解を正したかった。
　e）She wanted to write about how other people experience pain.
　　　他人がどのように痛みを経験しているのかを書きたかった。

Betsy がこの本を書こうと思い立ったきっかけについては，⓮の最後で述べられている。「自分の経験から，痛みの複雑さを研究したいと思った。そして痛みに苦しんでいる人が自分の経験していることを理解する手助けをしたい」というもの。これが a に該当する。

⑸ How does Joe feel about pain, according to the interview?
インタビューによると，ジョーは痛みについてどう感じているか。

a) He wishes he had felt less pain from a rib injury last year.
昨年の肋骨の怪我での痛みがもっと少なかったら良かったと思っている。

b) He would rather not think about pain because it is too complex.
あまりに複雑なので痛みについては考えたくないと思っている。

c) He is thankful for pain because it prevented a rib injury last year.
昨年肋骨の怪我を防いでくれたので，痛みに感謝している。

d) He is confused by pain because it is not always caused by a real injury.
痛みがいつも実際の怪我によって引き起こされるわけではないので困惑している。

e) He didn't feel so much pain from a rib injury because he didn't have many nociceptors.
侵害受容器の数が少なかったおかげで，肋骨の怪我でそれほど痛みを感じなかった。

❶❺の発言内容についての問題。Joe が I'd rather have a few less nociceptors myself と言っているのは，nociceptors が少なければ，痛みも減ったはずだと考えたからである。 a が正解。彼が骨折をしたのは事実であるから， c は誤り。

Set 11-B | 放送文

Artists and Tools

❶ Woman: Hi, we'd like two tickets for the guided tour of the Japanese print exhibit.

print 名 版画

❷ Museum cashier: I'm sorry, the tour started 15 minutes ago.

❸ Woman: Well, would we be able to join the group anyway?

❹ Museum cashier: Yes, that's fine, but I'll have to charge you the full ticket price.

charge 他 …に料金を請求する

❺ Woman: Okay, we'll do that.

❻ Museum cashier: The group should be in the large gallery on the second floor, to the right of the stairs.

❼ Woman: Great, thank you.

[Sound of woman and man rushing to join the tour]

❽ Tour guide: ...and what you see around you in this room is perhaps the most famous series of Japanese woodblock prints of all time. You'll notice that all the prints here share a common element: the distinctly conical Mt. Fuji. Indeed, these are *the Thirty-Six Views of Mount Fuji*, created by the Edo-era artist Hokusai and published by Nishimura Yohachi starting in 1830. They were an instant hit. Part of that of course was due to the fame and artistic mastery of Hokusai himself, who was already 70 years old at the time. But there was also another quite peculiar reason the series sold so well, and that was the color palette Hokusai used – well, one color in particular. If you have a look at the five prints lined up on this wall, which were in fact the first prints in the series, I think you'll be able to figure out what that color was. Anyone?

woodblock print 句 木版画

conical 形 円錐形の

mastery 名 熟達, 技量

peculiar 形 独特の, 妙な

📌 『富嶽三十六景』がヒットした理由：1. 北斎の知名度と技量，2. 北斎の色遣い

❾ Man: Blue!

❿ Guide: Right, blue. These five images were created entirely in shades of blue, in a style called aizuri-e, which literally means "blue printed pictures." The next five prints were semi-aizuri, that is, mostly blue with just a hint of pink, green, and black. The remaining images included a full range of

shade 名 色合い, 濃淡
literally 副 文字通り

a hint of ... 句 少量の…

colors, with heavy use of blue. But this was not any ordinary blue – at least not in Japan of the 1830s. It was a synthetic pigment imported from Europe called Prussian blue that had just begun to be widely available to artists at an affordable price. Prussian blue was all the rage in Japan back then – kind of like smartphones today! Nishimura wanted to make the most of the trend, so he asked Hokusai to make a series of blue prints. Yes, did you have a question?

❶ Woman: Why was that color so popular?

❷ Guide: In part, it symbolized the exotic and distant culture of Europe, where it came from. But it also had aesthetic appeal. Up till that point, Japanese artists had derived their blues from natural materials such as flower petals and indigo plants. In contrast the new color was a chemical product, and it could produce a wider range of more brilliant blues. It was also more abundant. Prussian blue had quite an impact on the style and content of Hokusai's work. You'll notice that most of the images in this room contain striking expanses of blue sky and water, which his earlier works do not. Some scholars believe Hokusai used blue to convey the importance of water and rebirth, which he associated with Mt. Fuji. Ironically, when these prints were first exhibited in Europe, people had no idea that the main ingredient in the blue ink had in fact originated close to their own home. They believed Hokusai had used native Japanese pigments, and even attributed the mysterious beauty of the images to Japan's indigo blues, which were not available in Europe at that time!

synthetic 形 合成の
pigment 名 顔料

affordable 形 手頃な値段の

all the rage 句 大流行して
いる

make the most of ... 句 …
を最大限に利用する

▶事実関係の把握：北斎の版
画には，ヨーロッパから輸
入されて普及し始め，人気
を博していた青の合成顔料
が用いられていた

symbolize 他 …を象徴する
aesthetic 形 美の，審美的な
appeal 名 魅力
derive A from B 句 Bから
Aを得る
petal 名 花びら
indigo 名 藍，インディゴ
brilliant 形 鮮やかな
abundant 形 豊富な
expanse 名 広がり

▶Prussian blue が北斎に与
えた影響：空と水を多く描
くようになった

convey 他 …を伝える
rebirth 名 再生
associate A with B 句 Aを
Bと結び付ける
ironically 副 皮肉なことに
ingredient 名 成分
attribute A to B 句 Aの原
因がBだと考える

▶「皮肉なことに (ironi-
cally)」の意味：ヨーロッ
パ人は，北斎の版画の美し
さは，日本独特の顔料を使
っているせいだと考えたが，
実はそれはヨーロッパ産の
顔料だった

Set 11-B | 放送文の日本語訳

芸術家と道具

❶女性：すみません，日本の版画展のガイド付きツアーのチケットを2枚いただけますか。

❷美術館のレジ係：申しわけありません。ツアーは15分前に出発しました。

❸女性：そうですか。途中から参加することはできますか。

❹美術館のレジ係：ええ，それは構いませんが，料金を全額お支払いいただかなければなりません。

❺女性：結構です。ではそれでお願いします。

❻美術館のレジ係：ツアーの方々は2階の大きな展示室にいるはずです。階段の右です。

❼女性：分かりました。ありがとう。

　　　　　　［女性と男性がツアーに合流しようと急ぐ音］

❽ツアーガイド：……この部屋に展示してあるのは，日本の木版画史上おそらく最も有名な連作です。全ての作品に共通の要素があることにお気付きでしょう。円錐形が特徴的な富士山ですね。そうです。これは『富嶽三十六景』です。江戸時代の芸術家，北斎によって制作され，西村与八によって1830年から出版されました。たちまち大成功を収めました。もちろんその理由の一部は，北斎自身の名声と芸術家としての技量にありました。当時彼は既に70歳でした。しかし，この連作の売れ行きが良かったことには，もう1つたいへん特殊な理由もありました。それは，北斎が使用した一連の色彩――それも，特にある1つの色でした。こちらの壁に展示してある5点の作品をご覧ください。これらはこの連作の最初期の作品なのですが，これを見ると，それが何色か分かると思います。どなたか，お分かりの方は？

❾男性：青！

❿ガイド：そうです。青ですね。この5点の作品は青の濃淡だけで表現されています。「藍摺絵（あいずりえ）」と呼ばれる技法です。文字通り，「藍色で摺られた絵」という意味です。その次の5点は藍摺に準ずるものです。つまりほとんど青ですが，わずかに淡紅色，緑，黒が使われています。これら以外の作品には，青を基調としつつ，あらゆる色が使われています。ところが，これは決して普通の青ではありませんでした。少なくとも1830年代の日本においては普通ではありませんでした。それは「プルシアンブルー」と呼ばれるヨーロッパから輸入された合成顔料で，手頃な値段で芸術家たちの間に普及し始めたところでした。当時の日本ではプルシアンブルーが大流行しました。今日のスマートフォンみたいなものです！　西村はこの流行を最大限に活用しようと考えました。そこで北斎に一連の藍摺の作品を作らせたのです。はい，ご質問ですね。

⓫女性：その色はどうしてそんなに人気があったのですか。

⓬ガイド：1つには，それがやってきた土地，ヨーロッパというエキゾチックで遠い土地の文化を象徴していたからです。しかし，それはまた審美的な魅力も具えていました。その時点まで，日本の芸術家たちは青を天然物質から採っていました。花びらや藍（インディゴ・プランツ）等です。それに対して，この新しい顔料は化学製品であり，より鮮やかな種々の青色を作り出すことができました。ま

たそれは量的にも豊富でした。プルシアンブルーは北斎の作品の様式と内容に大きな影響を与えました。この部屋のほとんどの作品に，青い空と海の驚くほどの広がりが描かれているのが分かりますね。それ以前の彼の作品はそうではありませんでした。北斎は水と再生の意義を伝えるために青を使った，そして彼はその意義を富士山と結び付けていた，と考える研究者もいます。皮肉なことに，これらの版画がヨーロッパで初めて展示された時，人々は，その青いインクの主要な成分が実は自分たちの故郷の近くに由来するものであるとは思いもしませんでした。彼らは，北斎は日本原産の顔料を使ったと考え，それらの作品の神秘的な美を，当時のヨーロッパでは入手できなかった日本のインディゴブルー（藍色）のおかげだとさえ考えたのです！

《 指針 》

葛飾北斎による『富嶽三十六景』については知っている人も多いだろう。ここでは，一連の作品に使われている青の顔料（プルシアンブルー）に焦点を当て，このツールが芸術家にどのような影響を与えたかについて語られる。聞き取りのポイントは以下の4つ。「プルシアンブルーとは何か」「なぜプルシアンブルーが人気を博したのか」「プルシアンブルーの使用によって北斎の画風はどう変わったか」「ヨーロッパで人々はどのような誤解をしたのか」。放送文の難易度はそれほど高くないが，設問の (4) (5) はやや難しい。

難易度

放送文	★★☆
設 問	★★☆
総 合	★★☆

☺☹))) スピーカー情報

Woman: 西海岸，カリフォルニア
Cashier: 中西部，イリノイ
Guide: 西海岸，カリフォルニア
Man: 西海岸，カリフォルニア

Set 11-B ｜ 設問解説

(1) Why does the cashier apologize to the woman?
レジ係が女性に謝っているのはなぜか。

a) Because she can't join the tour.
彼女がツアーに参加できないから。

b) Because the tickets were sold out.
チケットが売り切れていたから。

c) Because he gave her incorrect change.
彼が彼女に渡すお釣りを間違えたから。

d) Because she has to pay extra for her tickets.
彼女がチケット代として追加料金を支払わなければならないから。

e) Because she's missed the beginning of the tour.
彼女がツアーの最初の部分を聞き逃したから。

❷から，レジ係は，ツアーが15分前に始まってしまったことに対しI'm sorryと言っていることが分かる。正解は e 。この客は通常の料金を払って参加したので， d は誤り。

(2) According to the tour guide, why were *the Thirty-Six Views of Mount Fuji* so popular when they were first released?
ツアーガイドによれば，最初に売り出された時『富嶽三十六景』がそれほど人気を博したのはなぜか。

a) Because they were printed using a wide variety of colors.
様々な色を使って刷られていたから。

b) Because they were created by an up-and-coming young artist.
前途有望な若い芸術家の作品だったから。

c) Because they used a new blue pigment imported from Europe.
ヨーロッパから輸入された新しい青の顔料を使用していたから。

d) Because they depicted a mountain with great spiritual and cultural significance.
霊的・文化的に非常に重要な山を描いたものだったから。

e) Because they made effective use of geometric forms such as the conical Mount Fuji.
円錐形の富士山などの幾何学的な形態を効果的に利用していたから。

❽❿では，『富嶽三十六景』が人気を博した理由として，北斎自身の知名度と技量の他に，Prussian blueという青の顔料を使用したことが挙げられている。 c が正解。❽では，全ての作品に富士山が描かれていることが説明されているが，それと人気との関連性についての言及はない。

256

(3) According to the tour guide, which of the following is NOT a way in which Prussian blue differed from traditional blue pigments used in Japan?
ツアーガイドによれば，プルシアンブルーが日本で使用されていた伝統的な青の顔料と異なっていた点として適切でないのは次のうちどれか。

a) It was more widely available.
より入手しやすかった。

b) It was imported from Europe.
ヨーロッパから輸入された。

c) It produced more vivid colors.
より鮮やかな色を作り出した。

d) It was derived from chemicals rather than plants.
植物ではなく化学製品に由来するものだった。

e) It could be combined with other colors like pink and green.
淡紅色や緑等，他の色と混ぜ合わせることが可能だった。

❿では，プルシアンブルーがヨーロッパから輸入されたものであることが説明されており，これがｂに該当する。⓬では，プルシアンブルーと従来の青の顔料との違いについてさらに説明されている。the new color was a chemical product, and it could produce a wider range of more brilliant blues. It was also more abundant.という発言から分かるように，「化学製品由来だった」，「より鮮やかな幅広い青を表現可能だった」，「豊富にあった」という３点が指摘されており，これがそれぞれｄ，ｃ，ａに該当する。ｅについての言及はない。

(4) According to the tour guide, how did the availability of Prussian blue change Hokusai's work?
ツアーガイドによれば，プルシアンブルーが入手できるようになったことで，北斎の作品はどのように変化したか。

a) It made his prints more affordable for a mass audience.
彼の版画は多くの人に買いやすい価格になった。

b) It altered the type of landscape element he emphasized.
強調する景色の要素の種類が変わった。

c) It led him to explore sadder themes associated with blue.
青が連想させる悲しい主題を探究するようになった。

d) It encouraged him to draw in a more realistic, European style.
いっそう写実的な，ヨーロッパ的様式で描くようになった。

e) It enabled him to express natural scenes in a more dramatic way.
自然の風景をより劇的に表現できるようになった。

プルシアンブルーが北斎の作風に与えた影響については，⓬の中盤で説明されている。most of the images in this room contain striking expanses of blue sky and water, which his earlier works do notとあるように，以前は描かなかったような，広大な青い空や水を描くようになったのである。これを言い換えたｂが正

解となる。安価になったのは北斎の版画ではなくプルシアンブルーの顔料であるから, a は誤り。

（5）What was ironic about the European reaction to Hokusai's work, according to the guide?
ガイドによれば, 北斎の作品に対するヨーロッパ人の反応の, 何が皮肉だったのか。
 a ）They thought the prints were more exotic than they actually were.
  それらの版画を実際以上にエキゾチックと考えた。
 b ）They didn't realize Hokusai had been trained in European techniques.
  北斎がヨーロッパ的な技術の訓練を受けていたことに気づかなかった。
 c ）They mistakenly believed that Hokusai was influenced by European art.
  北斎がヨーロッパの芸術に影響を受けたと誤解していた。
 d ）They didn't know that European artists were also using Japanese indigo.
  ヨーロッパの芸術家たちもまた日本の藍を使用していることを知らなかった。
 e ）They were excited about the colors rather than the symbolism of the images.
  それらの作品の象徴より色彩に興奮した。

❷の後半のIronically, ... では, 『富嶽三十六景』が初めてヨーロッパで展示された時の, 「皮肉な」反応について述べられている。その内容は「ヨーロッパ人は, 『富嶽三十六景』の神秘的な美しさの原因は, 日本独特の顔料であるインディゴブルーを使っているからだと考えた。しかし, 実際は, 自分たちの住むヨーロッパを原産とするプルシアンブルーが使われていた」というものである。つまり, 彼らが「いかにも日本的だ」と感じていたものが, 実はヨーロッパ由来だったということであり, これを選択肢の a では the prints were more exotic than they actually were と表現している。exotic は「異国情緒のある」という意味の形容詞である。

Set 11-C | 放送文

Uncanny Valley

❶ It sounds like many a sci-fi story: a robot that doesn't know he is a robot, but instead thinks he is alive. In one version, the trait that makes the android human is his ability to love. But what really distinguishes the mechanical from the biological? Is it possible that one day, in the not-so-distant future, the line between the factory-made and the human-born will disappear? Many scientists say that this is not only probable, but likely.

❷ Some worry that when that day comes, we will be unable to tell humans and androids apart. Hiroshi Ishiguro, one of the most well-known makers of humanoid robots, thinks this is the case. He believes that in the future, robotics engineers will be able to make robots that can pass as humans. These researchers have long been attempting to copy human traits, movements, and appearance, thinking that people would connect more easily with robots if they looked like us. This is true, up to a point. The more an object resembles a human, the more positive a person's reaction to it is. Yet, surprisingly, it turns out that if an android looks too similar to a human, people are turned off by it. That is, the appearance of something almost—but not quite—human makes people feel uncomfortable, rather than connected to it. This sudden drop, from a positive reaction to a negative one, is called the "uncanny valley".

❸ There are several theories that seek to explain this effect. One states that since humans feel a similar dislike for dead bodies and false limbs, the uncanny valley comes from a fear of death and disease. Another claims that the inability of technology to match human behavior and movement exactly exaggerates the "wrongness," or inhumanness, of the robot. In this theory, the psychological tendency of humans to group objects comes into play. Researchers point to evidence that shows humans are less bothered

---

many a ... 句 多くの…
sci-fi 名 SF (science fiction)
trait 名 特徴
android 名 人造人間, アンドロイド
distinguish A from B 句 A を B と区別する

🔲 発言の主旨：人間とロボットの違いはなくなりつつある

tell A and B apart 句 A と B を見分ける
humanoid robot 句 人型ロボット
robotics 名 ロボット工学
pass as ... 句 …として通用する

turn off 句 …をうんざりさせる

uncanny 形 不気味な
🔲 uncanny valley とは：人が, ロボットなど人間に極めて似たものに対して嫌悪感を抱く現象
limb 名 手足 (の1つ), 肢

exaggerate 他 …を強調する

come into play 句 作用する

by robots that act like robots, or humans that act like humans. Conversely, humans that act like robots (or the opposite) make us uncomfortable because they fail to live up to expected behavior. Furthermore, one study has shown that it's not only humans who experience the uncanny valley effect. Monkeys also tend to avoid overly-realistic monkey models, meaning that this is not a uniquely human reaction.

❹　That is not to say that everyone agrees on the existence of the uncanny valley. Critics of the concept argue that people react negatively to realistic robots simply because we are shocked by new things. These critics point out that mankind has historically reacted with surprise and often rejection of anything foreign. After the novelty has become part of our everyday lives, however, we begin to see it as normal. Humans, after all, are used to adapting; once we become accustomed to robots, we won't even remember how different they used to seem.

❺　The entertainment industry is a case in point. For many years, animators worried about making their characters too realistic, in case their appearance made the audience uncomfortable, thereby reducing profits. That fear is rapidly disappearing, however, and more life-like cartoons are appearing onscreen. As artificial intelligence —and plain old CGI—becomes not only more realistic, but more common, humans will likely get used to the slight differences between true human appearance and human-like appearance. In fact, the tendency of some celebrities to experiment with body modifications like piercings, tattoos, and plastic surgery may help normalize nonhuman traits. In that case, perhaps it isn't only robots that are mimicking us, but us copying them, too.

🗂 uncanny valley の原因：
1. 死や病気を連想させるから，2. 本物の人間とのわずかな違いが，かえって違和感を強調するから

live up to … 句 …（期待など）に沿う，かなう

critic 名 批判する人

🗂 uncanny valley に対する批判：ロボットなどの目新しいものに拒否反応を示しているだけで，すぐに慣れるだろう

novelty 名 新奇なもの

case in point 句 好例，ぴったりした例

in case … 句 …するといけないので

cartoon 名 漫画，アニメ

artificial intelligence 句 人工知能

plain old 句 ありきたりな，普通の

🗂 uncanny valley が消えつつある例：アニメにおいて，かつては敬遠されていたリアルな人物描画が，最近は主流になっている

celebrity 名 有名人

modification 名 修正，改良，改造

plastic surgery 句 美容整形

normalize 他 …を標準化する

mimic 他 …を模倣する

Set 11-C ｜放送文の日本語訳

不気味の谷

❶　自分がロボットであることを知らない，それどころか自分が生きていると考えているロボット──。それは数あるSF小説のように聞こえます。あるバージョンでは，アンドロイドを人間にする特徴は，愛する能力であるとされています。しかし，機械的存在と生物学的存在とを真に区別するものは何でしょうか。遠くない将来のいつか，工場で作られたものと人間から生まれたものの間の境界線が消滅するなどということが起こり得るのでしょうか。多くの科学者が，それは可能性があるというだけでなく実際に起こりそうだと言っています。

❷　その日が訪れた時，私たちは人間とアンドロイドを見分けることができないだろうと憂慮する人もいます。人型ロボット開発者の最も著名な人物の1人，石黒浩は，まさにそうだと考えています。彼は，ロボット工学のエンジニアは，将来，人間として通用するロボットを作れるようになると考えています。これらの研究者たちは，長年，人間の特徴，動作，外見を複製しようとしてきました。ロボットが人間に似ている方が，人々がロボットと関わりを持ちやすいと考えたのです。これはある程度までは真理です。対象が人間に似ていれば似ているほど，それに対する人の反応は肯定的になります。しかし意外なことに，アンドロイドが人間に過度に似ていると，そのことで人々が嫌な気持ちになることが分かったのです。つまり，外見が人とほとんど同じなのに，完全に同じではないものは，それとの繋がりの意識ではなく不快感を与えるのです。肯定的な反応から否定的な反応へのこうした急落は，「不気味の谷」と呼ばれています。

❸　この作用が起こる理由を説明しようとする説はいくつかあります。その1つは，人間は死体や義肢に同様の嫌悪感を持つことから，不気味の谷は死や病気に対する恐怖に由来すると言います。また別の説は，テクノロジーは人間の行動や動作と完全に一致させることができないために，ロボットの「おかしさ」，つまり非人間性が強調されてしまうと言います。この説においては，対象をグループ化する人間の心理的傾向が作用しています。研究者たちは，人間はロボットらしい動作をするロボットや人間らしい振る舞いをする人間に対してはあまり不快に感じないことを示す証拠を指摘しています。反対に，ロボットのように振る舞う人間（あるいはその逆）は，期待通りの行動をしないため，我々を不快にするのです。さらに，不気味の谷の作用を経験するのが人間だけではないことを明らかにした研究もあります。サルもまた，過度にリアルなサルの模型を避ける傾向にあるので，これは人間に固有の反応ではないのです。

❹　しかし，だからと言って，全ての人が不気味の谷の存在に合意しているわけではありません。この概念の批判者は，人々がリアルなロボットに否定的な反応をするのは，単に我々が新しいものに衝撃を受けるからだと論じています。こういった批判者は，人類は歴史的に，あらゆる異質なものに対し，驚きとしばしば拒絶をもって反応してきたと指摘します。しかし，新奇なものが日常生活の一部になったあとは，我々はそれを標準と見なし始めます。結局のところ，人間は適応するようにできているのです。一旦ロボットに慣れてしまうと，我々は，それら

がいかに異質に見えていたかさえ思い出せなくなるでしょう。

❺　娯楽産業がその良い例です。長年，アニメ製作者は登場人物を過度にリアルに描くことに懸念を抱いていました。そうした外見が観客を不快にし，それによって収益が減じるといけないからでした。しかし，そのような心配は急速に解消されつつあり，より実物そっくりのアニメが現れつつあります。人工知能や普通のCGIがいっそうリアルであるだけでなくいっそう一般的になるにつれ，人間は，本物の人間の外見と人間のような外見の間のわずかな差異に慣れていくでしょう。実際，一部の有名人たちの，ピアスやタトゥーや美容整形などの身体改造を試みる傾向は，非人間的な特性の標準化に役立つかもしれません。そのような場合，おそらく，ロボットが我々を模倣するだけでなく，我々も彼らを模倣することになるでしょう。

《〈 指針 〉》

「不気味の谷（Uncanny Valley）」という心理作用を中心に，人間とロボットの差が縮まっていくことから生じうる問題点について述べた講義である。「不気味の谷」の作用が何故起こるのかについての諸説を紹介し，さらにこの作用が存在しないとする批判があることを指摘する。最後は，むしろこの批判と同じ立場に立って，アニメや身体改造にまで話を広げつつ，過度にリアルな人間的外観に我々が慣れてきたのではないかと主張する。放送文の聴解は難しい。「人は，人間に極めて近い造形物に対して嫌悪感を抱く」という現象が全体のテーマとなっており，これをいち早くつかんだ上で，話者が今どの立場から何を述べようとしているのかを考えながら聞き取るように心がけよう。

難易度

放送文	★★★
設　問	★★☆
総　合	★★☆

😊😐))) スピーカー情報

Lecturer: 西海岸，カリフォルニア

Set 11-C | 設問解説

(1) Based on the lecture, which statement would many scientists likely agree with?
   講義に基づけば，多数の科学者が賛成しそうな主張は次のうちどれか。

  a) Before long, robots will appear identical to humans.
    遠からず，ロボットは人間と同じに見えるようになるだろう。

  b) Robots that resemble humans too closely are dangerous.
    人間に似すぎたロボットは危険である。

  c) In the future, humans will probably be created in factories.
    将来，人間はおそらく工場で製造されるだろう。

  d) In the not-too-distant future, humans will be replaced by robots.
    遠くない将来，人間はロボットに取って代わられるだろう。

  e) The key difference between humans and robots is the ability to love.
    人間とロボットの主要な差異は愛する能力である。

❶の Many scientists say that this is not only probable, but likely. の this とは，その前文を指しており，「ロボットと人間を隔てる境界線が消滅する」ことを表す。よって a が正解。❷の冒頭の文も根拠となる。❶の the factory-made とは，工場で作られたロボットのことを指しており，c のように「人間が工場で製造される」ということは言われていない。また，e の内容は，SF小説でそのような設定になっているということであり，科学的な根拠を持つものではない。

(2) What is the "uncanny valley"?
   「不気味の谷」とはどのようなものか。

  a) Negative responses we make to non-human organisms.
    人間が人間以外の生物に対して示すネガティブな反応。

  b) The recent unexplained dip in the popularity of robots.
    ロボットの流行における，近年の解明されていない下落。

  c) The tendency to reject or fear robots that are too human-like.
    過度に人間に似たロボットを拒絶し恐れる傾向。

  d) A geographical location where many robots are manufactured.
    多数のロボットが製造される地理的な場所。

  e) The point at which people stop fearing robots and start liking them.
    人々がロボットを恐れるのをやめ，それらに好意をもち始める時点。

放送文全体のテーマである「不気味の谷（uncanny valley）」という現象については，❷の後半で説明される。ロボットなどが人間に近づけば近づくほど，人はそれに対し好印象を抱くが，あるレベルを超えて「人間に似過ぎてしまう」と，印象がネガティブなものへと「急落」するという現象である。この「急落」を「谷（valley）」にたとえている。これに合致した c が正解。b にあるような「流行の下落」が「谷」なのではない。

(3) Which of the following is NOT mentioned as a reason the uncanny valley effect exists?

不気味の谷の作用が存在する理由として言及されていないのは，次のうちどれか。

a) The fact that people may associate robots with death.
人々はロボットから死を連想する可能性があるという事実。

b) The human tendency to experiment with our own appearance.
自分自身の外見で実験を行う人間の傾向。

c) A natural behavioral tendency that humans share with other animals.
人間と他の動物に共通する生来の行動傾向。

d) The inability of engineers to make robots that are identical to humans.
エンジニアが，人間と同一のロボットを製造できないこと。

e) The failure of robots to behave as people expect man-made objects to behave.
ロボットが，人々が人工物に期待する行動をとれないこと。

不気味の谷の現象についての理由としては，❸で2つの説が紹介されている。1つは，「人間に極めて似ている物は，死や病気などを連想させる」というもの。これがaに該当する。もう1つは「科学技術では人間と全く同じ物は作れないので，その小さな違いが強調されてしまい，期待通りの行動をしないことで不快感を覚えてしまう」というもので，これがd及びeに該当する。さらに，「サルなど，他の動物にも同様の傾向が見られる」ということが紹介されており，これがcに相当する。bについては❺の最後で言及があるが，これはむしろ「uncanny valleyが消滅している」ことの論拠として提示されている。

(4) What is the argument against the existence of the uncanny valley?
不気味の谷の存在を否定する議論はどのようなものか。

a) People often dislike objects that are unfamiliar to them.
人々はしばしば，よく知らない対象を嫌悪する。

b) People are also afraid of other types of advanced technology.
人々は別の形式の先進技術も恐れる。

c) People get accustomed to an unfamiliar object as soon as they see it.
人々は見知らぬ物体を見るとすぐにそれに慣れる。

d) Most people are actually excited by the possibility of human-like robots.
ほとんどの人々は実際に，人間に似たロボットの可能性に興奮する。

e) The entertainment industry has made robots familiar, so they are no longer scary.
娯楽産業がロボットを見慣れたものにしたので，それらはもはや恐ろしくない。

「不気味の谷」の存在を否定する説については，❹で紹介されている。mankind has historically reacted with surprise and often rejection of anything foreignとあるように，「人は異質なものに対しては何でも拒否反応を起こす」というものである。これに合致するaが正解。

(5) How has the entertainment industry changed, according to the lecture?
講義によれば，娯楽産業はどのように変化したか。

a) Animators today worry more about declining profits.
今日のアニメ製作者は収益の減少をいっそう懸念している。

b) Animators in the past drew more realistic characters.
過去のアニメ製作者はいっそうリアルな登場人物を描いていた。

c) Animators today worry less about drawing overly realistic characters.
今日のアニメ製作者は過度にリアルな登場人物を描くことをあまり懸念していない。

d) Animators in the past worried more about drawing unrealistic characters.
過去のアニメ製作者はリアルではない登場人物を描くことをより懸念していた。

e) Animators in the past worried less about making audiences uncomfortable.
過去のアニメ製作者は観客を不快にすることをあまり懸念していなかった。

❺の内容理解を問う問題である。❹で述べられた，「不気味の谷」の存在を否定する説を受けて，❺ではその説を裏付けるような事例が紹介される。「昔のアニメは，観客の拒否反応を避けるために，リアルすぎる人物は描かなかった。しかし最近はCGIなどを用いてよりリアルなアニメが作られている」という内容である。これに合致するcが正解。

Set 12 | 解答

12A	(1) b	(2) b	(3) d	(4) a	(5) b
12B	(1) d	(2) d	(3) b	(4) a	(5) a
12C	(1) c	(2) c	(3) a	(4) b	(5) c

Set 12-A | 放送文

History of Letter Writing

❶ With the advent of modern technology and a corresponding increase in near-instantaneous communication, it is easy to forget the role letters and letter-writing once played in society. Yet for centuries, countries worked to establish primitive postal systems, using horses, birds, or human runners to relay messages across empires. Some rulers are even said to have used letters to play chess with others.

❷ For a long time, only the government sent letters and other mail, and usually only for matters of state or warfare. One reason for this was the difficulty of sending messages. For example, messengers on horseback had to be changed frequently as both horses and their riders became exhausted, making them a privilege only the wealthy and powerful could afford. Even then messages did not always get through, due to the poor quality of roads, the risk of bad weather, and other dangers of traveling. Another reason letter writing was not widespread was that the general population was unable to read. However, the invention of the printing press caused literacy rates to rise, mostly due to the increased availability of printed material. In England, from Shakespeare's time to the 1700s, the number of men able to read increased from 10 percent to an estimated 60 percent. The spirit of Europe's Enlightenment period had spread, and its thinkers used letters to inquire, discuss, and debate with philosophers in other countries.

❸ From there, letter writing gained popularity among the common people, not just scholars. By

advent 图 到来
corresponding 形 一致する, 対応する
instantaneous 形 即時の
establish 他 …を確立する
primitive 形 原始的な
relay 他 …を(中継ぎして)伝える

warfare 图 戦争

privilege 图 特権

📝 手紙が一般に普及しなかった理由：1. 手紙を届けるのが困難で，コストがかかった，2. 一般大衆の識字率が低かった

printing press 句 印刷機
literacy 图 識字

📝 手紙が一般に普及した原因：印刷の発明による識字率の上昇

Enlightenment 图 (18世紀ヨーロッパの) 啓蒙運動
inquire 自 尋ねる, 質問する

the early 1800s, women in England were also becoming more educated, with over half able to read and write. That led to an increase in personal correspondence between friends and family. The tools used to write letters, however, had not evolved much since the 1500s. Although metal nibs had been invented for use as the tips of pens, they were too expensive for most people. So, many still used feather quills as pens. Goose-feather pens were common, while swan and peacock feathers were treasured writing implements. The writer had to make her own quills based on her own preferences.

❹ As with other forms of communication, social norms controlled writing behavior. For instance, men and women were not allowed to write to each other unless they were related or engaged to be married. Another courtesy involved the matter of postage. Because the person receiving the letter paid per page, the writer of the letter tried to use as little paper as possible. This resulted in the "crossed letters" common at the time; once the letter writer had filled the page left to right, she turned the paper 90 degrees and wrote across her original lines. Looking at these crossed letters is similar to looking at check-patterned cloth.

❺ By the Victorian period in the mid-19th century, letter-writing had become an art form. The expression of self was further limited by a number of guidelines, much like other behaviors were in that era. Letter-writing guides were published to help the writer conform to societal expectations. Men were expected to use plain paper, while women could use decorated, or even perfume-scented, versions. Both sexes wrote with black ink, although blue was also acceptable, and used wax to seal their envelopes.

❻ Most importantly, perhaps, was the expectation that the writer be able to produce attractive and easily read handwriting. Penmanship, as the ability to write by hand was called, was very important to many Victorians. In fact, during this time a particular type of cursive handwriting,

correspondence 图 文通

nib 图 ペン先

quill 图 羽柄
peacock 图 クジャク
implement 图 道具

social norm 句 社会規範

courtesy 图 礼儀正しさ，気遣い
postage 图 郵便料金

▸ crossed letters とは：郵便料金を節約するために，同じ紙に，2方向に交差させて書いた手紙

▸ ビクトリア朝時代の手紙：様々なルールに縛られた，一種の芸術になる

conform to … 句 …に従う，順応する

wax 图 蠟，封蠟
seal 他 …に封をする

penmanship 图 書法，習字法

cursive 形 筆記体の

called copperplate, came into fashion. Copperplate was given its name because children learned to write their letters from model letters engraved on copper plates. There were many styles of copperplate, such as the French style and the Palace style. Many of these styles appear more similar to today's calligraphy than to modern cursive.

engrave 他 …を彫る，刻む

❼   Of course, some people today are only able to print, and cannot use these more ornamental types of handwriting at all; perhaps letter-writing will soon be a lost art of communication, like the language of the fan.

calligraphy 名 カリグラフィー，書道
print 自 活字体で書く
ornamental 形 装飾的な
the language of the fan 句 扇言葉（18世紀のフランス宮廷で女性に広まった，扇子を使うコミュニケーション法）

Set 12-A | 放送文の日本語訳

手紙の歴史

❶   現代テクノロジーの到来とそれに伴うほとんど即時のコミュニケーションの増加によって，手紙や手紙を書くことがかつて社会の中で担っていた役割は忘れられがちです。しかし，各国は何世紀にもわたって原始的な郵便制度の確立に努め，馬や鳥や人間の走者を使って帝国中にメッセージを届けようとしました。統治者の中には手紙を通じてチェスの対戦をした者もいたと言います。

❷   長い間，手紙やその他の郵便物を送るのは，政府のみ，しかも通例は国事や戦争のためのみでした。1つにはそれは，メッセージを送り届けることが困難だったからです。たとえば，馬による配達は，馬も人も疲労するため頻繁に交代しなければならないので，富裕な権力者にしか利用できませんでした。利用できる場合でさえ，道の悪さ，悪天候のリスク，その他移動に伴う危険のせいで，郵便物は必ずしも届くとは限りませんでした。手紙を書くことが普及しなかったもう1つの理由は，一般の人々が字を読めなかったことにあります。けれども，印刷機の発明によって識字率が上昇しました。それは主として印刷物の利用可能性が高まったことによるものでした。イングランドでは，シェイクスピアの時代から1700年代までに，文字を読むことのできる男性の割合が10パーセントから推定60パーセントに増加しました。ヨーロッパの啓蒙主義の精神が広まると，啓蒙思想家は手紙を使って他国の哲学者との間で，質問や討論，論争を行いました。

❸   その時から，手紙を書くことが，学者だけでなく一般大衆の間にも普及しました。英国では1800年代初期までに女性への教育も進み，半数以上の女性が読み書きができるようになっていました。それによって，友人や家族間の私的な文通が増加しました。しかし，手紙を書く道具は1500年代からあまり進歩していませんでした。ペンの先につけて使用する金属のペン先が発明されてはいましたが，ほとんどの人にとって高価すぎました。だから，多くの人々は依然として羽をペンとして用いていました。ガチョウの羽のペンが一般的でしたが，一方でハクチョウや

クジャクの羽は書くための道具として珍重されました。書く時は，各自が好みに応じて自分の羽ペンを作らなければなりませんでした。

❹　他の形のコミュニケーションの場合と同様に，書くという行為も社会規範によって制御されていました。たとえば，親族か婚約者どうしでない限り，男女はお互いに手紙をやりとりしてはいけませんでした。郵便料金を巡っても気を遣わなければなりませんでした。手紙は，受け取った人が分量に応じて料金を払ったので，書く人はできるだけ使う紙を少なくするよう努めました。そのため当時は「重ね書き」が一般的でした。これは，紙を一旦左から右に文字で埋めたあと，90度回転し，もとの行と交差させて書くというものです。重ね書きした手紙は格子縞の布のように見えます。

❺　19世紀半ばのビクトリア朝には，手紙を書くことは一種の芸術となっていました。その時代，自己表現を行うことは他の行動と同様，いくつもの指針によっていっそう制限されるようになっていました。手紙の書き方といった本が出版され，書き手が社会的期待に沿うように手引きしました。紙は，男性は無地を用いることが求められましたが，女性は装飾のついたものや，香りのあるものさえ用いることができました。男女ともに，青も許容されましたが，黒のインクで書き，封をする時には封蝋を用いました。

❻　おそらく最も重要だったのは，魅力的で読みやすい字が書けることでした。習字法（ペンマンシップ＝手書きの能力をこのように呼んだ）は多くのビクトリア朝人にとってたいへん重要でした。実際，この時代には，カッパープレートと呼ばれる特別な筆記体が流行しました。この名称は，子どもが字を練習するとき，銅板（カッパープレート）に彫られた手本の文字を用いていたことに由来します。カッパープレートには，フランス書体や宮廷書体など，様々な書体がありました。それらの多くは，現代の筆記体より今日のカリグラフィーに似ています。

❼　今日ではもちろん，活字体でしか書けず，こうした装飾的な手書きの書体が全く書けない人もいます。おそらく手紙を書くという行為は，「扇言葉」のように，コミュニケーション技術としてはやがて忘れられてしまうでしょう。

《　指針　》

「手紙の歴史」をテーマにした講義である。手紙の変遷が年代順に説明されている。聞き取る際にはいつの時代の話なのかを意識するようにしよう。また(5)のような設問には要注意。正解を導くには，放送文全体を見渡して考える必要がある。

難易度

😊😐))) スピーカー情報

Lecturer: 中西部, イリノイ

放送文 ★★☆

設 問 ★★☆

総 合 ★★☆

Set 12-A | 設問解説

(1) Which of the following was NOT true of the earliest postal systems?
最初期の郵便制度について適切でないのは次のうちどれか。

a) The post was set up mostly for use in governance.
郵便は主として統治に用いるために設立された。

b) Intellectuals often used the post to discuss scholarly questions.
知識人はしばしば学問上の問題について議論するために郵便を用いた。

c) Due to the low literacy rate, letter writing was not widespread.
識字率が低いため, 手紙を書くことは普及しなかった。

d) The post was sometimes unreliable, in part due to the difficulties of travel.
1つには移動が困難だったために, 郵便はときに当てにならなかった。

e) The cost of sending messengers naturally limited letters to the most powerful.
使いを出す費用のせいで, 手紙はおのずと最も有力な者に限定された。

最初期の郵便や手紙がどのようなものだったかについては, ❷で説明されている。only the government sent letters and other mail, and usually only for matters of state or warfareが a に合致し, messengers on horseback had to be changed frequently … making them a privilege only the wealthy and powerful could affordが e に合致する。さらにEven then messages did not always get through, due to the poor quality of roads …が d に, Another reason letter writing was not widespread was … が c に該当する。b の「知識人による手紙の利用」は❷の最後で触れられているが, これは「最初期の郵便」ではなく18世紀以降の話である。

(2) According to the lecture, what is one reason for the spread of letter writing?
講義によれば, 手紙を書くことが普及した1つの理由はどのようなものか。

a) Metal nibs were invented.
金属のペン先が発明された。

b) More people learned to read and write.
読み書きできる人々が増えた。

c) Transportation systems were developed.
交通が発達した。

270

d) Common people gained wealth, allowing them to pay postage.
一般大衆が富を獲得し，郵便料金を払うことができるようになった。

e) People had larger families that they needed to communicate with.
家族の規模が大きくなり，家族同士の通信が必要になった。

❷のthe invention of the printing press caused literacy rates to riseから❸の letter writing gained popularity among the common peopleにかけての箇所をもとに，ｂが正解だと判断する。

(3) How did people in pre-Victorian times save money when writing letters?
ビクトリア朝以前の人々は，手紙を書くときどのようにして費用を節約したか。

a) They sent only very short messages.
たいへん短い手紙しか送らなかった。

b) They reused checked cloth instead of paper.
紙の代わりに格子縞の布を再利用した。

c) They used one piece of paper again and again.
1枚の紙を何度も繰り返し使った。

d) They wrote in two directions on a single sheet of paper.
1枚の紙に2方向で文字を書いた。

e) The letter writer paid the postage, rather than the recipient.
手紙の受け手ではなく，書き手が郵便料金を払った。

❹で説明されているcrossed lettersについての問題。当時は手紙の受取人が，その手紙のページ数に応じた料金を支払うことになっていたので，書き手は相手への配慮としてページ数を節約するため，1枚の紙に縦・横の2方向で文字を書いたと言うのである。これに合致するｄが正解。「縦横に書いた手紙は，チェック柄の布のように見えた」とはあるが，ｂのように「布を再利用した」という事実は述べられていない。

(4) In what way did Victorian letter writing mimic Victorian society?
ビクトリア朝の手紙の書き方はビクトリア朝の社会をどのように反映していたか。

a) Writers had to follow social norms in their letters.
書き手は手紙の中で社会規範に従わなければならなかった。

b) People had a great deal of freedom when writing letters.
手紙を書く時，人々は大きな自由を享受していた。

c) There was no distinction between male and female roles.
男女の役割に区別がなかった。

d) Women had to obey more rules than men when writing letters.
手紙を書く時，女性は男性より多くの規則に従わなければならなかった。

e) People used typewriters to make their letters look more attractive.
手紙の見映えを良くするためにタイプライターを使った。

ビクトリア朝時代における手紙の慣習については❺と❻で説明される。このうち，❺のThe expression of self was further limited by a number of guidelines をもとに，ａを正解とする。「男性は無地の紙を使うものとされていたが，女性は様々な紙を使うことができた」という内容から，ｄは誤りだと分かる。

(5) Based on the lecture, what is probably the best reason that many people today do not use cursive?
講義に基づけば，今日多くの人々が筆記体を使わない一番の理由は何だと考えられるか。

a) Our families are smaller, requiring fewer letters.
今日では家族が小規模になっているので，手紙はあまり必要でない。

b) Computers have made hand-written letters unnecessary.
コンピュータによって手書きの手紙が不要になった。

c) Ornamental handwriting is considered unattractive today.
装飾的な手書き文字は今日では魅力的とは見なされない。

d) Postage is cheap, so we do not need to write crossed letters anymore.
郵便料金が安いので，私たちはもはや「重ね書き」をする必要がない。

e) People write far more letters than in the past, so they need to write faster.
昔に比べて書く手紙の数が増えたので，より速く書く必要がある。

放送文で直接言われていることではなく，放送文の内容をもとに推測して解く問題であることに注意。「筆記体（cursive）」の使用については❻で説明されている。ビクトリア朝時代には，手書きでの手紙が芸術の域にまで高められ，「カッパープレート（copperplate）」と呼ばれる手書きのスタイルが流行したという。では，そのような慣習がなぜ現代ではすっかり影を潜めてしまったのか。直接的な言及はないが，❶の冒頭の With the advent of modern technology and a corresponding increase in near-instantaneous communication, it is easy to forget the role letters and letter-writing once played in society. をもとに考えてみよう。そもそもコンピュータを用いた通信が主流の現代では，手書きで手紙を書くという慣習そのものがほぼ消滅しており，流麗な筆記体を用いる必然性がない。ｂを正解とするのが妥当であろう。

Set 12-B | 放送文

Wolves 1

❶　Wolves once roamed the North American continent in their thousands, but in the 19th century hunters set about systematically killing them using poison and traps. As many as 700,000 were wiped out during the 1870s alone. The US government continued to encourage the removal of these creatures, and the last wolf in Yellowstone National Park was killed in 1926. By the 1950s, they were on the brink of extinction, with only about 300 remaining in the country. So what led people to do this? Wolves' tendency to attack and kill sheep and other livestock provides part of the explanation, but it was also partly due to misunderstanding. Although they rarely approach humans, wolves are often portrayed in myths as evil, fearsome creatures. The unsettling sound of their howling at night probably added to their reputation. In today's lecture, though, I want to correct a new misunderstanding surrounding wolves.

❷　People's attitudes changed in the 1960s and 1970s with the growth of the conservation movement, and the federal government listed the wolf as an endangered species in 1974. In 1995, grey wolves from Canada were released into Yellowstone, and by 2009 the park had nearly 100. During the period when there were no wolves in the park, conservationists had become increasingly concerned about the effects that elk were having on the ecosystem. Without predatory wolves to control their numbers, the elk population had exploded. Elk fed freely on young aspen, willow and cottonwood trees, stopping them from reaching maturity. With fewer trees along the riverbanks, there was more erosion and less shade. This harmed the habitats of fish and songbirds. The removal of a predator from the top of the food chain had caused what scientists call a "negative trophic cascade."

❸　After the wolves were reintroduced, though,

roam 他 …を歩き回る
set about *do*ing 句 …し始める
systematically 副 組織的に
wipe out 句 …を全滅させる，殺す
on the brink of … 句 いまにも…しそうな
extinction 名 絶滅

☞北米でのオオカミ駆除の経緯：19世紀に駆除が始まり，1950年代には絶滅の危機に

livestock 名 家畜
myth 名 神話
fearsome 形 恐ろしい
unsettling 形 不安を掻き立てるような
howl 自 吠える

☞オオカミを駆除した理由：1. オオカミが家畜を攻撃した，2.「邪悪な動物だ」という誤った印象

conservation 名 保護
federal 形 連邦の

conservationist 名 環境保護論者
elk 名 エルク（アメリカアカシカ）
predatory 形 捕食性の
feed on … 句 …を餌にする
aspen 名 アスペン，ポプラ
willow 名 ヤナギ
cottonwood 名 ハコヤナギ
maturity 名 成熟期
habitat 名 生息環境
predator 名 捕食者
food chain 句 食物連鎖
trophic cascade 句 栄養カスケード（生態系の動物が捕食・被食関係を通じて段階的に影響を及ぼすこと）

elk numbers fell dramatically, and changes were observed in their behavior. Wolf biologist Douglas W. Smith, for example, noticed that elk had become more watchful and were feeding in areas that afforded a 360-degree view. They avoided areas that could conceal a wolf, and in these places, according to Smith, trees started to recover. A 2004 study by William Ripple and Robert Beschta of Oregon State University helped confirm this view. It found evidence that young willow trees were returning in narrow river valleys, where it was believed the chances of wolves attacking elk were highest.

❹ Repeated frequently in TV nature documentaries, this narrative of a positive trophic cascade in Yellowstone became familiar to many Americans. Now, though, there is growing evidence to contradict it. Elk numbers did decline, for instance, but not for the reason many suppose. A 2005 study showed that just 13 percent of elk deaths were linked to wolves, while 53 percent were caused by grizzly bears. Furthermore, a study published in 2010 found that aspen trees had not regrown despite the decline in the elk population. Even the claim that elk have become more nervous has been denied by Arthur Middleton from the University of Michigan, who found no change to elk feeding patterns in response to wolves.

❺ Does it matter that the reintroduction of wolves has not had the results many people suppose? After all, these large predators are now being successfully protected. Middleton says it matters for two reasons. Firstly, this story distracts people's attention away from other important environmental concerns. Secondly, people may lose faith in the scientists and environmentalists if they cannot explain clearly what is happening. Scientists need the trust of the public if they are to get support for their policy advice, and giving people mixed messages about wolves will not help their cause.

- 「負の栄養カスケード」とは：エルクの増加→若木の減少→河岸の浸食・木陰の減少→魚や鳥の生息域の被害

conceal 他 …を隠す
confirm 他 …を裏付ける

- オオカミの導入後に観察された変化：1. エルクの減少，2. エルクの行動が用心深くなった，3. 木々の再生

narrative 名 物語，話
contradict 他 …と矛盾する
grizzly bear 句 ハイイログマ，グリズリー

- その後の研究で分かったこと：1. エルクの減少の主因はオオカミではなくクマだった，2. エルクが減ってもポプラは再生しなかった，3. オオカミに対するエルクの行動に変化はなかった

in response to … 句 …に応じて

distract A from B 句 AをBからそらす
lose faith in … 句 …への信頼を失う

- オオカミの導入の効果について人々に誤解を抱かせたことの問題点：1. 人々の関心を他の重要な環境問題からそらせた，2. 科学者に対する信頼が失われた

cause 名 大義，理想，目標

Set 12-B | 放送文の日本語訳

オオカミ 1

❶　かつては非常に多くのオオカミが北米大陸を歩き回っていました。しかし19世紀，狩猟家が毒物とわなを使ってそれらを組織的に駆除することを始めました。1870年代だけで70万頭が殺されました。米国政府はこの動物の駆除を奨励し続け，イエローストーン国立公園で最後の1頭が殺されたのは1926年のことでした。1950年代にはオオカミは国内に約300頭しかおらず，絶滅の危機に瀕していました。では，何が人々をこのような行動に導いたのでしょうか。羊などの家畜を襲って殺すというオオカミの性質は，説明の1つではあります。しかしそれはまた，誤解によるものでもあったのです。オオカミは滅多に人間に近づきませんが，神話ではしばしば邪悪で恐ろしい生き物として描かれています。おそらく，オオカミの，不安を掻き立てる夜間の咆哮によって，そうした風評が増加したのでしょう。しかし，本日の講義では，オオカミにまつわる新たな1つの誤解を正したいと思います。

❷　環境保護運動の進展とともに，1960年代から1970年代に人々の態度が変化しました。連邦政府は1974年にオオカミを絶滅危惧種のリストに加えました。1995年，カナダのハイイロオオカミがイエローストーンに放され，2009年にはこの公園内に100頭近くが生息していました。公園内にオオカミがいなかった間，環境保護論者は次第にエルク（アメリカアカシカ）が生態系に及ぼしつつある影響を憂慮するようになっていきました。個体数を抑える捕食者としてのオオカミがいないために，エルクは爆発的に増加しました。エルクはポプラ，ヤナギ，ハコヤナギの若木を食い荒らし，成木となるのを妨げました。川岸の木が減少したために，浸食が進み，木陰が減りました。それによって魚や鳥の生息環境が損なわれました。食物連鎖の頂点にある捕食者の駆除は，科学者たちが「負の栄養カスケード」と呼ぶものをもたらしました。

❸　しかしオオカミが再導入されると，エルクの数は劇的に減少し，それらの行動に変化が現れました。たとえばオオカミを研究する生物学者，ダグラス・W・スミスは，エルクはいっそう用心深くなり，360度眺望の利く場所で餌を食べていると指摘しました。エルクはオオカミが潜む可能性のある場所を避け，そのような場所では，スミスによれば，木々が再生し始めました。オレゴン州立大学のウィリアム・リップルとロバート・ベシュタの2004年の研究がこの説を裏付けました。オオカミがエルクを襲う可能性が極めて高いと考えられていた狭い川谷に，ヤナギの若木が復活しつつある証拠を見出したのです。

❹　テレビの自然ドキュメンタリー番組で繰り返し取り上げられたために，イエローストーンにおけるこの正の栄養カスケードの話は多くのアメリカ人によく知られるようになりました。しかし今日では，これと矛盾する証拠も増加しつつあります。たとえば，エルクの個体数は確かに減少しましたが，それは多くの人々の考える理由によるものではありませんでした。2005年のある研究では，エルクの死のうちオオカミに関係があるのはわずか13%にすぎず，53%がグリズリー（ハイイログマ）によって引き起こされたものであることが明らかになりました。さ

らに，2010年に発表されたある研究は，エルクの生息数が減少したにもかかわらずポプラが再生しなかった事例を発見しました。エルクがいっそう臆病になったという主張でさえ，ミシガン大学のアーサー・ミドルトンによって否定されています。彼はエルクの食餌パターンにオオカミに応じた何の変化も見出しませんでした。

❺　オオカミの再導入が多くの人々の予測する結果をもたらさなかったことに，何か問題点があるでしょうか。なんといっても，この大型の捕食者は今日首尾よく保護されているのです。ミドルトンは，それは2つの理由から問題であると述べています。第1に，この話は人々の注意を，その他の重要な環境問題からそらしてしまうからです。第2に，科学者や環境問題の専門家が現実に起きていることがらについて明快に説明することができない場合，人々の信用を失ってしまうかもしれないからです。科学者が自らの政策的助言に支持を得ようとするなら，世間に信頼されることが必要です。そして，オオカミに関して人々に矛盾する情報を与えることは，科学者の大義の役に立たないでしょう。

《 指針 》

「オオカミ（wolves）」をテーマとした講義である。人々がオオカミについて抱いていた，とある「誤解（misunderstanding）」が話題の中心となるが，その誤解とは何なのかは後半のほうになってようやく明らかにされるため，慎重に聞き取りを進めないと，話の焦点を途中で見失ってしまうことになるだろう。個々の事実関係を把握していくだけでなく，全体の要旨を常に意識するようにしたい。

難易度

放送文	★★★
設　問	★★★
総　合	★★★

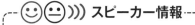 スピーカー情報

Lecturer: スコットランド

Set 12-B | 設問解説

(1) What is one thing the professor says about wolves in his introduction?
講義の導入部分で教授がオオカミについて述べていることがらはどれか。

a) They became extinct in 1926.
オオカミは1926年に絶滅した。

b) They were driven to the brink of extinction in the 1870s.
1870年代に絶滅の危機に瀕するにいたった。

c) It is a myth that wolves are too shy to approach human beings.
オオカミは臆病で人間に近づけないというのは神話である。

d) People's false impressions contributed to the decline in their numbers.
人々の誤った印象がそれらの数の減少の一因となった。

e) The US government tried to protect the wolf in the early 20th century.
米国政府は20世紀初期にオオカミの保護に努めた。

❶の内容把握を問う問題である。it was also partly due to misunderstandingとあり，オオカミが人間に近づくことは実際にはまれであるにもかかわらず，恐ろしい動物であるという「誤った印象」が広まり，オオカミの駆除という行為に人間を駆り立てたということが述べられている。これに合致するdが正解。1926年にオオカミが一掃されたのはイエローストーン国立公園でのことなので，aは誤り。絶滅の危機に瀕したのは1950年代であるから，bは誤り。

(2) Which of the following did NOT happen while there were no wolves in the park?
公園内にオオカミがいなかった時期に起こらなかったことは次のうちどれか。

a) A large increase in the number of elk.
エルクの数の大幅な増大。

b) The removal of soil due to a lack of trees.
木々がないことによる土壌の流失。

c) The effects called "negative trophic cascade."
「負の栄養カスケード」と呼ばれる影響。

d) The growth of more trees near the riverbanks.
川岸付近に生育する木々の増加。

e) Damage to the areas where fish and birds lived.
魚や鳥が生息する区域の被害。

❷の後半では，イエローストーンにオオカミが放たれる以前はどのような状況だったかが説明されている。「エルクの増加（a）」→「若木の減少」→「河岸の浸食（b），木陰の減少」→「魚や鳥の生息域の被害（e）」という順に連鎖的に影響が及び，これが「負の栄養カスケード（negative trophic cascade）（c）」という名称で呼ばれている。河岸の木々は減少したので，dの記述は誤りである。

(3) Which view did the 2004 study by Ripple and Beschta support?
リップルとベシュタによる2004年の研究が確証を与えたのはどの見解か。
a) Wolves were getting better at concealing themselves from elk.
オオカミはエルクから身を隠すのが上手になりつつあった。
b) Elk behavior changed as a result of the reintroduction of wolves.
オオカミの再導入の結果，エルクの行動が変化した。
c) After the reintroduction of wolves, the number of trees decreased.
オオカミの再導入の後，木々の数が減少した。
d) Douglas W. Smith's explanation for the rise in elk numbers was correct.
エルクの数の増加に対するダグラス・W・スミスの説明は正しかった。
e) The growth of young willow trees made it easier for wolves to hunt elk.
ヤナギの若木の成長はオオカミがエルクを捕食するのを容易にした。

　❸では，オオカミの導入後にイエローストーンでどのような変化が観察されたかが説明されている。リップルとベシュタの研究によって裏付けられたのは「エルクの減少」「エルクが用心深い行動をとるようになった」「木々の再生」などであり，2つ目が選択肢のbに合致する。「オオカミがエルクを捕食するような場所でヤナギの若木が再生した」という説明はあるが，eのような事実は語られていない。dは「エルクの数の増加」という箇所が誤り。

(4) What did the 2005 study tell us?
2005年の研究によって私たちが分かることは何か。
a) Grizzly bears killed more elk than wolves did.
グリズリーが殺したエルクの数はオオカミが殺した数より多かった。
b) Fewer Americans now watch nature documentaries.
今日では自然ドキュメンタリー番組を観るアメリカ人は減少している。
c) The growth of aspen trees was faster than expected.
ポプラの木の成長は予想以上に速かった。
d) Wolves were responsible for a majority of bear deaths.
クマの死の大多数はオオカミによってもたらされた。
e) There was no change in the feeding patterns of elk in response to wolves.
オオカミに反応して，エルクの食餌パターンには変化がなかった。

　❹では，❸にあったような「正の栄養カスケード」が，実は「誤解」であったということが述べられる。2005年の研究で明らかになったのは，「エルクの死の大半はグリズリーによるものだった」ということであり，aが正解となる。eは2005年の研究ではなく，その後の研究で分かったことである。

(5) What is one problem that Arthur Middleton fears may occur?
アーサー・ミドルトンが発生を危惧している問題は何か。
a) People will be less likely to believe scientists in future.
将来，人々は科学者をあまり信用しなくなるだろう。

278

b） People's attention will be distracted from protecting wolves.
人々の注意がオオカミの保護からそれていくだろう。

c） Scientists will advise governments to introduce wolves in other areas.
他の地域でも，オオカミを導入するよう科学者が政府に助言するだろう。

d） The case for reintroducing predators to the wild will be strengthened.
自然界への捕食者の再導入を支持する議論が活発になるだろう。

e） Scientists won't be able to get financial support from the government.
科学者たちは政府から財政援助を得られなくなるだろう。

❹で語られているように，「オオカミの導入によってイエローストーンの環境が再生した」という巷に流布した話が実は「誤解」だったということが明らかになった。それがどのような影響を及ぼすのか，Arthur Middletonの意見が❺で紹介されている。要点は2つ。まず「人々の関心を他の重要な環境問題からそらしてしまう」という点。イエローストーンで予想された効果が出なかったことによって，他の重要な環境問題への人々の関心が薄れてしまう，ということである。もう1つは「科学者に対する信頼が失われる」という点。これが選択肢のaに該当する。bがやや紛らわしいが，人々の注意がそれるのは「オオカミの保護から」ではなく「他の重要な環境問題から」である。

Set 12-C | 放送文

Wolves 2

❶ Rachael: So, Rahim, what did you make of Professor Sanchez's lecture this week? I mean wolves! I think it's awesome, although maybe just a little scary, that they are now back in the wild. I would love to see a pack of them running through the forest after their prey!

❷ Rahim: If you were close enough to see that, Rachael, you would probably be the prey! Right, Graham?

❸ Graham: Totally!

❹ Rahim: To be serious, though, I think the point he made about myths was a really good one. I've heard the same thing about sharks. They have been misunderstood for centuries. Just search for "sharks" on the Internet and often what you'll see are stories about sharks attacking surfers, or great whites ripping fishing boats to pieces, even though they rarely attack humans.

❺ Graham: Remember the movie *Jaws*? That was probably the worst news for sharks ever. It just confirmed all people's fears about them, which is really unfair. If you actually look at the lives of most sharks, they are far more complicated creatures than we give them credit for. And scientific research shows that when sharks do attack humans, it's usually because they mistake them for another marine animal.

❻ Rahim: That's right, Graham, and the other thing that most people forget is that we are entering their territory. Why do we think we have the right not to be attacked in the ocean? We belong on land, after all!

❼ Rachael: True, but I think that's partly down to human nature. We think we are superior beings, and therefore need to be in total control of all aspects of life and nature. I mean, it's hard to think of an environment that remains unaffected by human behavior. We're always trying to control it with dams, walls, fences, concrete, and pipes. We destroy forests, pollute the seas, and hunt animals

What do you make of ...? 句 …をどう思うか。

a pack of ... 句 … (犬・オオカミ) の群れ
prey 名 獲物

make a point 句 主張する
⚠ Rahimの発言の主旨: サメが実際に人間を襲うことは滅多にないのに，人に危害を加えた話ばかりが流布している
great white 句 ホホジロザメ

confirm 他 …を裏付ける，強める

give A credit for B 句 AのBを認める
mistake A for B 句 AをBと間違える

territory 名 なわばり

down to ... 句 (原因などが) …に行き着く，によるものである
in control of ... 句 …を支配している

often with no real thought about the future. We just want to be in control and satisfied right here, right now. Unless we change the way we approach life, I think the environment's in real trouble.

❽ Rahim: That's kind of depressing, Rachael. I know what you mean, but I don't think it's all bad. There are many conservation movements around, and many attempts to redress the ecological balance, such as the wolves the professor was talking about.

❾ Rachael: Yes, but most of the problems were caused by us in the first place.

❿ Graham: That reminds me of a great lecture the professor gave last year. He was talking about invasive species. While it's true that some species have moved naturally into ecosystems and caused havoc, so many times it has been the actions of humans, either deliberately, such as when Europeans released rabbits into the Australian outback, or accidentally, when insects, for example, catch a ride on container ships. The cane toad is a great example of the damage one animal can cause. It was deliberately introduced to Australia to eat a beetle called the cane beetle. This was a native beetle but it ate a lot of sugar cane, which was a key Australian export. So the toad was released. Ironically, the toad doesn't seem to have had much effect on the cane beetle, but the toad has caused damage to the plant and animal ecosystems in northeast Australia, and it continues to spread quickly.

⓫ Rahim: Well, I guess that just goes to show that we're not as smart as we think. Just as the professor was saying with the wolves, we don't always get it right.

⓬ Graham: But these days at least, we're using science rather than guesswork to figure out answers, which is one reason I decided to major in biology. I think science may be the only way to get us out of some of these situations.

⓭ Rachael: I hope you're right!

☞ Rachaelの発言の主旨：人間は，将来どのような結果になるかを考えずに，自然を破壊し続けている

depressing 形 気が滅入るような

redress 他 …を是正する

☞ Rahimの発言の主旨：人間は自然を破壊するだけではなく，自然保護活動も行っている

in the first place 句 そもそも

invasive species 句 侵入生物種
ecosystem 名 生態系
havoc 名 大破壊，大損害
deliberately 副 意図的に

catch a ride 句 （車などに）乗せてもらう
cane toad 句 オオヒキガエル
beetle 名 甲虫
cane beetle 句 サイカブト
sugar cane 句 サトウキビ
ironically 副 皮肉なことに

☞ 人の手により持ち込まれた侵入生物種の例：サトウキビの害虫であるサイカブト（cane beetle）を駆除するためにオオヒキガエル（cane toad）を導入したが，効果はなく，逆に生態系に被害を与えた

get it right 句 正しく理解する

guesswork 名 勘，当て推量

Set 12-C | 放送文の日本語訳

オオカミ 2

❶レイチェル：それで，ラヒーム，今週のサンチェス教授の講義をどう思った？　オオカミの講義のこと！　ちょっと怖いけれど，今オオカミが自然界に戻ってきているなんてすごいわ。私はオオカミの群れが獲物を追って森中を走り回っているところを是非見てみたい！

❷ラヒーム：レイチェル，見えるくらい近くにいたら，たぶん君が獲物にされると思うよ。ねえ，グレアム。

❸グレアム：まったくだ！

❹ラヒーム：でも真面目な話，神話について教授が言ったことは実に良かった。サメに関して同じような話を聞いたことがある。何世紀もの間，サメは誤解されてきた。インターネットで「サメ」を検索してみると，出てくるのはたいてい，サメがサーファーを襲ったとか，ホホジロザメが漁船をずたずたに引き裂いたとかいうような話だ。サメは滅多に人間を襲わないのに。

❺グレアム：『ジョーズ』っていう映画を覚えてる？　おそらくあれは，サメにとって過去最悪の災難だ。あれはサメに対する全ての人の恐怖を裏付けてしまった。全くフェアじゃない。実際にほとんどのサメの生活を見てみると，彼らは我々が思っているよりはるかに複雑な生物だ。科学的調査からも，サメが人間を攻撃するとき，それは大概，彼らが人間を他の海洋動物と間違えているんだってことが分かっている。

❻ラヒーム：そうだね，グレアム。それにもう1つ，ほとんどの人たちが忘れているのは，我々は彼らのなわばりに侵入しているんだってことだ。自分たちには海の中で攻撃されない権利があるって，人間はどうして思うのだろう。所詮我々は陸の動物なのに！

❼レイチェル：たしかに。でも，それはある程度，人間の本性によるものなのではないかしら。私たちは自分たちが優越的な存在だと思っている。だから，生物と自然の全ての局面を完全に支配している必要があると思っている。つまり，人間の活動による影響を受けないままの環境っていうものを想像するのは難しいのよ。私たちは常に環境をダムや壁やフェンスやコンクリートや管で支配しようとしている。しばしば，将来について実際に考えることもなしに，森林を破壊し，海を汚染し，動物を狩っている。私たちはただ，まさに今ここで，支配し満足を得ることだけを求めている。私たちが生物に対するアプローチの仕方を変えない限り，環境は本当に困ったことになると思うわ。

❽ラヒーム：気の滅入る話だね，レイチェル。君の言いたいことは分かるよ。でも僕は悪いことばかりじゃないと思う。たくさんの環境保護運動があちこちで起こっているし，生態学的均衡を回復する試みも多数行われている。教授が話していたオオカミの例もそうだ。

❾レイチェル：そうね。でも，そもそも問題のほとんどは私たちが起こしたものなのよ。

❿グレアム：それで思い出すのは，教授の去年の素晴らしい講義だな。教授は侵入生物種について話してくれて，たしかにいくつかの生物種は，生態系に自然に侵入

282

して破壊をもたらしたけれど，たいていそれは人間の仕業だったって。ヨーロッパ人がオーストラリアの奥地にウサギを放した時のように，意図的にやったこともあるし，たとえば昆虫がコンテナ船に乗り込んだ時のように，偶然に起きたこともある。オオヒキガエルは，1つの動物が引き起こしうる損害の好例だ。それはオーストラリアに，サイカブトと呼ばれる甲虫を捕食させるために意図的に導入されたんだ。サイカブトは在来種の甲虫だが，サトウキビを大量に食べた。サトウキビはオーストラリアの主要な輸出品だった。そこでヒキガエルが放された。皮肉なことに，ヒキガエルはサイカブトにはたいした効果を及ぼさなかったらしいんだが，オーストラリア北東部の植物と動物の生態系に損害を与えてしまった。今も急速に広がり続けているんだ。

⓫ラヒーム：やれやれ，我々が自分で思っているほど賢明じゃないってことが証明されたってわけだ。まさに，教授がオオカミの話で言っていた通りだ。我々は常に正しく理解しているわけではない——。

⓬グレアム：でも，少なくとも今日我々は，答えを見つけ出すのに当て推量ではなく科学を使っている。僕が生物学を専攻することにしたのも，一つにはそのためだ。僕は科学が，こうした状況のいくつかから我々を救い出す唯一の方法かもしれないと思っている。

⓭レイチェル：そうであって欲しいわ！

《 指針 》

Bに続く会話だが，「オオカミ」の話題から発展して，「人間と自然との関係」という大きなテーマになっている。前半は「サメに対する誤解」，後半は「侵入生物種」を中心に話が進む。3人の話者が明確に意見を対立させる場面はないが，人間の自然破壊に対して否定的なRachael，むしろ人間の環境保護活動に目を向けようとするRahim，そして科学的な考察を重視するGraham，という3人の立場・性格の違いに着目すると，会話の内容理解がより深まるだろう。

難易度

放送文 ★★☆
設　問 ★★☆
総　合 ★★☆

☺☹))) スピーカー情報

Rachael: 西海岸，カリフォルニア
Rahim: 西海岸，オレゴン
Graham: イングランド

Set 12-C | 設問解説

(1) What does Rahim suggest about sharks?
ラヒームがサメに関して示唆しているのはどれか。

a) They are actually quite friendly to humans.
実際は人間に対してかなり友好的である。

b) They are less territorial than scientists had previously believed.
科学者たちが従来考えていたほどなわばり行動をしない。

c) They get negative coverage even though they rarely pose a threat.
滅多に脅威を与えることがないにもかかわらず，否定的な報道をされている。

d) They have become more interesting to scientists since the *Jaws* movie.
映画『ジョーズ』以来，科学者たちにとっていっそう興味深いものとなっている。

e) They are a good example of an animal that remains a significant danger to humans.
依然として人類に対する深刻な脅威であり続けている動物の好例である。

❹でThey have been misunderstood ... even though they rarely attack humansとあるように，サメが実際に人間を襲うことは滅多にないのに，人に危害を与える恐ろしい生物だという情報がネットなどに多く出回っている，というのがRahimの主張である。これに合致するcが正解。サメが「滅多に人間を襲わない」とは言っているが，「人間に対して友好的である」とまでは言っていないので，aは誤り。dの『ジョーズ』については，❺でGrahamが「サメに対する誤解を強めたもの」として触れている。

(2) What point does Rachael attempt to make about human nature?
レイチェルが人間の本性について言おうとしているのはどういうことか。

a) It is important to understand that human nature is not always the same in all places and all situations.
人間の本性は，どんな場所や状況でも常に同じだとは言えないということを理解しておくのは重要である。

b) Humans tend to care more for their natural environment than the other two students believe they do.
残りの2人の学生が考えている以上に，人類は自然環境を大切にする傾向にある。

c) Humans will always try to dominate other species, even though it may not be in their long-term interests.
たとえそれが自分たちにとって長期的な利益にならないかもしれないとしても，人類は常に他の生物を支配しようとするだろう。

d) Most humans tend to be pessimistic about the future even though there are many conservation movements around.
各地で多数の環境保護運動が起こっているにもかかわらず，ほとんどの人間は将来に関して悲観する傾向にある。

e) Humans are superior beings and therefore have the right to control other animals and the environment they are in.
人間は他よりも優れた存在であり，故に他の動物やその環境を支配する権利がある。

❼での発言をもとにcを正解とする。eは，一般的に人間が考えている内容であり，Rachaelの考えではない。Rachael自身は，このような考え方に対して批判的である。

(3)　Why does Rahim bring up the subject of conservation?
　　ラヒームはなぜ自然保護の話題を持ち出しているのか。
a) To claim that some progress is being made.
　　いくつかの進展も見受けられると主張するため。
b) To show that he remembered last year's lecture.
　　彼が昨年の講義を覚えているということを示すため。
c) To point out that Europeans have caused the most problems.
　　ヨーロッパ人が最も多くの問題を引き起こしたと指摘するため。
d) To emphasize how humans totally dominate the environment.
　　人間が環境を完全に支配していることを強調するため。
e) To support Rachael's point about the environment being in trouble.
　　環境が困難に陥っているというレイチェルの主張を支持するため。

人間による環境破壊を批判するRachaelに対して，Rahimは❽でbut I don't think it's all badと反対の意を表明した上でThere are many conservation movements aroundと言い，多くの環境保護活動が行われていることを指摘している。つまり，自然の支配や破壊といったネガティブな面ばかりでなく，環境保護というプラスの進展もあるのだということを主張したいのである。aが正解。

(4)　What is one thing Graham tells us about the cane toad?
　　グレアムはオオヒキガエルについて我々にどのようなことを教えているか。
a) The toad was introduced to Australia to protect the cane beetle.
　　ヒキガエルはサイカブトを保護するためにオーストラリアに導入された。
b) The toad has had less effect on its intended target than was initially predicted.
　　ヒキガエルは，意図されたターゲットに対し，当初予想されたほどの効果をもたらさなかった。
c) It would have been better to introduce the toad earlier to protect cane sugar crops.
　　サトウキビの収穫を守るために，ヒキガエルをもっと早く導入すればよかっただろう。
d) The cane beetle has now become an endangered species because of the toad's introduction.
　　ヒキガエルの導入により，サイカブトは現在，絶滅危惧種になっている。

e) The toad is a good example of an animal that was accidentally brought into a foreign ecosystem.
ヒキガエルは，異質な生態系に偶然持ち込まれた動物の好例である。

❿では，人間によって持ち込まれた「侵入生物種（invasive species)」の代表例として「オオヒキガエル（cane toad)」が紹介される。オーストラリアで，サトウキビを食い荒らす「サイカブト（cane beetle)」を捕食させるために，意図的に導入されたが，その効果はあまりなく，それどころか生態系に被害を与えてしまった，という事実が述べられている。選択肢のbが正しい。its intended targetとは，もちろんサイカブトのことである。eはaccidentallyが誤り。オオヒキガエルは人間が故意に導入したものである。

(5) Which of the following sentences is true?
次の文のうち正しいものはどれか。
a) These people all agree that conservation is pointless.
これらの人々は全員，自然保護は無意味であるということで合意している。
b) Professor Sanchez's lectures are no longer interesting.
サンチェス教授の講義はもはや興味深くない。
c) Graham sees some hope as long as humans use science.
人類が科学を使用している限り，グレアムは希望を抱いている。
d) Rahim and Rachael have differing opinions about the movie *Jaws*.
ラヒームとレイチェルは映画『ジョーズ』に関して異なる意見をもっている。
e) Most invasive species have been deliberately brought into foreign environments.
ほとんどの侵入生物種は意図的に異質な環境に持ち込まれたものである。

放送文全体にかかわる問題である。⓬のGrahamの発言から，cを正解とする。science may be the only way to get us out of some of these situationsというセリフには，科学に対して彼が抱いている希望が窺える。aやbの内容を示唆するような発言はどこにもない。また，映画『ジョーズ』についてはGrahamの発言に対しRahimがThat's rightと言っているだけで，3人の間で意見の不一致は見られない。よってdも誤り。❿では，侵入生物種が意図的に持ち込まれた場合と，偶然持ち込まれた例が紹介されており，eも誤り。

Profile

三木秀則（みき ひでのり）
筑波大学附属駒場高校，東京大学文学部卒。鉄緑会英語科の主任として，これまでに東京大学をはじめ，国立大医学部などの難関大学に数多くの合格者を送り込む。中1から高3まで，すべての英語教材の開発を担当。リスニング・文法・作文を統合した独自の教材は，全国トップレベルの中高生の間で強い支持を得ている。『改訂版 鉄緑会 東大英単語熟語 鉄壁』，及び『改訂版 鉄緑会 東大英単語熟語 鉄壁CD』（共にKADOKAWA）を執筆。

鉄緑会（てつりょくかい）
1983年，東京代々木に中高6年一貫の有名進学校の生徒を対象とした，東京大学受験指導の専門塾として設立された。以来今日まで，開成，筑駒，桜蔭といった首都圏難関校の最上位層が己を研鑽する場として集い，その独自の6年間カリキュラムの徹底した指導により，毎年極めて高い合格率で圧倒的多数が東大合格を手にしている。歴代の鉄緑会卒業生も，現在では医学界・法曹界・政官界・学術界と，国内外を問わず幅広く活躍している。

編集協力
株式会社オフィス宮崎

英文執筆
George A. Bailey
Winifred Bird
Steven Davis
Amy Holdsworth
Christian Opperman

翻訳
秋山淑子
坪野圭介
森冨美子

英文校正
Simon Siddall

校正
小西道子
坂本安子
白石実都子
小内 一
鷗来堂

録音・編集
冨手一樹（株式会社巧芸創作）

ナレーション
Aileen Chizuru Inoue
Ann Slater
Chris Wells
Deirdre Merrell Ikeda
Dominic Allen
Donald Whyte
Emma Howard
Eric Kelso
Josh Keller
Julia Yermakov
Katie Adler
Michael Rhys
Nina Handjeva-Weller
Peter Von Gomm

装丁・アートディレクション
深山典子

DTP
星島正明

CD2枚付　改訂版　鉄緑会　東大英語リスニング

2021年11月5日　初版発行
2024年7月5日　3版発行

編／鉄緑会英語科
発行者／山下 直久
発行／株式会社KADOKAWA
〒102-8177　東京都千代田区富士見2-13-3
電話0570-002-301（ナビダイヤル）

印刷所／大日本印刷株式会社

●お問い合わせ
https://www.kadokawa.co.jp/（「お問い合わせ」へお進みください）
※内容によっては、お答えできない場合があります。
※サポートは日本国内のみとさせていただきます。
※Japanese text only